ABOUT THE AUTHOR

 Nick Redfern works full time as an author, lecturer, and journalist. He writes about a wide range of unsolved mysteries, including Bigfoot, UFOs, the Loch Ness Monster, alien encounters, and government conspiracies. His many books include *Control*, *The Zombie Book*, *The Bigfoot Book*, *The Monster Book*, *Secret History*, *Secret Societies*, and *The New World Order Book*. He writes regularly for *Mysterious Universe*. He has appeared on numerous television shows, including History Channel's *Monster Quest* and *UFO Hunters*; VH1's *Legend Hunters*; National Geographic Channel's *The Truth about UFOs* and *Paranatural*; the BBC's *Out of this World*; MSNBC's *Countdown*; and SyFy Channel's *Proof Positive*. Nick lives just a few miles from Dallas, Texas' infamous Grassy Knoll and can be contacted at his blog:

http://nickredfernfortean.blogspot.com.

ASSASSINATIONS
THE PLOTS, POLITICS, AND POWERS BEHIND HISTORY-CHANGING MURDERS

Visible Ink Press®
43311 Joy Rd., #414
Canton, MI 48187-2075

Visible Ink Press is a registered trademark of Visible Ink Press LLC.

Most Visible Ink Press books are available at special quantity discounts when purchased in bulk by corporations, organizations, or groups. Customized printings, special imprints, messages, and excerpts can be produced to meet your needs. For more information, contact Special Markets Director, Visible Ink Press, www.visibleink.com, or 734-667-3211.

Managing Editor: Kevin S. Hile
Art Director: Mary Claire Krzewinski
Typesetting: Marco Divita
Proofreaders: Larry Baker and Shoshana Hurwitz
Indexer: Shoshana Hurwitz

Front cover images: Martin Luther King Jr. (Library of Congress), McKinley assassination (Library of Congress), Jacqueline Kennedy (U.S. government). Back cover images: space shuttle Challenger disaster (NASA), Diana, Princess of Wales, and Dodi Al-Fayed Memorial (Bobak Ha'Eri), Lincoln assassination (Heritage Auctions).

ISBN: 978-1-57859-690-4

Cataloguing-in-Publication Data is on file at the Library of Congress.

Printed in the United States of America.

10 9 8 7 6 5 4 3 2 1

ASSASSINATIONS

THE PLOTS, POLITICS, AND POWERS BEHIND HISTORY-CHANGING MURDERS

OTHER VISIBLE INK PRESS BOOKS BY NICK REDFERN

The Alien Book: A Guide to Extraterrestrial Beings on Earth
ISBN: 978-1-57859-687-4

Area 51: The Revealing Truth of UFOs, Secret Aircraft, Cover-ups & Conspiracies
ISBN 978-1-57859-672-0

The Bigfoot Book: The Encyclopedia of Sasquatch, Yeti, and Cryptid Primates
ISBN: 978-1-57859-561-7

Control: MKUltra, Chemtrails, and the Conspiracy to Suppress the Masses
ISBN: 978-1-57859-638-6

Cover-Ups & Secrets: The Complete Guide to Government Conspiracies, Manipulations & Deceptions
ISBN: 978-1-57859-679-9

The Monster Book: Creatures, Beasts, and Fiends of Nature
ISBN: 978-1-57859-575-4

The New World Order Book
ISBN: 978-1-57859-615-7

Secret History: Conspiracies from Ancient Aliens to the New World Order
ISBN: 978-1-57859-479-5

Secret Societies: The Complete Guide to Histories, Rites, and Rituals
ISBN: 978-1-57859-483-2

The Zombie Book: The Encyclopedia of the Living Dead
With Brad Steiger
ISBN: 978-1-57859-504-4

ALSO FROM VISIBLE INK PRESS

Alien Mysteries, Conspiracies, and Cover-Ups
by Kevin D. Randle
ISBN: 978-1-57859-418-4

Ancient Gods: Lost Histories, Hidden Truths, and the Conspiracy of Silence
by Jim Willis
ISBN: 978-1-57859-614-0

Angels A to Z, 2nd edition
by Evelyn Dorothy Oliver, Ph.D., and James R Lewis, Ph.D.
ISBN: 978-1-57859-212-8

Armageddon Now: The End of the World A to Z
by Jim Willis and Barbara Willis
ISBN: 978-1-57859-168-8

The Astrology Book: The Encyclopedia of Heavenly Influences, 2nd edition
by James R. Lewis
ISBN: 978-1-57859-144-2

Celebrity Ghosts and Notorious Hauntings
by Marie D Jones
ISBN: 978-1-57859-689-8

Conspiracies and Secret Societies: The Complete Dossier, 2nd edition
by Brad Steiger and Sherry Hansen Steiger
ISBN: 978-1-57859-368-2

Demons, the Devil, and Fallen Angels
by Marie D. Jones and Larry Flaxman
ISBN: 978-1-57859-613-3

The Dream Encyclopedia, 2nd edition
by James R Lewis, Ph.D., and Evelyn Dorothy Oliver, Ph.D.
ISBN: 978-1-57859-216-6

The Dream Interpretation Dictionary: Symbols, Signs, and Meanings
By J. M. DeBord
ISBN: 978-1-57859-637-9

The Encyclopedia of Religious Phenomena
by J. Gordon Melton
ISBN: 978-1-57859-209-8

The Fortune-Telling Book: The Encyclopedia of Divination and Soothsaying
by Raymond Buckland
ISBN: 978-1-57859-147-3

The Government UFO Files: The Conspiracy of Cover-Up
By Kevin D. Randle
ISBN: 978-1-57859-477-1

Haunted: Malevolent Ghosts, Night Terrors, and Threatening Phantoms
by Brad Steiger
ISBN: 978-1-57859-620-1

Hidden Realms, Lost Civilizations, and Beings from Other Worlds
by Jerome Clark
ISBN: 978-1-57859-175-6

The Horror Show Guide: The Ultimate Frightfest of Movies
By Mike May
ISBN: 978-1-57859-420-7

The Illuminati: The Secret Society That Hijacked the World
By Jim Marrs
ISBN: 978-1-57859-619-5

Lost Civilizations: The Secret Histories and Suppressed Technologies of the Ancients
by Jim Willis
ISBN: 978-1-57859-706-2

Real Aliens, Space Beings, and Creatures from Other Worlds,
by Brad Steiger and Sherry Hansen Steiger
ISBN: 978-1-57859-333-0

Real Encounters, Different Dimensions, and Otherworldly Beings
by Brad Steiger with Sherry Hansen Steiger
ISBN: 978-1-57859-455-9

Real Ghosts, Restless Spirits, and Haunted Places, 2nd edition
by Brad Steiger
ISBN: 978-1-57859-401-6

Real Miracles, Divine Intervention, and Feats of Incredible Survival
by Brad Steiger and Sherry Hansen Steiger
ISBN: 978-1-57859-214-2

Real Monsters, Gruesome Critters, and Beasts from the Darkside
by Brad Steiger and Sherry Hansen Steiger
ISBN: 978-1-57859-220-3

Real Vampires, Night Stalkers, and Creatures from the Darkside
by Brad Steiger
ISBN: 978-1-57859-255-5

Real Visitors, Voices from Beyond, and Parallel Dimensions
By Brad Steiger and Sherry Hansen Steiger
ISBN: 978-1-57859-541-9

Real Zombies, the Living Dead, and Creatures of the Apocalypse
by Brad Steiger
ISBN: 978-1-57859-296-8

The Religion Book: Places, Prophets, Saints, and Seers
by Jim Willis
ISBN: 978-1-57859-151-0

The Sci-Fi Movie Guide: The Universe of Film from Alien to Zardoz
By Chris Barsanti
ISBN: 978-1-57859-503-7

The Spirit Book: The Encyclopedia of Clairvoyance, Channeling, and Spirit Communication
by Raymond Buckland
ISBN: 978-1-57859-172-5

Supernatural Gods: Spiritual Mysteries, Psychic Experiences, and Scientific Truths
by Jim Willis
ISBN: 978-1-57859-660-7

UFO Dossier: 100 Years of Government Secrets, Conspiracies, and Cover-Ups
By Kevin D. Randle
ISBN: 978-1-57859-564-8

Unexplained! Strange Sightings, Incredible Occurrences, and Puzzling Physical Phenomena, 3rd edition
by Jerome Clark
ISBN: 978-1-57859-344-6

The Vampire Book: The Encyclopedia of the Undead, 3rd edition
by J. Gordon Melton
ISBN: 978-1-57859-281-4

The Werewolf Book: The Encyclopedia of Shape-Shifting Beings, 2nd edition
by Brad Steiger
ISBN: 978-1-57859-367-5

The Witch Book: The Encyclopedia of Witchcraft, Wicca, and Neo-Paganism
by Raymond Buckland
ISBN: 978-1-57859-114-5

"REAL NIGHTMARES" E-BOOKS BY BRAD STEIGER

Book 1: *True and Truly Scary Unexplained Phenomenon*

Book 2: *The Unexplained Phenomena and Tales of the Unknown*

Book 3: *Things That Go Bump in the Night*

Book 4: *Things That Prowl and Growl in the Night*

Book 5: *Fiends That Want Your Blood*

Book 6: *Unexpected Visitors and Unwanted Guests*

Book 7: *Dark and Deadly Demons*

Book 8: *Phantoms, Apparitions, and Ghosts*

Book 9: *Alien Strangers and Foreign Worlds*

Book 10: *Ghastly and Grisly Spooks*

Book 11: *Secret Schemes and Conspiring Cabals*

Book 12: *Freaks, Fiends, and Evil Spirits*

PLEASE VISIT US AT VISIBLEINKPRESS.COM

ASSASSINATIONS

THE PLOTS, POLITICS, AND POWERS BEHIND HISTORY-CHANGING MURDERS

NICK REDFERN

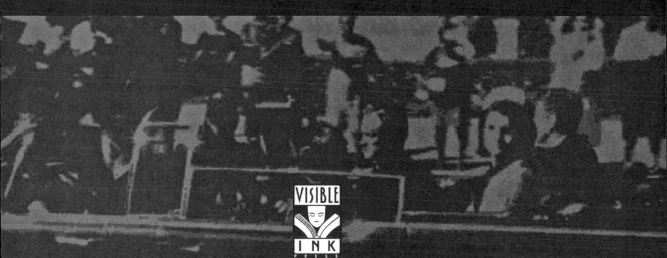

VISIBLE
INK
PRESS

ACKNOWLEDGMENTS

I would like to offer my very sincere thanks to my tireless agent, Lisa Hagan, and to everyone at Visible Ink Press, particularly Roger Janecke and Kevin Hile.

CONTENTS

Acknowledgments   [viii]

Photo Sources   [xi]

Introduction [xiii]

Photo Sources

A1DsVu (Wikicommons): p. 256.
Anthony22 (Wikicommons): p. 136.
Vassia Atanassova: p. 176.
Gray Barker: p. 391.
George Barris: p. 90.
Albert K. Bender: p. 388.
Katherine Bowman: p. 346.
Brady National Photographic Art Gallery: p. 13.
Dan Battle Brook: p. 165.
California Department of Corrections: p. 158.
CBS Television: p. 134.
Chrolka (Wikicommons): p. 287.
Creator22 (Wikicommons): p. 183.
Dallas Morning News: pp. 106, 117.
Dutch National Archives: p. 182.
Ecuadorian Foreign Ministry: p. 364.
B. D. Engler: p. 314.
Equinox: p. 282.
Erik1980 (Wikicommons): p. 231.
Executive Office of the President of the United States: pp. 209, 212.
Flickr: p. 268 (Allawi).
Franklin D. Roosevelt Presidential Library and Museum: p. 127.
Evan Freed: p. 155.
Gerald R. Ford Presidential Library and Museum: p. 220.
German Federal Archive: p. 207.
Bobak Ha'Eri: p. 233.
Maxwell Hamilton: p. 236.
Anton Holoborodko: p. 354.
Iraqi News Agency: p. 267.

Stephen Jones: p. 294.
Dan Keck: p. 334.
T. Kiya: p. 242.
Library of Congress: pp. 16, 80, 126, 140, 156.
Lower Saxony State Museum: p. 2.
LuxAmber (Wikicommons): p. 338.
Lyndon Baines Johnson Library and Museum: p. 121.
James McNellis: p. 358.
Museo Che Guevara, Havana, Cuba: p. 86.
NariceA (Wikicommons): p. 250.
NASA/Aubrey Gemignani: p. 376.
National Aeronautic and Space Administration: pp. 197, 201.
National Institute of Standards and Technology: p. 262.
National Reconnaissance Office: p. 60.
Bert Parry: p. 91.
Mark Pilkington: p. 383.
Puck magazine: p. 18.
Nick Romanenko: p. 247.
Ronald Reagan Presidential Library: p. 181.
Roswell Daily Record: p. 29.
Shutterstock: pp. 12, 26, 34, 36, 53, 58, 62, 71, 75, 81, 102, 115, 130, 150, 199, 204, 266, 274, 280, 284, 288, 299, 302, 325, 330, 344, 352, 365, 370, 372, 380, 394.
Simon & Schuster: p. 308.
Smerus (Wikicommons): p. 323.
John Mathew Smith / www.celebrity-photos.com: p. 228.
U.S. Air Force: pp. 28, 49, 100, 188, 300, 359.

U.S. Central Intelligence Agency: pp. 64, 84, 218.

U.S. Coast Guard: p. 168.

U.S. Department of Energy: p. 42.

U.S. Department of State: pp. 304, 319.

U.S. Federal Bureau of Investigation: pp. 143, 259.

U.S. Government: pp. 46, 94, 119, 177, 223, 268 (Chalabi).

U.S. Navy: p. 192.

U.S. Public Health Service: p. 258.

U.S. War Department: p. 109.

Yellow Pages: p. 31.

Z22 (Wikicommons): p. 317.

Public domain: pp. 6, 8, 14, 15, 19 (top and bottom), 20, 22, 70, 186, 272, 296, 349.

INTRODUCTION

Ruthless killers and murderers for hire are here, there, and everywhere. They lurk in the shadows, ready to pounce. They terminate to order, and in the process, they change the course of humankind. They are among the world's most cold-hearted, deadly, and emotionless figures. They are assassins. In *Assassinations: The Plots, Politics, and Powers behind History-changing Murders* you will quickly find yourself immersed in a world that is filled with killings made to seem like suicides, murders that were designed to look like heart attacks and overdoses, and accidents that, in reality, were carefully orchestrated wipeouts. While it is the case that the twentieth to the twenty-first centuries have proved to be the most intriguing eras in which suspicious deaths have occurred, there is nothing new at all about suspicious deaths and "guns for hire."

With that all said, let's take a look at some of the questions that will be answered in the pages of this book:

- Did Marilyn Monroe take her own life in August 1962? Was a contract put out on her?

- Did Lee Harvey Oswald really kill JFK? Or, was Oswald the patsy he claimed to be?

- Was Jack the Ripper, who terrified London in 1888, a madman or a ruthless secret agent of the British government, killing to order?

- Did the United States' first Secretary of Defense, James Forrestal, kill himself, or was he thrown out of a window to his death in May 1949?

- What led to the demise of Danny Casolaro, an investigative journalist, who, at the time of his death in 1991, was investigating a powerful cabal known as "The Octopus"?

- Was Diana, Princess of Wales, the victim of a car accident or of a carefully orchestrated plot?

- Can soundwaves and microwaves kill people at the flick of a switch?

- Was John Lennon's death not all that it appeared to be?

- Why are so many scientists dying under suspicious circumstances in the age of terror?

Learn the answers to these questions and many more within the pages of this book.

EARLY YEARS

A ny mention of assassinations inevitably evokes imagery of sinister men in black suits, prowling around in the darkness and the shadows, armed with a trusty pistol and silencer, and ready to take out their designated target. Sure, that's certainly a big part of the story. It's a fact, however, that assassinations have a long and controversial history, as we shall now see. In 2012, the U.K.'s *Telegraph* newspaper ran an article titled "Pharaoh's Murder Riddle Solved after 3,000 Years." In part, it stated the following:

> Forensic technology suggests Ramses III, a king revered as a god, met his death at the hand of a killer, or killers, sent by his conniving wife and ambitious son. And a cadaver known as the "Screaming Mummy" could be that of the son himself, possibly forced to commit suicide after the plot, they added. Computed tomography (CT) imaging of the mummy of Ramses III shows that the pharaoh's windpipe and major arteries were slashed, inflicting a wound 70 millimeters (2.75 inches) wide and reaching almost to the spine, the investigators said. The cut severed all the soft tissue on the front of the neck. "I have almost no doubt about the fact that Ramses III was killed by this cut in his throat," palaeopathologist Albert Zink of the EURAC Institute for Mummies and the Iceman in Italy told AFP.

Then, there's the matter of none other than Julius Caesar, who came to an untimely end in 44 B.C.E.—at the hands of his very own senators. *History* states:

> Julius Caesar, the 'dictator for life' of the Roman Empire, is murdered by his own senators at a meeting in a hall next to Pompey's

Theatre. The conspiracy against Caesar encompassed as many as sixty noblemen, including Caesar's own protégé, Marcus Brutus. Caesar was scheduled to leave Rome to fight in a war on March 18 and had appointed loyal members of his army to rule the Empire in his absence. The Republican senators, already chafing at having to abide by Caesar's decrees, were particularly angry about the prospect of taking orders from Caesar's underlings. Cassius Longinus started the plot against the dictator, quickly getting his brother-in-law Marcus Brutus to join.

Caesar should have been well aware that many of the senators hated him, but he dismissed his security force not long before his assassination. Reportedly, Caesar was handed a warning note as he entered the senate meeting that day but did not read it. After he entered the hall, Caesar was surrounded by senators holding daggers. Servilius Casca struck the first blow, hitting Caesar in the neck and drawing blood. The other senators all joined in, stabbing him repeatedly about the head.

The saga of the secret society of the Garduña is highly controversial for one specific reason: historians cannot agree on whether or not it really exist-

One of the most infamous assassinations in all of history was that of Julius Caesar, who was killed by Roman senators despite being warned of the danger (1865 painting by Karl von Piloty, *The Murder of Caesar*).

ed. The story goes that the group had its origins in Spain, and at some unspecified period in the Middle Ages, but probably at some point in the early 1400s in, or around, Toledo. The tale continues that the Garduña was comprised of both former prisoners and escapees who engaged in just about any and all unlawful acts in exchange for money. Assassinations, burglaries, and the destruction of property were always high on the list. Reportedly, the Garduña existed for more than four centuries—with the bulk of its activities undertaken during the Spanish Inquisition, which was established in 1478 and lasted until 1834.

On the other hand, there is the research of a pair of Spanish researchers and historians, Hipólito Sanchiz and León Arsenal. They dug very deeply into the story of the Garduña and found that references to the Garduña did not date back any further than the 1800s, specifically to the pages of a book titled *Misterios de la inquisición española y otras sociedades secretas de España*. It was written by Víctor de Fereal and Manuel de Cuendías and was published in 1850. As a result of their research, Sanchiz and Arsenal concluded that in all likelihood the stories surrounding the Garduña were far more suited to fiction than to fact.

It has been suggested that the stories of the Garduña inspired—or even joined forces with, at times—the Camorra, an early Mafia-like organization that operated out of southern Italy and is believed to have come to prominence in the 1600s. However, they may have existed much earlier, possibly as many as two centuries earlier. As is the case with so many secret societies, the truth (or lack of) behind the story of the Garduña remains a mystery.

One of the most notorious of all Italian secret societies was the Camorra—a group ultimately absorbed into the much feared and powerful Mafia. The Camorra was one of many bands of criminals that operated out of Naples, Italy, during the 1800s. The majority of those bands were loose-knit in nature and, due to their lack of organizational skills, were largely ineffective. In terms of their activities, however, that was most certainly not the case when it came to the Camorra. Although not entirely proven, there are indications that the origins of the Camorra may actually date back as far as the 1400s, albeit in Spain and before eventually making their stealthy way to Italy. What began as a small and secret society of criminals soon mutated into something very different. They provoked terror and fear among the people of Naples, particularly so when they began to engage in large-scale, widespread crimes, such as blackmail, robberies, burglaries, extortion, and even ruthless assassinations.

> The incredible power and influence that the Camorra ultimately wielded led them to infiltrate local law enforcement, the corrupt Bourbon monarchy, and the military.

The incredible power and influence that the Camorra ultimately wielded led them to infiltrate local law enforcement, the corrupt Bourbon monarchy, and the military. Dirty and deadly deeds that the Royals, the Army, and politicians may not have wished to have gotten involved in were handled by the Camorra—for substantial fees and with not even a single question asked. Or else. Nevertheless, by the early 1860s things began to change. It was specifically due to what became known as Italian Unification. On this matter, the U.S. Department of State notes:

> The northern Italian states held elections in 1859 and 1860 and voted to join the Kingdom of Piedmont-Sardinia, a major step towards unification, while Piedmont-Sardinia ceded Savoy and Nice to France. Giuseppi Garibaldi, a native of Piedmont-Sardinia, was instrumental in bringing the southern Italian states into the unification process. In 1860, Garibaldi cobbled together an army (referred to as the "Thousand") to march into the southern part of the peninsula. Landing first in Sicily and then moving onwards into Naples, Garibaldi and his men overthrew the Bourbon monarchy and turned over the southern territories to Victor Emmanuel II, King of Piedmont-Sardinia. In early 1861 a national parliament convened and proclaimed the Kingdom of Italy, with Victor Emmanuel II as its king. At this point, there were only two major territories outside of the parameters of the new Kingdom of Italy: Rome and Venetia.

One of the results of unification—and of the overthrowing of the Bourbon monarchy—was that steps were finally taken to reel in the Camorra and bring their reign of crime, intimidation, and murder to an end. For decades, the military—following just about every conceivable lead available—hunted down the Camorra, and mercilessly so, too. In addition, its attempts to come to power in the 1901 Neapolitan election were thwarted. Nevertheless, the Camorra were not done yet: many of the members—realizing they were fighting a losing battle—secretly made their way to the United States where, after more than a few turf wars, they were absorbed into the Mafia.

And it has made a remarkable comeback, as the FBI notes: "The word 'Camorra' means gang. The Camorra first appeared in the mid-1800s in Naples, Italy, as a prison gang. Once released, members formed clans in the cities and continued to grow in power. The Camorra has more than 100 clans and approximately 7,000 members, making it the largest of the Italian organized crime groups. In the 1970s, the Sicilian Mafia convinced the Camorra to convert their cigarette smuggling routes into drug smuggling routes with the Sicilian Mafia's assistance. Not all Camorra leaders agreed, leading to the Camorra Wars that cost 400 lives. Opponents of drug trafficking lost the war. The Camorra made a fortune in reconstruction after an earthquake ravaged the Campania region in 1980. Now it specializes in cigarette smuggling and receives payoffs from other criminal groups for any cigarette traffic through

Italy. The Camorra is also involved in money laundering, extortion, alien smuggling, robbery, blackmail, kidnapping, political corruption, and counterfeiting. It is believed that nearly 200 Camorra affiliates reside in this country, many of whom arrived during the Camorra Wars."

Moving on....

Global Security says the following of the Carbonari, a secret political society that became notorious in Italy and France around 1818, though it had existed for a number of years earlier: "Freemasons could enter the Carbonari as masters at once. The openly avowed aim of the Carbonari was political: they sought to bring about a constitutional monarchy or a republic, and to defend the rights of the people against all forms of absolutism. They did not hesitate to compass their ends by assassination and armed revolt. As early as the first years of the nineteenth century the society was widespread in Neapolitan territory, especially in the Abruzzi and Calabria. Not only men of low birth, but also government officials of high rank, officers, and even members of the clergy belonged to it."

Writer Juri Lina, a noted expert on the Carbonari and its history and activities, reveals: "The headquarters of the Carbonari was located in Rome. In the 1820s the movement had 700,000 armed members. They claimed that they could enlighten the world with the holy fire (illuminism!). The symbol of their message of truth was charcoal, the source of light. An upside-down tree symbolized the murdered king. They advocated removal of the wolves (tyrants) in the forest (society). The members of the same hut called themselves *boni cugini* (good cousins). Non-Carbonari were called *pagani* (heathens). The Carbonari were divided into two classes: apprentices and masters. No apprentice could rise to the degree of master until the end of six months. The Carbonari colors were blue (hope), red (love) and black (faith). At their gatherings they displayed five glowing triangles symbolizing the Illuminati five-point program."

Tom Frascella, who has carefully studied the Carbonari Society, says: "The Carbonari society had many secret rituals and members were required to take certain oaths of mutual support. Upon acceptance members would learn code words by which fellow members could recognize each other. Members would refer to each other as 'buoni cugini' or good cousins. Their secret lodges were called 'vendita' or sales. Many of their rituals and ceremonies contained a mixture of both Christian and pagan references and symbols."

Their goals and ideology were, in their own words, as follows: "Crush the enemy whoever he may be; crush the powerful by means of lies and calumnies; but especially crush him in the egg. It is to the youth we must go. It is that which we must seduce; it is that which we must bring under the banner of the secret societies. In order to advance by steps, calculated but sure, in that perilous way, two things are of the first necessity. You ought to have the air of being simple as doves, but you must be prudent as the serpent. Your fathers, your children, your wives themselves, ought always to be ignorant of the secret, which you carry in your bosoms. If it pleases you, in order the better to deceive the inquisitorial eye, to go often to confession, you are, as by right authorized, to preserve the most absolute silence regarding these things. You know that the least revelation, that the slightest indication escaped from you in the tribunal of penance, or elsewhere, can bring on great calamities and that the sentence of death is already pronounced upon the revealers, whether voluntary or involuntary."

The final word goes to Tom Frascella: "After 1834 the Carbonari Movement slowly stops being center stage and the Giovane Italia Society comes to the forefront as a political movement. However the two movements are probably better regarded as an evolutionary development of practical political thought."

Now, we come to one of the most mysterious and controversial bodies, the Illuminati.

Although what is known officially as the Order of the Illuminati did not come into being until the 1700s, the word "Illuminati" has origins that date back to at least the 1400s. In Spain, at that time, those who immersed themselves in the world of the black arts identified occultists, alchemists, and witches as having been given "the light." We're talking about nothing less than a supernatural form of "illumination" that gave them extraordinary powers, hence the term "Illuminati." As for the Order of the Illuminati, it was created on May 1, 1776. The man behind the mysterious group was Adam Weishaupt. The location: Ingolstadt, Bavaria. At the time, Weishaupt was approaching his thirties and worked as a professor of religious law. As Brad Steiger notes, Weishaupt "blended mysticism into the workings of the brotherhood in order to make his agenda of republicanism appear to be more mysterious than those of a political reform group."

The group had decidedly small-scale origins: it began with just five members, one being Weishaupt himself. The Illuminati was not destined to stay that way, however. Bit by bit, the group began to grow, to the point

Adam Weishaupt is associated with forming the mysterious group known as the Illuminati, a society credited for instigating historically important events that shaped the world.

where, by 1780, the membership was around five dozen and extended to six cities. Certainly, many were attracted to Weishaupt's group as a result of the fact that it paralleled the Masons—specifically in relation to levels and orders of hierarchy that could be achieved. Indeed, Weishaupt was careful to point out to his followers that the further they immersed themselves in the domain of the Illuminati, the greater the level of illuminated, supernatural knowledge they would achieve.

History has shown that Weishaupt was not alone in ensuring that the Illuminati grew from strength to strength. He was aided to a very significant degree by Adolph Franz Friedrich Ludwig Knigge, better known as Baron von Knigge. A renowned and influential figure with an expert knowledge of all things of an occult nature, von Knigge was a powerful individual who had risen through the ranks of the Masons. He shared Weishaupt's desire for political revolution. In no time, and as a result of von Knigge's contacts and ability to entice others to the cause, the Illuminati grew to a group of several hundred. The Illuminati was not a group open to everyone, however. In fact, quite the opposite: the powerful, the rich, and the well connected were those that Weishaupt and von Knigge worked hard to bring onboard. Rituals and rites for those who wished to be a part of Weishaupt's vision were established, as was the wearing of specific clothes—or, as Brad Steiger described them, "bizarre costumes." The membership expanded ever further.

By the mid-1780s, the Illuminati was no longer a group with hundreds of followers but thousands. In 1784, however, there was dissent in the ranks. That April, von Knigge and Weishaupt had a major falling-out, which led to von Knigge walking away from the group. There was another problem, too: the occult "illumination" that Weishaupt had promised his followers failed to appear. Many of them became disillusioned, suspecting that Weishaupt actually had very little interest in the domain of the occult but had instead sought out the rich and powerful as a means to help his plans for a revolution. The outcome was that many walked away from the Illuminati, fearful that it was becoming a manipulative, sinister body with hidden agendas. Soon, the Illuminati was no more. On this issue, let's turn again to Brad Steiger:

> In June 1784 Karl Theodor [the Duke of Bavaria] issued an edict outlawing all secret societies in his province. In March 1785 another edict specifically condemned the Illuminati. Weishaupt had already fled to a neighboring province, where he hoped to inspire the loyal members of the Illuminati to continue as a society. In 1787 the duke issued a final edict against the Order of the Illuminati, and Weishaupt apparently faded into obscurity.

Or did it? Does the Illuminati still exist? Is it one of the major bodies in the secret cultivation of a New World Order? These are the questions we will address now.

In 1784, Karl Theodor, the Duke of Bavaria, outlawed secret societies—specifically, the Illuminati—but there is plenty of evidence that this only drove these groups deeper underground.

The Jeremiah Project says: "Many believe the Illuminati are the masterminds behind events that will lead to the establishment of such a New World Order, and see connections between the Illuminati, Freemasonry, the Trilateral Commission, British Imperialism, International Zionism and communism that all lead back to a bid for world domination. *In more recent years the Illuminati has allegedly been involved in the assassination of John F. Kennedy* [italics mine] and has been at the forefront of indoctrinating the American public into their socialist one-world agenda. It is difficult to uncover the facts regarding the modern day role of the Illuminati as most of the information is cloaked in secrecy. What we must do instead is to look at the available evidence and relationships in the context of contemporary world events, and form some common sense conclusions based on that inquiry."

The Jeremiah Project also notes: "The Illuminati was presumed to have been dispersed by the end of the century but some people such as David Icke, Ryan Burke and Morgan Gricar have argued that the Bavarian Illuminati survived and believe that Illuminati members chose instead to conceal themselves and their plans within the cloak of Freemasonry, under which auspices they continue to thrive. They have maintained a stranglehold on the political, financial and social administration of the United States and other nations acting as a shadowy power behind the throne, controlling world affairs through present day governments and corporations."

Henry Makow reveals an extremely disturbing NWO–Illuminati story:

A woman who was raised in the Illuminati cult describes a powerful secret organization comprising one per cent of the U.S. population that has infiltrated all social institutions and is covertly preparing a military takeover. Her revelations cast the "war on terror" and "homeland security" in their true light.

"Svali" is the pseudonym of the woman, age 45, who was a mind "programmer" for the cult until 1996. She was the sixth head trainer in the San Diego branch and had 30 trainers reporting to her. She has risked her life to warn humanity of the Illuminati's covert power and agenda.

She describes a sadistic Satanic cult led by the richest and most powerful people in the world. It is largely homosexual and pedophile, practices animal sacrifice and ritual murder. It works "hand in glove" with the CIA and Freemasonry. It is Aryan supremacist (German is spoken at the top) but welcomes Jewish apostates. It controls the world traffic in drugs, guns, pornography and prostitution. It may be the hand behind political assassination, and "terrorism," including Sept. 11, the Maryland sniper and the Bali bomb blast. It has infiltrated government on a local, state and national level; education and financial institutions; religion and the media. Based in Europe, it plans a "world order" that will make its earlier attempts, Nazism and Communism, look like picnics.

The website *Warning Illuminati* appropriately warns us:

There is a worldwide conspiracy being orchestrated by an extremely powerful and influential group of *genetically related individuals* (at least at the highest echelons) which include many of the world's wealthiest people, top political leaders, and corporate elite, as well as members of the so-called Black Nobility of Europe (dominated by the British Crown) whose goal is to create a One World (fascist) Government, stripped of nationalistic and regional boundaries, that is obedient to their agenda. Their intention is to effect complete and total control over every human being on the planet and to dramatically reduce the world's population by 5.5 billion people. While the name *New World Order* is a term frequently used today when referring to this group, it's more useful to identify the principal organizations, institutions, and individuals who make up this vast interlocking spiderweb of elite conspirators.

The Illuminati is the oldest term commonly used to refer to the 13 *bloodline families* (and their offshoots) that make up a major portion of this controlling elite. Most members of the Illuminati are also members in the highest ranks of numerous secretive and occult societies which in many cases extend straight back into the ancient world. The upper levels of the tightly compartmentalized (need-to-know-basis) Illuminati structural pyramid include planning committees and organizations that the public has little or no knowledge of. The upper levels of the Illuminati pyramid include secretive committees with names such as: the Council of 3, the Council of 5, the Council of 7, the Council of 9, the Council of 13, the Council of 33, the Grand Druid Council, the Committee of 300 (also called the "Olympians") and the Committee of 500 among others.

PRESIDENT LINCOLN TAKEN OUT

Any mention of presidential assassinations that changed the face of the United States will, probably first and foremost, conjure up imagery relative to the November 22, 1963, assassination of President John F. Kennedy at Dealey Plaza in Dallas, Texas. Long before JFK was killed, however (whether by Lee Harvey Oswald, the Cubans, the Mafia, or the KGB), there was the murder of President Abraham Lincoln in April 1865.

Unlike so many presidents of the twentieth century, Lincoln was not born into a rich, powerful family. It was exactly the opposite: Lincoln was very much a self-made man, one who was brought up in near-poverty in Hardin County, Kentucky. Lincoln was determined to make a significant life for himself, however, and he achieved exactly that—and much more. Prior to his election as president of the United States in November 1860, Lincoln had worked as a lawyer, a state representative, and a U.S. representative. From there, it was a case of the sky being the limit until, that is, a man named John Wilkes Booth ended it all. There are, however, widely held beliefs that Booth did not act alone when he shot and killed Lincoln. Powerful bankers, the Confederates, the Jesuits, or possibly even high-ranking Masons, it has been suggested, may have been in on the deadly act.

To understand the conventional theory, that Booth was the culprit, we have to go back to the dawning of the 1860s. In the presidential election of 1860, Lincoln gained a great deal of support from those who demanded an end to slavery—as did Lincoln himself. There were, however, significant numbers who were vehemently against the abolition of slavery. They were the people of Georgia, Mississippi, Texas, South Carolina, Louisiana, Alabama, and Florida. So vehemently antiabolition were they, they created what became known as the Confederate States of America. Tensions began to mount between North and South, to the point when, on April 12, 1861, civil war broke out. It continued until May 9, 1865, and saw the South soundly defeated. Slavery was no more, and the Confederate States of America was gone, too. It was a decisive victory for the president, who celebrated a new beginning for the United States and its people. Unfortunately, Lincoln would not have long to celebrate. Someone was planning a quick demise for the nation's victorious leader.

It's ironic that John Wilkes Booth was so anti-Lincoln for this particular reason: despite his hatred of the president, Booth chose never to enlist with the Confederate military and do in-the-field battle with the North. That's not to say he was a coward, though. Rather, Booth forged deep and intriguing links to the world of espionage, acting for the Confederates in decidedly "James Bond, 007"-style. Demonstrating his loathing for the president, more than a year before Lincoln was killed, Booth had secretly devised an operation to have the president kidnapped and held until such a time that he authorized the release of a large number of Southern soldiers. Things really reached their peak in early

Lincoln's assassin, John Wilkes Booth, is shown jumping from the presidential box onto the stage at Ford's Theatre in this 1865 illustration.

April 1865, however. That was when Booth, outraged by Lincoln's plans to allow black people to vote, decided that kidnapping wasn't enough for Lincoln: nothing less than the president's death would satisfy Booth.

The date on which America was changed was April 14, 1865. The location was the Washington, D.C.-based Ford's Theatre, where Lincoln and his wife, Mary, were due to watch Tom Taylor's play *Our American Cousin*. It was during an intermission that disaster struck. Lincoln's main bodyguard was a man named John Parker. During the intermission, Parker left the president and headed for a drink or two at the Star Saloon, which stood adjacent to the theater. It was the perfect moment for Booth to strike—and strike he did. It was shortly before 10:15 P.M. when Booth stealthily made his way to the balcony seats in which Lincoln and Mary were sitting and fired a bullet at the president's head.

Pandemonium broke out. Booth was almost apprehended, by one Major Henry Rathbone, but managed to escape by plunging a knife into the major. As for the president, his hours were numbered. One of the theater attendees was Dr. Charles Leale, who raced to the rapidly fading Lincoln. Despite frantic attempts to save his life, Lincoln died the next day after plunging into a coma for more than eight hours. As for Booth, he fled the theater and outwitted and outmaneuvered his military pursuers for almost two weeks. A standoff occurred at a Virginia farm, where Booth was shot to death by Sergeant Thomas "Boston" Corbett.

When it comes to the conspiracy theories concerning the death of President Abraham Lincoln, they differ significantly from the killing of President John F. Kennedy in November 1963. Whereas most conspiracy researchers of the JFK affair suggest Lee Harvey Oswald was nothing but a convenient patsy who never fired even a single bullet, most Lincoln assassination investigators are convinced Booth was the gunman. A big question, however, exists: was Booth the brains behind the operation, or was someone else pulling the strings? To try to answer that question, let's start with the Masonic theory.

Researcher John Daniel lays the blame squarely on the tentacles of British-based Masonry. He suggests that the reason why powerful figures in the British establishment

Major Henry Reed Rathbone almost captured the assassin but was stabbed by Booth, who managed to escape immediate arrest. Rathbone was tormented by his failure for the rest of his life.

wanted President Lincoln gone were twofold. First, having Lincoln assassinated would splinter the United States into two less-than-powerful sections, both of which could be conquered more easily than could one unified nation. Second, Daniel argued that the Brits wished to create a central bank under their control.

Such a bank would likely have been established under the powerful Rothschilds, who, history has shown, did offer the Lincoln government a loan—one with an extremely high interest rate. The Rothschilds were convinced that Lincoln would have no choice but to accept the loan to help get the United States back on its feet. Lincoln chose not to, however. The Rothschilds were soundly rebuffed.

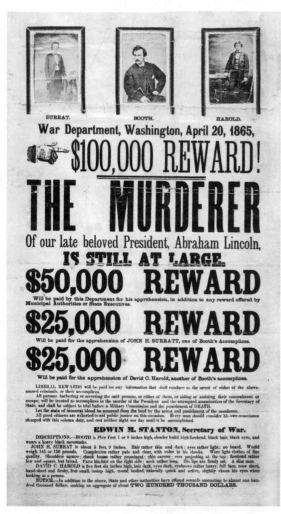

The wanted poster for John Wilkes Booth and his co-conspirators.

Daniel says: "Had it not been for Abraham Lincoln, English Freemasonry would have succeeded. When Lincoln restored the Union, the British Brotherhood, out of revenge, plotted his assassination. The Knights of the Golden Circle, bankrolled by British Masonic interests, selected John Wilkes Booth, a 33rd degree Mason and member of Mazzini's Young America, for the task."

As for how the crime was hidden, Daniel concludes that Edwin Stanton—both a Freemason and the secretary of war during the Lincoln Administration—coordinated the effort to bury the truth. He says that it was Stanton who ordered the blocking of all the roads out of Washington, D.C., aside from the one from which John Wilkes Booth was able to escape and make his way to Virginia. On top of that, Daniel does not believe that Booth died at the Virginia farm that the history books assure us he did: "Stanton then arranged for a drunk man to be found, similar in build and appearance to Booth. This man was to be murdered and his body burned in a barn adjacent to the only road not guarded by the military. Stanton just happened to be on that road when he 'found' the murdered man, certifying that the charred body was the remains of John Wilkes Booth. The real John Wilkes Booth escaped."

Moving on, we have the Jesuit-based conspiracy theory.

The idea that President Lincoln's assassination was orchestrated by Jesuits has its origins in events that occurred in 1856 in Urbana, Illinois. In that year, while employed as a lawyer, Lincoln successfully offered defense to a Canadian Catholic priest named Charles Chiniquy. The case revolved around the claim that Chiniquy had slandered Catholic bishop Anthony O'Regan. When an Illinois Catholic named Peter Spink filed suit against Chiniquy, Lincoln was the man who came to the rescue. And although the court's decision did not rule totally in favor of Chiniquy, an agreement was, at least and at last, reached.

Rather intriguingly, when the trial was over, Chiniquy developed deep concerns that the Jesuits—better known as the Society of Jesus or, as they are sometimes called, "God's Marines"—would take revenge on Lincoln for humiliating Spink and, as a result, the entire Catholic Church. More disturbingly, Chiniquy learned of an association between the Jesuits and John Wilkes Booth. It was a discovery that, in 1906, prompted Chiniquy to go public with his conclusion that the Jesuits were indeed guilty of killing the president—via the deadly actions of Booth.

An equally controversial theory suggests that none other than Lincoln's vice president, Andrew Johnson, ran the operation to have Lincoln permanently removed from office—or that, at the very least, Johnson knew of the planned killing and deliberately did nothing to stop it from occurring. The latter was a theory that even Lincoln's wife, Mary, came to believe. As unbelievable or as unlikely as such a theory might sound, it is a fact that Booth and Johnson crossed paths in February 1864, when Booth—who worked as an actor—performed at Wood's Theatre in Nashville, Tennessee, Johnson's home state. Even more damning, in terms of establishing a connection, two years earlier, in 1862, both men shared a mistress.

On top of that, although Johnson and Lincoln amounted to a political pair, they were certainly not friends. Johnson did not share Lincoln's views concerning the abolition of slavery. Lincoln had dropped incumbent vice president Hannibal Hamlin, a fellow Republican, in favor of Johnson, however, when it was decided that by choosing Johnson—as a southerner—it would send a message to the people that Lincoln was doing his utmost to reunite the country.

Because of a legal case Lincoln had worked on to clear Chiniquy of charges he slandered the local bishop, the judge did not rule totally in Chiniquy's favor, spurring later reprisals that led to a Jesuit conspiracy theory.

An exploration of all possible scenarios surrounding the assassination of President Lincoln included a look at Vice President Andrew Johnson, but, in the end, no conspiracy was found.

Such was the extent to which the finger-pointing in Johnson's direction extended that a congressional assassination committee was created to address the claims of Johnson's complicity in the killing of the president. It found no evidence of guilt on the part of Johnson.

More than 150 years have now passed since President Abraham Lincoln was assassinated by John Wilkes Booth. It's doubtful that Booth was a wholly innocent patsy—as has been suggested in the case of Lee Harvey Oswald roughly a century later. As for the possibility that Booth was the main man in a deep, dark conspiracy, however, theories continue to circulate years and years later that suggest that the killing of the president was not just the work of one crazed man.

JACK THE RIPPER OR JACK THE ASSASSIN?

In the latter part of 1888, a deadly figure roamed the shadowy and foggy back-streets of Whitechapel, London, England, by night, violently slaughtering prostitutes and provoking terror throughout the entire capital. He quickly became—and still remains to this very day—the world's most notorious serial killer. He was, in case you haven't by now guessed, Jack the Ripper. But what makes the Ripper so infamous, more than a century after his terrible crimes were committed, is that his identity remains a mystery. And everyone loves a mystery.

So, who might Jack have been? The theories are almost endless. Indeed, no fewer than thirty potential suspects have been identified. They include a powerful Freemason, a surgeon, a doctor, a poet, and even a member of the British Royal Family. What follows is a list of those individuals who have had more fingers pointed at them than any others.

Without doubt, the most controversial theory for whom, exactly, Jack the Ripper might have been is that he was a member of the British Royal Family, specifically Prince Albert Victor, the Duke of Clarence. It was a theory that first surfaced in the early 1960s, specifically in the pages of a book by French author Philippe Jullian. In the 1967 English-language version, Jullian wrote:

> Before he died, poor Clarence was a great anxiety to his family. He was quite characterless and would soon have fallen a prey to some intriguer or group of roués, of which his regiment was full. They indulged in every form of debauchery, and on one occasion the police discovered the Duke in a *maison de recontre* of a particularly equivocal nature during a raid. The young man's evil reputation soon spread. The rumor gained ground that he was Jack the Ripper.

Additional rumors suggested that Albert had caught syphilis from a London prostitute and, in a deranged state of mind caused by the increasing effects of his condition, roamed the Whitechapel district of London in search of prostitutes, upon whom he could take out his rage and revenge. Nothing concrete, however, has surfaced—so far, at least—to suggest the prince was Jack. That hasn't stopped the theory from thriving, however.

A variation on the theory that the Duke of Clarence was Jack the Ripper is that he was not the killer but was connected to him in a roundabout fashion. The duke, theorists suggest, secretly married a woman who was a Catholic. This was too much for Queen Victoria, so a dark plan was put into place. Sir William Withey Gull, the 1st Baronet of Brook Street and a noted physician and Freemason, took on the grim task of killing the friends of the young woman in question who knew of the secret marriage. Gull, then, trying to protect the royals from scandal, was the man behind the Ripper legend. And to ensure that the killings were not traceable back to the highest levels of the British Royal Family, the legend of the serial killer, Jack the Ripper, was created as a convenient cover and diversion. Maybe.

The mystery of just who the notorious Whitechapel murderer was, and what motivated him, was addressed in this 1889 issue of *Puck* magazine.

As early as the 1890s, American newspapers were reporting on the rumor that Jack was actually a prominent figure in London medicine, one who, according to the man's wife, had displayed violent characteristics at the height of the killings. Supposedly, the story got back to the man's coworkers. They quickly visited the family home and found a number of undisclosed items that strongly suggested the man was indeed Jack the Ripper. He was reportedly hospitalized for his own good and died soon after. Perhaps of some significance, Gull—who famously coined the term "anorexia nervosa"—died in 1890, just two years after the Ripper murders took place.

In 1970, the late English physician Thomas Edmund Alexander Stowell stated that Gull was not the Ripper but was the killer's doctor. Although Stowell did not come straight to the point and name Jack, his words and description of the man make it clear that he was talking about the Duke of Clarence.

Six years later, in 1976, the Gull theory was advanced at length in the pages of Stephen Knight's book *Jack the Ripper: The*

Final Solution. Knight's book was lauded at the time, but the story he told—of Gull, of a huge Masonic conspiracy, and of terrible murders that were linked to the British monarchy—has since been denounced, even by leading figures in the Jack the Ripper research community.

John Hamill, of the Freemasons' United Grand Lodge of England, said: "The Stephen Knight thesis is based upon the claim that the main protagonists, the Prime Minister Lord Salisbury, Sir Charles Warren, Sir James Anderson and Sir William Gull, were all high-ranking Freemasons. Knight knew his claim to be false for, in 1973, I received a phone call from him in the Library, in which he asked for confirmation of their membership. After a lengthy search I informed him that only Sir Charles Warren had been a Freemason. Regrettably, he chose to ignore this answer as it ruined his story."

One person who often pops up in Ripper research is John Pizer, an admittedly unsavory Polish Jew who worked in Whitechapel as a bootmaker and who was known locally as "Leather Apron." Strongly suspected of having assaulted a number of prostitutes in the area and with a conviction for stabbing already on record, Pizer was arrested by Police Sergeant William Thicke in September 1888—perhaps with much justification, it might be argued.

Unfortunately for Thicke, Pizer had alibis for two of the murders. At the time of Jack the Ripper's second killing, Pizer was speaking with a police officer. The two of them were watching a huge fire as it engulfed the London Docks. Nevertheless, the investigation of Pizer continued, which revealed there had been bad blood between Pizer and Thicke for years.

Although Pizer had the perfect alibi, elements of the London press openly named him as Jack the Ripper. Pizer had his revenge, however: a bit of legal wrangling ensured

One of the earliest suspects in the Jack the Ripper mystery was Prince Albert Victor, Duke of Clarence. While he had a bad reputation, he was never a proven killer.

Partly due to a popular book by Stephen Knight about Jack the Ripper in which Gull is portrayed as the killer, William Withey Gull was a likely suspect to many peoples' minds.

monetary compensation for the controversial bootmaker. And, in a strange bit of irony that no doubt pleased Pizer—and as British Home Office papers of 1889 reveal—Sergeant Thicke was himself once accused of being the Ripper.

Thomas Cream, a doctor who specialized in abortions (which, for the numerous prostitutes of Whitechapel in the late 1800s, would have been many), often surfaced in those domains in which Ripper investigators dwell. In 1881, Cream was jailed for poisoning in Illinois. On his release in 1891, however, he moved to London, where his murders continued. He was hanged by the neck at Newgate Prison in 1892. Legend says that Cream was literally halfway through admitting to being the Ripper when the rope snapped his neck, although it's a claim that has yet to be confirmed.

There is a problem here: Cream was in jail in the United States in 1888, the year in which the Ripper murders occurred. Or was he? Some Ripper researchers suggest Cream bribed his way out of his U.S. prison years earlier and was secretly replaced by a lookalike. Was it all too good to be true? As with just about every suspect in the Ripper affair, the jury remains steadfastly out.

On New Year's Eve 1888, the body of Montague John Druitt, a barrister from Dorset, England, was hauled out of the River Thames. Druitt, who also doubled as an assistant schoolmaster, was suspected by Assistant Chief Constable Sir Melville Macnaghten of being Jack the Ripper. Macnaghten was no fool: he rose to the position of assistant commissioner of the London Metropolitan Police.

It is a fact that mental illness ran through the Druitt family: both his mother and grandmother were deranged souls. There was also talk that Druitt had taken his life for fear that word might get out that he was homosexual. The fact that the Ripper murders ceased after Druitt's suicide only served to amplify the theory that he was the killer. For example, in his 1906 book *The Mysteries of Modern London*, poet and novelist George Robert Sims wrote that the Ripper had avoided the gallows by throwing himself into the Thames just after the Ripper murders ended—which is exactly what Druitt did. A near-identical statement was made by Sir John Moylan, the Home Office's undersecretary of state.

Druitt became a suspect because he committed suicide by drowning shortly after the last murder attributed to Jack the Ripper. Further investigation led to many doubts about that assumption.

If Druitt was Jack the Ripper, then he took with him to the grave the secrets of his homicidal, double life.

William Henry Bury, originally from London's East End, might be considered the ideal candidate for Jack the Ripper. Shortly after the horrific murders occurred, he moved to Dundee, Scotland. While living there, Bury killed his wife, Ellen. Notably, Ellen was a former prostitute and was the victim of vicious cuts to her stomach. The fact that Jack the Ripper solely targeted prostitutes and took a great deal of glee in slicing and dicing his victims did not pass by unnoticed.

Bury freely admitted to having killed his wife. He was quickly found guilty of her murder and soon thereafter hanged for his crime. Interestingly, the hangman himself, a character named James Berry, told just about anyone who cared to ask about Bury that he, Bury, was Jack the Ripper. Had Bury made a secret confession to the man who ended his life? It's difficult to say for sure, but Berry was sufficiently sure in his own mind. He told the story in 1927 to *Thomson's Weekly News*.

One of the biggest problems facing the police in the Ripper affair was that the killer always acted in an elusive fashion. But one man claimed to have gotten a close-up look at him. That man was George Hutchinson, a laborer. Hutchinson's story revolved around the life and death of Jack the Ripper's final victim, Mary Jane Kelly.

According to Hutchinson's somewhat unlikely claim made to the police, at around 2:00 A.M., just a few hours before Kelly's death, he had seen her with a suspicious-looking character. As Kelly and Hutchinson crossed paths, and as the former walked toward Thrawl Street, she was approached by a man wearing a hat. He was determined to ensure that Hutchinson didn't get a good look at his face. Oddly, Hutchinson then contradicted himself by asserting that the man was in his mid-thirties, wore a long coat, had a "stern" look on his face, and sported a thin moustache, slightly curled at the ends.

Allegedly somewhat concerned for Kelly's safety, Hutchinson decided to keep careful watch on Kelly's rented room, to where she took the man, and where she was violently torn to pieces only hours later. Despite hanging around for a while, Hutchinson never saw Kelly or the man leave the room. The astonishingly detailed nature of Hutchinson's report led some in London's police force to wonder if he, himself, was the Ripper, trying to cover his tracks by providing a detailed, false description of the killer.

Between April and October 1888, Joseph "Danny" Barnett was in a relationship with Jack's final victim, Mary Jane Kelly. At the time, Barnett was working at Billingsgate Fish Market. With money coming in, there was no more need for Kelly to walk the streets. Unfortunately, in October, Barnett lost his job, and Kelly had to return to selling herself for pennies. After a violent quarrel, the two split up. Nevertheless, Barnett—after the initial drama had calmed down—continued to give Mary money when he had some to spare.

As a result, intriguing theories have been suggested concerning Barnett's possible role as Jack the Ripper. First, there is the scenario of Barnett killing Kelly's prostitute friends as a means to scare Kelly out of earning her living on the streets of London. A second theory suggests that during their violent argument, Barnett killed Kelly—whether by accident or design is unknown. But to try to avoid suspicions that he was the killer, Barnett chose to hideously mutilate her body in a fashion befitting the Ripper as a means to camouflage his own actions. Since the Ripper was on everyone's minds, Barnett would fall under the radar.

One of the strangest stories concerning the identity of Jack the Ripper revolves around a Russian doctor named Alexander Pedachenko. It's a story that has conspiratorial overtones to it since Pedachenko was also a member of the Okhrana, a "secret police" unit focused on fighting terrorists and revolutionaries.

The story that links Pedachenko to Jack the Ripper's murderous spree in Whitechapel sounds unlikely but is nonetheless thought provoking. Supposedly, Pedachenko, working secretly with two colleagues, went on homicidal rampages around London's East End.

According to the strange and controversial story, Pedachenko embarked on the mad killing spree with one specific goal in mind: to make the finest minds of Scotland Yard look foolish and lacking in credibility due to their inability to solve the crimes. That the story was supposed to have surfaced from Grigori Rasputin, the famous healer, mystic, and "Mad Monk" who had an unrelenting hold on the Russian Royal Family, only made matters even more controversial.

In 1889, just one year after Jack the Ripper brought overwhelming fear to Whitechapel, a man named Francis Thompson penned a short story titled "The End Crowns the Work." It told of a poet who sacrificed young women to ancient gods as a means to ensure he became successful in his career in the field of poetry. Thompson was a keen poet himself, who also spent time living in the very heart of Whitechapel. For a while, he had to resort to sleeping on the streets of the district, when his planned career as a full-time poet

The success of a short story of a poet who sacrifices women to gods in order to enhance his career as a poet turned Francis Thompson into a suspect in the Jack the Ripper mystery.

spectacularly collapsed around him. In addition, Thompson studied for six years to be a surgeon. It was training that, of course, made Thompson very familiar with both human anatomy and knives.

Ripper theorists have suggested that Thompson's story—of young girls and sacrificial rites—might very well have been based upon Thompson's own warped and deranged attempts to achieve literary success by killing—and, in his crazed mind, sacrificing—London's East End prostitutes. Interestingly, while down and destitute in London, Thompson actually lived for a short period with a prostitute who, soon thereafter, disappeared.

Beyond any shadow of doubt, the most important development in decades—perhaps *ever*—in the saga of Jack the Ripper surfaced in September 2014. It revolved around a man named Aaron Kosminski. Born in 1865 in Kłodawa, Poland, Kosminski moved to England with his family in the 1880s at the age of sixteen.

There are several notable things about Kosminski: he lived in Whitechapel when the Ripper murders occurred, he suffered from acute mental illness and was placed in an insane asylum, and the police had suspected him of being Jack the Ripper. He was plagued night and day by voices in his head, he was scared of eating food prepared by anyone but himself, and he had an even bigger fear of bathing. Due to his psychological state, Kosminski spent time in two institutions: Colney Hatch Lunatic Asylum and Leavesden Asylum, the latter being where he died at the age of fifty-three, chiefly due to severe malnutrition provoked by anorexia.

In terms of the Jack the Ripper connections, in 1894, the aforementioned Sir Melville Macnaghten, who, at the time, was the assistant chief constable of the London Metropolitan Police, recorded in a memo that Kosminski was considered a suspect. Far more telling, Macnaghten described Kosminski as someone who had a "great hatred of women" and who had "strong homicidal tendencies."

In September 2014, Britain's *Daily Mail* newspaper revealed the results of a mitochondrial DNA analysis, which demonstrated the presence of Kosminski's semen on a shawl owned by one of the Ripper's victims, Catherine Eddowes. Critics, however, have pointed out that the shawl was "in the same room" as two of Eddowes's descendants in 2007, which means they could have contaminated the shawl with the DNA at that time rather than back in 1888.

Writer Tom Head noted: "Finding Kosminski's mtDNA in a semen stain on the shawl is *much* more impressive, and is much harder to explain. Contrary to Ripperologist Richard Cobb's claim that the stain could be explained by Kosminski's history with prostitutes in the area, the likelihood that Kosminski's mtDNA just *happened* to end up on a shawl that had already been described as an artifact of the murder scene seems prohibitively remote to me."

It was thanks to Russell Edwards, the author of the book *Naming Jack the Ripper*, that the shawl surfaced: he purchased it at an auction, and he ultimately had it tested for DNA evidence. Edwards says: "I've got the only piece of forensic evidence in the whole history of the case. I've spent fourteen years working on it, and we have definitively solved the mystery of who Jack the Ripper was. Only non-believers that want to perpetuate the myth will doubt. This is it now—we have unmasked him."

Of course, given the history of Jack the Ripper and the controversies surrounding him, it's likely that the last word *won't* be the last word, after all.

MURDERING UFO INVESTIGATORS

The term "flying saucer" was created in the summer of 1947. It was on June 24 of that year that a pilot named Kenneth Arnold had an amazing encounter with a squadron of strange-looking aircraft in the skies near Mt. Rainier, Washington State. Word of Arnold's now legendary encounter soon got out—to both the world's media and the U.S. military. Since Arnold described the craft as flying like a saucer would if it was skimmed across a body of water, the mysterious vehicles became known as flying saucers. Over the years, "unidentified flying object (UFO)" has become the more popular term. Since 1947, thousands of people have researched and investigated the phenomenon, all determined to find the answers to the riddle of the saucers. But what if UFO researchers don't just get close to the truth, but get *too* close? Might their lives be in danger? Could they be taken out of circulation by hired gunmen? The answer to those questions is undeniably yes. There are many cases on record where people allied to the world of UFO research have died under highly mysterious and controversial circumstances. And it's not just UFO investigators who have had their lives cut short as a result of digging into things that certain powerful people want them kept away from at all costs. The list also includes politicians and famous figures in the world of entertainment, as we'll now see.

In this sinister saga, there are suicides that may not have been suicides after all. There are people who have vanished off the face of Earth. There are deaths of flying saucer investigators that are attributed to natural causes but which, time-wise, seem to be far too convenient. Is all of this evidence nothing more than coincidence? Are people looking for evidence of murder and trying to force the facts to fit? No, not at all. All the evidence points in the direction of a ruthless cabal that will not think twice about taking out of circulation those who know too much about UFOs. If you are thinking of entering the world of UFO research, you may first want to consider the following before doing so.

We can find evidence of mysterious deaths in what was arguably the very first UFO event of the modern era. On June 21, 1947, a squadron of UFOs was seen flying over Maury Island, Puget Sound, Washington State. One of the craft exploded in midair, showering huge amounts of debris into the harbor below. A few pieces of that mysterious material were recovered by a man named Harold Dahl, who worked at the harbor. He handed it over to his boss, Fred Crisman. Interestingly, Crisman was later identified by New Orleans district attorney Jim Garrison as the second gunman in the November 22, 1963, assassination of President John F. Kennedy.

The U.S military soon got word of what had gone down at Maury Island and quickly dispatched two military officers to the area to investigate what had happened. They were Lieutenant Frank Mercer Brown and Captain William Lee Davidson, both of U.S. Army Intelligence. There are good indications that even in that early era, powerful figures were already running the ship. Although the military wanted answers to what had come down at Maury Island, those same powerful figures were determined to ensure that their secrets didn't get out. There was a very good reason for that.

Michael Riconosciuto is someone who has had long-standing involvement in the field of intelligence operations; he says that the Maury Island

Allegedly, this is where the first major sighting of UFOs took place, on June 21, 1947, an event complete with one of the mysterious flying discs exploding and spreading material onto the island and into the waters.

UFOs were actually nuclear-powered aircraft built in secret by elements of the government. No wonder those pulling the strings couldn't allow the facts to come out. The result was that Lieutenant Brown and Captain Davidson were soon dead: after collecting the wreckage, the pair took to the skies with the intent of flying to Wright Field near Dayton, Ohio, where the material was due to be examined by base scientists. It never happened, though: Brown and Davidson's aircraft caught fire in midair, killing both men in the process. On top of that, two journalists, Ted Morello and Paul Lance, who were looking into the explosion over Maury Island, also died under dubious circumstances. The mystery was quickly locked down, and with just about every one of any significance dead—and Dahl having had his life threatened by a Man in Black-type character, no less—the saga came to an end.

Many commentators (including Captain Edward Ruppelt of Project Blue Book fame; Blue Book was a UFO investigation program of the U.S. Air Force that folded in 1969) have stated that the entire Maury Island event was nothing more than an unfortunate hoax that had a tragic outcome for Brown and Davidson. However, the intense and dedicated research of conspiracy researcher Kenn Thomas has shown that the affair might not be as clear as has previously been assumed. Most significant are Fred Crisman's links with the intelligence community. In 1968, Crisman was subpoenaed by New Orleans district attorney Jim Garrison as part of Garrison's investigation into the assassination of President John F. Kennedy.

Moreover, according to the leaked "Majestic 12 1st Annual Report Annex C" (Majestic 12 allegedly was a high-level UFO research project of the government), some of the debris from Maury Island was turned over by Crisman (referred to as a CIC or counterintelligence corps agent) to a CIA agent named Shaw. The Annual Report states:

> The death of two Air Force counterintelligence officers in the crash of their B-25 aircraft en route to Hamilton AFB, California, after interviewing two auxiliary CG men who reported six UFOs over Maury Island, Washington, in June 1947. CIC agent Crisman had spoken to Kenneth Arnold, who on June 26th,1947, had reported a flight of UFOs over Mt. Rainier, Washington, and filed his report after he had spoken to Captain Davidson and Lieutenant Brown. The material given to Davidson and Brown was believed to come from Maury Island and may be celestial fragments containing metal from a nuclear reactor from a UFO. Fragments were turned over to CIA agent Shaw, and Crisman was ordered to the Alaskan Air Defense Command for assignment in Project IVY.

Kenn Thomas suggests that this was a reference to Clay Shaw, one of three people that Jim Garrison attempted to indict during his quest for the

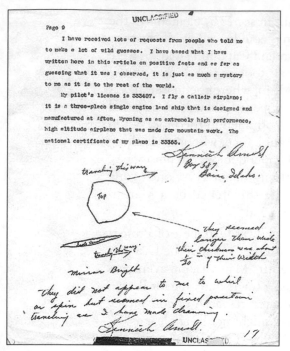

UNCLASSIFIED

Page 9

I have received lots of requests from people who told me to make a lot of wild guesses. I have based what I have written here in this article on positive facts and as far as guessing what it was I observed, it is just as much a mystery to me as it is to the rest of the world.

My pilot's license is 333487. I fly a Callair airplane; it is a three-place single engine land ship that is designed and manufactured at Afton, Wyoming as an extremely high performance, high altitude airplane that was made for mountain work. The national certificate of my plane is 33355.

Kenneth Arnold
Boy 387
Boise, Idaho.

A photocopy of notes taken by Kenneth Arnold showing what he saw over Mt. Rainer from his aircraft. This was just a week before the Roswell UFO crash.

truth surrounding the JFK assassination. And although Shaw was eventually acquitted, his role as a CIA asset has since been well documented and admitted officially by the CIA. For his part, Garrison claimed that his prosecution of Shaw was a "toe-hold" to a larger conspiracy in which Crisman may have been an assassin working on behalf of the aerospace industry, which had its own reasons for wanting JFK dead. In a well-known report titled "The Torbitt Document," Crisman is named as one of the three "hoboes" picked up in the railyard behind the infamous Grassy Knoll at Dealey Plaza in Dallas where, some maintain, a second gunman was located during the killing of Kennedy.

The fog of time has effectively resulted in certain aspects of the Maury Island case remaining unresolved, perhaps even permanently. For some, the case is still seen as nothing but a tragic hoax. For others, however, it is perceived as one of the most important cases of all, involving the actual recovery of debris from a malfunctioning UFO; the involvement of shadowy players on the periphery of the intelligence community; the possible deliberate murder of Air Force personnel in possession of the strange materials recovered at Maury Island; and even direct or indirect links to the JFK assassination of November 22, 1963, in Dallas, Texas.

Now, it's time to turn our attention to the most famous UFO case of all: Roswell. What else? It was in early July 1947 that something strange crashed on the Foster Ranch in Lincoln County, New Mexico. The wreckage of whatever it was that had come down was strewn across a distance of around six hundred feet. The rancher who found the material—William Ware "Mack" Brazel—contacted the local police, who then contacted the old Roswell Army Air Field. In no time at all, the military descended on the ranch, quickly collecting the materials and warning Brazel not to talk about what he had seen—which, evidence and testimony suggest, included not just the wreckage but also a number of mangled, rapidly decomposing bodies. While UFO researchers champion the case, there are strong indications that what came down was a top-secret, experimental vehicle of the U.S. military that spiraled out of control and crashed on the ranch. As for the bodies, they were almost certainly not alien in origin but rather human guinea pigs used in an early high-altitude exposure flight: they were handicapped people, secretly taken from a nearby hospital—Fort Stanton—which housed people with both mental and physical handicaps. The dark experiment was hidden behind a curtain of cover stories, including the rumor that a UFO from another world had come down. The ruse worked: even to this very day, the idea that the Roswell affair involved aliens is championed by just about every UFO researcher who has ever addressed the matter. Arguably, though, using handicapped people in experiments against their will is far more controversial than the theory that extraterrestrials lost their lives in New Mexico in July 1947.

To ensure that the case was forever confused, the military, only days after recovering the materials, said that the wreckage was not from a UFO after all but was rather from a weather balloon. In 1994, the Air Force changed its position again—this time it claimed that the balloon was not a weather balloon but rather a Mogul balloon, a huge balloon designed to monitor early Soviet atomic bomb tests. As for the stories of bodies found at the site, the U.S. government, in 1997, said they were nothing but crash test dum-

This story ran in the local *Roswell Daily Record* about the capture of a UFO at a nearby ranch.

mies. The cover stories are still in place to this very day, ensuring that the far darker "secret experiment" angle never gets out.

Miriam Bush was someone who knew exactly what happened on the Foster Ranch in early 1947. Not only that, she paid for that knowledge with her life. Bush has, at times, been incorrectly described as a nurse who worked at the military hospital at the Roswell Army Air Field. She was not: Bush was actually an executive secretary at the base. The distinction may sound small, but the fact is that Bush's position meant that she would have been in a prime position to see the mangled bodies when they were secretly brought to the base. Bush's immediate superior was Lieutenant Colonel Harold Warne, who played a significant role in the autopsies of the dead people used in the experiment.

It's hardly surprising, given the circumstances and the subsequent warnings issued to Bush and others in the base hospital at the time, that Bush became deeply paranoid and even in fear of her life. Although she had been told by high-ranking personnel at the base to never discuss what she had seen, Bush secretly chose to confide in her family, who she warned not to tell anyone what had happened and what she knew. For Bush, though, the Roswell affair came to dominate her life: she became even more paranoid, entered into a loveless marriage, and soon started seriously drinking. She would soon become a full-blown alcoholic. Such were the effects of what can happen when one finds oneself tangled in a conspiracy as disturbing and dark as the Roswell event surely was.

Even though Miriam Bush did not tell anyone else—outside of her family—about what she had seen at the Roswell base, namely, the bodies found on the Foster Ranch, she could never quite shake off the feeling that she was still being watched. She probably was: there are rumors that on two occasions, listening devices were placed on her home telephone, once in 1969 and once in 1982.

For Miriam Bush, matters came to a head—and to a shocking and suspicious end—in the late 1980s. Without warning, in December 1989, she took off for San Jose, California, and checked into a local motel under her sister's name—a strange action, further suggesting that she was concerned she was being watched. After all, why would she try to obfuscate her real identity if she had nothing to hide? The very next day, Bush was found dead in her motel room; a tightly tied plastic bag was around her neck. Marks on her arms indicated that a scuffle occurred at some point after she checked in the motel. Despite the evidence suggesting she was murdered, the official conclusion was that Bush had taken her own life. Whatever Miriam Bush knew about the Roswell affair, and whatever the full extent of her specific role into the events of 1947 was, went with her to the grave. Might she have been taken out of circulation by a hired assassin? There really is not a more likely explanation.

It's worth noting too that two other key figures in the Roswell affair also descended into full-blown alcoholism—all because of the trauma surrounding the incident and their roles in it. One of them was Dee Proctor. At the time of the Roswell crash in July 1947, Proctor was just a young boy who regularly did chores on the ranch of his neighbor, William Brazel. Proctor just happened to be with Brazel when the wreckage was found. Not long after finding the wreckage of the vehicle that had come down, Brazel and Proctor found something else: several mangled bodies of unknown origin. Both man and boy were severely threatened by the authorities. They were sternly told that their lives would be in mortal danger if they ever talked. Just like Miriam Bush, Dee Proctor was deeply scarred by the experience and ended up as a reclusive alcoholic. Major Jesse Marcel Sr., who was also on the crash site shortly after the incident took place, could only find solace in booze. He too became an alcoholic. Proctor hardly ever discussed the case with anyone. Marcel, decades later, gave several interviews to both ufologists and the media. He touched on the matter of the strange debris, but any discussion of the bodies was out of bounds. Just like Bush, both Proctor and Marcel took their secrets with them when the Grim Reaper came calling.

Guy Banister was a man who has become inextricably linked to the infamous events that occurred at Dealey Plaza in Dallas, Texas, on November 22, 1963. I am, of course, talking about the assassination of President John F. Kennedy. For many of those who conclude that a conspiracy was at the heart of the killing of the president, Banister is seen as one of the key conspirators, rubbing shoulders with the likes of Lee Harvey Oswald and David Ferrie. For those who don't see a conspiracy, his connection is perceived as being, at best, tenuous. Born in 1901, Banister spent twenty years with the FBI—specifically from 1934 to 1954. One year later, in 1955, he took on the position of assistant superintendent of the New Orleans Police Department. Then, in 1957, he established a private-detective agency, Guy Banister Associates, Inc., which he ran until his death in June 1964 at the age of sixty-three. But there's something else about Banister that's worth noting. In the summer of 1947 while with the FBI, Banister investigated a number of UFO reports for his boss, FBI director J. Edgar Hoover. Without doubt the most visible case that fell into Banister's jurisdiction occurred in Twin Falls, Idaho, in July 1947.

On July 11, the *Oregon Journal* published an article titled "FBI Describes Idaho 'Saucer' in Detail" that reported the following: "FBI Agent W. G. Banister said an object

Former special agent for the FBI, and later superintendent of the New Orleans Police, Guy Banister became involved in many curious cases from the JFK assassination to the investigation of UFOs which appeared to be a 'flying disc' was found early today at Twin Falls, Idaho and turned over to federal authorities there. Banister, special agent in charge of the FBI in Montana and Idaho, said the bureau had reported the discovery to the army at Fort Douglas, Utah. An FBI agent in Twin Falls inspected the 'saucer' and described it as similar to the 'cymbals used by a drummer in a band placed face to face.'"

The *Oregon Journal* continued: "The object measured 30.5 inches in diameter with a metal dome on one side and a plastic dome about 14 inches high on the opposite side, anchored in place by what appeared to be stove bolts. The gadget is gold painted on one side and silver (either stainless steel, aluminum, or tin) on the other. It appeared to have been turned out by machine, reports from Twin Falls said. The FBI agent declined to elaborate further. At Fort Douglas, a high-ranking officer, who declined to permit use of his name, would not comment. He refused either to confirm or deny that army authorities had heard of the reported discovery or were investigating it."

Within hours, the matter was resolved, as the *Boston Post* noted on July 12: "Assistant Police Chief L. D. McCracken said tonight four juveniles had admitted making a metallic disc found this morning in the yard of Mrs. T. H. Thompson of Twin Falls. McCracken said that he was tipped that one of the boys knew about the case. The boys explained it took them two days to make the 'saucer,' which resembled band cymbals placed together and with frosted plexiglass dome. McCracken said that army officers who came to Twin Falls from Fort Douglas, Utah, had taken the disc to Salt Lake City."

The newspaper added: "The object measured 30.5 inches in diameter with a metal dome on one side and a plastic dome about 14 inches high on the opposite side, anchored in place by what appeared to be stove bolts. The gadget was gold painted on one side and silver on the other. The object was found by Mrs. F. W. Easterbrooks, who said she heard a thudding noise about 2:30 A.M. She ran outside, saw the 'disc' in an adjoining yard and called police."

While the prank explanation was certainly correct, it's intriguing to note that only hours before the matter was resolved in a down-to-earth fashion, Banister was briefed by military personnel from Fort Douglas, Utah, on what was known about the "flying disc" issue at that time. The full story of what Banister was told—or was not told—remains unresolved. Banister was not done with UFOs, however. He soon investigated yet another Twin Falls-based report, this one from August 13. I quote from FBI records declassified under the terms of the Freedom of Information Act:

"…[deleted] of Twin Falls, Idaho … and two sons Billie, age ten, Keith, age eight, saw an object nine miles northwest of Twin Falls, resembling [a] flying disc. [Deleted] stated this object was proceeding down Salmon River at terrific speed estimated by him at one thousand miles per hour. [Deleted] and sons described object to newspapers as twenty feet long, ten feet wide and ten feet thick, light sky blue in color and also observed flames emanating from sides of object." Banister informed FBI headquarters that he would keep them "promptly and fully informed" of any relevant and additional data that might surface. Nothing of any significance did.

On August 19, yet another UFO report reached Banister. On this occasion, a married couple and a family friend viewed a triangular formation of ten UFOs flying over Twin Falls at around 9:30 P.M. They reportedly resembled flying saucers and were "illuminated." Banister evidently took the matter seriously. He wrote in his report: "In event Bureau in possession of any information concerning experimental activities on part of Army Air Forces which may explain these phenomena, advice would be greatly appreciated. It is believed continued appearance of such objects without official explanation may result in hysteria and panic [at] Twin Falls." In total, Banister investigated no fewer than nine UFO reports in the July–August 1947 time frame alone.

Guy Banister: a man who will probably forever be tied to the JFK assassination, someone who received a behind-closed-doors briefing on UFOs from the U.S. military in the summer of 1947, and an agent of the FBI who undertook a number of UFO investigations in his official capacity with the Bureau. Not only that, in 1944, Banister was at the forefront of an investigation into the landing of a Japanese "Fugo" balloon-bomb in Kalispell, Montana. The late John Keel suspected that what came down at Roswell, New Mexico, in 1947 was a "Fugo" balloon, or a then-modernized variation on it. Taking all of the above into consideration, there's little wonder that Guy Banister is perceived by many as an enigmatic character.

There is yet another famous case that has for many years been perceived as a ufological classic but that also falls under the "secret balloon" category. It occurred just half a year after Roswell. It's the strange and ultimately tragic affair of Kentucky Air National Guard pilot Captain Thomas P. Mantell, who, many UFO believers accept, lost his life chasing a UFO on the afternoon of January 7, 1948. He did not; Mantell died chasing a balloon. Matters began when personnel at Godman Army Air Field, Kentucky, caught sight of something in the sky they perceived as very strange: a large and extremely reflective object that appeared to be circular in design. No one could identify it. It was, then, hardly surprising that talk of flying saucers was quickly all-encompassing.

Fortunately, or so it seemed at the time, a squadron of four P-51 *Mustang* aircraft, under the command of Captain Mantell, was heading toward Godman Army Airfield. One of the pilots was low on fuel, another one expressed concern about pursuing the object due to his lack of an oxygen mask, and a third was ordered to shadow to the ground the pilot who had worries about losing consciousness due to oxygen deprivation. That left only Captain Mantell to pursue the object.

Reports of flying saucers, or UFOs, first started getting traction in the late 1940s, becoming a pop culture phenomenon by the 1950s, especially with the help of popular sci-fi B movies.

At a height of around 15,000 feet, Mantell called into the base and said that he could see the UFO quite clearly. He pushed his plane further through the skies, ultimately reaching a height of approximately 25,000 feet. Then, nothing. Apart, that is, from death for the captain: having reached such an altitude without oxygen, Mantell passed out, and his plane plummeted to the ground. For many in ufology, the case is a UFO classic. They are wrong. Rumors suggest that Mantell's plane was blasted out of the sky, in essence to prevent him from getting too close to a classified vehicle of the kind test-flown near Maury Island, Washington, in June 1947.

In 1955, one of the most controversial of all the many and varied UFO books published in the fifties was released—and, for the UFO field, to a distinct fanfare. Its title was *The Case for the UFO*. The author was Morris K. Jessup. His book was a detailed study of the theoretical power sources for UFOs: what was it that made them fly? How could they perform such incredible aerial feats, such as coming to a complete stop in the skies, hovering at incredible heights? Jessup believed that the vitally important answers lay in the domain of gravity or, as he saw it, antigravity. Jessup may well have been on to something, as it wasn't long at all before the world of officialdom was on Jessup's back—specifically senior figures in the U.S. Navy. It was one particularly intriguing office of the Navy that was watching Jessup—a "special weapons" division. Clearly, someone in the U.S. Navy was interested in, and perhaps even concerned by, Jessup's findings and theories. Maybe that same office of the Navy was worried that Jessup just might stumble onto the same technology that was being used to fly Uncle Sam's very own UFOs—those UFOs that the military were very happy for the public to perceive as alien spacecraft, as the perception helped the military's long-term plan to fabricate an alien invasion.

Just like Miriam Bush and Dee Proctor in relation to Roswell, Morris Jessup became deeply worried—paranoid, even—that he was being spied on by certain elements of the U.S. government. On several occasions, he noticed that certain items in his office had clearly been moved, strongly suggesting that when he was out of his home, someone was having a stealthy look around. The ante was upped to a significant degree when Jessup had a face-to-face interview with Navy representatives who wanted to speak with him about his book, his theories concerning antigravity, and the technology referred to in his book. That wasn't all they wanted to talk about, though. The Navy officers who met with Jessup also wanted to know what Jessup knew about the so-called Philadelphia Experiment of 1943. It was said to have been a top-secret program designed to make warships magnetically invisible. So, the story went, the experiment—which occurred in the Philadelphia Navy Yard, hence the name of the program—went wrong and caused the ship to become literally invisible, injuring a number of the crew and killing some, too. There are even tales that some of the crew vanished from the ship, never to be seen again. Jessup, scared and stressed, blew the whistle on what he knew of the experiment and told the Navy all that he knew, which was exactly what the Navy wanted.

Of course, given the fact that Jessup was already in a deep state of fear and paranoia, this visit from the Navy only increased his anxieties. He saw Men in Black lurking outside of his home. Hang-up calls in the middle of the night became regular occurrences. Mail arrived tampered: opened and resealed. Clearly, someone—or some agency—was trying to derail Jessup and his research. And they were doing a very good job, too. In fact, from Jessup's perspective, it was way too good a job.

In the early evening of April 20, 1959, the lifeless body of Morris Jessup was found in his car, which was parked in Matheson Hammock Park in Miami, Florida. The car's engine was still running, and a hosepipe, affixed to the exhaust, had been fed through the driver's side window. Jessup was dead from the effects of carbon monoxide. Jessup's body was found by a man named John Goode, who worked at the park. Shocked at the sight before him, Goode quickly called the police, who arrived in no time at all.

While it certainly looked as if Jessup had killed himself, not everyone was quite so sure that things were as clear-cut as that. The window through which the hose ran was stuffed with a couple of towels to prevent air from getting in and carbon monoxide from getting out. Curiously, Jessup's wife, Rubeye, confirmed that the towels were not theirs. Why, if Jessup took his own life, did he not take towels from the family home? What would have been the point of buying new towels? And if he did buy such towels, where was the receipt from the store they were purchased from? It certainly wasn't in the car or in any of Jessup's pockets. Equally suspicious is the fact that on the very night before his death, Jessup was in a very upbeat, fired-up mood: he spent more than an hour chatting on the phone with a good friend, Dr. Manson Valentine, expressing his enthusiasm for his latest work and plans for further investigations. Jessup even told Valentine that they should have lunch together the next day, as Jessup had something incredible to reveal. Valentine never got to see what it was that Jessup had uncovered—and he never saw Jessup again, either. Suicide or murder? The jury still can't make up its mind, almost sixty years later.

Finally....

As anyone and everyone with knowledge of the UFO phenomenon will be aware, the entire subject is steeped in controversy. But some aspects of

More connected to the possibility of alien visitations than almost anyplace else in the world, Roswell, New Mexico, capitalizes on their history with the UFO Museum, which is a popular tourist attraction.

the UFO phenomenon are more controversial than others. And then there are those aspects that are *really* controversial. All of which brings us yet again to the matter of UFOs and suspicious deaths. In 1997 I interviewed the well-known British UFO investigator Jenny Randles regarding a strange series of events she found herself in back in the latter part of 1986. It was a very curious saga involving allegedly classified documents, dead aliens, crashed flying saucers, and much more. It all began in October 1986, when Randles came into contact with a man who had then recently left his employment with the British Army. According to the man, he had in his possession a large stash of still classified material on UFOs that he had acquired under very controversial circumstances. Despite the admittedly sensational nature of the story, Randles agreed to meet with the man—who Randles referred to only as Robert—at a location in the English town of Eccles, near where Randles lived. Peter Hough, a friend of Randles and a fellow UFO investigator, also attended the meeting.

The story that Robert told was as remarkable as it was inflammatory. Roughly a year or so earlier, an American individual, employed by the U.S. military and working at Wright-Patterson Air Force Base in Dayton, Ohio, came across a large batch of computerized files while engaged in repairing one particular system at the base. And we're not talking about just a few pages of material. According to what Robert told Randles and Hough, the number of pages was huge. The man allegedly printed around *six hundred* pages of material, which wasn't even anywhere near the overall total.

It turned out that the man in question was allegedly friends with Robert's commanding officer in the British Army, the two having met in an exchange program. Fearful about what he had gotten himself into, the computer specialist gave the hundreds of pages of material on those aforementioned crashed saucers and alien autopsies to the CO. It wasn't long before there was disturbing news: the specialist was killed in a car "accident," supposedly while under the influence of booze. That was not the only issue surrounding controversial deaths that Randles heard of from Robert, as will soon become clear.

Back in 1997, when I spoke with Jenny Randles about all this, she told me: "Robert's CO explained that he was due to take on a new position with the British Army and he needed to offload the UFO files. Was Robert the man for the job?" He most certainly was. At first, as he admitted, Robert found the whole thing exciting. High-level secrets concerning Uncle Sam's collection of deceased extraterrestrials, alien technology, and more all dominated Robert's amazed mind. It was like something out of a Robert Ludlum or Tom Clancy novel. But it wasn't long before reality set in, and Robert went from being excited to deeply worried. After all, if the files were the real deal, then he was in potential, deep trouble. It was this worry that led Robert to approach Randles with a view to handing the material over to her.

The plan failed. About a week after the meeting between Robert, Randles, and Hough took place, Robert got back in touch. He claimed that in the intervening week, what were described as his "former employers" paid him a visit, took him to a military installation in the south of England, and intensely grilled him about those files. Robert claimed he had no choice but to hand over the approximately six hundred pages. Failure to do so might backfire on his wife and children, Robert was ominously told. On handing the material over, those same "former employers" informed Robert that the files were nothing but the result of "a prank." Given the large size of the file, it seems unlikely that someone would have gone to such a massive degree to perpetrate a hoax—and, even if it was nothing more than a time-consuming joke, what would have been the motivation?

> Robert claimed he had no choice but to hand over the approximately 600 pages. Failure to do so might backfire on his wife and children, he was ominously told.

Many might say that Robert was nothing more than a fantasy-prone character, who was stringing along Randles and Hough for his own obscure amusement. But that is unlikely. Randles, having been on the receiving end of conspiratorial tales in the past, elected to do a bit of digging into Robert. It turns out that when the initial meeting was over, Randles and Hough had the presence of mind to note the license plate number on Robert's car. They then shared that number with a trusted source in the British Police Force, who agreed to run the plate number through the force's database and see who it belonged to. The outcome was quite intriguing.

Randles told me: "It turned out that what [Robert] had told us proved to be correct. The name he had given us was his real name. He lived where he said he lived. He had recently been in the Army. And his car had been registered in precisely the same month that his Army career had come to an end."

And there's something else, too: one of the documents contained in the vast stash of material was titled "Elimination of Non-Military Personnel." Randles said to me: "[Robert] said that this was a document discussing the ways in which witnesses who had come into possession of too much information on UFOs were silenced. And although this sounds very much like something out of a spy film, from his detailed discussion of a number of case histories in the file, the one tactic that was used most often—particularly with people in influential positions—was to offer them high-paid jobs in government departments. They had pretty much determined that where money was concerned, people usually comply."

Randles added: "But, there was a discussion of the so-called Men in Black—people going around warning people about national security and intimidating them into silence. However, Robert told us that this tactic was only used on those whose instability was considered to be significant enough that, if they ever told their story publicly, it would not be considered credible."

Then there was one final tactic: if financial incentives didn't work, and "instability" wasn't relevant, there was always *termination*. Robert stressed to Randles that this last-resort tactic was rarely ever used, primarily because of the dicey and fraught nature of trying to make a murder look like a suicide or an accident. Yet, again we see how getting way too close to the truth behind the UFO phenomenon can end in fatal tragedy.

BLOWING THE WHISTLE

Back in 1998, I wrote a book titled *The FBI Files*. It told the story of the Bureau's involvement in the UFO phenomenon; contactee cases; the alleged Aztec, New Mexico, UFO crash of 1948; the cattle mutilation mystery; and even FBI records on the sinister Men in Black. Chapter 4 of the book was titled "The Oak Ridge Invasion," a reference to the name of an atomic energy facility located in Tennessee. As so often happens when I write a book, people who personally know something of its contents or subject matter will contact me and share the relevant information. And that is precisely what happened with regard to that specific chapter of my book. It was a study of FBI files that had been declassified under the terms of the Freedom of Information Act, which described various UFO encounters at the Oak Ridge National Laboratory from the late 1940s to the early 1950s.

One of the people who contacted me through my publisher, Simon & Schuster, was an elderly woman who worked at Oak Ridge in 1947 and had read my book. She added that she had some information that I was sure to find of deep interest but which she preferred to tell me about specifically in person. As I was living in the U.K. at that time, there wasn't much of a chance of me meeting up with her anytime soon. I asked if she could put her revelations onto paper, but I couldn't persuade her. Nor would she share them with me over the telephone or via email.

It wasn't until I moved to the United States in 2001 that I was able to connect with the woman. In the summer, I traveled around much of the West Coast, chiefly to do a series of lectures for various UFO groups in California. I put out a feeler to the woman, explaining my new circumstances and asking if we could now, finally, talk about the UFO secrets that had fallen into her lap.

On July 28, 2001, I had lunch with the then-seventy-nine-year-old woman at a Los Angeles restaurant, and we chatted extensively. She was driven to the restaurant by a family member, a much younger man who seemed to be equally as worried and concerned as she was. Nevertheless, she agreed to share what she knew, provided that her name was never published (she was, however, required to provide Simon & Schuster's legal people with a detailed release form, as were each and all of the other whistleblowers). So, I sat back and listened carefully, amazed.

I referred to her in the book as the Black Widow. There was a highly relevant reason for this, a reason which was not mentioned in my 2005 book that described her revelations, *Body Snatchers in the Desert*: her husband, whom she married in 1972, was African American. She, however, was not. They were both just into their very early fifties when they married and had twenty-four happy years together, despite some unforgivable racist comments from her ignorant family. It was in 1996 that her husband passed away, hence the title I gave her: the Black Widow.

When we met, knowing that she had read *The FBI Files*, my natural assumption was that she wanted to tell me something about UFO encounters at the Oak Ridge facility. Makes sense, right? No. I was wrong; what she actually wanted to share with me was certain information that, if provable, would radically alter the face of ufology and blow the Roswell case right out of the water. As we ate, I wondered, with a fair degree of excitement, what I had gotten myself into. It wasn't long before I had the answer to that loaded question.

The Oak Ridge, Tennessee, facility, shown here around 1950, was part of the Manhattan Project but was called the Energy Research and Development Administration.

The Black Widow, born in 1922, had worked at Oak Ridge from the mid-1940s to the early 1950s. While there, and on three occasions between May and July 1947, she saw a number of unusual-looking bodies brought to the facility under stringent security. She said some of them looked Japanese, while others displayed signs of certain medical conditions, such as dwarfism, oversized heads, and bulging eyes. A few of the bodies were extensively damaged, as if they had been involved in violent accidents, which, as it happens, proved to be the case. In all, fifteen such bodies were brought to Oak Ridge under great secrecy, I was told; all of them were reportedly used against their wills in certain high-altitude, balloon-based experiments in New Mexico, one of which led to the Roswell "UFO crash" legend—or, more likely, became a part of the massive cover-up. The Black Widow said: "Those bodies—the Roswell bodies—they weren't aliens. The government could care less about those stories about alien bodies found at Roswell—except to hide the truth."

> Everything, the Black Widow said, was hidden beneath a mass of fabricated tales of flying saucers and little men from the stars.

She added: "I don't know anything at all about how these people were brought [to the United States], but I heard at Oak Ridge that some of them were in the States in late 1945 and brought over with Japanese doctors and Nazi doctors who had been doing similar experiments. That's when some of this began." The story continued that at least some of the people used in the tests were American prisoners given the opportunity to cut the lengths of their sentences—if, that is, they were willing to take a chance and take part in the dicey experiments. Reportedly, a number did take the bait but failed to survive the flights. Some of the handicapped people did not come from Japan but rather from "hospitals and asylums" in the United States.

All of the material evidence was said to have been eventually destroyed—chiefly because the operations didn't provide much in the way of results and because of the outright illegality of the experiments. Everything, the Black Widow said, was hidden beneath a mass of fabricated tales of flying saucers and little men from the stars. She doubted that anything of any significance still existed—certainly not the bodies or the balloons, and probably not even the old records, which she believed were burned to oblivion to ensure nothing could ever be proved, decades later. Unless, however, some of them were preserved for secret, historical purposes, which is not at all impossible. I hope they were. If not, it may be nigh on impossible to conclusively prove *anything* about Roswell—ever.

There was one other aspect of the Black Widow's story that needs to be addressed: it was the overwhelming fear she exhibited at our meeting. It was ever present throughout our 2001 lunch; it was undeniable. She tried to disguise that fear with smiles and laughter, but she was certainly no Oscar-winning Hollywood actor. That's for sure. Seeing through her façade was like seeing through freshly polished glass. In *Body Snatchers in the Desert*, I said that she "possessed the sad and somewhat sunken eyes of a person with the weight of the world on her shoulders. She was clearly looking for someone to speak with; but, equally, she was very concerned about the ramifications of doing so, 'if the government finds out.'"

In my original manuscript, I detailed why she was so scared, but that section didn't make the cut. The reason? The publisher was highly concerned about the Black Widow's claims to me that certain people who had gotten too close to the truth of Roswell, and who couldn't keep their mouths shut, had been *murdered by the government*. So the story went, certain hired assets, who regularly worked with the intelligence community on "troublesome" situations, were secretly contracted to terminate those who threatened the status quo and its dangerous secret.

Interestingly, the Black Widow made a mention to me of a long-retired nurse from Roswell who had died under extremely questionable circumstances "a few years ago." I didn't know it at the time, but it's highly possible that she was referring to a woman named Miriam Bush. Miriam was not actually a nurse; in 1947, she was an executive secretary at the Roswell Army Air Field (RAAF) hospital. She worked for a medical officer, Lieutenant Colonel Harold Warne, and saw the bodies found on the Foster Ranch—specifically when they were brought into the confines of the hospital. They were, as nearly everyone claimed, small, damaged, and unusual looking. This trauma-filled experience clearly affected Miriam to a huge degree. The whole thing was like an albatross around her neck. That huge, ominous bird never left her.

Miriam's private life was a mess, and she became alcoholic—as did, by the way, both Major Jesse Marcel and Dee Proctor, a sign, perhaps, of the tremendous burden of hiding what they may have known. And, in the late 1980s, Miriam became fearful that she was being watched and followed. *She was*. Miriam Bush was found dead in a motel room just outside of San Jose, California, in December 1989. A plastic bag was around her head, and her arms were bruised and scratched. The verdict? Suicide. Yes, really.

When the story of Miriam Bush surfaced—years after I spoke with the Black Widow, and also a couple of years after *Body Snatchers in the Desert* was published—my mind instantly swung back to the Black Widow's comments relative to the highly suspicious death of a certain "nurse" from Roswell. Was it Miriam Bush? I don't know. But logically, it would make sense. If so, though, how did the Black Widow know this? After all, Miriam was based in Roswell, New Mexico, and the Black Widow worked in Tennessee. I have no answer to that question; I wish I did. But I do know that the Black Widow's major concern about speaking on the record was the fear that she would end up like the woman from Roswell—a woman who happened to be in the wrong place at the wrong time in 1947, and who paid for it with her life, years later.

A DEADLY FALL

May 22, 1949, was the date on which the first U.S. secretary of defense, James Forrestal, died. The official record is that he died at 1:50 A.M., although there were no witnesses. As will quickly become apparent, the circumstances surrounding Forrestal's final hours are swamped in controversy. All that we know with absolute certainty is that Forrestal's body was found on a third-floor canopy of the Bethesda Naval Hospital in Maryland. Did he take a fatal leap out of the window of the thirteenth floor of the hospital, his mind in turmoil and suicide on his mind? Was it an accident? Or, was Forrestal assassinated? Let's have a look at this undeniably strange and disturbing affair. We'll begin with a bit of important background on the man himself. Forrestal was born just eight years before the dawning of the twentieth century in Dutchess County, New York, and, after completing his education at Princeton University, took a job with a Wall Street-based company, William A. Read and Co. A skilled figure in the field of economics, Forrestal quickly made a significant amount of money. At the age of thirty-four, he married *Vogue* journalist Josephine Ogden. It was hardly the ideal situation, though. Ogden was an alcoholic who flew off the handle at just about any given moment. Forrestal had his flaws, too: he was a very unemotional person. For Forrestal, getting close to people was incredibly difficult. At some point, he pretty much gave up trying. In 1940, however, things changed for Forrestal, massively so.

It was in that year that Forrestal decided to take his career in a very different direction: with the U.S. government. Amazingly, it wasn't too long before he was offered the prestigious position of undersecretary of the Navy. Hardly surprisingly, Forrestal quickly accepted the position. From there, things really took off: he was soon given the job of secretary of the Navy. Things were taken to an even greater scale when, in 1947—the year in which the National Security Act was passed and the CIA was created—Forrestal was approached, by the presidential office, no less, to take on the role of the very first secretary of defense. President Harry S. Truman was more than happy with his choice for the position. Matters soon began to change, however, and not at all in a good way—to say the very least.

It wasn't long before Forrestal began to exhibit psychological problems. Depression, caused by his huge workloads, were said to have been the primary cause. Matters only got worse: the depression deepened, anxiety attacks kicked in, and a notable dose of paranoia overwhelmed him. For the U.S. government, as the secretary of defense, Forrestal was a major asset to the infrastructure of the United States; this was not good at all. His psychological issues, however, had him secretly marked by President Truman as a potential danger to the orderly running of the Department of Defense. Bit by bit, and throughout 1948, Forrestal's fraught state of mind got even worse. Eventually, action had to be taken. And it most certainly was. Forrestal lost his job as the secretary of defense. The next thing for the government was to try to help For-

The disturbing condition of James Forrestal, the first U.S. secretary of defense who caused Truman to replace him due to his erratic behavior, saw him hospitalized for his feelings of paranoia, which may have been increased by the recent activity of so-called flying saucers.

restal get well. Of course, no one wanted the man to suffer or plunge into a state of life-threatening proportions. So, a decision was made to have Forrestal admitted to the aforementioned Bethesda Naval Hospital, where, hopefully, he could recover. Most worrying for Truman's team, however, was the genuine fear that a destabilized Forrestal just might go off the rails and divulge some of the U.S. government's most guarded secrets. It was a dangerous and unpredictable time. It would soon turn deadly.

Just a few days before he ended up in the naval hospital, Forrestal had a curious experience that had distinct Men in Black overtones attached to it. On the day in question, Forrestal received a visit from a friend named Ferdinand Eberstadt, who was deeply concerned about Forrestal's fragile and paranoid state of mind. Eberstadt, a lawyer, banker, and author of a historic 1945 document, "Task Force Report on National Security Organization," was floored by what he saw when he arrived at Forrestal's home. All of the curtains were closed. Forrestal told his friend—in hushed tones—that listening devices were all over the house. Sinister characters were watching his every move. His life was in danger.

To demonstrate this to Eberstadt, Forrestal carefully opened one of the blinds and pointed, knowingly, in the direction of a pair of shabbily dressed men on the street corner. "They" were a part of it, Forrestal assured Eberstadt. In no time at all, the doorbell to Forrestal's home was heard ringing. The last thing Forrestal wanted to do was answer the door. Fortunately, one of his staff was on hand to do exactly that. A brief conversation took place, which neither Forrestal nor Eberstadt were able to hear. The facts, however, quickly came to Forrestal from his aide.

According to what the two men were told, the visitor at the door was trying to generate support that would hopefully allow him to become postmaster in his hometown. Could he come in and speak with Forrestal and have him offer some help and advice? Due to Forrestal's chaotic mindset, the man was quickly turned away. Eberstadt and Forrestal watched carefully as the man walked directly toward the two badly dressed men that *already* had Forrestal in a state of turmoil. It was even more evidence of a conspiracy against him, Forrestal grimly concluded, when he saw the three clearly engaging in conversation.

Maybe the whole thing was blown out of proportion by a man descending into a collective state of paranoia, fear, and nervous collapse. Certainly, that's what happened. But it's worth noting that this odd affair, which occurred during Eberstadt's visit, has several Men in Black-themed parallels to it. First, the Men in Black are typically described as looking not quite right: they are extremely pale-skinned, they often have bulging eyes (hidden behind wraparound shades), and (very bizarrely) are at times described as wearing wigs and makeup. The inference is that they are not human. Forrestal's visitor on the day in question was described by his staff as very odd looking.

That the man tried to gain access to Forrestal's home—by claiming to be seeking support for a potential job as a postmaster—mirrors the 1960s-era reports of MIB finding ways into the homes of UFO witnesses by claiming to be military personnel or police officers. In the same time frame, Women in Black were posing as census takers and as gypsies. They were clearly neither. The MIB are often described as wearing clothes that are shabby, dirty, and occasionally give off an odor like dirt. The two characters that the "odd-looking" man walked toward (and began speaking to) were badly dressed. And there's the fact that the men amounted to a trio. Particularly in the 1950s and 1960s, the MIB turned up in threes at the homes of witnesses to UFOs.

It must be stressed that none of this proves James Forrestal was murdered. It must be said, however, that the day in question was a very weird one. And not just for Forrestal, but also for Eberstadt. Even he had to admit it was all a bit odd. And it's worth noting the words of Dennis Stacy, a long-time and well-respected figure in ufology who runs Anomalist Books with Patrick Huyghe. Of that MIB-like affair, Stacy observed in a 1993 article for *Flying Saucer Review* magazine titled "Forrestal's Fall: Did He Jump, or Was He Pushed?" that "the whole thing has the appearance of a one-act play staged for Forrestal's 'benefit.'"

Notably, Stacy added that the affair "begins to smack of orchestration aimed at unsettling an already unstable Forrestal." Thought-provoking words, indeed.

On April 2, 1949, Forrestal was taken to the hospital—for his own good and for that of the U.S. government, too. It was apparent to the doctors and nurses that Forrestal was in a dangerous state. Forrestal was absolutely sure that dangerous characters were watching his every move. Who those characters might have been all very much depended on Forrestal's frame of mind: sometimes, they were Russian agents. On other occasions, they were spies in the U.S. government. As for the latter, Forrestal thought they were from J. Edgar Hoover's FBI. Forrestal's mind was spinning—and far from in a good way. On top of that, Forrestal stopped eating for a while. Not a good sign. It's important to note that when Forrestal was admitted to Bethesda, he was in what amounted to solitary confinement, and the windows of the room were modified so they couldn't be opened. Notably, when Forrestal's family inquired why such actions had been taken, Captain George N. Raines, the chief psychiatrist at Bethesda, said it was to prevent Forrestal from leaping out of the windows and killing himself—which, some believe, is exactly what happened on the fateful night that Forrestal's life met its end.

> It's important to note that when Forrestal was admitted to Bethesda, he was in what amounted to solitary confinement, and the windows of the room were modified so they couldn't be opened.

After a few weeks in the hospital, there was a clear, welcome improvement for Forrestal. Both the doctors and the nurses concurred. On top of that, his appetite started to return. He even ate a huge steak in the presence of Rear Admiral Morton Willcutts, who had come to see his old friend. It really did appear that good times were ahead. That all changed, however, only two nights later. Death was just around the corner.

It was a death shrouded in mystery. Let's see what we know for sure about those final hours for someone who held some of the U.S. government's most important secrets. The man assigned to keep a careful watch on Forrestal was U.S. Navy corpsman Edward Prise. Because of the time they spent together, the pair became good friends. As the night got longer, Forrestal told Prise that he didn't need a sleeping pill and was going to read for a while. That seemed to be a good thing. After Prise's shift was over, another military man, Robert Wayne Harrison Jr., replaced him. Forrestal's end was almost upon him.

At some point into his shift, Harrison left the room to run an errand. From that point onward, facts become murky and unclear. When Harrison got back to the room, he was shocked to see that Forrestal was not in his bed and the room's windows were open. Harrison raced to the window; the cord of Forrestal's dressing gown was tied to the radiator near the window. Clearly, the goal was death by strangulation. It turned out, however, that Forrestal's weight caused the cord to snap and Forrestal fell ten floors to his death, which absolutely no one could have had a chance of surviving. The official theory is that Forrestal—left alone in his room—took his own life, possibly in a brief moment when his mind swung back to that dangerous state of depression and anxiety. The big question, however, is: could Forrestal have been pushed? The reason: to make sure he could never, ever reveal what he may have been exposed to by the government.

It's vital to note that Forrestal's fears of being watched were not groundless.

It should also be stressed that at the time of his death, Forrestal was in one of his best states of mind of the last few months. Moreover, Edward Prise revealed that Forrestal had told him he would like Prise to become Forrestal's personal driver. In other words, Forrestal seemed to be making plans for a good future—and not for the end of his life. Then, there's the matter of Forrestal's brother, Henry. On the day of Forrestal's death, Henry marched into the hospital, demanding that Forrestal be released into his, Henry's, care. If someone on "the inside" wanted Forrestal dead, then allowing Henry Forrestal to take his brother home would have been disastrous. Forrestal would have been totally out of the control of those who may have wanted him dead, something powerful players may not have wanted. It is, then, rather telling that Forrestal died the night before Henry was due to take his brother back to his house.

That's not all, though: there's also the matter of why, precisely, Robert Wayne Harrison Jr. left the room. That was completely against the grain: official orders were that Forrestal was never, ever to be left alone. And yet, on the very night that Forrestal died, he *was* left alone. Henry Forrestal was deeply con-

General Nathan Twining, who was U.S. Air Force chief of staff from 1953 to 1957, was the author of "AMC Opinion Concerning 'Flying Discs.'"

cerned about the circumstances surrounding his brother's death, to the point that he came to believe that his brother had indeed been murdered. But why, exactly, would someone want Forrestal gone? We now come to the most controversial theory of all. It all revolves around timing.

It was on April 26, 1947, that the U.S. government unveiled the National Security Act. Two months later, on June 24, Kenneth Arnold encountered a squadron of flying saucers over Mt. Rainier, Washington State—thus ushering in the beginning of the UFO phenomenon. Just about a week later, the still controversial Roswell, New Mexico, "UFO crash" occurred. And on September 17, 1947, President Truman insisted that Forrestal be sworn in as the first secretary of defense—as in immediately and not under the regular, much slower process of placing someone into the presidential infrastructure. One day later, the CIA was created; it went on to play a significant role in the history of U.S. government UFO investigations. It's hardly surprising that within the UFO research community, there are a significant number of investigators who believe that Forrestal was wiped out to prevent him—in his fraught state—from spilling the beans on what he knew about UFOs and Roswell. If this all sounds like a plot from *The X-Files*, it's significant to note that something else occurred on September 19, 1947. On the same day that Forrestal became secretary of defense, a highly classified U.S. military document was prepared. Its title was "AMC [Air Materiel Command] Opinion Concerning 'Flying Discs.'" The document was written by General Nathan Twining. In the document, Twining wrote: "The phenomenon reported is something real and not visionary or fictitious.… There are objects probably approximating the shape of a disc, of such appreciable size as to appear to be as large as man-made aircraft."

Did someone in the U.S. government want James Forrestal gone? As in forever? And all as a result of fears that Forrestal might have been on the verge of revealing to the public, and to the media, what he had learned about UFOs? The full answers elude us. The significant time frame—which ties UFOs with the creation of both the CIA and the National Security Act—suggests that, incredibly, Forrestal really was callously thrown out of that thirteenth-floor window at the Bethesda Naval Hospital. And just maybe, the reason revolved around the sudden and growing presence of extraterrestrials in our world.

HOW TO KILL, CIA STYLE

Assassins have played significant roles in the history of secret societies, as this book demonstrates on repeated occasions. Few people know more about the ancient art of assassination, however, than the CIA. How can we be so sure? The answer is quite astonishing: in the early 1950s, the CIA drafted a document for those personnel working undercover, and in the field, and whose work involved "taking out of circulation" certain people deemed by the CIA to be undesirables. We're talking about foreign leaders, dangerous dictators, and more. The document is appropriately titled "A Study of Assassination." The CIA has been very careful to delete from the available pages the name of the author. But the content is largely uncensored.

The unknown author of the document states:

Assassination is a term thought to be derived from "Hashish," a drug similar to marijuana, said to have been used by Hasan-Dan-Sabah to induce motivation in his followers, who were assigned to carry out political and other murders, usually at the cost of their lives. It is here used to describe the planned killing of a person who is not under the legal jurisdiction of the killer, who is not physically in the hands of the killer, who has been selected by a resistance organization for death, and whose death provides positive advantages to that organization.

Assassination is an extreme measure not normally used in clandestine operations. It should be assumed that it will never be ordered or authorized by any U.S. Headquarters, though the latter may in rare instances agree to its execution by members of an associated foreign service. This reticence is partly due to the necessity for committing communications to paper. No assassination instructions should ever be written or recorded. Consequently, the decision to employ this technique must nearly always be reached in the field, at the area where the act will take place. Decision and instructions should be confined to an absolute minimum of persons. Ideally, only one person will be involved. No report may be made, but usually the act will be properly covered by normal news services, whose output is available to all concerned.

The clearly well-informed CIA figure who penned the document then stated:

Murder is not morally justifiable. Self-defense may be argued if the victim has knowledge which may destroy the resistance organization if divulged. Assassination of persons responsible for atrocities or reprisals may be regarded as just punishment. Killing a political leader whose burgeoning career is a clear and present danger to the cause of freedom may be held necessary. But assassination can seldom be employed with a clear conscience. Persons who are morally squeamish should not attempt it.

The techniques employed will vary according to whether the subject is unaware of his danger, aware but unguarded, or guarded. They will also be affected by whether or not the assassin is to be killed with the subject hereafter, assassinations in which the subject is unaware will be termed "simple"; those where the subject is aware but unguarded will be termed "chase"; those where the victim is guarded will be termed "guarded." If the assassin is to die with the subject, the act will be called "lost."

Moving on, the CIA source behind the document adds this:

If the assassin is to escape, the adjective will be "safe." It should be noted that no compromises should exist here. The assassin must not fall alive into enemy hands. A further type division is caused by the need to conceal the fact that the subject was actually the victim of assassination, rather than an accident or natural causes. If such concealment is desirable the operation will be called "secret"; if concealment is immaterial, the act will be called "open"; while if the assassination requires publicity to be effective it will be termed "terroristic."

Of course, when one is dealing with such a controversial topic, it's vital that agents of the CIA know exactly how to kill a person, how to do so quickly, and how to make it look like anything but an assassination: "The essential point of assassination is the death of the subject. A human being may be killed in many ways but sureness is often overlooked by those who may be emotionally unstrung by the seriousness of this act they intend to commit. The specific technique employed will depend upon a large number of variables, but should be constant in one point: Death must be absolutely certain. The attempt on Hitler's life failed because the conspiracy did not give this matter proper attention."

The author had more to say on this matter, which makes one wonder if he, himself, had experience as an "in the field" assassin:

> It is possible to kill a man with the bare hands, but very few are skillful enough to do it well. Even a highly trained Judo expert will hesitate to risk killing by hand unless he has absolutely no alternative. However, the simplest local tools are often the most efficient means of assassination. A hammer, axe, wrench, screwdriver, fire poker, kitchen knife, lamp stand, or anything hard, heavy and handy will suffice. A length of rope or wire or a belt will do if the assassin is strong and agile. All such improvised weapons have the important advantage of availability and apparent innocence. The obviously lethal machine gun failed to kill Trotsky where an item of sporting goods succeeded.

Would-be killers for hire were told that....

> ...for secret assassination, either simple or chase, the contrived accident is the most effective technique. When successfully executed, it causes little excitement and is only casually investigated. The most efficient accident, in simple assassination, is a fall of 75 feet or more onto a hard surface. Elevator shafts, stair wells, unscreened windows and bridges will serve. Bridge falls into water are not reliable. In simple cases a private meeting with the subject may be arranged at a properly cased location. The act may be executed by sudden, vigorous [deleted] of the ankles, tipping the subject over the edge. If the assassin immediately sets up an outcry, playing the "horrified witness," no alibi or surreptitious withdrawal is necessary. In chase cases it will usually be necessary to stun or drug the subject before dropping

While it is possible to kill someone with your bare hands, a tool, such as a knife, is more likely to guarantee success. Assassins are not known for killing just with their hands for this reason.

him. Care is required to insure that no wound or condition not attributable to the fall is discernible after death.

Remember those words above: "The most efficient accident, in simple assassination, is a fall of 75 feet or more onto a hard surface." These words are positively chilling, particularly so when one remembers the final minutes of the life of the first U.S. secretary of defense, James Forrestal, as described in the previous chapter.

And the deadly list went on and on:

Falls into the sea or swiftly flowing rivers may suffice if the subject cannot swim. It will be more reliable if the assassin can arrange to attempt rescue, as he can thus be sure of the subject's death and at the same time establish a workable alibi. If the subject's personal habits make it feasible, alcohol may be used [several words deleted] to prepare him for a contrived accident of any kind. Falls before trains or subway cars are usually effective, but require exact timing and can seldom be free from unexpected observation.

As for assassinations involving cars and even trucks, the CIA had that area covered, too:

Automobile accidents are a less satisfactory means of assassination. If the subject is deliberately run down, very exact timing is necesary and investigation is likely to be thorough. If the subject's car is tampered with, reliability is very low. The subject may be stunned or drugged and then placed in the car, but this is only reliable when the car can be run off a high cliff or into deep water without observation. Arson can cause accidental death if the subject is drugged and left in a burning building. Reliability is not satisfactory unless the building is isolated and highly combustible.

Drugs and medicines all played a role in the early, formative years of the CIA's assassins:

In all types of assassination except terroristic, drugs can be very effective. If the assassin is trained as a doctor or nurse and the subject is under medical care, this is an easy and rare method. An overdose of morphine administered as a sedative will cause death without disturbance and is difficult to detect. The size of the dose will depend upon whether the subject has been using narcotics regularly. If not, two grains will suffice. If the subject drinks heavily, morphine or a similar narcotic can be injected at the passing out stage, and the cause of death will often be held to be acute alcoholism. Specific poisons, such as arsenic or strychnine, are effective but their possession or procurement is incriminating, and accurate dosage is problematical.

Then, we get to see how guns played major roles in the matter of death by the CIA:

> Firearms are often used in assassination, often very ineffectively. The assassin usually has insufficient technical knowledge of the limitations of weapons, and expects more range, accuracy and killing power than can be provided with reliability. Since certainty of death is the major requirement, firearms should be used which can provide destructive power at least 100% in excess of that thought to be necessary, and ranges should be half that considered practical for the weapon. Firearms have other drawbacks. Their possession is often incriminating. They may be difficult to obtain…. However, there are many cases in which firearms are probably more efficient than any other means.

Explosives, said the CIA, were also valuable tools when it came to eliminating the enemy:

> Bombs and demolition charges of various sorts have been used frequently in assassination. Such devices, in terroristic and open assassination, can provide safety and overcome guard barriers, but it is curious that bombs have often been the implement of lost assassinations. The major factor which affects reliability is the use of explosives for assassination. The charge must be very large and the detonation must be controlled exactly as to time by the assassin who can observe the subject. A small or moderate explosive charge is highly unreliable as a cause of death, and time delay or booby-trap devices are extremely prone to kill the wrong man. In addition to the moral aspects of indiscriminate killing, the death of casual bystanders can often produce public reactions unfavorable to the cause for which the assassination is carried out.

Could there be a more dangerous document than "A Study of Assassination"? Probably not.

MANIPULATING THE MIND TO A FATAL DEGREE

Now, it's time to take a look at the very controversial death of a man named Frank Olson; in the early 1950s, he was at the forefront of what has popularly become known as mind control. Olson was also likely terminated with extreme prejudice. Before we get to the matter of Olson's death, though, let's first take a look at how and why so much research of mind manipulation took place in that era.

Within the annals of research into conspiracy theories, there is perhaps no more emotive term than that of the aforementioned mind control. Indeed, mention those two words to anyone who is even remotely aware of the term, and it will invariably and inevitably (and wholly justifiably, too) provoke imagery and comments pertaining to political assassinations, dark and disturbing CIA chicanery, sexual slavery, secret government projects—and even alien abductions and subliminal advertising on the part of the world's media and advertising agencies. Yes: the specter of mind control is one that has firmly worked its ominous way into numerous facets of modern-day society. And it has been doing so for years. Consider, for example, the following.

"I can hypnotize a man, without his knowledge or consent, into committing treason against the United States," asserted Dr. George Estabrooks, Ph.D., chairman of the Department of Psychology at Colgate University, way back in 1942, before a select group of personnel attached themselves to the U.S. War Department.

Estabrooks added: "Two hundred trained foreign operators, working in the United States, could develop a uniquely dangerous army of hypnotically controlled Sixth Columnists."

Hypnosis can be used in therapy, for example, to break people's addictions. The CIA has also explored its use for more unsavory purposes.

Estabrooks's pièce-de-résistance, however, was to capitalize on an ingenious plan that had been postulated as far back as the First World War.

As he explained:

During World War One, a leading psychologist made a startling proposal to the navy. He offered to take a submarine steered by a captured U-boat captain, placed under his hypnotic control, through enemy mine fields to attack the German fleet. Washington nixed the stratagem as too risky. First, because there was no disguised method by which the captain's mind could be outflanked. Second, because today's technique of day-by-day breaking down of ethical conflicts brainwashing was still unknown.

The indirect approach to hypnotism would, I believe, change the navy's answer today. Personally, I am convinced that hypnosis is a bristling, dangerous armament which makes it doubly imperative to avoid the war of tomorrow.

A perfect example of the way in which the will of a person could be completely controlled and manipulated was amply and graphically spelled out in an article that Dr. George Estabrooks wrote in April 1971 for the now defunct publication *Science Digest*. Titled "Hypnosis Comes of Age," it stated the following:

Communication in war is always a headache. Codes can be broken. A professional spy may or may not stay bought. Your own man may have unquestionable loyalty, but his judgment is always open to question.

The "hypnotic courier," on the other hand, provides a unique solution. I was involved in preparing many subjects for this work during World War II. One successful case involved an Army Service Corps Captain whom we'll call George Smith.

Captain Smith had undergone months of training. He was an excellent subject but did not realize it. I had removed from him, by post-hypnotic suggestion, all recollection of ever having been hypnotized.

First I had the Service Corps call the captain to Washington and tell him they needed a report of the mechanical equipment of

Division X headquartered in Tokyo. Smith was ordered to leave by jet next morning, pick up the report and return at once. Consciously, that was all he knew, and it was the story he gave to his wife and friends.

Then I put him under deep hypnosis, and gave him—orally—a vital message to be delivered directly on his arrival in Japan to a certain colonel—let's say his name was Brown—of military intelligence.

Outside of myself, Colonel Brown was the only person who could hypnotize Captain Smith. This is "locking."

I performed it by saying to the hypnotized Captain: "Until further orders from me, only Colonel Brown and I can hypnotize you. We will use a signal phrase *the moon is clear*. Whenever you hear this phrase from Brown or myself you will pass instantly into deep hypnosis.

When Captain Smith re-awakened, he had no conscious memory of what happened in trance. All that he was aware of was that he must head for Tokyo to pick up a division report.

On arrival there, Smith reported to Brown, who hypnotized him with the signal phrase. Under hypnosis, Smith delivered my message and received one to bring back. Awakened, he was given the division report and returned home by jet. There I hypnotized him once more with the signal phrase, and he spieled off Brown's answer that had been dutifully tucked away in his unconscious mind.

And with the early, groundbreaking work of George Estabrooks now concisely spelled out for one and all to read, digest, and muse upon, let me acquaint you with a concise history of the world of mind control, mind manipulation, and what could accurately be termed mind slavery.

The picture is not a pretty one—not at all.

Although the U.S. intelligence community, military, and government have undertaken countless official (and off-the-record, too) projects pertaining to both mind control and mind manipulation, without any doubt whatsoever, the most notorious of all was Project MKUltra: a clandestine operation—sometimes spelled MK-Ultra or MK-ULTRA—that operated out of the CIA's Office of Scientific Intelligence beginning during the Cold War era of the early 1950s.

The date of the project's actual termination is a somewhat hazy one; however, it is known that it was definitely in operation as late as the latter part of the 1960s—and, not surprisingly and regretfully, has since been replaced by far more controversial and deeply hidden projects.

To demonstrate the level of secrecy that surrounded Project MKUltra, even though it had kicked off at the dawn of the Fifties, its existence was largely unknown outside of the intelligence world until 1975....

To demonstrate the level of secrecy that surrounded Project MKUltra, even though it had kicked off at the dawn of the fifties, its existence was largely unknown outside of the intelligence world until 1975—when the Church Committee and the Rockefeller Commission began making their own investigations of the CIA's mind-control-related activities—in part to determine if (a) the CIA had engaged in illegal activity, (b) the personal rights of citizens had been violated, and (c) if the projects at issue had resulted in fatalities, which they most assuredly and unfortunately did.

Rather conveniently, and highly suspiciously, too, it was asserted at the height of the inquiries in 1975 that two years earlier, CIA director Richard Helms had ordered the destruction of the Agency's MKUltra files. Fortunately, this did not stop the Church Committee or the Rockefeller Commission—both of whom had the courage and tenacity to forge ahead with their investigations, relying on sworn testimony from players in MKUltra, where documentation was no longer available for scrutiny, study, and evaluation.

The story that unfolded was both dark and disturbing in equal degrees. Indeed, the scope of the project—and allied operations, too—was spelled out in an August 1977 document titled "The Senate MK-Ultra Hearings" that was prepared by the Senate Select Committee on Intelligence and the Committee on Human Resources as a result of its probing into the secret world of the CIA.

As the document explained:

Research and development programs to find materials which could be used to alter human behavior were initiated in the late 1940s and early 1950s. These experimental programs originally included testing of drugs involving witting human subjects, and culminated in tests using unwitting, non-volunteer human subjects. These tests were designed to determine the potential effects of chemical or biological agents when used operationally against individuals unaware that they had received a drug.

The Committee then turned its attention to the overwhelming secrecy that surrounded these early 1940s/1950s projects:

The testing programs were considered highly sensitive by the intelligence

In 1975, a commission was sworn in to keep tabs on CIA activity and Project MKUltra. The goal was to make sure programs conducted by these agencies were not going to be a liability to the U.S. government.

agencies administering them. Few people, even within the agencies, knew of the programs and there is no evidence that either the Executive Branch or Congress were ever informed of them.

The highly compartmented nature of these programs may be explained in part by an observation made by the CIA Inspector General that, "the knowledge that the Agency is engaging in unethical and illicit activities would have serious repercussions in political and diplomatic circles and would be detrimental to the accomplishment of its missions."

The research and development programs, particularly the covert testing programs, resulted in massive abridgments of the rights of American citizens, sometimes with tragic consequences, too. As prime evidence of this, the Committee uncovered details on the deaths of two Americans who were firmly attributed to the programs at issue, while other participants in the testing programs were said to still be suffering from the residual effects of the tests as late as the mid-1970s.

And as the Committee starkly noted: "While some controlled testing of these substances might be defended, the nature of the tests, their scale, and the fact that they were continued for years after the danger of surreptitious administration of LSD to unwitting individuals was known, demonstrate a fundamental disregard for the value of human life."

There was far more to come: the Select Committee's investigation of the testing and use of chemical and biological agents also raised serious questions about the adequacy of command and control procedures within the Central Intelligence Agency and military intelligence and also about the nature of the relationships among the intelligence agencies, other governmental agencies, and private institutions and individuals that were also allied to the early mind-control studies.

For example, the Committee was highly disturbed to learn that with respect to the mind-control and mind-manipulation projects, the CIA's normal administrative controls were controversially and completely waived for programs involving chemical and biological agents—supposedly to protect their security, but more likely to protect those CIA personnel who knew they were verging upon (if not outright surpassing) breaking the law.

But it is perhaps the following statement from the Committee that demonstrates the level of controversy that has surrounded the issue of mind-control-based projects:

The decision to institute one of the Army's LSD field testing projects had been based, at least in part, on the

> The Select Committee's investigation of the testing and use of chemical and biological agents also raised serious questions about the adequacy of command and control procedures within the Central Intelligence Agency and military intelligence....

finding that no long-term residual effects had ever resulted from the drug's administration. The CIA's failure to inform the Army of a death which resulted from the surreptitious administration of LSD to unwitting Americans, may well have resulted in the institution of an unnecessary and potentially lethal program.

The Committee added:

The development, testing, and use of chemical and biological agents by intelligence agencies raise serious questions about the relationship between the intelligence community and foreign governments, other agencies of the Federal Government, and other institutions and individuals.

The questions raised range from the legitimacy of American complicity in actions abroad which violate American and foreign laws to the possible compromise of the integrity of public and private institutions used as cover by intelligence agencies.

While MKUltra was certainly the most infamous of all the CIA-initiated mind-control programs, it was very far from being an isolated one. Indeed, numerous subprojects, postprojects, and operations initiated by other agencies were brought to the Committee's attention. One was Project Chatter, which the Committee described thus:

Mescaline, a drug harvested from peyote, was one of the chemicals used in human experiments. Peyote resembles an artichoke—hence the name of one of the programs: Project Artichoke.

Project Chatter was a Navy program that began in the fall of 1947. Responding to reports of amazing results achieved by the Soviets in using truth drugs, the program focused on the identification and the testing of such drugs for use in interrogations and in the recruitment of agents. The research included laboratory experiments on animals and human subjects involving *Anabasis aphylla*, scopolamine, and mescaline in order to determine their speech-inducing qualities. Overseas experiments were conducted as part of the project. The project expanded substantially during the Korean War, and ended shortly after the war, in 1953.

Then there were Projects Bluebird and Artichoke. Again, the Committee dug deep and uncovered some controversial and eye-opening data and testimony:

The earliest of the CIA's major programs involving the use of chemical and biological agents, Project Bluebird, was approved by the Director in 1950. Its objectives were: (a) discovering means of conditioning personnel to prevent unauthorized extraction of information from them by known means, (b) investigating the possibility of control of an individual by application of special interrogation techniques, (c) memory enhancement, and (d) establishing defensive means for preventing hostile control of Agency personnel.

The Committee added with respect to Bluebird:

As a result of interrogations conducted overseas during the project, another goal was added—the evaluation of offensive uses of unconventional interrogation techniques, including hypnosis and drugs. In August 1951, the project was renamed Artichoke. Project Artichoke included in-house experiments on interrogation techniques, conducted 'under medical and security controls which would ensure that no damage was done to individuals who volunteer for the experiments. Overseas interrogations utilizing a combination of sodium pentothal and hypnosis after physical and psychiatric examinations of the subjects were also part of Artichoke.

Interestingly, the Committee noted that "information about Project Artichoke after the fall of 1953 is scarce. The CIA maintains that the project ended in 1956, but evidence suggests that Office of Security and Office of Medical Services use of 'special interrogation' techniques continued for several years thereafter."

MKNaomi was another major CIA program in this area. In 1967, the CIA summarized the purposes of MKNaomi thus: "(a) To provide for a covert support base to meet clandestine operational requirements. (b) To stockpile severely incapacitating and lethal materials for the specific use of TSD [Technical Services Division]. (c) To maintain in operational readiness special and unique items for the dissemination of biological and chemical materials. (d) To provide for the required surveillance, testing, upgrading, and evaluation of materials and items in order to assure absence of defects and complete predictability of results to be expected under operational conditions."

Under an agreement reached with the Army in 1952, the Special Operations Division (SOD) at Fort Detrick was to assist the CIA in developing, testing, and maintaining bio-

Under an agreement reached with the Army in 1952, the Special Operations Division (SOD) at Fort Detrick was to assist CIA in developing, testing, and maintaining biological agents and delivery systems....

logical agents and delivery systems—some of which were directly related to mind-control experimentation. By this agreement, the CIA finally acquired the knowledge, skill, and facilities of the Army to develop biological weapons specifically suited for CIA use.

The Committee also noted:

SOD developed darts coated with biological agents and pills containing several different biological agents which could remain potent for weeks or months. SOD developed a special gun for firing darts coated with a chemical which could allow CIA agents to incapacitate a guard dog, enter an installation secretly, and return the dog to consciousness when leaving. SOD scientists were unable to develop a similar incapacitant [sic] for humans. SOD also physically transferred to CIA personnel biological agents in "bulk" form, and delivery devices, including some containing biological agents.

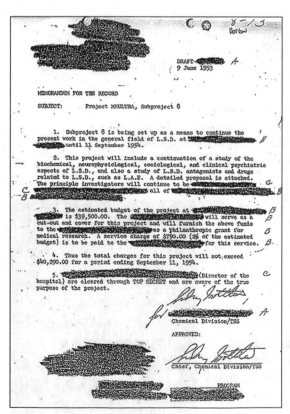

A 1953 memo bearing Sidney Gottlieb's signature approved the MKUltra project involving top-secret experiments with LSD.

In addition to the CIA's interest in using biological weapons and mind control against humans, it also asked the SOD to study use of biological agents against crops and animals. In its 1967 memorandum, the CIA stated:

Three methods and systems for carrying out a covert attack against crops and causing severe crop loss have been developed and evaluated under field conditions. This was accomplished in anticipation of a requirement which was later developed but was subsequently scrubbed just prior to putting into action.

The Committee concluded with respect to MKNaomi that the project was "terminated in 1970. On November 25, 1969, President Nixon renounced the use of any form of biological weapons that kill or incapacitate and ordered the disposal of existing stocks of bacteriological weapons. On February 14, 1970, the President clarified the extent of his earlier order and indicated that toxins—chemicals that are not living organisms but are produced by living organisms—were considered biological weapons subject to his previous directive and were to be destroyed. Although instructed to relinquish control of material held for the CIA by SOD, a CIA scientist acquired approximately 11 grams of shellfish toxin from SOD personnel at Fort Detrick which were stored in a little-used CIA laboratory where it went undetected for five years."

Recognizing, however, that when it came to mind control and manipulation, MKUltra was the one project that more than any other was worth pursuing as part of its efforts to determine the extent to which the CIA had bent and broken the law and flouted the rights of citizens, the Committee had far more to say on the operation.

Time and again, the Committee returned to Project MKUltra. Not surprising, as it was, after all, the principal CIA program involving the research and development of chemical and biological agents and was, in the words of the Committee: "…concerned with the research and development of chemical, biological, and radiological materials capable of employment in clandestine operations to control human behavior."

The inspector general's survey of MKUltra, in 1963, noted the following reasons for the profound level of sensitivity that surrounded the program:

A. Research in the manipulation of human behavior is considered by many authorities in medicine and related fields to be professionally unethical, therefore the reputation of professional participants in the MKUltra program are on occasion in jeopardy.

B. Some MKUltra activities raise questions of legality implicit in the original charter.

C. A final phase of the testing of MKUltra products places the rights and interests of U.S. citizens in jeopardy.

D. Public disclosure of some aspects of MKUltra activity could induce serious adverse reaction in U.S. public opinion, as well as stimulate offensive and defensive action in this field on the part of foreign intelligence services.

Over the at least ten-year life span of the program, many "additional avenues to the control of human behavior" were designated as being wholly appropriate for investigation under the MKUltra charter. These included "radiation, electroshock, various fields of psychology, psychiatry, sociology, and anthropology, graphology, harassment substances, and paramilitary devices and materials."

Needless to say, this was a grim list.

A 1955 MKUltra document provides a good example of the scope of the effort to understand the effects of mind-

> Over the at least ten-year life span of the program, many "additional avenues to the control of human behavior" were designated as being wholly appropriate for investigation under the MKUltra charter.

altering substances on human beings and lists those same substances as follows. In the CIA's own words:

1. Substances which will promote illogical thinking and impulsiveness to the point where the recipient would be discredited in public.

2. Substances which increase the efficiency of mentation and perception.

3. Materials which will prevent or counteract the intoxicating effect of alcohol.

4. Materials which will promote the intoxicating effect of alcohol.

5. Materials which will produce the signs and symptoms of recognized diseases in a reversible way so that they may be used for malingering, etc.

6. Materials which will render the induction of hypnosis easier or otherwise enhance its usefulness.

7. Substances which will enhance the ability of individuals to withstand privation, torture and coercion during interrogation and so-called "brain-washing."

8. Materials and physical methods which will produce amnesia for events preceding and during their use.

9. Physical methods of producing shock and confusion over extended periods of time and capable of surreptitious use.

10. Substances which produce physical disablement such as paralysis of the legs, acute anemia, etc.

11. Substances which will produce "pure" euphoria with no subsequent let-down.

12. Substances which alter personality structure in such a way that the tendency of the recipient to become dependent upon another person is enhanced.

13. A material which will cause mental confusion of such a type that the individual under its influence will find it difficult to maintain a fabrication under questioning.

14. Substances which will lower the ambition and general working efficiency of men when administered in undetectable amounts.

15. Substances which promote weakness or distortion of the eyesight or hearing faculties, preferably without permanent effects.

16. A knockout pill which can surreptitiously be administered in drinks, food, cigarettes, as an aerosol, etc., which will be safe to use, provide a maximum of amnesia, and be suitable for use by agent types on an ad hoc basis.

17. A material which can be surreptitiously administered by the above routes and which in very small amounts will make it impossible for a man to perform any physical activity whatsoever.

In other words, when it came to mind manipulation, more than half a century ago, the CIA already had all bases covered.

A special procedure, designated MKDelta, was established to govern the use of MKUltra materials when specifically utilized in overseas operations. Such materials were used on a number of occasions. According to the Committee: "Because MKUltra records were destroyed, it is impossible to reconstruct the operational use of MKUltra materials by the CIA overseas; it has been determined that the use of these materials abroad began in 1953, and possibly as early as 1950."

The Committee expanded further:

Drugs were used primarily as an aid to interrogations, but MKUltra/MKDelta materials were also used for harassment, discrediting, or disabling purposes. According to an Inspector General Survey of the Technical Services Division of the CIA in 1957—an inspection which did not discover the MKUltra project involving the surreptitious administration of LSD to unwitting, non-volunteer subjects—the CIA had developed six drugs for operational use and they had been used in six different operations on a total of thirty-three subjects. By 1963 the number of operations and subjects had increased substantially.

Aside from the CIA, the Committee learned that the Army was up to its neck in mind-control-related projects, too. In its 1977 report, the Committee wrote:

There were three major phases in the Army's testing of LSD. In the first, LSD was administered to more than 1,000 American soldiers who volunteered to be subjects in chemical warfare experiments. In the second phase, Material Testing Program EA 1729, 95 volunteers received LSD in clinical experiments designed to evaluate potential intelligence uses of the drug. In the third phase, Projects Third Chance and Derby Hat, 16 unwitting non-volunteer subjects were interrogated after receiving LSD as part of operational field tests.

But what of the post-MKUltra era? Did the official world really cease its operations and destroy its files *en masse*, in 1973, as had been alleged? Probably not: in a 1977 interview, fourteen-year CIA veteran Victor Marchetti stated that the CIA's claim that MKUltra was abandoned was nothing more than a "cover story."

AND ANOTHER DEADLY FALL

H. P. Albarelli Jr. is the author of an immense, 826-page book titled *A Terrible Mistake*. It's an investigation of the mysterious 1953 death of Frank Olson, a brilliant chemist who, in the early 1950s, worked for the U.S. Army's Special Operations Division. Although Olson was at the forefront of researching mind-altering technology—such as MKUltra—his work was not destined to last. Nor was his life. Olson died on November 28, 1953, as a result of an, ahem, "fall" from the tenth floor of the Statler Hotel in Manhattan.

When it comes to the matter of Frank Olson's undeniably strange and suspicious death, there are two overriding theories as to what happened on that particular night. The theory that has been endorsed by the U.S. government (and specifically the CIA) is that Olson fell or jumped of his own volition. The very different scenario upheld by conspiracy theories and Olson's family is that the poor man was pushed to his death—whether deliberately or by mistake. Let us take a look at what we know with certainty. On November 18, 1953, Olson headed out to Deep Creek Lake in Maryland. This was no vacation, however. Rather, Olson was on top-secret government work. The purpose was to determine how successfully the MKUltra and other associated programs were working. And that's when things went outrageously and recklessly wrong. Unknown to Olson, his glass of Cointreau was spiked with lysergic acid diethylamide, or LSD. The reason was to allow a select team to see how Olson responded to the mind-bending drug. In Olson's case, it didn't work well at all. In fact, a good case can be made that it was this overdosing of Olson that led to his death. Some might say indirectly. I say directly.

We know now who the man was who gave Olson the hit that changed his life and bent his mind to the fullest extent possible. It was Sidney Gottlieb.

Frank Olson died under mysterious circumstances in a fall from his hotel room at the Statler Hotel in Manhattan (now known as the Pennsylvania Hotel).

A product of New York's Bronx, Gottlieb obtained a Ph.D. in chemistry from the California Institute of Technology and a master's degree in speech therapy. In 1951 he was offered the position as head of the Chemical Division of the CIA's Technical Services Staff (TSS), a job that focused to a great extent on two issues: the development of lethal poisons for use in clandestine assassination operations and understanding, harnessing, and manipulating the human brain—mind control, in other words. It was Gottlieb's work in these fields that led him to become known within the U.S. intelligence community as the Black Sorcerer. It proved to be a very apt title, indeed.

In April 1953, Gottlieb began coordinating the work of the CIA's MKUltra project, which was activated on the orders of CIA director Allen Dulles. Gottlieb routinely administered LSD, as well as a variety of other psychoactive drugs, to unwitting subjects as he sought to develop "techniques that would crush the human psyche to the point that it would admit anything." It can be said with a high degree of certainty that Gottlieb succeeded in crushing Olson's mind—and to Olson's cost.

A few days after the Deep Creek Lake incident, Olson approached his boss, Vincent Ruwet, out of the blue and told him that he was quitting the mind-control programs. Ruwet no doubt knew that someone had meddled with Olson's mind. But whether Ruwet was involved in the spiking remains unclear. All that Ruwet really knew was that Olson was most definitely not himself anymore. Of equal concern to Ruwet was the fact that Olson knew all about nearly all of the most guarded facts and results of not just the Army's mind-controlling drug-based programs but those of the CIA's, too. That issue alone made Olson a national security threat—or, at the very least, a potential security threat. Already going through Ruwet's mind was the image of a disgruntled Olson spilling his guts to the nation's most prominent newspapers. The secrets of MKUltra spilled all across the front page of the *New York Times*? For Ruwet, it didn't even bear thinking about. But Ruwet did think about it; he even discussed the worrisome situation with colleagues.

Such was the state that Olson's mind was plunged into in an alarmingly short time, Ruwet decided that the best approach to take was to find Olson a good psychiatrist. That was quickly done. Then, it was suggested that it would be good for Olson, the psychiatrist, and Robert Lashbrook, who at the time was the assistant chief of the CIA's Chemical Branch, to meet. The plan was to try to put all things right with Olson. Certainly, there was a great deal to put right. For example, files demonstrate that in the days leading up to his death, Olson was exhibiting levels of stress, panic attacks, overwhelming paranoia, and psychological collapse.

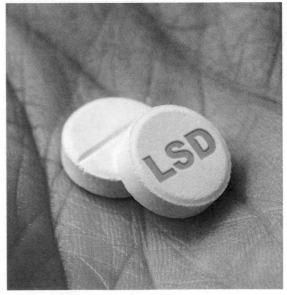

It must be said that had Gottlieb not dosed Olson with LSD ... the fraught situation would never have surfaced its head.

It must be said that had Gottlieb not dosed Olson with LSD—and altered Olson's mind and turned him into a potential threat to the United States (as Gottlieb and Lashbrook saw it, at least)—the fraught situation would never have surfaced. In other words, Olson was the victim, and Gottlieb and his colleagues were the ones who should have been hauled over the coals, perhaps even by Congress. Such a thing never happened, however. At around 2:30 A.M. on November 28, Olson plummeted from the tenth-floor window of Room 1018A at Manhattan's Statler Hotel. So we are assured, anyway. That assurance does not sit well with many. Nor do the facts, which did not even get any light shed on them until the 1970s—which was the time frame when both the Church Committee and the Rockefeller Commisson started to take a very close look at the final weeks, days, hours, minutes, and seconds of Frank Olson's life.

When the cat was finally after the bag—after a period of around three decades, no less—the CIA, when pushed, and pushed again, stated in a roundabout fashion that yes, Olson probably had been hit by something mind-altering and life-changing. Incredibly, Olson knew absolutely nothing about all of this: it had been hidden by the CIA since the moment Olson lost his life. Of course, just because Olson was hit by LSD doesn't necessarily mean that he was murdered. Even the Church Committee and the Rockefeller Commisson that addressed the controversial death admitted that. There was still, however, more than a few figures who wanted the whole issue cleared up and to the satisfaction of Frank Olson's family, who were enraged by the whole controversy. It's rather telling that the U.S. government made a $750,000 payment to the Olson family.

Lysergic acid diethylamide (better known as the mind-altering drug LSD) was used by the CIA to see if its properties would lend themselves well to mind control.

Olson's son, Eric—who could never let go of the matter, and he can hardly be blamed for that—was far from satisfied. Such were the suspicions that Olson had about his father's death, he arranged in the 1990s for his father's body to be exhumed and examined for anything suspicious. It turned out that there were indeed reasons to be suspicious. An examination of Frank Olson's corpse by Professor James E. Starrs of George Washington University showed conclusively that Olson had suffered from blunt-force trauma prior to his assumed death from a fall that no one could stand a chance of surviving. It wasn't long before the emotive word "homicide" entered into the controversy. Matters did not end there.

Perhaps inevitably, with the death of Frank Olson more than forty years old, it remained very difficult to come to a definitive conclusion that Olson was murdered.

There's another issue that we should not overlook. You will recall that in an earlier chapter, the matter of the CIA's manual "A Study of Assassination" was addressed. The writer of the document—whose name, remember, has never, ever been disclosed—revealed the best ways to kill someone and make such a killing appear to be a suicide or an accident. Keep the following in mind when it comes to that blunt-force trauma that Olson's body exhibited when examined. The CIA noted that "blows should be directed to the temple, the area just below and behind the ear, and the lower, rear portion of the skull. Of course, if the blow is very heavy, any portion of the skull will do." Whoever wiped out Frank Olson clearly spent a great deal of time digesting the words of that highly controversial document.

We should also not forget that the death of Frank Olson in November 1953 eerily mirrored the equally controversial death of the first secretary of defense, James Forrestal, in May 1949: fatal descent from a high building. Now, let's address an equally controversial case that involved Sidney Gottlieb and an innocent figure who was callously used to test new drugs—completely without his knowledge. What this demonstrates, as you will see, is further evidence that Gottlieb was a ruthless, amoral character—which probably made him the ideal person to perform such undeniably inexcusable experimentation. Read on.

I'll focus on the story of a man named Stanley Glickman. *Salon.com* notes: "Until his death in 1992, Glickman insisted that a CIA agent, who for 40 years he consistently described as having a clubfoot, had slipped him a mind-bending mickey in a glass of Chartreuse liqueur at a bar in Paris in 1952, driving Glickman mad and destroying his life."

The story of Glickman is, ultimately, a tragic and turbulent one. At the time of his strange encounter, Glickman, an American, was living and working in Paris, France. He was in his mid-twenties and life was good: he spent time at the Académie de la Grande Chaumière and got to hang out with modernist painter and sculptor Fernand Léger. Then, one night, things changed. In the latter part of 1952, Glickman met with a friend in the Paris-based Cafe Select. It was while the pair was hanging out and drinking coffee that something very weird happened. Two American men came into the cafe and soon engaged Glickman in a deep debate. Hank Albarelli's 2009 book A *Terrible Mistake* chronicles the history of MKUltra in detailed fashion and addresses the Glickman affair. Albarelli notes that "the two strangers fell into a heated debate with Glickman about *politics, power, and patriotism* [italics mine]."

The confrontational debate finally came to an end, at which point the two men offered Glickman a drink. Unwisely, he accepted it. As history has shown, it was just about the worst move that Glickman ever could have made. He soon found himself plunged into a psychedelic nightmare. Glickman felt as if he was floating above the table. His perceptions, said Albarelli, "became distorted." The mysterious men watched "intently" as Glickman's hallucinations became ever more graphic and terrifying. The odd pair soon thereafter exited the café. The incident affected Glickman's whole life from thereon: delusions and a sense of going insane gripped him for weeks after he was hit by the mind-bending cocktail. Glickman was finally given shock treatment at the American Hospital of Paris, but he was never quite the same again. Glickman gave up painting, moved back to the United States (New York), and ran an antiques shop for the rest of his life.

> As history has shown, it was just about the worst move that Glickman ever could have made. He soon found himself plunged into the hearts of a psychedelic nightmare.

Notably, Glickman stated that one of the two men who engaged him had a very noticeable limp. This has given rise to the genuinely intriguing theory that the limping man was one Sidney Gottlieb. He was a chemist and one of the key figures in the CIA's "mind-control" program, MKUltra. Gottlieb just happened to have a clubfoot. In Gottlieb's 1999 obituary, the U.K.'s *Independent* newspaper stated: "Gottlieb's contribution was to oversee MKUltra. From the early 1950s through most of the 1960s hundreds of American citizens were administered mind-altering drugs. One mental patient in Kentucky was given LSD for 174 consecutive days. In all the agency conducted 149 mind-control experiments. At least one 'participant' died as a result of the experiments and several others went mad."

The Alliance for Human Research Protection states that in 1977, Glickman "learned about Gottlieb and CIA's LSD experiments on unwitting involuntary subjects from the Kennedy congressional hearings. Glickman sued in 1981, but the trial was delayed 17 years on technical grounds, by which time Glickman had died in 1992."

There is also the matter of yet another incident that provoked terror and trauma for—in this case—two victims, which almost certainly involved

Sidney Gottlieb. It all happened in 1973. The location: Pascagoula, Mississippi. The affair has gone down in history as one of the world's most famous UFO encounters. In reality, though, it may have had nothing to do with aliens. But it just might have had a huge amount to do with hallucinogens. On October 11, 1973, the lives of two men were turned upside down: they stayed that way for a very long time. In fact, it's fair to say that both men were changed by the ordeal but in very different ways. The night promised a good night of fishing for Calvin Parker and Charles Hickson. For a while, that promise was fulfilled. Around 9:00 P.M., though, all thoughts of catching a few tasty fish disappeared. As the two men sat on the bank, they could see a light getting closer and closer. They had no idea what it was. Their attention was really caught when the light veered slightly and came directly toward them. The sudden air of mystery was now one of terror. The light, they could now see, was a somewhat oval-shaped device, big enough to hold more than a few people, that gave off a hum that caused both men to almost vomit. Both Parker and Hickson felt confused, disoriented, and dizzy. Then, some kind of doorway opened.

> The pair, unable to run ... could only watch in horror as three, humanoid figures with large, clawed hands ... levitated across the waters of the Mississippi River and in their direction.

The pair, unable to run or do pretty much anything at all as a result of the disabling technology used on them, could only watch in horror as three humanoid figures with large, clawed hands—similar to lobster claws, the pair later opined—levitated across the waters of the Mississippi River and in their direction. They were suddenly seized by the crew of the craft.

If that was not enough to deal with, both men found themselves suddenly paralyzed from head to toe. They were carried onto the craft and then given the usual alien-abduction experience: intrusive experiments and a sense of being used like a mouse in a lab. For all intents and purposes, that is exactly what they were. When the event finally ended, the men were unceremoniously dumped back on the edge of the river.

I mentioned earlier how the close encounter of the terrifying kind caused very different reactions on the part of Parker and Hickson. The former went pretty much silent, shunned the media, and ultimately had a nervous breakdown. Hickson, meanwhile, positively embraced the encounter, chatted with the media whenever they wanted to speak with him, and even wrote a book on the incident. Its title was *UFO Contact at Pascagoula*, cowritten with William Mendez.

The story is not quite over, though. There is another aspect to the case that many UFO enthusiasts have overlooked. They have done so at their cost. There is very little doubt that Charles Hickson and Calvin Parker experienced something very strange, something that radically changed their lives and that they never, ever forgot. But it does not necessarily mean that they encountered aliens on the night they decided to go fishing. There is an alternative theory for the Pascagoula incident that is far more plausible than the idea that aliens decided to take a couple of fishermen for a ride. In the other scenario, both men were certainly taken for a ride: of the deceptive kind.

So many UFO investigators focused on the Hickson–Parker case. But they should have been looking at the location. Barely any distance at all from where Hickson and Parker were fishing is a stretch of land called Horn Island. It looks inviting and picturesque, which it is. But sometimes, appearances are deceiving. From the 1940s onward, the U.S. military used Horn Island to test all manner of chemical-warfare-based technologies—which could be used against enemy forces on the battlefield. By the 1950s, the U.S. Army's Chemical Corps were running the show. By then, the facility was undertaking work for the CIA's MKUltra project. The official story is that the work on Horn Island was closed down years before the Hickson and Parker incident. The locals, though, say this is nonsense. They talk about highly classified experiments undertaken at Horn Island in the late 1960s and early 1970s involving 3-Quinuclidinyl benzilate (BZ or, most popularly, "Buzz"). Its mind-altering properties are impressive in the extreme: terrifying hallucinations are often reported. A sense of having been placed into a dreamlike state is described. Colors become more vivid, and sounds become more notable.

Taking into consideration the time frame, the location, and the drugged-out state that Hickson and Parker found themselves in, consider this:

Home to the CIA's MKUltra experiments with psychoactive chemicals that have gone on for a disputed period of time, Horn Island was still being used by the government as late as 1970.

Buzz is described by the National Academy of Sciences as an "anticholinergic delirium, a non-specific syndrome of cognitive dysfunction, hallucinations, and inability to perform tasks."

Imagine being plunged into a state of mind in which hallucinations quickly develop as a result of an aerosol-based agent directed at you from a military helicopter. That same helicopter, in your drugged-out state, turns into a brightly lit UFO. Perhaps the masklike faces, and clawed hands, which the pair described, were really full-body protection suits, helmets, and thick gloves, worn by the abductors and seen by two men rendered into states of mind in which hallucinations were running wild?

If we look at things from an unbiased perspective, and not with an "I want to believe"-driven head on our shoulders, the idea of a secret experiment—one that was an outgrowth of the MKUltra program of the early 1950s—becomes far more likely than an alien intrusion ever could.

The official story is that the people of the town were the victims of a certain fungus called ergot, which can affect rye. It does far more to the person who eats the infected rye: it provokes graphic and terrifying hallucinations....

A few last words on this strange incident: on at least two known occasions, Frank Olson visited the facilities at Horn Island. Just perhaps, from the 1950s onward, an arm of MKUltra was meddling with the minds of American citizens as a means to, among other things, fabricate alien encounters by exposing them to brain-screwing technologies and drugs. Perhaps Olson knew of the UFO program, and it was that which got him killed. The story, and the truth behind the death of Olson, I suspect, are far from being over.

One final story concerning Olson, which someone might kill to keep the secret. It revolves around a little French town called Pont-Saint-Esprit, which is located in the southern part of the country. The tranquil town is filled with history dating back to the 1700s. Today, however, it is a decidedly infamous locale—chiefly as a result of a series of events that took place on August 15, 1951. On that day, all hell broke loose around Pont-Saint-Esprit, and numerous townsfolk took on the forms of marauding animals—in their minds, at least. The official story is that the people of the town were the victims of a fungus called ergot, which can affect rye. It does far more to the person who eats the infected rye: it provokes graphic and terrifying hallucinations, as werewolf/shapeshifter authority Linda Godfrey makes clear. In her 2006 book *Hunting the American Werewolf*, she says that "ergot is now widely regarded as a possible cause of the bestial madness. According to this theory, it was not demonic influence but the ingestion of *Claviceps purpurea* (which contains a compound similar to LSD), which led to the demented behavior and thus, executions, of many alleged witches, werewolves, and vampires."

The day began as a normal one for the people of this picturesque, old town. By sundown, however, it was like a scene from *The Walking Dead*: what seemed to amount to raging infection was everywhere, and those free of that same, perceived infection cowered behind locked doors, fearful of becoming the next victims of whatever it was that had cursed Pont-Saint-Esprit. Hundreds of people rampaged around town. Others swore they saw their fellow townsfolk change into hideous creatures. All told, close to 260 people were affected. Seven died. And more than four dozen were so psychologically traumatized that they were temporarily held at local asylums both for the good of themselves and for the unaffected people of the town.

But was ergot really the cause of the devastation and death? Here's where things become really controversial. One of those who investigated the mystery of what erupted that day was Frank Olson. While liaising with French intelligence counterparts, he traveled to France in both 1950 and 1951, the latter being the year in which the town of Pont-Saint-Esprit experienced bedlam, as Albarelli notes in his book. The French were as interested as the Americans (and the Russians and the Brits, too, as it transpired) in how the human mind could be clandestinely manipulated. In view of all this, it's very notable that Olson's name turns up in previously classified CIA documents on the events at Pont-Saint-Esprit. One such document, which has surfaced through the terms of the U.S. Freedom of Information Act—the title of which is blacked out for national security reasons—states: "Re: Pont-Saint-Esprit and F. Olson files. SO Span/France Operation file, including Olson. Intel files. Hand carry to Berlin—tell him to see to it that these are buried."

While this communication is couched in cagey and careful language, it appears to link Olson to Pont-Saint-Esprit, and it makes it abundantly clear that whatever really happened—which led to people believing they and their friends were changing into wild beasts—had to be kept hidden at all costs. "Buried," even. Whatever the answer to the strange affair, the people of Pont-Saint-Esprit have not forgotten that terrible day when the townsfolk became monsters—in their minds but not physically.

With so many secrets swirling around his head, it's perhaps not surprising that someone thought that Olson just had to go.

ATTEMPTS TO KILL CASTRO

To understand the sheer extent to which the CIA sought to have Cuba's Fidel Castro assassinated, it's important to understand the nature of the time frame: the 1960s. It was a fraught and dangerous era in which fears of nuclear war were absolutely rife. In 2016, in a very refreshing fashion, the CIA placed into the public domain a time frame of what, essentially, led the CIA to try to have Castro ousted—as in forever. The CIA papers state:

> Fifty-five years ago, more than a thousand Cuban exiles stormed the beaches at the Bay of Pigs, Cuba, intending to ignite an uprising that would overthrow the government of Fidel Castro. This week, we look back at the events that unfolded and at the key players whose covert performances played out for all the world to see. In the 1950s, a young, charismatic Cuban nationalist named Fidel Castro led a guerrilla army against the forces of General Fulgencio Batista from a base camp deep within the Sierra Maestra Mountains, the largest mountain range in Cuba. Castro's goal was to overthrow Batista, the US-backed leader of Cuba. After three years of guerrilla warfare, Castro and his ragtag army descended from the mountains and entered Havana on January 1, 1959, forcing Batista to flee the country. Castro took control of the Cuban Government's 30,000-man army and declared himself Prime Minister.

The CIA continued, detailing the history between the United States and Cuba and much more, including the insertion of the Soviet Union into the situation:

The leader of Cuba for nearly fifty years, Fidel Castro was often in the sights of the CIA for a variety of reasons.

For nearly 50 years, Cuba had been America's playground and agricultural center. Many wealthy Americans lived in Cuba and had established thriving businesses there. In fact, a significant portion of Cuba's sugar plantations were owned by North Americans. With Castro's self-appointment to Prime Minister, that changed. In February 1960, Cuba signed an agreement to buy oil from the Soviet Union. When the US-owned refineries in the country refused to process the oil, Castro seized the firms, and the US broke off diplomatic relations with the Cuban regime. To the chagrin of the Eisenhower administration, Castro established increasingly close ties with the Soviet Union while delivering fiery condemnations of the US. The American-Cuban relationship deteriorated further when Castro established diplomatic relations with our Cold War rival, the Soviet Union. Castro and Soviet Premier Nikita Khrushchev signed a series of pacts that resulted in large deliveries of economic and military aid in 1960. Within a year, Castro proclaimed himself a communist, formally allied his country with the Soviet Union, and seized remaining American and foreign-owned assets. The establishment of a Communist state 90 miles off the coast of Florida raised obvious security concerns in Washington and did not sit well with President Eisenhower. Eisenhower authorized the CIA to conduct a covert operation to rid the island of its self-appointed leader.

Things were about to become dicey and dangerous, as CIA papers note:

For simplicity, the Bay of Pigs invasion plan can be broken down into three phases: Phase One: Destroy as many of Castro's combat aircraft as possible so that when the Brigade invaded the beach, Castro's air force would have no retaliatory capabilities. To do this, pilots of Brigade 2506 planned to bomb three of Castro's air force bases. The cover story for these bombings was simple. Pilots in the Brigade would pose as pilots in the Fuerza Aérea Revolucionaria (FAR), Castro's Air Force. Allegedly, they would become disgruntled, take their aircrafts, shoot up their own air force bases, and then fly to the US to defect. This first airstrike was supposed to take place two days prior to the invasion (phase three). B-26 training Phase Two: Destroy any remaining combat planes in Castro's fleet that weren't taken out during phase one. Pilots in Brigade 2506 planned to drop bombs on Castro's air force bases in the morning hours prior to the main invasion (phase three) to destroy any remaining combat planes in Castro's fleet. This would ensure the Brigade members invading the beach would not have to contend with Castro's aircraft dropping bombs and firing mercilessly on them from above during the actual invasion. Phase Three: The invasion. The Brigade would invade Cuba by sea and air. Some members would invade Cuba on the beaches of Trinidad; others would parachute in farther inland. The Brigade pilots would fly air cover missions over the beach. The old colonial city of Trinidad was chosen as the invasion site because it offered many significant features. It

The tranquil beach at Trinidad was selected as the main point of invasion for the United States during the Bay of Pigs invasion. President Kennedy believed this spot would be best to allow for plausible deniability in the future.

was an anti-Castro town with existing counter-revolutionary groups. It had good port facilities. The beachhead was easily defensible and, should the Brigade need to execute their escape plan, the Escambray Mountains were there to offer solitude.... As the number of days till the invasion shortened, Kennedy's concern that the operation would not remain covert grew. He was adamant the hand of the US Government remain hidden at all costs.

The papers reveal much more:

Kennedy thought changing the invasion site from Trinidad would make future deniability of US involvement more plausible, so he gave the CIA four days to come up with a new one. And so, a month before the operation was set to get underway, the landing location changed from Trinidad to the Bay of Pigs. This presented an array of problems, namely, the Bay of Pigs was one of Castro's favorite fishing holes. He knew the land like the back of his hand. He vacationed there frequently and invested in the Cuban peasants surrounding the bay, garnering their loyalty and admiration. Additionally, the Escambray Mountains, the designated escape site, was 50 miles away through hostile territory. The bay was also far from large groups of civilians, a necessary commodity for instigating an uprising, which may be a moot point, as the bay was surrounded by the largest swamp in Cuba, making it physically impossible for any Cubans wanting to join the revolt to actually do so. Early on the morning of April 15, phase one was deployed. Six Cuban-piloted B-26 bombers struck two airfields, three military bases, and Antonio Maceo Airport in an attempt to destroy the Cuban air force. Their planes had been refurbished to match those of the FAR; each equipped with bombs, rockets and machine guns. About 90 minutes later a "defecting" pilot, a member of Brigade 2506, took off in his American-made getaway plane, also disguised as a FAR aircraft. His plane, however, received extra attention. Dirt was rubbed on the markings to make it look worn. A phony flight log was in the cockpit along with various other items typically found in Cuban military aircraft. Finally, because a defector shooting up his own base would most likely encounter resistance, his plane was shot full of bullet holes. B-26 disguised to look like Cuban aircraft The "defector's" destination was the Miami International Airport. He radioed a "mayday" distress signal from off the coast of Florida and informed US authorities that he was defecting from the Cuban Air Force, having engine trouble, and requested permission to land. Upon landing, he was taken into custody by US Customs and Immigration and Naturalization. Reciting his cover story, he explained that he was defecting from Cuba, but before doing so had attacked his own air base and that two colleagues had also defected and had attacked other Cuban air bases. Damage assessments of the airstrikes vary, but it is believed that 80 percent of Castro's combat aircraft were disabled. Assuming Castro had an inventory of as many as 30 combat aircraft, that left six functioning aircraft available at his disposal on the day of the Bay of Pigs invasion. Castro vehemently denied that the attacks on his airfields had been by rebellious members of the FAR and immediately blamed the US. He also quickly concluded that these strikes were an indication of something larger brewing. He preemptively rounded up thousands of potential dissidents and herded them into theatres, stadiums and military bases to squelch the possibility of a spontaneous uprising to overthrow his regime.

As the CIA notes:

Following Castro's orders, Raúl Roa, the Cuban Foreign Minister, called an emergency session of the United Nations Political and Security Committee in New York on the afternoon of April 15. The session was attended by US Ambassador to the UN, Adlai Stevenson. Stevenson held up pictures of the planes as he adamantly stated the US had nothing to do with the airstrikes. He insisted that the attacks were conducted by defectors from Castro's own air force. The pictures, however, proved to be the unraveling of the cover story. On close inspection, one could make out a metal nose on the plane flown by the defector; FAR aircraft noses were plastic. Ambassador Stevenson, who was unaware of the covert operation, was furious when the truth was revealed. This was bad news for President Kennedy whose number one priority was hiding the hand of the US Government, which was becoming more exposed as the operation proceeded. Lying to the UN had serious consequences and a second strike would put the United States in an awkward position internationally. Political considerations trumped the military importance of a "D-Day" air strike. Late in the evening of April 16, Kennedy made the decision to cancel the air strikes set to destroy the remaining fleet of Cuban bombers.

The decision was so last minute that the Brigade pilots were sitting on the runway, taxied in position for takeoff when they were told to stand down. Ironically, however, the air support sched-

FIGURE 30
PUERTO CABEZAS. B-26. TAIL ASSEMBLY DETAIL, CUBAN INSIGNIA, FAR,
AND TAIL NUMBERS IDENTICAL TO CASTRO'S B-26'S.

Shown here is a Douglas A-26 Invader "B-26" bomber aircraft disguised as a Cuban model in preparation for the Bay of Pigs invasion.

uled to provide cover to the invading Brigade on the beach could proceed as planned. This last-minute cancellation forced leadership to work furiously through the midnight hours, reworking and revising their plans, racing the sun as it climbed into a cloudless sky the morning of April 17, 1961: D-Day.

Matters were most assuredly heating up, as the CIA now reveals:

The Bay of Pigs invasion began with the launch of eight pairs of aircraft flown by Brigade pilots over the Bay of Pigs. But, like all else, that number too had been scaled back at the last minute, which left large patches of time when no aircraft would be providing air support for the invading Brigade. The FAR had read the remnants of the April 15 strikes like tea leaves and correctly predicted a second attack. This time, they were prepared. As the sun's orange rays stretched across the Caribbean Sea, the members of Brigade 2506 prepared to return home. Not as citizens, not as vacationers, but as invaders. As their vessels drew ever nearer to shore, they saw their island as never before: not as a warm, welcoming place, but as a hostile, yet, strangely familiar territory. They had been training for this moment, anticipating it and envisioning it for the past year. Now it was upon them. This was their opportunity to make a difference in the country in which they had lived, the country which they had loved, the country from which they had fled. This was their chance to turn the tide. Yet, it was an ocean tide and unforeseen coral reefs that made it increasingly difficult for the Brigade to even reach the shore.

Most of the men lost their weapons and equipment to the turquoise waters. Once ashore, they were met instantly by Cuban armed forces who outnumbered them. The salvaged and undamaged Cuban planes that had survived the April 15 strikes, the very planes that should have been destroyed that morning had Kennedy not canceled the planned strike, were now flying overhead wreaking mayhem on the Brigade. The invasion did not go as planned, and the exiles soon found themselves outgunned, outmanned, outnumbered and outplanned by Castro's troops. Castro's first priority was sinking the ships that invaded

Cuban waters. The USS *Houston*, an American troop and supply vessel, was damaged by several FAR rockets, its captain then intentionally beached it on the western side of the bay. The FAR also machine gunned the two landing craft and other supply vessels that had brought the Brigade into the Bay of Pigs. They hit the USS *Rio Escondido*, which was loaded with aviation fuel, causing a terrific explosion before it sank like a stone. Meanwhile, the paratroopers dropped in. One set missed their target and lost most of their equipment, and two other men were injured when their static line cable broke. A portion of the equipment that was airdropped sank in the swamps. The Brigade did have some successes. Several paratroopers hit their targets and were able to hold their positions and block roads for two days. The Brigade pilots providing air cover support successfully destroyed tanks and other armor and halted an advancement of Cuban militia cadets. Neither side made any significant advances as the invasion and fighting continued into the third day. The deteriorating operation convinced President Kennedy to authorize six unmarked fighter jets from the aircraft carrier USS *Essex* to provide combat air patrol for the Brigade's aircraft for one hour on April 19. But not without strict limitations; they could not instigate air combat or attack ground targets. Limitations, however, wasn't the biggest problem: timing was. Somewhere, among the last-minute changes and cables going back and forth, there was a miscommunication. As the six jets sat on deck awaiting their scheduled departure time, the Brigade's aircraft flew over them an hour ahead of schedule. The jets immediately launched after them, but they were unable to reach the invasion area in time to protect the Brigade's aircraft. Brigade 2506's pleas for air and naval support were refused at the highest US Government levels, although several CIA contract pilots dropped munitions and supplies, resulting in the deaths of four of them: Pete Ray, Leo Baker, Riley Shamburger, and Wade Gray. Kennedy refused to authorize any extension beyond the hour granted. To this day, there has been no resolution as to what caused this discrepancy in timing. Without direct air support—no artillery and no weapons—and completely outnumbered by Castro's forces, members of the Brigade either surrendered or returned to the turquoise water from which they had come. Two American destroyers attempted to move into the Bay of Pigs to evacuate these members, but gunfire from Cuban forces made that impossible. In the following days, US entities continued to monitor the waters surrounding the bay in search of survivors, with only a handful being rescued. A few members of the Brigade managed to escape and went into hiding, but soon surrendered due to a lack of food and water. When all was said and done, more than seventy-five percent of Brigade 2506 ended up in Cuban prisons.

Due to the fiasco that the Bay of Pigs invasion became, plans were secretly put in place to get rid of Castro on a permanent basis: assassination was the next approach. Despite the incredible extent of the attempts undertaken by U.S. intelligence to have Castro taken permanently out of circulation, the man seemed to have nine lives, as we shall now see.

Because of the failure of the Bay of Pigs attack, the new goal set for the CIA was to assassinate Castro (pictured).

On November 10, 2017, Jeremy B. White stated in the *Independent*: "On the day John F Kennedy died, the CIA was working to kill Fidel Castro with a poisoned pen. Mr. Kennedy was assassinated in Dallas in 1963, but Mr Castro survived a CIA plot to kill him with a lethal ballpoint pen. In the end, the Cuban leader outlasted his American rival by more than five decades. The machinations against Cuba's communist leader are revealed in a new batch of declassified documents relating to Mr. Kennedy's assassination. The National Archives has been steadily making thousands of documents available to the public, helping to illuminate both the government's scramble to investigate the President's death and the Cold War geopolitics playing out around them."

That was not all, however. From *NBC News*, we learn the following: "Fidel Castro survived no fewer than 634 attempts on his life, according to his former secret service chief. Whether that figure is accurate or not, Cuba's iconic dictator provided an almost-mythical adversary for what became an obsessive, error-prone assassination campaign by the CIA. The agency's attempts to kill Castro ranged from the calamitous to the comical. Many of them were detailed by the Church Committee, a special Senate subcommittee headed by Democratic Sen. Frank Church in 1975."

NBC News continues: "Perhaps the most famous attempt to kill Castro came in

1960 when the CIA poisoned a box of his favorite cigars. Just a year after Castro seized power, the agency spiked the cigars with a botulinum toxin strong enough to kill anybody who put one in their mouth. The cigars were delivered to an "an unidentified person" in 1961, according to the subcommittee, but it's unclear what happened to them after that. Needless to say, they were never chewed by 'El Comandante.'"

Mental Floss reveals the following: "Marita Lorenz, just one of many women Castro counted as a mistress, allegedly accepted a deal from the CIA in which she would feed him capsules filled with poison. She managed to get as far as smuggling the pills into his bedroom in her jar of cold cream, but the pills dissolved in the cream and she doubted her ability to force-feed Castro face lotion, and she also just chickened out. According to Lorenz, Castro somehow figured out her plan and offered her his gun. 'I can't do it, Fidel,' she told him."

Mental Floss also highlights yet another attempt on Castro's life: "Knowing that Castro liked to scuba dive, the CIA made plans to plant an explosive device in a conch shell at his favorite spot. They plotted to make the shell brightly colored and unusual looking so it would be sure to attract Castro's attention, drawing him close enough to kill him when the bomb inside went off."

As history has shown, despite an astonishing number of attempts—largely planned by the CIA—to terminate Fidel Castro, each and every one of them failed.

THE MYSTERIOUS DEATH OF MARILYN MONROE

There can be no doubt that when it comes to Hollywood legends, they don't get more legendary than Marilyn Monroe, the ultimate blonde bombshell. Born in 1925, she became one of the biggest stars of Hollywood's Golden Age, starring in such hit movies as *Bus Stop*, *Some Like It Hot*, and *Gentlemen Prefer Blondes*. With worldwide fame, millions of adoring fans, and a lifestyle that saw her mixing with the rich, the famous, and the leading lights of both Hollywood and the world of politics, Monroe's life should have been a dream. It was, however, more like a nightmare: failed marriages, depression, anxiety, a fragile state of mind, and a cast of characters who used and abused Monroe were all parts of the short life of the famous star, one whose life tragically came to an end at just thirty-six. It was a death that, more than half a century after it occurred, still provokes a mass of debate.

That Monroe is acknowledged to have had affairs with both President John F. Kennedy and his brother, Robert Kennedy (the attorney general in the JFK Administration), has led to suspicions that she was murdered as a result of certain top-secret data shared with her by the Kennedy brothers as a means to impress her into the bedroom before being callously dumped. There's no doubt that Monroe was a prestigious keeper of journals—one of which, dubbed "The Red Book," reportedly contained the facts surrounding a wealth of data on such topics as the U.S. government's plans to invade Cuba, a CIA–Mafia connection, attempts to have Cuba's Fidel Castro assassinated, and even crashed UFOs and dead aliens—all provided by the recklessly talkative Kennedy boys.

If Marilyn Monroe was considered a potential security threat for what she knew, surely we should see some evidence of it, correct? Yes, correct. And

The beautiful actress Marilyn Monroe was the subject of much controversy based on her mysterious death at age thirty-six in 1962.

we do see that evidence, thanks to the Freedom of Information Act. Previously classified documents reveal that as far back as 1955, both the FBI and the CIA were watching Monroe closely as a result of her visa application that same year to visit the former Soviet Union.

The FBI's files also show that J. Edgar Hoover was keeping watch on all the rumors of links between Monroe and both JFK and RFK. Her links to Mob buddy Frank Sinatra were also secretly noted and frowned upon by officialdom. The secret surveillance of Monroe would likely have continued had something not intervened. That "something" was her death on August 5, 1962.

Despite extensive investigations, the passing of Marilyn Monroe remains the enigma it was back in 1962. The story begins on August 4, one day before the actress's death. The afternoon was taken up by a visit to Monroe's Brentwood home in Los Angeles by her psychiatrist, Dr. Ralph Greenson. He was attempting to get Monroe out of her depressive state of mind. A few hours later, at around 7:00 P.M., Monroe chatted on the phone with Joe DiMaggio Jr. (the son of her former husband, baseball legend Joe DiMaggio), who later said she was in a good frame of mind. Not long after that, actor Peter Lawford invited Marilyn over to his house for dinner, but she chose not to go. Lawford was reportedly concerned by Monroe's stoned, slurry tones and decided to call her again later. This is where things become confusing—and potentially conspiratorial.

So the story goes, Lawford tried to reach Monroe several times again that night, all to no avail. He was, however, able to speak with her housekeeper, Eunice Murray, who assured Lawford that all was well. He was not so sure. Murray would later state that at roughly 10:00 P.M., she saw a light coming from Monroe's bedroom but heard nothing, and she assumed the actress had fallen asleep and left the light on.

Around half an hour later (exact timelines are difficult to nail down), rumors were circulating that Marilyn had overdosed, which were confirmed by Monroe's lawyer, Mickey Rudin, and her publicist, Arthur P. Jacobs. At approximately 1:00 A.M., Lawford got a call from Rudin, stating the star was dead. That is somewhat curious, however, as at 3:00 A.M.—two hours later—Murray reportedly tried to wake Monroe by knocking on the bedroom door and the French windows.

Dr. Greenson was soon on the scene again, having been phoned by Murray; he quickly smashed the windows to gain entry. Sure enough, the world's most famous blonde was no more. The police soon arrived to find a scene filled with confusion and suspicious activity. Murray was hastily washing the bedsheets when the investigating officers descended on Marilyn's home. Both Greenson and Murray made changes to their stories, specifically in regard to who called whom and when and in relation to the particular time at which they believed she died—around 4:00 A.M. This was completely at odds with the conclusion of the undertaker, Guy Hockett, who put the time of death at around 9:30 P.M., a significant number of hours earlier. On top of that, the pathologist, Dr. Thomas Noguchi, was suspicious of the fact that even if Monroe had taken an overdose—of what was deemed to be Nembutal—she had not swallowed it, via a glass of water, for example. A study of her intestines demonstrated that. How the drugs got into the system of the actress remained a puzzle. Actually, everything remained a puzzle—and still does.

Marilyn Monroe was laid to rest on August 8, 1962, at the Westwood Village Memorial Park Cemetery in Los Angeles. Was her death due to a combination of her fragile state of mind, anger, and turmoil at the way the Kennedy brothers treated her and over-whelming depression? Such a scenario isn't impossible. It's worth noting, however, that not long after Marilyn's death, the FBI received startling information, which was not declassified until decades later, that shed shocking new light on the strange saga.

One of the most fascinating—and deeply controversial—pieces of documenta-tion that has surfaced concerning the death of Marilyn Monroe originated with an unknown individual that the FBI identified, in its now declassified dossier on the Hollywood legend, as a "former Special Agent, who is currently Field Representative, Appointment Section, Governor's Office, State of California."

Written and sent to the FBI in 1963, its contents are eye-opening in the extreme, since they suggest that the attorney general himself, Bobby Kennedy, was involved in a plot to "induce" Monroe's suicide. The lengthy docu-ment to the FBI begins as follows: "Robert

Marilyn Monroe passed away on August 5, 1962, in the early morning hours. While the drug Nembutal was in her system, she apparently had not swallowed it, which suggests it was injected.

Kennedy had been having a romance and sex affair over a period of time with Marilyn Monroe. He had met her, the first date being arranged by his sister and brother-in-law, Mr. and Mrs. Peter Lawford. Robert Kennedy had been spending much time in Hollywood during the last part of 1961 and early 1962, in connection with his trying to have a film made of his book dealing with the crime investigations. He used to meet with producer Jerry Wald. He was reported to be intensely jealous of the fact that they had been making a film of John F. Kennedy's book of the PT boat story."

The unidentified special agent of the FBI continued that RFK was "deeply involved emotionally" with Marilyn Monroe and had repeatedly promised to divorce his wife to marry Marilyn. Eventually, however, she realized that Bobby had no intention of marrying her and almost certainly never had any such plans. Adding to that woe was the fact that, as the Bureau was also informed, "about this time, twentieth century Fox studio had decided to cancel [Monroe's] contract. She had become very unreliable, being late for set, etc. In addition, the studio was in financial difficulty due to the large expenditures caused in the filming of 'Cleopatra.' The studio notified Marilyn that they were canceling her contract. This was right in the middle of a picture she was making. They decided to replace her with actress Lee Remick."

The spiraling bad luck, in both her private life and her acting career, prompted Monroe to turn to Bobby Kennedy yet again, even though it was clear to her that the relationship was doomed to go nowhere. It was a decision that may well have cost Marilyn her life, as the words of the FBI's confidante demonstrate:

> Marilyn telephoned Robert Kennedy from her home at Brentwood, California, person-to-person, at the Department of Justice, Washington, D.C., to tell him the bad news. Robert Kennedy told her not to worry about the contract—he would take care of everything. When nothing was done, she again called him from her home to the Department of Justice, person-to-person, and on this occasion they had unpleasant words.

> She was reported to have threatened to make public their affair. On the day that Marilyn died, Robert Kennedy was in town, and registered at the Beverly Hills Hotel. By coincidence, this is across the street from the house in which a number of years earlier his father, Joseph Kennedy, had lived for a time, common-law, with Gloria Swanson.

It was at this point in the informant's story that things turned decidedly dark. Hardly surprising, since he outlined something controversial in the extreme: a cold-hearted plot to manipulate Marilyn Monroe into taking her own life. It began like this, FBI documents state:

Peter Lawford knew from Marilyn's friends that she often made suicide threats and that she was inclined to fake a suicide attempt in order to arouse sympathy. Lawford is reported as having made a "special arrangement" with Marilyn's psychiatrist, Dr. Ralph Greenson, of Beverly Hills. The psychiatrist was treating Marilyn for emotional problems and getting her off the use of barbiturates. On her last visit to him, he prescribed [illegible] tablets, and gave her a prescription for 60 of them, which was unusual in quantity, especially since she saw him frequently.

That "special arrangement" had one goal: the death of the Hollywood goddess. The statement to the FBI continues:

[Monroe's] housekeeper put the bottle of pills on the night table. It is reported the housekeeper and Marilyn's personal secretary and press agent, Pat Newcomb, were cooperating in the plan to induce suicide. Pat Newcomb was rewarded for her cooperation by being put on the head of the Federal payroll as top assistant to George Stevens, Jr., head of the Motion Pictures Activities Division of the U.S. Information Service. His father, George Stevens, Sr., is a left-wing Hollywood director, who is well known for specializing in the making of slanted and left-wing pictures. One of these was the "Diary of Anne Frank."

On the day of Marilyn's death, said the "former Special Agent," Robert Kennedy checked out of the Beverly Hills Hotel and flew from Los Angeles International Airport via Western Airlines to San Francisco, where he checked into the St. Francis Hotel, which was owned by a Mr. London, a friend of Kennedy's. From there, Kennedy phoned Lawford "to find out if Marilyn was dead yet."

FBI records reveal what reportedly happened next: "Peter Lawford had called Marilyn's number and spoke with her, and then checked again later to make sure she did not answer. Marilyn expected to have her stomach pumped out and to get sympathy through her suicide attempt. The psychiatrist left word for Marilyn to take a drive in the fresh air, but did not come to see her until after she was known to be dead.

"Marilyn received a call from Joe DiMaggio, Jr., who was in the U.S. Marines, stationed at Camp Pendleton, California. They were very friendly. Marilyn told him she was getting very sleepy. The last call she attempted to make was to Peter Lawford to return a call she had made to her. Joe DiMaggio, Sr., knows the whole story and is reported to have stated when Robert Kennedy gets out of office, he intends to kill him. [Deleted] knew of the affair between Robert Kennedy and Marilyn."

The story was not over, however; in fact, far from it. The FBI's source had far more to add:

Robert F. Kennedy, Marilyn Monroe, and John F. Kennedy are shown here backstage during the birthday celebration for JFK.

While Robert Kennedy was carrying on his sex affair with Marilyn Monroe, on a few occasions, John F. Kennedy came out and had sex parties with [deleted], an actress. Chief of Police Parker, of the Los Angeles Police Department, has the toll call tickets obtained from the telephone company on the calls made from Marilyn's residence telephone. They are in his safe at Los Angeles Headquarters.

From there, things got even more controversial:

Florabel Muir, the columnist, has considerable information and knowledge of the Robert F. Kennedy and Marilyn Monroe affair. She personally saw the telephone call records. Marilyn Monroe's psychiatrist, although he knew she had taken the pills, did not come to her home until after she was dead. He made contact with the coroner and an arrangement was made for a psychiatric board of inquiry to be appointed by the coroner, an unheard of procedure in the area. This was so the findings could be recorded that she was emotionally unbalanced. It was reported this arrangement was to discredit any statements she may have made before she died.

During the period of time that Robert F. Kennedy was having his sex affair with Marilyn Monroe, on one occasion a sex party was conducted at which several other persons were present. Tap recording was secretly made and is in the possession of a Los Angeles private detective agency. The detective wants $5,000 for a certified copy of the recording, in which all the voices are identifiable.

We may never know for sure if and to what extent the data provided to the FBI was acted upon. We can say one thing for certain, however: just as with the deaths of JFK, Robert Kennedy, and Martin Luther King, nagging suspicions remain that the official explanation may not be the correct one. Now, let's take a look at the most controversial aspect of all concerning Marilyn Monroe: namely, that she was assassinated because of the UFO secrets that President Kennedy had shared with her as a means to impress her into bed.

ASSASSINATED BECAUSE OF ALIENS?

UFOs and the death of Marilyn Monroe: are they all connected? It's a hugely charged saga that dates back to the mid-1990s and is clearly not going to go away anytime soon. The vast majority of the story is reliant on a controversial document of questionable origins and of equally questionable authenticity. Allegedly, it's a CIA document dated August 3, 1962, which deals with Marilyn Monroe's supposed knowledge of Roswell and UFO-themed conspiracies. And matters relative to what is referred to as a "secret base." Now, where might that be...?

What is particularly interesting about the "Monroe document" is not so much what it says but what it specifically doesn't say. Despite what many researchers have said, there is not even a single reference in the document to aliens, extraterrestrials, flying saucers, or UFOs. In fact, the wording could actually push the whole story down a different path, as you will soon see. But first, let's see how and under what circumstances the controversial, one-page document surfaced.

It all began in 1995 at a press conference in Los Angeles held by Milo Speriglio, a man with a deep interest in the circumstances surrounding Marilyn's death. Speriglio was so interested in her final day in August 1962 that he wrote three books on the issues of her life and her still controversial death: *Crypt 33*, *The Marilyn Conspiracy*, and *Marilyn Monroe: Murder Cover-Up*. Until 1995, Speriglio had not made any kind of connection between Monroe and UFOs. So, what was it that prompted Speriglio to head off into new and highly inflammatory territory? It was a revelation from well-known ufology figure Timothy Cooper.

Today, many people within ufology might not recognize that name. But in the 1990s, Cooper was involved in a controversy that stemmed from the fact that he claimed to have received a wealth of old, sensational, leaked documents from retired figures in the intelligence community—almost all of them on crashed UFOs, Roswell, dead aliens, and the notorious Majestic 12 group. Rather notably, the initial batch came to Cooper from a source in Nevada.

There's no doubt that the documents existed (and still exist). You can find PDF versions of most of them at Ryan Wood's *MajesticDocuments.com* website. There are literally hundreds of pages. The big question is: are they the real deal? When the papers were made available, there were those researchers who believed that the documents were 100 percent real. Some investigators, though, considered them to be government disinformation. And others firmly believed that Cooper had created them himself, perhaps for fame, notoriety, or money. Possibly, all three. The controversy raged on for a while but finally imploded upon itself with barely a sigh. The Marilyn document was one of those that Cooper claimed to have received from one of his various sources or, as we might justifiably call them, "ufological Snowdens."

I know quite a bit about the Cooper papers (including the Marilyn Monroe document), as the following extract from my 2017 book *The Roswell UFO Conspiracy* makes clear:

> It's a little known fact that in late 2001 Tim Cooper sold all of his voluminous UFO files to Dr. Robert M. Wood. Bob is the author of *Alien Viruses* and the father of Ryan Wood, who has spent years researching alleged crashed UFO incidents—all detailed in his book, *Majic Eyes Only*. It is even less well-known that in the early days of 2002, Bob hired me to spend a week in an Orange County, California-based motel-room, surrounded by all of the thousands upon thousands of pages of Cooper's voluminous collection of the cosmic sort.

> The plan was for me to catalog all of the material, to compile each and every piece of it into chronological order, and to summarize the content of each document, every letter, and every Freedom of Information request that Cooper had submitted to government agencies—which is precisely what I did. It was a week in which I most definitely earned my loot. It was also a week that paralleled the infamous story told by Hunter S. Thompson in his classic gonzo saga, *Fear and Loathing in Las Vegas*. Whereas Thompson was hunkered down with his whisky, margaritas and shrimp cocktails, for me it was cases of cold beer and club sandwiches.

> Contained within that huge amount of material at my disposal was the Monroe document—the "original copy" that Cooper is said to have received from one of his shadowy sources. There were also a number of FOIA requests

from Cooper that he had sent to various military and intelligence agencies in search of any and all files on Marilyn Monroe. Cooper was clearly seeking out as much as he could find on Marilyn and UFOs—regardless of the actual origin of the document. For around eight weeks, Speriglio did absolutely nothing with the document, aside from sitting on it and pondering on what his next move should be. What Speriglio finally did was to hold that aforementioned press conference. And that's how the story began and how the document and its contents spilled over into the UFO research community.

> The Marilyn document was one of those that Cooper claimed to have received from one of his various sources or, as we might justifiably call them, "ufological Snowdens."

One of the lesser-known aspects of this story is that Speriglio made a very brief comment to the effect that copies of the document were in the hands of what he described as "two federal agencies." At the press conference, Speriglio flatly refused to reveal the identities of the two agencies. And he refused to reveal the names when questioned later, too. So far, nothing of any substance has ever surfaced in relation to what exactly, if anything, those two agencies may have done with the document.

Now, let's take a look at the contents of the document.

Most of those contents are focused on conversations between two people: newspaper columnist Dorothy Kilgallen and a friend of hers named Howard Rothberg. The former was a well-known figure in the field of celebrity journalism in the 1950s, and she was deeply interested in the JFK assassination. As an aside, when the Speriglio–Cooper document surfaced, I fired off FOIA requests to the CIA and the FBI and received copies of their files on Kilgallen. The CIA papers were few and brief, to say the least. The FBI, however, mailed me close to 170 pages on Kilgallen, demonstrating that she was someone who was watched very closely by J. Edgar Hoover's special agents.

As for what the purported CIA document states, there is this: "Rothberg discussed the apparent comeback of [Marilyn Monroe] with Kilgallen and the break up with the Kennedys. Rothberg told Kilgallen that she was attending Hollywood parties hosted by the 'inner circle' among Hollywood's elite and was becoming the talk of the town again. Rothberg indicated in so many words, that she had secrets to tell, no doubt arising from her trists [sic] with the President and the Attorney General."

Now, we get to the crux of the story. The document reveals: "One such [illegible] mentions the visit by the President at a secret air base for the purpose of inspecting things from outer space. Kilgallen replied that she knew what might be the source of the visit. In the mid-fifties Kilgallen learned of secret effort by US and UK governments to identify the origins of crashed spacecraft and dead bodies, from a British government official. Kilgallen believed the story may have come from the [illegible] in the late forties. Kilgallen said that if the story is true, it could cause terrible embarrassment to Jack and his plans to have NASA put men on the moon."

It is true that Dorothy Kilgallen wrote briefly about UFOs back in 1955. While vacationing in the United Kingdom in that year, Kilgallen was on the receiving end of a very odd story, as she noted: "I can report today on a story which is positively spooky, not to mention chilling. British scientists and airmen, after examining the wreckage of one mysterious flying ship, are convinced these strange aerial objects are not optical illusions or Soviet inventions, but are flying saucers which originate on another planet. The source of my information is a British official of cabinet rank who prefers to remain unidentified."

That same "British official of cabinet rank" reportedly advised Kilgallen of the following: "We believe, on the basis of our inquiry thus far, that the saucers were staffed by small men—probably under four feet tall. It's frightening, but there's no denying the flying saucers come from another planet."

Kilgallen had more to say: "This official quoted scientists as saying a flying ship of this type could not have possibly been constructed on Earth. The British Government, I learned, is withholding an official report on the 'flying saucer' examination at this time, possibly because it does not wish to frighten the public. When my husband and I arrived here from a brief vacation, I had no premonition that I would be catapulting myself into the controversy over whether flying saucers are real or imaginary."

The references in the document to Marilyn having "secrets to tell" (secrets supposedly shared with her by JFK and RFK) have led a number of UFO investigators to conclude that Marilyn was killed because of what she knew about the Roswell, New Mexico, event of July 1947. The alleged CIA document goes on to refer to Monroe's "diary of secrets," to "what the newspapers would do with such disclosures" and how she had "threatened to hold a press conference and would tell all." A countdown to death, all in the name of maintaining UFO secrecy? Well, yes, that's how it seems. But within the domain of ufology, practically nothing is as it seems.

Project Moon Dust was conducted at the Air Force Missile Development Center (1958 photo shown here), which was part of the Holloman Air Force Base near Alamogordo, New Mexico.

It's important to note that at the top of the document, there is a reference to a Project Moon Dust. Over the years, ufologists have given a great deal of attention to this U.S. military program, which, in government circles, is also referred to as Moondust. Its origins date back to the 1950s. The reason why so much attention has been placed upon Project Moon

Dust is because of its potential connection to the issue of alleged crashed and recovered UFOs held by elements of the U.S. military—crash retrievals, or C/Rs as they are generally known. But was Moon Dust really the key operation in secretly locating and recovering crashed ships from faraway worlds?

No, it was not. A November 3, 1961, U.S. Air Force document states: "In addition to their staff duty assignments, intelligence team personnel have peacetime duty functions in support of such Air Force projects as Moondust, Bluefly, and UFO, and other AFCIN directed quick reaction projects which require intelligence team operational capabilities.... Unidentified Flying Objects (UFO): Headquarters USAF has established a program for investigation of reliably reported unidentified flying objects within the United States. AFR 200-2 delineates 1127th collection responsibilities...."

That all sounds very interesting, but if you take a careful look at all of the Moon Dust documents in the public domain (which I have done), it becomes very clear that when military officials were referring to "UFOs" in their files, they were *not* talking about alien spacecraft. Rather, they were referencing probable space debris that originated with the former Soviet Union. Which brings me back to the document that got Milo Speriglio fired up.

Keep Moon Dust in mind as you read the following. You'll recall that earlier I stated the following: "Despite what many researchers have said, there is not even a single reference in the document to dead aliens, extraterrestrials, flying saucers, or UFOs. Not a single one." That's absolutely true. What it really says is that JFK allegedly traveled to "a secret air base for the purpose of inspecting things from outer space." No references to aliens or to extraterrestrial ships. The document also refers to "crashed spacecraft and dead bodies." But again, no specific references to mangled E.T.s or wrecked saucers.

Now, some might say that references to "dead bodies," "things from outer space," and "crashed spacecraft" are references to the Roswell event and to deceased aliens. On the other hand, however, the very fact that the document references Project Moon Dust suggests another possibility. Namely, that the subject matter may have been a failed—and still unknown—early Soviet manned mission into space. One that predated Yuri Gagarin's flight into outer space on April 12, 1961. There is another bit of data that supports this scenario. Recall that the document states: "Kilgallen said that if the story is true, it could cause terrible embarrassment to Jack and his plans to have NASA put men on the moon." For ufologists, this is—or should be—a problem.

Why on Earth would widespread knowledge of the existence of aliens "cause terrible embarrassment to Jack and his plans to have NASA put me on the moon"? The answer is: it wouldn't. If such information on aliens reached the public, it certainly would have caused widespread fear, wonder, and amazement among the public—and within the government, too. But specifically provoking embarrassment for NASA in relation to plans to put a man on the Moon? That doesn't make any sense. If, however, those "dead bodies" were Soviet cosmonauts, if the "crashed spacecraft" was a Russian rocket, and if the Soviets did have a number of unsuccessful manned missions that predated Gagarin—and that such information threatened to surface during the time Kennedy was in office—then, yes, that would have caused significant embarrassment for the JFK administration and, possibly, for NASA, too.

So, where does all of this leave us? Admittedly, since the Marilyn document first surfaced in 1995, my views and opinions have gone back and forth. I think it's probably a hoax. Mainly because it gives ufology just about all the things it wants and yearns for: the references to "dead bodies" and "crashed spacecraft" inevitably provoke Roswell-like imagery. The mention of a "secret air base" effortlessly points us in the direction of Area 51, thus adding another layer of sensational conspiracy to the story. The JFK–UFO angle reinforces the belief in some quarters that Kennedy was whacked because of what he knew about Roswell. The same with Marilyn, too. It's *The X-Files*-meets-*Dark Skies*-meets-Oliver Stone's *JFK*.

But I have to admit, I do find it intriguing that whoever really wrote the document, they were extremely vague in terms of what they were talking about. I have seen more than a few questionable UFO documents in my time, and the one thing that nearly all of them share is an explicit, collective reference to E.T.s, to aliens, to flying saucers, and to extraterrestrial craft. In other words, there is no doubt about the subject matter: creatures from other worlds.

Area 51 is by far the most notable military base connected with UFOs and possible failed alien missions that could provide some evidence of truth to the mysteries.

For me, though, the Marilyn document remains interesting because of the undeniable haziness of what it says. Or of what it doesn't say. It doesn't tell the reader that aliens crashed anywhere—despite the assumptions of ufology. So, maybe, with that in mind, there is something to the document, after all. That's not a case of me fence-sitting. As I said, I *think* it's a hoax. But if it is, then a great deal of thought went into it. As did a great deal of restraint—in terms of the unclear subject matter. Maybe, there's another answer: that we're seeing a document crafted by disinformation experts to confuse ufology for reasons presently unknown.

In light of all the above, it's not surprising the document is still "alive and kicking" close to a quarter of a century after it surfaced.

Finally, it's worth noting that the FBI took a deep interest in a certain book on the death of Marilyn Monroe. It may come as a surprise to many to learn that agencies of government often review published books. I'm going to share with you a timely example, as the relevant documentation can be found in the newly released files on the JFK assassination of November 22, 1963, at Dealey Plaza, in Dallas, Texas. The now declassified, fourteen-page file tells an interesting story of a man named Frank A. Capell and his book *The Strange Death of Marilyn Monroe*. An FBI Airtel of July 2, 1964, states the following:

> On instant date, captioned individual [Frank A. Capell] advised he is about to publish a 70-page paperback book dealing with the suicide of MARILYN MONROE. He said the book is titled 'The Strange Death of Marilyn Monroe' and will sell for $2.00 per copy. CAPELL advised that the book should be ready for sale on or about 7/10/64, and that he will furnish a copy of this book for the Bureau's information.

The FBI document continues: "He advised that the book will make reference to Attorney General ROBERT KENNEDY and KENNEDY's friendship with Miss MONROE. He advised that he will indicate that the evidence shows that KENNEDY and MONROE were intimate and that KENNEDY was in MONROE's apartment at the time of her death. He advised that he will attempt to show that some Communists were evidently working behind the scenes, inasmuch as a physician who signed the death certificate was a Communist." The FBI special agent in charge at the New York office of the FBI added: "It was noted that CAPELL appeared very emotional and aggressive when he advised of this book and was unable to state the exact purpose for having written it."

A background check on author Capell revealed the following, which is extracted from an FBI document of July 7, 1964: "He publishes 'The Herald of Freedom,' an anticommunist newsletter of an exposé type. He has been interviewed in recent months by Agents of our New York Office concerning numerous allegations he had made against a number of prominent individuals. Some allegations of Capell are from public sources and are apparently true, some are completely false and others are extremely questionable and not subject to corroboration. Capell has consistently refused to divulge his alleged sources to our Agents. The above allegation concerning the Attorney General has been previously circulated and has been branded as false as the Attorney General was actually in San Francisco with his wife at the time Marilyn Monroe committed suicide."

The document concluded: "It is recommended that the attached letter be sent to the Attorney General to advise him of the contemplated publication of the above book." Sure enough, on the very same day, Attorney General Kennedy was informed about Capell and his then-forthcoming book.

A week later, the FBI had in its possession a copy of Capell's book. A document was prepared by the FBI's R. W. Smith, who wrote the following on its contents: "The New York Office has now furnished us with a copy of this 70-page book. The book claims that Miss Monroe's involvement with Kennedy 'was well known to her friends and reporters in the Hollywood area,' but was never publicized. It is alleged that 'there are person-to-person telephone calls, living witnesses, tape recordings and certain writings to attest the closeness of their friendship.'"

Smith added: "The author suggests that Miss Monroe 'was led to believe his intentions were serious,' and that Kennedy had promised to divorce his wife and marry her. When he failed to do so, the book charges, she 'threatened to expose their relationship,' which would have ruined his presidential aspirations. It was then that Kennedy decided 'to take drastic action.'"

The Smith document continues: "According to the book, Kennedy used 'the Communist Conspiracy which is expert in the scientific elimination of its enemies' to dispose of Miss Monroe by making her murder appear to be a suicide. This could have been achieved without great difficulty, the author points out, because her personal physician, Dr. Hyman Engelberg, was a communist." Note: Engelberg was a member of the Communist Party from around 1939 to 1948.

Much of the rest of the dossier concerns certain other extracts from Capell's book. One states: "On page 70, reference is made to an anonymous letter quoted in a column of Walter Winchell datelined May 25, 1964, at Hollywood, California, which told of a 23-year-old Beverly Hills blonde who had been 'terrorized for months by the same person who caused Marilyn Monroe's death.... You can check this with FBI Special Agent in Charge, Mr. Grapp in L.A.... Her initials are M. J.'"

The FBI knew exactly who "M. J." was. The document notes: "Our Los Angeles Office reported that 'M. J.' was Mary Lou Jones, a would-be actress of no talent, who is apparently mentally disturbed. Miss Jones complained to the Beverly Hills, California, Police Department that she was being followed and harassed by unidentified men, but her allegations were completely unsubstantiated by the police."

A few other minor issues aside, that, in essence, is the nature and content of the document collection. So, with that all said, let's take a further look at Frank Capell's *The Strange Death of Marilyn Monroe*. Reviewer David Marshall says of Capell's book that it makes you want to go and "wash your hands, and when that doesn't do the trick, take a shower and have a strong drink to wash the taste out of your mouth."

Few people had time for Capell's claims—which is not at all surprising, given his highly unlikely scenario of a bunch of commies murdering the world's most legendary blonde.

LEE HARVEY OSWALD AND AN EARLIER ASSASSINATION ATTEMPT

Make mention of the name Lee Harvey Oswald, and most people will immediately and quite understandably think of the tragic events that occurred at Dealey Plaza in Dallas, Texas, on November 22, 1963. Oswald was killed two days later by a local nightclub owner with Mafia ties. His name was Jack Ruby. The fact is that because of Ruby's dirty deed, Oswald never went to trial. It's an assumption that Oswald was the gunman (or one of several gunmen) at the Grassy Knoll when JFK was killed. A theory is all it's likely to remain, given the large passage of time since November 1963. And the fact that just about anyone with firsthand knowledge of the affair is now dead themselves practically ensures that the mystery is almost certainly not going to be resolved to the satisfaction of everyone with an opinion on the matter.

It's a lesser-known fact that some researchers suggest that Oswald was involved in an earlier assassination operation—albeit one that failed. Much of what we know of this other affair comes from the controversial Warren Commission that addressed the murder of the president and concluded that Oswald was the killer. On this other intriguing issue, the Warren Commission members began as follows, under the heading of "The Attempt on the Life of Maj. Gen. Edwin A. Walker":

> At approximately 9 P.M., on April 10, 1963, in Dallas, Tex., Maj. Gen. Edwin A. Walker, an active and controversial figure on the American political scene since his resignation from the U.S. Army in 1961, narrowly escaped death when a rifle bullet fired from outside his home passed near his head as he was seated at his desk. There were no eyewitnesses, although a 14-year-old boy in a neighboring house claimed that immediately after the shoot-

ing he saw two men, in separate cars, drive out of a church parking lot adjacent to Walker's home. A friend of Walker's testified that two nights before the shooting he saw 'two men around the house peeking in windows.' General Walker gave this information to the police before the shooting, but it did not help solve the crime. Although the bullet was recovered from Walker's house, in the absence of a weapon it was of little investigatory value. General Walker hired two investigators to determine whether a former employee might have been involved in the shooting. Their results were negative. Until December 3, 1963, the Walker shooting remained unsolved.

One of the most intriguing of all the aspects of this particular story reads as follows:

The Commission evaluated the following evidence in considering whether Lee Harvey Oswald fired the shot which almost killed General Walker: (1) A note which Oswald left for his wife on the evening of the shooting, (2) photographs found among Oswald's possessions after the assassination of President Kennedy, (3) firearm identification of the bullet found in Walker's home, and (4) admissions and other statements made to Marina Oswald by Oswald concerning the shooting.

Note left by Oswald: on December 2, 1963, Mrs. Ruth Paine turned over to the police some of the Oswalds' belongings, including a Russian volume entitled *Book of Useful Advice*. In this book was an undated note written in Russian. In translation, the note read as follows:

1. This is the key to the mailbox which is located in the main post office in the city on Ervay Street. This is the same street where the drugstore, in which you always waited is located. You will find the mailbox in the post office which is located 4 blocks from the drugstore on that street. I paid for the box last month so don't worry about it. 2. Send the information as to what has happened to me to the Embassy and include newspaper clippings (should there be anything about me in the newspapers). I believe that the Embassy will

Jack Ruby killed Lee Harvey Oswald in plain sight of dozens of witnesses who were there plus millions of television viewers.

come quickly to your assistance on learning everything. 3. I paid the house rent on the 2d so don't worry about it. 4. Recently I also paid for water and gas. 5. The money from work will possibly be coming. The money will be sent to our post office box. Go to the bank and cash the check. 6. You can either throw out or give my clothing, etc. away. Do not keep these. However, I prefer that you hold on to my personal papers (military, civil, etc.). 7. Certain of my documents are in the small blue valise. 8. The address book can be found on my table in the study should need same. 9. We have friends here. The Red Cross also will help you. 10. I left you as much money as I could, $60 on the second of the month. You and the baby can live for another 2 months using $10 per week. 11. If I am alive and taken prisoner, the city jail is located at the end of the bridge through which we always passed on going to the city (right in the beginning of the city after crossing the bridge).

The members of the Warren Commission added:

Prior to the Walker shooting on April 10, Oswald had been attending typing classes on Monday, Tuesday, and Thursday evenings. He had quit these classes at least a week before the shooting, which occurred on a Wednesday night. According to Marina Oswald's testimony, on the night of the Walker shooting, her husband left their apartment on Neely Street shortly after dinner. She thought he was attending a class or was on his own business. When he failed to return by 10 or 10:30 P.M., Marina Oswald went to his room and discovered the note. She testified: "When he came back I asked him what had happened. He was very pale. I don't remember the exact time, but it was very late. And he told me not to ask him any questions. He only told me he had shot at General Walker." Oswald told his wife that he did not know whether he had hit Walker; according to Marina Oswald when he learned on the radio and in the newspapers the next day that he had missed, he said that he "was very sorry that he had not hit him." Marina Oswald's testimony was fully supported by the note itself which appeared to be the work of a man expecting to be killed, or imprisoned, or to disappear. The last paragraph directed her to the jail and the other paragraphs instructed her on the disposal of Oswald's personal effects and the management of her affairs if he should not return.

The Warren Commission was far from being done with this controversial affair:

It is clear that the note was written while the Oswalds were living in Dallas before they moved to New Orleans in the spring of 1963.

The references to house rent and payments for water and gas indicated that the note was written when they were living in a rented apartment; therefore, it could not have been written while Marina Oswald was living with the Paines. Moreover, the reference in paragraph 3 to paying "the house rent on the 2d" would be consistent with the period when the Oswalds were living on Neely Street since the apartment was rented on March 3, 1963.

Oswald had paid the first month's rent in advance on March 2, 1963, and the second month's rent was paid on either April 2 or April 3. The main post office "on Ervay Street" refers to the post office where Oswald rented box 2915 from October 9, 1962, to May 14, 1963. Another statement which limits the time when it could have been written is the reference "you and the baby," which would indicate that it was probably written before the birth of Oswald's second child on October 20, 1963. Oswald had apparently mistaken the county jail for the city jail. From Neely Street the Oswalds would have traveled downtown on the Beckley bus, across the Commerce Street viaduct and into downtown Dallas through the Triple Underpass. Either the viaduct or the underpass might have been the "bridge" mentioned in the last paragraph of the note. The county jail is at the corner of Houston and Main Streets "right in the beginning of the city" after one travels through the underpass.

The commission secured illuminating information from Marina Oswald, as the relevant papers demonstrate, which led to a debate concerning certain intriguing photos:

In her testimony before the Commission in February 1964, Marina Oswald stated that when Oswald returned home on the night of the Walker shooting, he told her that he had been planning the attempt for 2 months. He showed her a notebook 3 days later containing photographs of General Walker's home and a map of the area where the house was located. Although Oswald destroyed the notebook, three photographs found among Oswald's possessions after the assassination were identified by Marina Oswald as photographs of General Walker's house. Two of these photographs were taken from the rear of Walker's house. The Commission confirmed, by comparison with other photographs, that these were, indeed, photographs of the rear of Walker's house. An examination of the window at the rear of the house, the wall through which the bullet passed, and the fence behind the house indicated that the bullet was fired from a position near the point where one of the photographs was taken.

The third photograph identified by Marina Oswald depicts the entrance to General Walker's driveway from a back alley. Also seen in the picture is the fence on which Walker's assailant apparently rested the rifle. An examination of certain construction work appearing in the background of this photograph revealed that the picture was taken between March 8 and 12, 1963, and most probably on either March 9 or March 10. Oswald purchased the money order for the rifle on March 12, the rifle was shipped on March 20, and the shooting occurred on April 10.

A photography expert with the FBI was able to determine that this picture was taken with the Imperial Reflex camera owned by Lee Harvey Oswald.

A fourth photograph, showing a stretch of railroad tracks, was also identified by Marina Oswald as having been taken by her husband, presumably in connection with the Walker shooting. Investigation

Lee Harvey Oswald was determined to be the assassin of not only John F. Kennedy but also, apparently, Major General Edwin A. Walker (pictured).

determined that this photograph was taken approximately seven-tenths of a mile from Walker's house. Another photograph of railroad tracks found among Oswald's possessions was not identified by his wife, but investigation revealed that it was taken from a point slightly less than half a mile from General Walker's house. Marina Oswald stated that when she asked her husband what he had done with the rifle, he replied that he had buried it in the ground or hidden it in some bushes and that he also mentioned a railroad track in this connection. She testified that several days later Oswald recovered his rifle and brought it back to their apartment.

In a section titled "Firearms identification," the Warren Commission reported:

In the room beyond the one in which General Walker was sitting on the night of the shooting the Dallas police recovered a badly mutilated bullet which had come to rest on a stack of paper. The Dallas City County Investigation Laboratory tried to determine the type of weapon which fired the bullet. The oral report was negative because of the battered condition of the bullet. On November 30, 1963, the FBI requested the bullet for ballistics examination; the Dallas Police Department forwarded it on December 2, 1963.

Robert A. Frazier, an FBI ballistics identification expert, testified that he was "unable to reach a conclusion" as to whether or not the bullet recovered from Walker's house had been fired from the rifle found on the sixth floor of the Texas School Book Depository Building. He concluded that "the general rifling characteristics of the rifle are of the same type as those found on the bullet and, further, on this basis the bullet could have been fired from the rifle on the basis of its land and groove impressions." Frazier testified further that the FBI avoids the category of "probable" identification. Unless the missile or cartridge case can be identified as coming from a particular weapon to the exclusion of all others, the FBI refuses to draw any conclusion as to probability. Frazier testified, however, that he found no microscopic characteristics or other evidence which would indicate that the bullet was not fired from the Mannlicher-Carcano rifle owned by Lee Harvey Oswald. It was a 6.5-millimeter bullet and, according to Frazier, "relatively few" types of rifles could produce the characteristics found on the bullet. Joseph D. Nicol, superintendent of the Illinois Bureau of Criminal Identification and Investigation, conducted an independent examination of this bullet and concluded "that there is a fair probability" that the bullet was fired from the rifle used in the assassination of President Kennedy. In explaining the difference between his policy and that of the FBI on the matter of probable identification, Nicol said: "I am aware of their position. This is not, I am sure, arrived at without careful consideration. However, to say that because one does not find sufficient marks for identification that it is a negative, I think is going overboard in the other direction. And for purposes of probative value, for whatever it might be worth, in the absence of very definite negative evidence, I think it is permissible to say that in an exhibit such as there is enough on it to say that it could have come, and even perhaps a little stronger, to say that it probably came from this, without going so far as to say to the exclusion of all other guns. This I could not do."

In its final words on this particular affair, the Warren Commission noted the following:

Although the Commission recognizes that neither expert was able to state that the bullet which missed General Walker was fired from Oswald's rifle to the exclusion of all others, this testimony was considered probative when combined with the other testimony linking Oswald to the shooting. Additional corroborative evidence.—The admissions made to Marina Oswald by her husband are an important element in the evidence that Lee Harvey Oswald fired the shot at General Walker. As shown above, the note and the photographs of Walker's house and of the nearby railroad tracks provide important corroboration for her account of the incident. Other details described by Marina Oswald coincide with facts developed independently of her statements. She testified that her husband had postponed his attempt to kill Walker until that Wednesday because he had heard that there was to be a gathering at the church next door to Walker's house on that evening. He indicated that he wanted more people in the vicinity at the time of the attempt so that his arrival and departure would not attract great attention. An official of this church told FBI agents that services are held every Wednesday at the church except during the month of August.

Marina Oswald also testified that her husband had used a bus to return home. A study of the bus routes indicates that Oswald could have taken any one of several different buses to Walker's house or to a point near the railroad tracks where he may have concealed the rifle. It would have been possible for him to take different routes in approaching and leaving the scene of the shooting.

Conclusion—Based on (1) the contents of the note which Oswald left for his wife on April 10, 1963, (2) the photographs found among Oswald's possessions, (3) the testimony of firearms identification experts, and (4) the testimony of Marina Oswald, the Commission has concluded that Lee Harvey Oswald attempted to take the life of Maj. Gen. Edwin A. Walker (Resigned, U.S. Army) on April 10, 1963. The finding that Lee Harvey Oswald attempted to murder a public figure in April 1963 was considered of probative value in this investigation, although the Commission's conclusion concerning the identity of the assassin was based on evidence independent of the finding that Oswald attempted to kill General Walker.

> The claim that the rifle allegedly used to kill President Kennedy matched the one that Oswald—also allegedly—attempted to assassinate Walker with has been dismissed.

Taking into consideration the many twists and turns that dominated the short life of Lee Harvey Oswald, it's not a surprise that the theory suggesting he shot—and tried to kill—General Walker has been disputed. Critics note that

Marina gave controversial, contradictory data to the Warren Commission. The claim that the rifle allegedly used to kill President Kennedy matched the one that Oswald—also allegedly—attempted to assassinate Walker with has been dismissed. Certainly, the most plausible scenario of Oswald's links to this whole controversy comes from the *22 November 1963* website:

"Oswald's supposed motive for shooting at Walker was political. Walker was well known for his very right-wing views. He had been forced to resign from the Army for indoctrinating his troops with the ideas of the John Birch Society and for announcing publicly that President Truman, among other prominent American politicians, was a communist sympathizer. Although the alleged presidential assassin was officially supposed to have been a communist, the known facts of Lee Harvey Oswald's career show that he was closely associated with one or more US intelligence agencies, and that his pro-communist public persona was highly likely to have been a fake.

"With no plausible motive and no substantial grounds for believing that Oswald was involved in the attempted shooting of Walker, and no strong evidence that Oswald was guilty of the JFK assassination, it seems that the Walker shooting was attributed to Oswald by the FBI and the Warren Commission purely to support the notion that Oswald was a leftist malcontent with a propensity for violence."

DEATH AT DEALEY PLAZA

November 22, 1963, was, without any doubt whatsoever, one of the darkest days in American history. That was the date on which President John F. Kennedy was shot and killed at Dealey Plaza in Dallas, Texas. Numerous theories have been put forward to try to determine who the real killer of JFK was. Or, maybe, killers. To understand what it was that led to the president's death, we have to take a look at the government's own words on the matter. The U.S. Government Publishing Office provides the following summary of the lead-up to that tragic event that shook not just the nation but the entire world:

> In June 1963, President John F. Kennedy met with Vice President Lyndon B. Johnson and Texas Governor John Connally in El Paso, Texas. They discussed the upcoming 1964 presidential election. President Kennedy had not yet announced that he would be running again, but according to the JFK Library, 'it was clear that President Kennedy was going to run and he seemed confident about his chances for re-election.' At the meeting, they determined the need to carry the two states in the South that had the most electoral votes to win in the upcoming election. Campaigning in Florida and Texas became high priority.

> In November, President Kennedy set off to campaign in those states. On November 21, the president, accompanied by the first lady, boarded Air Force One to head to Texas. After visiting San Antonio, Houston, and Fort Worth, on November 22, the Kennedys took a quick 13-minute flight from Fort Worth to Dallas. When they landed at Love Field, an adoring crowd was there to greet them. Mrs. Kennedy received a bouquet of red roses

upon arriving in Dallas. She carried them with her to the limousine, where Governor Connally and his wife, Nellie, who had yellow roses, were already sitting.

The specially fabricated Lincoln automobile had a plastic bubble top, but agents had instructions from the President that the only time the bubble top was to be used was if there was inclement weather, or if Mrs. Kennedy's hair was getting out of place from strong winds. Though it had been drizzling earlier in the morning, the skies had cleared for their ride around Dallas. Thus, no need for the bubble top.

The excited onlookers could see the Kennedys and Connallys up-close-and-personal as they drove through downtown Dallas. The cheering crowds continued to grow and grow. Secret Service Agent for Mrs. Kennedy, Clint Hill, hopped on the back of the car several times in case he needed to fend off rowdy fans who were flooding the left-hand side of the street along which Mrs. Kennedy was riding. The plan was to stop at the Trade Mart where President Kennedy was scheduled to speak at a luncheon. That meant the car needed to decelerate to make the sharp turn from Houston onto Elm Street. As the car was passing the Texas School Book Depository, at around 12:30 P.M., shots were fired, striking the president in the head and neck and the governor in the back. The beautiful red and yellow roses from earlier in the day were scattered throughout the car.

Almost immediately, Lee Harvey Oswald was arrested and held for the assassination of John F. Kennedy. Two days later, Oswald was shot and killed on live television while being transferred from police headquarters to the county jail. Ninety-nine minutes after the president's death, Vice President Johnson took the oath of office with a brave Jackie Kennedy by his side on Air Force One.

Further illuminating and important data comes from the John F. Kennedy Presidential Library and Museum:

John F. Kennedy was sworn in as the 35th president on January 20, 1961. In his inaugural speech he spoke of the need for all Americans to be active citizens. "Ask not what your country can do for you, ask what you can do for your country," he said. He also asked the nations of the world to join together to fight what he called the "common enemies of man: tyranny, poverty, disease, and war itself." President Kennedy, together with his wife and two children, brought a new, youthful spirit to the White House. The Kennedys believed that the White House should be

An "X" marks the spot where President Kennedy was assassinated at Dealey Plaza in Dallas, Texas.

a place to celebrate American history, culture, and achievement. They invited artists, writers, scientists, poets, musicians, actors, and athletes to visit them. Jacqueline Kennedy also shared her husband's interest in American history. Gathering some of the finest art and furniture the United States had produced, she restored all the rooms in the White House to make it a place that truly reflected America's history and artistic creativity. Everyone was impressed and appreciated her hard work.

The White House also seemed like a fun place because of the Kennedys' two young children, Caroline and John-John. There was a pre-school, a swimming pool, and a tree-house outside on the White House lawn. President Kennedy was probably the busiest man in the country, but he still found time to laugh and play with his children. However, the president also had many worries. One of the things he worried about most was the possibility of nuclear war between the United States and the Soviet Union. He knew that if there was a war, millions of people would die. Since World War II, there had been a lot of anger and suspicion between the two countries but never any shooting between Soviet and American troops. This "Cold War," which was unlike any other war the world had seen, was really a struggle between the Soviet Union's communist system of government and the United States' democratic system. Because they distrusted each other, both countries spent enormous amounts of money building nuclear weapons. There were many times when the struggle between the Soviet Union and the United States could have ended in nuclear war, such as in Cuba during the 1962 missile crisis or over the divided city of Berlin.

President Kennedy worked long hours, getting up at seven and not going to bed until eleven or twelve at night, or later. He read six newspapers while he ate breakfast, had meetings with important people throughout the day, and read reports from his advisers. He wanted to make sure that he made the best decisions for his country. "I am asking each of you to be new pioneers in that New Frontier," he said. The New Frontier was not a place but a way of thinking and acting. President Kennedy wanted the United States to move forward into the future with new discoveries in science and improvements in education, employment and other fields. He wanted democracy and freedom for the whole world.

Sadly, JFK's plans were snuffed out in terrible, irreversible fashion, as history has shown. Now, let's take a look at the theories that have been put forward to try to determine who was the assassin (or assassins) that ended the life of the much-loved president. In the slightly more than half a century that has now passed since President John F. Kennedy was shot and killed in Dallas, a wealth of theories has been put forward to explain his death. Those theories range from plausible to paranoid and bizarre to out of this world. On November 29, 1963, an investigation began that still provokes huge debate in conspiracy-themed circles decades after JFK's death. The ten-month-long study was undertaken by the President's Commission on the Assassination of President Kennedy, better known as the Warren Commission, which took its name from its chairman, Chief Justice Earl Warren. The commission's job was to determine who shot JFK. According to the Warren Commission, it was Oswald. And it was *only* Oswald. Not everyone agreed with that controversial conclusion, however.

In 1978, fourteen years after the Warren Commission laid all the blame firmly on the shoulders of Oswald, the U.S. House Select Committee on Assassinations came to a different conclusion. The lone gunman, said the committee, was not such a lone gunman, after all. President Kennedy's death was the result of a full-on conspiracy. The HSCA agreed with the Warren

Commission that Kennedy was killed by Oswald and no one else. The committee went one step further, however, by concluding that Oswald was not the only gunman prowling around Dallas on that deadly day. Forensic analysis suggested to the HSCA's investigators that *four* shots rang out, not the three that the Warren Commission attributed to Oswald. That's to say there was another gunman. In the minds of the HSCA's staff, this mysterious second character completely missed his target. Nevertheless, a pair of shooters meant a conspiracy was at the heart of the JFK assassination.

Was JFK the victim of both an assassin and friendly fire? Two men, totally unconnected to each other but who, in a strange set of circumstances, ultimately sealed the fate of the president? This was the theory postulated in a 1992 book, *Mortal Error: The Shot That Killed JFK* by Bonar Menninger. The scenario presented by Menninger had Oswald as the chief culprit but not the only one. George Hickey was a Secret Service agent traveling in the vehicle immediately following the presidential car. After the bullets fired by Oswald

Waving to the crowds in Dallas while riding in the presidential motorcade, few spectators could imagine what was only moments away when this photo was taken.

slammed into JFK, Menninger suggested, Hickey accidentally discharged his weapon, delivering the fatal head shot that killed Kennedy. In 1992, when *Mortal Error* was published, Hickey was still alive. He was not pleased to see himself portrayed as the second gunman in the Kennedy assassination. Unfortunately for Hickey, he let three years pass before trying to take legal action against the publisher, St. Martin's Press. U.S. District Court Judge Alexander Harvey II dismissed the defamation case on the grounds that Hickey had waited too long to file suit. In 1998, however, Hickey received an undisclosed sum of money from St. Martin's Press that led Hickey's attorney, Mark S. Zaid, to state: "We're very satisfied with the settlement."

Prior to his death in 1976, Johnny Roselli was a notorious and much-feared figure in the Chicago, Illinois, Mafia. His influence and power extended to the heart of Tinseltown and the slots and tables of Vegas. In 1960, Roselli was quietly contacted by a man named Robert Maheu, a former employee of the CIA and the FBI. A startling proposal was put to Roselli. The CIA, Maheu explained, wanted Roselli's help in taking care of Fidel Castro. In Mob-speak, "taking care of" meant "whacking." Thus was born a controversial program that saw the CIA and the Mob work together hand in glove. As history has shown, Roselli and his goons never did take out Castro, but, say conspiracy theorists, they may have ended the life of JFK with help from the CIA. The Mob was no fan of the Kennedy Administration. Robert Kennedy, as attorney general, went after the Mafia in definitive witch-hunt style. Did the Mob decide to return the favor? Maybe it did. Following Kennedy's killing, Roselli and a number of other mobsters, including Santo Trafficante Jr. and Carlos Marcello, were suspected of having been implicated. Even the House Select Committee on Assassinations admitted there were "credible associations relating both Lee Harvey Oswald and Jack Ruby to figures having a relationship, albeit tenuous, with Marcello's crime family or organization." Just perhaps, it's not such a whacked-out theory, after all.

JFK taken out of circulation to prevent him from revealing the truth about what really crashed at Roswell, New Mexico, in 1947? So say UFO researchers, on getting elected in 1960, JFK got the lowdown on all things E.T.-based in a secret briefing from the CIA: "Bad news, Mr. President: E.T. is real. Worse news: he really doesn't like us." Kennedy was determined to warn the public of the alien menace. A secret and ruthless cabal in the heart of officialdom, however, was having none of it. The president had to go before he spilled the bug-eyed beans. It sounds crazy. But even crazier, the JFK assassination really *is* littered with characters that were tied to the strange world of flying saucers.

Back in 1947, a man named Fred Crisman claimed to have recovered debris from an exploded UFO in Tacoma, Washington. Crisman also alluded to having worked for decades as a deep-cover agent with U.S. intelligence. Jim

Garrison was New Orleans's district attorney from 1961 to 1973 and the man portrayed by Kevin Costner in Oliver Stone's *JFK*. In 1968, Garrison subpoenaed Crisman while investigating JFK's death. The reason: Crisman had connections to a CIA asset believed by many researchers to have been linked to the killing of Kennedy. His name was Clay Shaw. The case against Shaw collapsed, and Crisman breathed a big sigh of relief.

Guy Banister, a retired FBI agent at the time of the JFK assassination, was also linked to Shaw by Garrison. As the Freedom of Information Act has shown, Banister undertook numerous UFO investigations for the FBI in 1947. There's even a Lee Harvey Oswald connection. In October 1962, Oswald went to work for a Texas-based company called Jaggars-Chiles-Stovall. It undertook classified photo analysis connected to the CIA's U-2 spy plane program. Where was the U-2 developed? Area 51, that's where. And we all know what goes on out there, right?

One of the oddest theories concerning the Kennedy assassination tumbled out in the pages of a 1975 book, *Appointment in Dallas*. It was written by Hugh McDonald, formerly of the LAPD. According to McDonald, Oswald was indeed a patsy but in a very strange fashion. Oswald was supposedly told, by shadowy sources, that his expertise was needed in Dallas on November 22, 1963. But Oswald wasn't required to kill the president. Quite the contrary, Oswald was told to ensure that all his bullets *missed* JFK. The operation, Oswald was assured, was designed to demonstrate how inadequate the Secret Service was by staging a mock assassination attempt of the president. Unbeknownst to Oswald, however, a team of *real* assassins was at Dealey Plaza. Their bullets, however, did not miss. The gunmen made quick exits, leaving Oswald as the man guaranteed to take the fall—simply because he really *did* fire bullets across Dealey Plaza. A panicked Oswald, realizing he had been set up, fled the scene, thus setting in motion the wheels that led to his arrest and death.

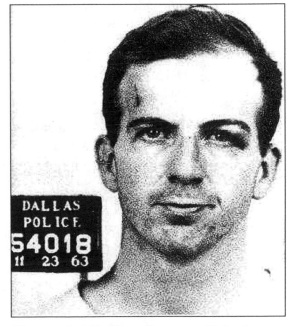

Forget Oswald. JFK was killed by the man behind the wheel in full view of the people of Dallas and thousands of cameras. That was the outrageous claim of one of the most vocal conspiracy theorists of the 1980s and 1990s. His name was Milton William "Bill" Cooper. The man who Cooper fingered as the guilty party was William Greer, a Secret Ser-

The man who killed Kennedy was specified as Lee Harvey Oswald, but some questions remain that put his guilt—and whether he acted alone—into question.

vice agent who drove the presidential limousine on the day that JFK was destined not to leave Dallas alive. When shots echoed around Dealey Plaza, Greer slowed the car down and turned back to look at the president. For Cooper, Greer's actions were not due to confusion caused by the chaos breaking out all around him. No. Cooper claimed that analysis of the famous footage taken by Abraham Zapruder on the Grassy Knoll on November 22 showed Greer pointing some form of device at JFK. That device, Cooper maintained to anyone who would listen, was nothing less than a sci-fi-style weapon developed by government personnel who had acquired the technology from extraterrestrials. By the time Cooper got on his rant, which began in the late 1980s, Greer wasn't around to defend himself. He passed away in 1985 from cancer, having retired from the Secret Service in 1966 as a result of problems caused by a stomach ulcer. In a strange piece of irony, Cooper himself died by the bullet. In the summer of 1998, he was formerly charged with tax evasion. Cooper told the government what to go and do. What the government did, on November 5, 2001, was to dispatch deputies to Cooper's Arizona home. A shoot-out soon erupted, resulting in Cooper's death.

In October 1959, Lee Harvey Oswald—a self-admitted Marxist—made his way to the Soviet Union. Oswald reached Moscow on October 16 and announced that he wished to remain in Russia. Although the Soviets were, initially, reluctant to allow Oswald residency, that soon changed. It wasn't long before Oswald had a job and a home. In 1961, he had a wife, Marina. Fatherhood soon followed. Claiming to have become disillusioned with a dull life in the Soviet Union, however, Oswald moved his family to the United States in 1962. Was Oswald recruited by the KGB during his time in Russia? Did his return to the States actually have nothing to do with disillusionment? Had the elite of the Kremlin convinced Oswald to kill Kennedy? One person who has commented on such matters is Ion Mihai Pacepa. In 1978, Pacepa, a general with Romania's Department of State Security, defected to the United States. One of Pacepa's revelations was that JFK was killed on the orders of Soviet premier Nikita Khrushchev. Still seething from backing down in the Cuban Missile Crisis of 1962, Khrushchev was determined to exact his revenge. Oswald was chosen to ensure that revenge was achieved. Notably, Pacepa asserted that Khrushchev made a last-minute decision not to go ahead with the plan to kill JFK. Unfortunately, the Russians failed to make timely contact with Oswald and inform him of the change in plans. The countdown to assassination could not be stopped.

As far back as the late 1950s, the CIA planned to have Cuba's president, Fidel Castro, assassinated. The Kennedy Administration sought to destabilize the Cuban government on many occasions. Castro was enraged. Not as enraged as he became in the wake of the Bay of Pigs invasion of 1961 and the missile crisis of 1962, however. So angered was Castro that he decided to teach the United States a terrible lesson by having the most powerful man on the planet, JFK, murdered. Or, so this particular conspiracy theory goes. None other than Kennedy's successor, Lyndon B. Johnson, suspected the Cubans were behind the president's killing. Stating that he could "accept that [Oswald] pulled the trigger," Johnson felt that Castro had a significant hand in matters somewhere. Not surprisingly, Castro consistently denounced such claims. Castro also asserted, perhaps with justification, that had the United States proved Cuba was involved, his country would have been wiped off the map. Castro was certainly not a fan of JFK. But would he have risked the very existence of Cuba to see Kennedy killed? The question lives on.

In January 1961, outgoing president Dwight D. Eisenhower made a speech, part of which has become inextricably tied to the murder of JFK. Eisenhower said: "In the councils of government, we must guard against the

In the spirit of a full investigation of the assassination of President Kennedy, a commission headed by Earl Warren was tasked with reporting the facts to President Johnson. Today, however, many doubt the conclusions made in the original report.

acquisition of unwarranted influence, whether sought or unsought, by the military-industrial complex." In the minds of many JFK assassination researchers, it is this military-industrial complex that we should look to for the answers on the fifty-six-year-old killing of the president. JFK had a vision of creating a state of lasting peace between the United States and the Soviet Union. In short, Kennedy wanted to end the Cold War. Powerful figures in the military, the intelligence community, and companies that raked in millions of dollars in lucrative defense contracts secretly agreed to do the unthinkable. Profits from war were more important than the life and goals of the president.

Today, more than half a century after President John F. Kennedy was assassinated, we're still none the wiser as to what really went down. Or didn't. Those who see conspiracies around every corner will continue to see them. As for those who don't, well, they won't. And in all likelihood, the full and unexpurgated facts, whether pointing in the direction of deep conspiracy or Lee Harvey Oswald, will never surface. One thing does seem likely, however. In another fifty years, when the hundredth anniversary of the JFK assassination looms large, theorizing, finger-pointing, and Deep Throat-style testimony will still be the order of the day. But definitive answers? Don't bet on it.

One final thing: Those who are skeptical of the theory that the JFK assassination was 100 percent free of conspiracy state that if there was a conspiracy, we would see evidence of it. They claim that all of the official documentation on what went down at Dealey Plaza on November 22, 1963, is now in the public domain. So, as that line of thinking goes, if the papers are now available to see, how can there have been any kind of cover-up? The fact is, though, that certain files are not in the public domain at all. In fact, they are suspiciously missing, as you will now see.

All of this brings us to a man named Robert E. Jones. At the time of the assassination, Jones was a colonel in the U.S. Army. When, in the 1970s, the House Select Committee on Assassinations launched a deep inquiry to try to answer, once and for all, the riddle of who killed JFK, Colonel Jones claimed to know something significant. In 1978, he went before the committee and shared what he knew—that when the president was murdered, there were around a dozen military personnel on site. It was Jones's impression, at the time, that the group was there to help provide protection for the president in much the same way that the Secret Service did. It has since been suggested by JFK researchers that the military team was not there to protect the president—but that it was really a carefully camouflaged hit squad.

There is an interesting afterword to all of this: as far back as the summer of 1963, the HSCA learned, Colonel Jones had been involved in a top-secret investigation of Oswald's activities. As a result of this investigation, official files were, of course, compiled. The files were held, said Jones, by the 112th Military Intelligence Group. They contained data on how, in the immediate aftermath of the shooting of JFK, Jones contacted the FBI with what he knew of Oswald and his actions leading up to the events of November 22, 1963. The House Select Committee on Assassinations looked carefully at what Colonel Jones had to say.

The HSCA did its best to track down the military intelligence file on Oswald, which Colonel Jones knew of because he was a key figure in the collation of it. Unfortunately, the HSCA's best was not good enough. According to the HSCA's records: "Access to Oswald's military intelligence file, which the Department of Defense never gave to the Warren Commission, was not possible because the Department of Defense had destroyed the file as part of a general program aimed at eliminating all of its files pertaining to non-military personnel."

The HSCA asked the military about the nature of the destruction. The HSCA was told that it was "not possible" to state with certainty when the Oswald files were destroyed. It was also impossible to determine "who accomplished the actual physical destruction of the dossier." Neither could it be ascertained who ordered the "destruction or deletion." And just for good measure, the military added to the HSCA: "The exact material contained in the dossier cannot be determined."

As the above demonstrates, regardless of what we are getting to see now, the fact is that years ago, vital documents that could have shed further light on the assassination of President Kennedy were destroyed. In all likelihood, we'll *never* know what those destroyed papers contained.

WORDS FROM THE WARREN COMMISSION

Although the Warren Commission concluded that there was no conspiracy in the November 22, 1963, shooting of President John F. Kennedy, the fact is that the committee's report does detail a history of assassinations in the United States. It is well worth taking a look at what the commission had to say on (a) the killing of JFK and (b) its observations on earlier assassinations. The committee's words on the death of President James A. Garfield began as follows:

> President James A. Garfield was shot in the back by Charles J. Guiteau on July 2, 1881, in Washington, D.C. Guiteau, a religious fanatic and would-be officeholder, had been denied access to the White House after he had asked to be appointed U.S. Ambassador to Austria. When Garfield appointed James A. Blaine as Secretary of State, an incensed Guiteau apparently believed that the President had betrayed a faction of the Republican Party.
>
> In the ensuing murder trial, there was no suggestion that the defendant was involved in any conspiracy. Guiteau maintained that he had acted as an agent of God in a political emergency and therefore was not guilty of wrongdoing. Despite a history of mental illness in Guiteau's family, the insanity defense presented by his counsel failed. Guiteau was declared sane, found guilty and hanged before a large crowd. Contrary to events following the Lincoln assassination, no theories of possible conspiracy surfaced in the wake of Garfield's slaying.

The committee then addressed the matter of the assassination of President William McKinley in 1901:

While attending the Pan-American Exposition at Buffalo, N.Y., on September 6, 1901, President William McKinley was shot. He died 8 days later, the victim of assassin Leon F. Czolgosz, a factory worker and anarchist. Although an anarchist group had published a warning about Czolgosz 5 days before McKinley was shot and Czolgosz insisted he had acted alone, many believed that the assassination was the result of an anarchist plot. Czolgosz refused to testify at his own trial which was held 4 days after McKinley's funeral. After 34 minutes of deliberation, the jury found him guilty of murder. Czolgosz did not appeal the verdict, and he was executed in the electric chair.

McKinley's assassination came after a wave of anarchist terrorism in Europe. Between 1894 and 1900, anarchist assassins had killed M. F. Sadi Carnot, President of France; Elizabeth, Empress of Austria; and Humbert I, King of Italy. Following McKinley's death vigilantes in the United States attacked anarchist communities. Anarchist leaders such as Emma Goldman were arrested. Responding to a plea by the new President, Theodore Roosevelt, Congress passed a series of restrictive measures that limited the activities of anarchists and added alien anarchists to the list of excluded immigrants. Despite a spate of frenzied charges of an anarchist conspiracy, no plot was ever proven, and the theories appeared to collapse shortly after the execution of Czolgosz.

Then, there was this from the Warren Commission:

Three Presidents who preceded John F. Kennedy were the target of attempted assassinations. On January 30, 1835, Richard Lawrence tried to kill President Andrew Jackson on the steps of the U.S. Capitol, but both pistols he carried misfired, and Jackson was not injured. Following the attempt, some of Jackson's supporters charged a Whig conspiracy, but this allegation was never substantiated. Lawrence was found not guilty by reason of insanity and spent the rest of his life in mental institutions.

On February 15, 1933, in Miami, Fla., President-elect Franklin D. Roosevelt

President William McKinley was assassinated by an anarchist named Leon Czolgosz, who had become radicalized after losing his job after the Panic of 1893 caused a depression.

was fired upon by Giuseppe Zangara, an unemployed Italian immigrant bricklayer. Zangara missed Roosevelt, but mortally wounded Chicago Mayor Anton Cermak. Zangara was tried, found guilty of murder and executed. No conspiracy was charged in the shooting.

Two Puerto Rican nationalists attacked Blair House, the temporary residence of President Harry S. Truman in Washington, D.C., on November 1, 1950, with the apparent intention of assassinating the President. A White House guard and one of the nationalists, Griselio Torresola, were killed in the ensuing gun battle. The surviving nationalist, Oscar Collazo, explained that the action against Truman had been sparked by news of a revolt in Puerto Rico. He believed the assassination would call the attention of the American people to the appalling economic conditions in his country. The two would-be assassins were acting in league with P. Albizu Campos, president of the Nationalist Party of Puerto Rico. Truman was not harmed during the assault. Collazo was tried and sentenced to death, but President Truman commuted the sentence to life imprisonment.

Now, let's see what the Warren Commission concluded on the JFK assassination—a conclusion that was at odds with just about everyone else who dug deep into the still controversial affair:

> The President's Commission on the Assassination of President Kennedy (Warren Commission) concluded that President Kennedy was struck by two bullets that were fired from above and behind him. According to the Commission, one bullet hit the President near the base of the back of the neck, slightly to the right of the spine, and exited from the front of the neck. The other entered the right rear of the President's head and exited from the right side of the head, causing a large wound.

The Commission based its findings primarily upon the testimony of the doctors who had treated the President at Parkland Memorial Hospital in Dallas and the doctors who performed the

This bullet was removed from the injured William Sinnott, who was serving as President Franklin D. Roosevelt's bodyguard when Giuseppe Zangara tried to kill the president. The attacker missed Roosevelt but hit five others, wounding four and killing the mayor of Chicago, Anton Cermak.

autopsy on the President at the Naval Medical Center in Bethesda, Md.

In forming this conclusion, neither the members of the Warren Commission, nor its staff, nor the doctors who had performed the autopsy, took advantage of the X-rays and photographs of the President that were taken during the course of the autopsy. The reason for the failure of the Warren Commission to examine these primary materials is that there was a commitment to make public all evidence examined by the Commission. The Commission was concerned that publication of the autopsy X-rays and photographs would be an invasion of the privacy of the Kennedy family. The Commission's decision to rely solely on the testimony of the doctors precluded the possibility that the Commission might make use of a review of the autopsy evidence by independent medical experts to determine if they concurred with the findings of the doctors at Parkland and Bethesda.

A determination of the number and location of the President's wounds was critical to resolving the question of whether there was more than one assassin. The secrecy that surrounded the autopsy proceedings, therefore, has led to considerable skepticism toward the Commission's findings. Concern has been expressed that authorities were less than candid, since the Navy doctor in charge of the autopsy conducted at Bethesda Naval Hospital destroyed his notes, and the Warren Commission decided to forego an opportunity to view the X-rays and photographs or to permit anyone else to inspect them. The skepticism has been reinforced by a film taken of the Presidential motorcade at the moment of the assassination by an amateur movie photographer, Abraham Zapruder. In the Zapruder film, the President's head is apparently thrown backward as the front right side of the skull appears to explode, suggesting to critics of the Warren Commission's findings that the President was struck by a bullet that entered the front of the head. Such a bullet, it has been argued, was fired by a gunman positioned on the grassy knoll, a park-like area to the right and to the front of where the moving limousine was located at the instant of the fatal shot.

To this day, more than half a century since JFK was murdered, the conclusions of the Warren Commission remain, for the most part, the official stance of the U.S. government.

MICROWAVED TO DEATH

This story revolves around a man named Ernest Arthur Bryant, a resident of an old village in the English county of Devon called Scoriton. Or, as some prefer to spell it, Scorriton. As for Devon, it's an ancient and mysterious land, made famous by the fact that Sir Arthur Conan Doyle set his classic Sherlock Holmes novel *The Hound of the Baskervilles* in Devon's Dartmoor National Park. On April 24, 1965, Bryant (who served with the British Commandos in World War II) saw something amazing hovering over a field close to his home: a flying saucer. Bryant stared, shocked and amazed, for a few moments and then made his cautious way to the field. As he did so, seemingly in response to his actions, the circular-shaped craft gently touched to the ground.

As Bryant arrived, a group of three human-like beings attired in shiny, silver suits motioned to him not to come any closer. He did as he was told. Bryant looked on, stunned, and noticed that the beings had overly long foreheads, seemed to have problems breathing in Earth's atmosphere, and, somewhat oddly, had no thumbs. One of the beings then moved toward Bryant and reeled off typical, absurd, Space Brother-themed spiel. The entity claimed his name was "Yamski" and that he and his comrades hailed from Venus.

The alien then made a comment along the lines of, "If only Des were here." Or, suggested Bryant, it may have been "Les," rather than "Des." This, along with the "Yamski" name, is all very interesting, since only one day before the encounter, the world's most famous contactee, George Adamski, died. Plus, Adamski's coauthor on his *Flying Saucers Have Landed* book was Desmond Leslie.

Also in typical contactee/Space Brother style, Bryant was given a "tour" of the UFO, which was, allegedly, split into three sections. The aliens then

The area that is now Dartmoor National Park in Devon, England, was the setting both for Sir Arthur Conan Doyle's *The Hound of the Baskervilles* and an alien encounter experienced by an ill-fated local man.

made a cryptic statement suggesting they would contact Bryant again. As Bryant watched from a safe distance, the UFO then rose into the sky and vanished from sight.

Although Bryant was determined to keep the incident under wraps, it didn't stay like that for long: both the local media and UFO researchers were soon on the case. Flying saucer investigator Norman Oliver looked into the matter deeply and, in 1967, Eileen Buckle penned an entire book on the affair, titled *The Scoriton Mystery*. Bryant's story would, in all likelihood, have remained as just another contactee case were it not for one notable and very strange thing.

In the late 1970s, UFO researcher Rich Reynolds was contacted by a man named Bosco Nedelcovic, who suggested that Bryant's encounter had very little to do with aliens and much more to do with secret experimentation of a very down-to-earth nature. Nedelcovic (who worked for the U.S. Department of State's Agency for International Development and who also had ties to the CIA) claimed that Bryant was the victim of a form of sophisticated mind control, somewhat akin to the kind of work undertaken by the CIA's MKUltra program.

Nedelcovic told Reynolds of a number of bogus "UFO episodes" in both the United States and the United Kingdom, in which individuals were led to believe they had UFO encounters when, in fact, they experienced something very different. Nedelcovic alluded to how these events involved "visual displays, radar displacement, and artifact droppings." One of those events, said Nedelcovic, was the Bryant case.

Nedelcovic also revealed how the operation proceeded, which involved "experimental drugs used to induce specific hallucinatory material" as well as "microwave transmissions." On this latter point, Reynolds was told by Nedelcovic that "the injudicious use of microwave technology" led to a disastrous outcome for Bryant. As history has shown, Bryant died in 1967 from the effects of a brain tumor.

Interestingly, in his 1969 book *UFO: Flying Saucers over Britain?*, author Robert Chapman noted: "There remains a possibility" that Bryant "might have had the UFO sighting planted in his mind through hypnotism." Chapman noted that there was "no evidence" to warrant such a belief, yet it is interesting that he even chose to bring up the matter in the first place, given that this was pretty much exactly what Bosco Nedelcovic was asserting a decade or so later.

All of the above suggests there is far more to the UFO encounter and tragic death of Bryant than meets the eye. And with the fiftieth anniversary of the incident now fast approaching, it would be the ideal time for someone to (a) readdress the Bryant case and the claims of Bosco Nedelcovic and (b) undertake a new, in-depth study of this tragic, controversial, and fatal affair.

A REPORTER MEETS THE GRIM REAPER

As was noted earlier, journalist Dorothy Kilgallen was a friend to Hollywood legend Marilyn Monroe. As we also saw, Monroe died under extremely dubious and mysterious circumstances. Monroe may even have been assassinated to ensure that she did not reveal what she knew from the Kennedy brothers about some of the U.S. government's most protected secrets. It's disturbing to note that three years after Monroe, Kilgallen was also dead. It hardly needs saying, but yes, the circumstances surrounding Kilgallen's death were as controversial as those regarding Monroe's untimely ending.

Born in Chicago in July 1913, Kilgallen, without the benefit of a college degree, soared up the ranks in the field of journalism. She became one of the most popular—and, at times, hated and even feared—figures in the media. Kilgallen also moved effortlessly in the worlds of high society, Hollywood, politics, government secrecy, and deep and dark conspiracies. She was buddies with Marilyn Monroe, as we have seen, and she hung out with Ernest Hemingway. Kilgallen was also the subject of extensive surveillance by several agencies of the U.S. intelligence community. Indeed, the FBI surveillance file on Kilgallen runs to hundreds of pages. This latter point is hardly surprising, however, as will soon become very apparent.

Kilgallen's life was somewhat fraught: her April 1940 marriage to Broadway producer Richard Kollmar was not a happy one. While things began okay, they certainly didn't stay that way: the pair eventually drifted apart, emotionally and sexually, which resulted in Kilgallen having a number of affairs, including a long-standing one with singer Johnnie Ray. Kollmar, meanwhile, descended into full-blown alcoholism and finally took his own life.

Author Mark Shaw says of Kilgallen: "Called by famed attorney F. Lee Bailey 'A very bright and very good reporter of criminal cases, the best there was,' 'One of the greatest women writers in the world,' by Ernest Hemingway, and by the *New York Post*, 'The most powerful female voice in America,' Dorothy Kilgallen was a *What's My Line?* television star, radio personality, celebrated journalist, revered investigative reporter and author. One of the most courageous journalists in history, Kilgallen was a larger-than-life true Renaissance woman and the first female media icon whose accomplishments rival modern day legends like Oprah Winfrey, Barbara Walters, and Diane Sawyer. During the 1950s, and '60s, the college dropout-turned-feisty-journalist with the light-up smile, Irish wit, and high society manners who achieved phenomenal success in a man's world, made enemies ranging from show business celebrities to government officials to those in the underworld."

In his 2016 book on the life and death of Kilgallen, titled *The Reporter Who Knew Too Much*, author Mark Shaw makes it clear that Kilgallen's first and overriding passion was journalism—of the investigative type, of the celebrity kind, and of the downright dangerous-to-your-health variety. She was gutsy, driven, ambitious, and very well connected. All of which brings us to the matter of not so much Kilgallen's *life* but her *death*. She died, at the age of just fifty-two, on November 8, 1965, in her New York townhouse. Shaw makes it clear that Kilgallen's death was almost certainly not the suicide or accidental death that so many powerful players wanted it to be. Indeed, Kilgallen's still controversial death is the absolute cornerstone of Shaw's 329-page book.

Certainly, Kilgallen had enemies of the kind that few would want, including the Mob. Frank Sinatra outright despised her. And she had little regard for the Mob pal, either. Add to that Kilgallen's persistent efforts to uncover the truth behind the November 22, 1963, assassination of President John F. Kennedy, the fatal shooting of Lee Harvey Oswald by Jack Ruby, and the subsequent arrest and trial of Ruby, and what you have is a definitively dangerous brew. Kilgallen had enemies elsewhere, too. The CIA was hardly overjoyed when she became the first journalist to reveal that the agency was working with the Mafia—chiefly in relation to plots to get rid of Fidel Castro. She also covered the notorious Profu-

Dorothy Kilgallen was a Hearst newspaper reporter whose rise to fame was based on her career as an excellent writer and having an interest in unusual criminal cases. She was also a regular contestant on the hit TV game show *What's My Line?*

mo Affair that rocked the U.K. establishment (and entertained the public) in the summer of 1963, when the worlds of prostitutes and government officials blended into one.

There can be little doubt, as Shaw makes clear, that things began to get dangerous for Kilgallen when she got her hooks into the aforementioned shooting of JFK back in 1963. She was particularly intrigued by Jack Ruby's role in the whole affair. Maybe even a bit obsessed with it, too. What was his real motivation? Was he "just following orders"? What links did he have to Oswald?

Kilgallen began to compile what would ultimately become a large file on her findings. It mysteriously vanished after her death and never resurfaced. Her dislike of FBI boss J. Edgar Hoover only increased when he maintained that the only person involved in the death of the president was Oswald. Incidentally, Kilgallen's FBI and CIA files are now both in the public domain, thanks to the provisions of the Freedom of Information Act. Kilgallen closely followed Ruby's trial for killing Oswald, pondering deeply on how things were made so easy for Ruby to have killed Oswald on November 24, 1963. It's a testament to her tenacity and determined character that Kilgallen was the only journalist to get an interview with Ruby while the trial was still going on. She was also leaked specific pages about Ruby from the Warren Commission report before it was made openly available.

As Kilgallen's research into the intricacies of the whole JFK affair increased, she became somewhat worried, then frightened; she was concerned that her life was in danger. As Shaw reveals in his book, she was in major danger. Kilgallen made a mystery-filled trip to New Orleans. Her hairdresser, Marc Sinclaire, said (and is quoted by Shaw): "Her life had been threatened." All of which leads up to the matter of her puzzling, controversy-filled death and the discovery of her dead in bed on November 8, 1965.

Shaw, without doubt the leading expert in the Kilgallen controversy, confidently rips apart the official line—maybe suicide, perhaps accidental death—and in his book heads off into territory filled with what may have been a hired killer, a mole in Kilgallen's inner circle, and even the influence of the Mafia (Mob don Carlos Marcello is a particular target in terms of who may have been behind the murder). Shaw spends a lot of time focusing on the levels of drugs and alcohol in her system and reveals the flaws in Kilgallen's autopsy. A good case is made that Dorothy was deliberately drugged—to the point where she ultimately died. There is also the matter of a mysterious man she met with at the Regency Hotel bar in New York just hours before her death.

The *New York Post* gave Shaw's book on Kilgallen's death a positive review: "Shaw makes a compelling argument that Kilgallen was the victim of foul play, likely orchestrated by New Orleans Mafia don Carlos Marcello, who feared the results of her 18-month investigation for a tell-all book that would accuse Marcello of masterminding the JFK and Lee Harvey Oswald assassinations. The possibility that Marcello was responsible for JFK's death came up in the 1991 Oliver Stone movie *JFK*, but New Orleans District Attorney Jim Garrison, who launched a probe, dismissed the idea. 'He missed it,' Shaw says. 'He didn't have access to Kilgallen's research.' Kilgallen died weeks before a planned second trip to New Orleans for a meeting with a secret informant, telling a friend it was 'cloak and daggerish.' 'I'm going to break the real story and have the biggest scoop of the century,' she told her lawyer. Her death brought all that to a halt. 'The killers won, because she was eliminated and erased from any historical record about the JFK assassination,' Shaw says. Her JFK book was never published."

It should be noted that Mark Shaw's book was not the first one to address the mystery-filled death of Dorothy Kilgallen. On the website *Kennedys and King*, James DiEugenio wrote an excellent article on the Kilgallen controversy in 2017. In part, he said: "Prior to Shaw's book, there had been three major sources about Kilgallen's life and (quite) puzzling death. The first was Lee Israel's biography titled *Kilgallen*. Published in hardcover in 1979, it went on to be a *New York Times* bestseller in paperback."

Midwest Today demonstrated just how hazardous it can be for a journalist who decides to dig into the world of government secrecy, conspiracy theorizing, and hired assassins: "Dorothy was one of the very few American journalists who immediately assailed the investigation into the death of the President, and scored a world exclusive when she obtained an advance copy of the Warren Commission's controversial report—which infuriated President Lyndon Johnson, who had not yet even seen it. She proceeded to publicly challenge its numerous gaps, contradictions and outright lies. Ms. Kilgallen also launched a private inquiry which took her to New Orleans and resulted in her drawing the scrutiny—and scorn—of FBI director J. Edgar Hoover and LBJ. FBI agents were even dispatched to her private residence in New York to interrogate her, but she said she'd rather die than reveal her source(s). She soon did just that. For many years, agencies of the federal government like the CIA and FBI followed Dorothy and her friends, as is well documented in declassified files. Her phones were tapped, and she had to arrange clandestine meetings with sources, hoping that her various subterfuges would keep her safe. Near the end of her life, she very much felt she was in danger—and indeed she was."

While in the midst of writing a tell-all book linking New Orleans Mafia don Carlos Marcello to the JFK assassination, Dorothy Kilgallen was found dead from a mix of alcohol and barbiturates. She is buried at the Gate of Heaven Cemetery in Hawthorne, New York.

The last word goes to George W. Bailey, who has an interest in the death of Dorothy Kilgallen and who runs the *Oswald's Mother* blog. He says of Kilgallen: "Her husband, Richard Kollmar, was asleep in the fourth story of the townhouse. He gave inconsistent accounts of what happened that night. He claimed that Dorothy arrived home at 11:30 P.M., in good spirits, and went off to write her column. But those who saw her in the Regency lounge reported her being there far past midnight 2 A.M. Later, when asked by friends about Dorothy's JFK investigation, he replied, 'I'm afraid that will have to go to the grave with me.' And it did when Kollmar died of a drug overdose in 1971."

MARTIN LUTHER KING AND A DEADLY BULLET

Very few people would dispute that Martin Luther King Jr. was the foremost, leading, and most influential figure in the arena of civil rights in the twentieth century. King, who was born on January 15, 1929, in Atlanta, Georgia, was a man whose words inspired millions of African Americans—and still do. He changed the face of American society and culture. He was awarded the Nobel Peace Prize in 1964. And he died—before he was even forty—under circumstances that many theorists and researchers believe were dominated by conspiracy and cover-up.

The official story of the shooting of Martin Luther King Jr. goes like this: in early February 1968, a major dispute broke out in Memphis, Tennessee. Local African Americans, employed in the city's sanitation industry, were becoming more and more angered by the fact that their wages were significantly lower than those of their white colleagues. The result was that they went on strike, protesting against what they saw as an outrageous, racist practice on the part of Memphis's mayor, Henry Loeb. King agreed with them, to such an extent that he decided to fly out to Memphis to offer his support for the striking workers and to condemn the practices of Loeb. King could not have known it at the time, but his actions had just firmly sealed his fate.

The countdown to King's final moments really began on April 3. That was when King spoke before an audience at Memphis's Church of God in Christ—which, today, has five million, predominantly African American, followers. Looking back on the day in question, one can practically see the air of menace and death growing before King's very eyes. When he was due to fly to Memphis, King's flight was almost canceled—the result of a claim that there was an explosive device aboard. Fortunately, that proved not to be the case.

The ominous atmosphere was not about to go away anytime soon, however. While he passionately delivered a speech to the large throng at the Church of God in Christ, a huge storm wailed and thundered outside. The rain poured, the heavens flashed, and the sky boomed.

Somewhat eerily, what turned out to be King's final public speech was cloaked with references to finality, to death, and to God. King told the audience:

> I don't know what will happen now. We've got some difficult days ahead. But it doesn't matter with me now, because I've been to the mountaintop. And I don't mind. Like anybody, I would like to live a long life. Longevity has its place. But I'm not concerned about that now. I just want to do God's will. And He's allowed me to go up to the mountain. And I've looked over and I've seen the Promised Land. I may not get there with you. But I want you to know tonight, that we, as a people, will get to the Promised Land. And so, I'm happy, tonight. I'm not worried about anything; I'm not fearing any man. My eyes have seen the glory of the coming of the Lord.

Followers of Christianity might say that the Lord, hearing King's words, came calling on him—and very soon, too.

While he was visiting Memphis, King stayed in Room 306 at the Lorraine Motel, which he shared with Reverend Ralph David Abernathy—who, after King's death, ran the Poor People's Campaign, which saw thousands of angry African Americans descending upon Washington, D.C., to protest their living conditions.

At 6:01 P.M. on April 4, King's life violently and viciously ended. King was standing on a second-floor balcony of the motel. Suddenly, a single shot rang out. It wrought immediate and irreversible devastation on King: it slammed into his cheek, utterly shattering his right jawbone, breaking into shards a number of vertebrae, and creating a gaping hole in his jugular vein. One of these injuries alone, could have proved fatal. With all of them, however, King really didn't stand a chance. He was unconscious even before he hit the balcony floor.

Promoting the idea that black trash collectors in Memphis should be paid the same as white ones, Martin Luther King Jr. flew there to promote that idea through peaceful protest. It was there that he would be assassinated.

Despite the fact that King was driven at breakneck speed to Memphis's St. Joseph Hospital, and despite the very best efforts of the hospital's medical staff, King could not be saved. A little more than an hour after he was shot, King was dead. He was just thirty-nine years of age. Adding to the odd and unsettling sense of finality that surrounded King's last days, when his body was autopsied, it was determined that his heart was in very bad shape—which may well have taken him to an early grave anyway, even if he had avoided that deadly bullet. As for who shot and killed King, this is where things become decidedly murky.

The official version of events is actually quite straightforward. Not long after that fatal shot rang out, a man named James Earl Ray was seen leaving—with possibly incriminating speed—a lodging house that was situated on the other side of the road from the Lorraine Motel. That Ray, at the time, was renting a room at the house, is not a matter of any doubt. Nor is the fact that less than a week before the shooting, Ray purchased a rifle, using a bogus name. That very same rifle—along with a pair of binoculars, no less—was found in a bundle covered in Ray's fingerprints. It must be noted, too, that Ray had a long and checkered history as a career criminal.

He was found guilty of burglary in 1949, served two years in prison for armed robbery in 1952, and was convicted of mail fraud three years later. In 1959, after yet another armed robbery, Ray was hit with a two-decade sentence. The sentence didn't last, however. In 1967, Ray escaped from the Missouri State Penitentiary in Jefferson City, after which he spent time in, variously, Mexico, Los Angeles, and Birmingham, Alabama, where, on March 30, 1968, he purchased a Remington Gamemaster 760 .30-06 caliber rifle and twenty bullets.

In the aftermath of the shooting, Ray made his careful, stealthy way to the Canadian city of Toronto, where he had previously secured a bogus ID. Exactly one month after he returned to the city, Ray used that same faked documentation to fly to the United Kingdom. It was at London's Heathrow Airport that Ray was finally arrested—while trying to leave the United Kingdom for pastures new. He was quickly returned to the United States and, ultimately, was charged with the murder of Martin Luther King Jr. Not only that, Ray offered up that yes, he did shoot and kill King. The date of the confession was March 10, 1969—Ray's forty-first birthday. For his actions, Ray got ninety-nine years. He died, still incarcerated, on April 23, 1998, from the effects of hepatitis C. He was seventy years old.

Just like Lee Harvey Oswald, James Earl Ray was portrayed as a definitive lone gunman, even by himself. At least, he was for a short period: only seventy-two hours after admit-

In 1967, Ray escaped from the Missouri State Penitentiary in Jefferson City, after which he spent time in, variously, Mexico, Los Angeles, and Birmingham, Alabama, where, on March 30, 1968, he purchased a Remington Gamemaster 760 .30-06 caliber rifle and twenty bullets.

ting to having shot and killed King, Ray, by now in custody, had a sudden and radical change of mind. Not only that, he made some curious statements concerning the assassination of the civil rights legend. According to Ray's odd words, while he was not the man who shot and killed King, he just might have been: he said he was "partially responsible without knowing it." Then, there was the matter of a mysterious character known as "Raoul."

According to Ray, he met the enigmatic Raoul in Canada sometime after escaping from the Missouri State Penitentiary. Writer Pat Shannan said of the Ray–Raoul connection that Raoul "quickly began to give James money in exchange for his help with importing some kind of contraband."

Shannan continued: "In Memphis on April 4th, the afternoon of the murder, Raoul had suggested that James go to a movie, but James declined. After several tries at getting rid of James for awhile, Raoul finally sent him on an errand only minutes before King was shot. James said that he was going to get the worn tires changed on the Mustang but that the man at the tire store was too busy and could not get to it that day. When James returned to the flophouse/Lorraine Motel location, it was surrounded by police cars with flashing lights, and he decided it would be prudent to leave the area, as it certainly was not a place for an escaped con to be hanging around."

It was, said Ray, Raoul who told him to purchase the rifle, who instructed Ray to meet with him in Memphis, and who even told Ray in which boardinghouse he should rent a room. The story continues that, although he did not realize it at the time, Ray was being set up as the fall guy in the assassination. A case for this *can* be made: the bundle containing the rifle and binoculars was dumped in the doorway of a building adjacent to the rooming house.

The website *What Really Happened* notes: "Less than two minutes after the fatal shot was fired, a bundle containing the 30.06 Remington rifle allegedly used in the assassination and some of Ray's belongings was conveniently found in the doorway of the Canipe Amusement Company next door to the boarding house. Ray would have had to fire the shot that killed King from his contorted position in the bathroom, exit the sniper's nest, go to his room to collect his belongings and wrap and tie it all in a bundle, leave his room, run down the stairs and out of the boarding house, stash the bundle next door, and then get away from the scene unnoticed—all within two minutes!"

Ray may have been a long-term criminal, but he was certainly no fool. Why leave the incriminating evidence, along with his fingerprints, right below the room in which he allegedly carried out the assassination—for one and all to see?

In June 2000, the U.S. Department of Justice released a document titled "Investigation of Recent Allegations Regarding the Assassination of Dr. Martin Luther King, Jr." It contains a fascinating section titled "Findings Regarding Raoul."

On August 26, 1998, the attorney general directed the Civil Rights Division of the U.S. Department of Justice, assisted by the Criminal Division, to investigate two separate, then-recent allegations related to the April 4, 1968, assassination of King. The allegations emanate from two people: Loyd Jowers, a former Memphis tavern owner, and Donald Wilson, a former agent with the FBI.

In 1993, twenty-five years after the murder, Jowers claimed that he had participated in a conspiracy to kill King, along with an alleged Mafia figure, Memphis police officers, and a man named Raoul. According to Jowers, one of the conspirators shot Dr. King from behind his tavern.

Wilson alleged in 1998 that shortly after the assassination, while working as an FBI agent, he took papers from the abandoned car of James Earl Ray. Wilson claims he concealed them for thirty years. Some of the papers contained references to Raoul and figures associated with the November 1963 assassination of President John F. Kennedy. According to Wilson, someone who later worked in the White House subsequently stole the other papers he took from Ray's car, including one with the telephone number of an FBI office.

The Department of Justice had much to say on all this:

> Both the Jowers and the Wilson allegations suggest that persons other than or in addition to James Earl Ray participated in the assassination. Ray, within days of entering his guilty plea in 1969, attempted to withdraw it. Until his death in April 1998, he maintained that he did not shoot Dr. King and was framed by a man he knew only as Raoul. For 30 years, others have similarly alleged that Ray was Raoul's unwitting pawn and that a conspiracy orchestrated Dr. King's murder.
>
> These varied theories have generated several comprehensive government investigations regarding the assassination, none of which confirmed the existence of any conspiracy. However, in *King v. Jowers*, a recent civil suit in a Tennessee state court, a jury returned a

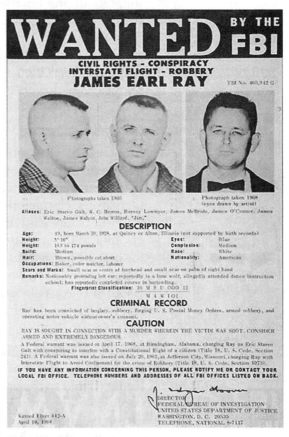

James Earl Ray, shown in this wanted poster, quickly became the primary suspect in Dr. Martin Luther King Jr.'s death.

verdict finding that Jowers and unnamed others, including unspecified government agencies, participated in a conspiracy to assassinate Dr. King.

The DoJ was not persuaded by the words of Jowers and Wilson:

Our mission was to consider whether the Jowers or the Wilson allegations are true and, if so, to detect whether anyone implicated engaged in criminal conduct by participating in the assassination. We have concluded that neither allegation is credible. Jowers and Wilson have both contradicted their own accounts. Moreover, we did not find sufficient, reliable evidence to corroborate either of their claims. Instead, we found significant evidence to refute them.

Nothing new was presented during *King v. Jowers* to alter our findings or to warrant federal investigation of the trial's conflicting, far-ranging hearsay allegations of a government-directed plot involving the Mafia and African American ministers closely associated with Dr. King. Ultimately, we found nothing to disturb the 1969 judicial determination that James Earl Ray murdered Dr. King or to confirm that Raoul or anyone else implicated by Jowers or suggested by the Wilson papers participated in the assassination.

The DoJ also noted:

More than 30 years after the crime, there still is no reliable information suggesting Raoul's last name, address, telephone number, nationality, appearance, friends, family, location, or any other identifying characteristics. The total lack of evidence as to Raoul's existence is telling in light of the fact that Ray's defenders, official investigations, and others have vigorously searched for him for more than 30 years. The dearth of evidence is also significant since Ray often claimed that he was repeatedly with Raoul in various places, cities, and countries, and many of Ray's associations unrelated to the assassination have been verified.

Because the uncorroborated allegations regarding Raoul originated with James Earl Ray, we ultimately considered Ray's statements about him. Ray's accounts detailing his activities with Raoul related to the assassination are not only self-serving, but confused and contradictory, especially when compared to his accounts of activities unrelated to the assassination. Thus, Ray's statements suggest that Raoul is simply Ray's creation. For these reasons, we have concluded there is no reliable evidence that a Raoul participated in the assassination.

As persuasive as many might find the words of the Department of Justice to be, the story does not end there. It's now time for us to take a look at the controversial world of mind control. It is a fact that after he escaped from prison, in 1967, Ray underwent plastic surgery—reportedly, notes Brad Steiger—on the orders of Raoul. Steiger says:

> A link to MK-ULTRA, the CIA's mind-control project, may have occurred when Ray was recuperating from the plastic surgery. Dr. William Joseph Bryan, Jr. had programmed individuals when he was with the air force as chief of Medical Survival Training, the air force's covert mind-control section. Bryan, whom some called pompous and arrogant, liked nothing better than to talk about himself and his accomplishments. He was known as an expert on brainwashing, and he served as a consultant on *The Manchurian Candidate*, a motion picture that portrayed a programmed political assassin. In informal discussions, Bryan 'leaked' that he had programmed Sirhan Sirhan and James Earl Ray to commit assassinations and to forget their participation in the act.

The *It Was Johnson* website (which is dedicated to the study of the theory that President John F. Kennedy's death was orchestrated by his successor, President Lyndon B. Johnson) notes: "Dr. Bryan, like many other figures directly involved in the murders of the Kennedy brothers and King, would die under mysterious circumstances in the spring of 1977; this at a time when the JFK case was reopened and key witnesses and conspirators everywhere conveniently died (e.g. John Rosselli, Sam Giancana). In Bryan's case, the coroner determined he died of natural causes before any autopsy was performed."

The Ray family was determined to have their say, too. In April 2008, Ray's brother, John Larry Ray, wrote and published a book on the death of his sibling. Its title was *Truth at Last*. *The Birmingham News* noted, in an article penned by Rahkia Nance: "For years, John Larry Ray has tried to reveal what he says is an uncovered page in history about his older brother's role in the assassination of Martin Luther King Jr. He always has contended James Earl Ray was a government 'patsy,' the fall guy for a sophisticated government plot."

Nance noted that John Larry Ray stated that his brother had been "caught in a web of hypnosis, brainwashing and government-backed mind-control programs that all began with the shooting of a black soldier, named Washington, in 1948. As a military police officer in Germany, James Earl Ray was directed to shoot the soldier, only identified as Washington, who had been arrested for beating up Jews. Army records showed that prior to the incident, Ray had received two spinal taps, which John Larry suggests may have been part of a drug experiment," one that may have involved the administering of LSD and other hallucinogens.

The shooting, Ray said in his book, "identified James Earl Ray as a programmable personality and would eventually thrust him into the center of the King assassination. Upon his general discharge from the Army in 1948, James Earl Ray would spend the next 20 years falling deeper into the government network, first used as an undercover operative investigating Communists and eventually landing in and out of prisons, supposedly under the guidance of federal agents."

Was Martin Luther King Jr. murdered by nothing more than a violent career criminal, one who had killed *another* black man some twenty years earlier? Or, were King and James Earl Ray *both* victims in this strange and (so far) unending saga? The final word, for now, goes to Ray's brother, John Larry Ray, who said: "James got caught up in something he didn't understand. He didn't know what was going down."

WHAT THE U.S. GOVERNMENT SAYS ABOUT MLK

The U.S. House Select Committee on Assassinations has made its views on the Martin Luther King Jr. assassination very clear. Interestingly, as you'll see, the committee's conclusions did not mirror the approach of the Warren Commission that investigated the November 22, 1963, killing of President John F. Kennedy at Dealey Plaza in Dallas, Texas. Whereas the Warren Commission dismissed each and every conspiracy theory, the King committee took a very different—even refreshing—approach to its investigation. It began as follows, with three primary points that were carefully presented:

> The committee concluded that there was a likelihood of conspiracy in the assassination of Dr. King. To summarize, several findings were central to the committee's conspiracy conclusion. First, James Earl Ray was the assassin of Dr. King, and Raoul, as described by Ray, did not exist. In reaching these conclusions, the committee rejected the possibility that James Earl Ray was an unwitting fall guy manipulated by others. The committee found, rather, that Ray acted with full knowledge of what he was doing in the murder of Dr. King.

> Second, an analysis of Ray's conduct before the assassination provided compelling indications of conspiracy. Ray was not, in fact, a man without significant associations. His financing, in all likelihood supplied by the Alton bank robbery in July 1967, was strong evidence of significant criminal associations with his brothers during the pre-assassination period. Further, his campaign activities in California, viewed against the background of his 1967–68 fugitive status, his apolitical nature and his consis-

tent refusal to admit the activities, also strongly suggested involvement with others. Ray's trip to New Orleans, too, was significant. The abrupt nature of his departure from Los Angeles, the risks he took on the road, his receipt of money during the visit and the speedy termination of his mission all indicated Ray's involvement with others in an important meeting with a preplanned purpose.

Third, the analysis of Ray's motive was crucial to the conspiracy conclusion. After examining Ray's behavior, his character and his racial attitudes, the committee found it could not concur with any of the accepted explanations for Ray as a lone assassin. Historically, Ray was a financially motivated criminal. While unsympathetic to the civil rights movement, he did not manifest the type of virulent racism that might have motivated the assassination in the absence of other factors. While the committee recognized the presence of other possible motives—racism or psychological needs—it concluded that the expectation of financial gain was Ray's primary motivation. The committee's finding on motive, therefore, carried conspiratorial implications.

Just as significant in the committee's ultimate conclusions on conspiracy was the evidence bearing on the complicity of the brothers, John and Jerry Ray. Three factors, negative in character, raised the possibility of the involvement of one or both brothers.

There was another three-part aspect to all of this, too. The committee said:

First, despite an exhaustive and far-reaching field investigation, neither the committee nor previous investigators were able to identify significant associates of the assassin other than his brothers. The possibility of their involvement in the assassination was necessarily increased by the absence of alternatives.

Second, despite an offer of assistance from the Justice Department, Ray refused to provide credible evidence on the subject of conspiracy. His self-sacrificial posture was possibly explained as an effort to protect his brothers.

Third, the Ray brothers consistently attempted to conceal the true scope of their pre-assassination contact with each other. John and James denied any contact at all. This conduct could be explained by a sense of family loyalty. Nevertheless, it also raised the possibility that pre-assassination contact, if revealed, would lead to implication in a conspiracy.

The committee added further weight to its theory:

Additional positive factors ultimately convinced the committee of the likelihood of the involvement of one or both brothers in the assassination. James was, of course, a fugitive from Missouri State Penitentiary. Automatically, this should have led him to limit the duration of meetings with his brothers. Nevertheless, substantial contact in a variety of forms apparently persisted throughout the pre-assassination period. Much of this contact, moreover, was criminal in nature. Both John and Jerry met with and assisted James during the months immediately following his escape from Missouri State Penitentiary. In addition, John clearly had foreknowledge of the escape plans and provided James with an alias and social security number for immediate use. More significantly, the committee found it highly likely that John and James robbed the Bank of Alton in Alton, Ill., on July 13, 1967. Jerry knew of the robbery and assisted in distributing the proceeds to James throughout his fugitive travels. There was evidence of the receipt of money by James from a brother as late as February 1968, only weeks before the assassination. Further, the committee concluded that James' trip to New Orleans in December 1967 could best be understood as a meeting with one or both of his brothers, with circumstantial evidence suggesting it was Jerry Ray. The purpose of that meeting, beyond the transfer of funds, could not be firmly established, but its sinister significance was clear. Finally, there was strong circumstantial evidence of the involvement of a brother in a consulting capacity during Ray's purchase of the murder weapon itself, although the evidence was insufficient to determine the identity of the brother or the nature of the contact.

Nevertheless, the evidence with respect to Ray and his brothers contained one serious flaw: by itself, it provided no convincing explanation for their combination in a plot on Dr. King's life. The committee did receive strong evidence of pronounced racist attitudes in both John and Jerry. Yet, the committee believed it unlikely that James or his brothers would have killed Dr. King solely for racial reasons. The development of additional evidence on a credible St. Louis-based plot, therefore, became a crucial element in the committee's conspiracy analysis.

The committee found that there was substantial evidence to establish the existence of a St. Louis-based conspiracy to finance the assassination of Dr. King. A serious effort to solicit Russell Byers was made by John Sutherland and John Kauffmann in late

The Martin Luther King Jr. Memorial was designed by famous Chinese sculptor Lei Yixin. Located in Washington, D.C., next to the Franklin D. Roosevelt Memorial at the National Mall, the statue opened to the public in 2011 and bears the words of Dr. King's famous "I Have a Dream" speech.

1966 or early 1967, apparently on behalf of a wider authority. In addition, knowledge of Kauffmann's role in the effort to broker the assassination was circulated and frequently mentioned at his Buff Acres Motel in 1967. According to witness A, it was perceived as a standing offer. The committee frankly acknowledged that it was unable to uncover a direct link between the principals of the St. Louis conspiracy and James Earl Ray or his brothers. There was no direct evidence that the Sutherland offer was accepted by Ray, or a representative, prior to the assassination. In addition, despite an intensive effort, no evidence was found of a payoff to Ray or a representative either before or after the assassination.

Winding down to the end, the committee that looked into the murder of MLK stated these words:

Despite this, the committee believed that there was a likelihood that word of the standing offer on Dr. King's life reached James Earl Ray prior to the assassination. This conclusion was based on several considerations. John was a permanent resident of St. Louis from October 1966 forward. Ray himself was in the St. Louis area on at least two occasions during his early fugitive period once immediately after his escape, and again in July 1967 when he participated in the robbery of the Bank of Alton. It was possible that either John or James or both received word of the standing offer through criminal associates in the St. Louis area. It was more likely, however, that John Ray heard of the offer through AIP [American Independent Party] campaign activities in and around the Grapevine Tavern. George Wallace's Presidential bid stirred up intense support in the Grapevine's neighborhood—the south St. Louis area. Race relations and the civil rights movement became subjects of daily, and increasingly polarized, debate. At the same time, Dr. King's efforts in the civil rights movement were expanding to encompass opposition to the Vietnam war and support for the economically oppressed—to culminate in a Poor People's Campaign in Washington. The committee found it reasonable to believe that with an increase in the intensity of the St. Louis AIP campaign effort, and the heightened visibility of Dr. King. discussion of the Sutherland offer could well have come to James Earl Ray's attention. This possibility was only strengthened by Sutherland's heavy involvement in the AIP effort in St. Louis. Kauffmann also did significant work with Sutherland on behalf of the party. In addition, the committee found at least two individuals who knew Sutherland, were active in the AIP campaign, and who had been in the Grapevine Tavern. Finally, John Ray's tavern was used as a local distribution point for AIP campaign literature and paraphernalia. It was in these campaign activities that the committee found the most likely connective between James Earl Ray and the St. Louis conspiracy. In sum, the committee believed that the weight of the evidence bearing on James and his brothers, taken in combination with the evidence of the St. Louis-based conspiracy, established the likelihood of a conspiracy in the death of Dr. King.

Because of a failure of the evidence, the committee's ultimate conclusion must, however, be phrased in terms of alternatives. The committee believed that the St. Louis conspiracy provided an explanation for the involvement of Ray and one or both brothers in the assassination. The manner of their involvement could have taken one of two forms. James Earl Ray may simply have been aware of the offer and acted with a general expectation of payment after the assassination; or he may have acted, not only with an awareness of the offer, but also after reaching a specific agreement, either directly or through one or both brothers, with Kauffmann or Sutherland. The legal consequences of the alternative possibilities are, of course, different. Without a specific agreement with the Sutherland group, the conspiracy that eventuated in Dr. King's death would extend only to Ray and his brother(s); with a specific agreement, the conspiracy would also encompass Sutherland and his group. In the absence of additional evidence, the committee could not make a more definite statement. The committee believed, nevertheless, that the evidence provided the likely outlines of conspiracy in the assassination of Dr. King.

It is unfortunate that this information was not developed in 1968, when it could have been pursued by law enforcement agencies equipped with tools not available to the committee and at a time when the principals were still alive and witness' memories were more precise. It is a matter on which reasonable people may legitimately differ, but the committee believed that the conspiracy that eventuated in Dr. King's death in 1968 could have been brought to justice in 1968.

THE GOVERNMENT AND RFK

It is, perhaps, predictable that the government concluded there was no conspiracy in the 1968 death of Robert Kennedy, as we shall see in the next chapter. First, though, let's take a look at what the John F. Kennedy Library has to say about RFK and his important place in history:

> Robert Francis Kennedy was born on November 20, 1925, in Brookline, Massachusetts, the seventh child in the closely knit and competitive family of Rose and Joseph P. Kennedy. "I was the seventh of nine children," he later recalled, "and when you come from that far down you have to struggle to survive." He attended Milton Academy and, after wartime service in the Navy, received his degree in government from Harvard University in 1948. He earned his law degree from the University of Virginia Law School three years later. Perhaps more important for his education was the Kennedy family dinner table, where his parents involved their children in discussions of history and current affairs. "I can hardly remember a mealtime," Robert Kennedy said, "when the conversation was not dominated by what Franklin D. Roosevelt was doing or what was happening in the world."
>
> In 1950, Robert Kennedy married Ethel Skakel of Greenwich, Connecticut, daughter of Ann Brannack Skakel and George Skakel, founder of Great Lakes Carbon Corporation. Robert and Ethel Kennedy later had eleven children. In 1952, he made his political debut as manager of his older brother John's successful campaign for the US Senate from Massachusetts. The following

year, he served briefly on the staff of the Senate Subcommittee on Investigations, chaired by Senator Joseph McCarthy.

Disturbed by McCarthy's controversial tactics, Kennedy resigned from the staff after six months. He later returned to the Senate Subcommittee on Investigations as chief counsel for the Democratic minority, in which capacity he wrote a report condemning McCarthy's investigation of alleged Communists in the Army. His later work as Chief Counsel for the Senate Rackets Committee investigating corruption in trade unions won him national recognition for exposing Teamsters' Union leaders Jimmy Hoffa and David Beck.

In 1960, he was the tireless and effective manager of John F. Kennedy's presidential campaign. After the election, he was appointed Attorney General in President Kennedy's cabinet. While Attorney General, he won respect for his diligent, effective and nonpartisan administration of the Department of Justice. Attorney General Kennedy launched a successful drive against organized crime, and convictions against organized crime figures rose by 800% during his tenure. He also became increasingly committed to helping African Americans win the right to vote, attend integrated schools and use public accommodations. He demonstrated his commitment to civil rights during a 1961 speech at the University of Georgia Law School: "We will not stand by or be aloof. We will move. I happen to believe that the 1954 [Supreme Court school desegregation] decision was right. But my belief does not matter. It is the law. Some of you may believe the decision was wrong. That does not matter. It is the law." In September 1962, Attorney General Kennedy sent US Marshals and troops to Oxford, Mississippi to enforce a federal court order admitting the first African American student— James Meredith—to the University of Mississippi.

The riot that had followed Meredith's registration at "Ole Miss" had left two dead and hundreds injured. Robert Kennedy believed that voting was the key to achieving racial justice and collaborated with President Kennedy in proposing the most far-reaching civil rights statute since Reconstruction, the Civil Rights Act of 1964, which passed eight months after President Kennedy's death. Robert Kennedy was not only President Kennedy's Attorney General, he was also his closest advisor and confidant. As a result of this unique relationship, the Attorney General played a key role in several critical foreign policy decisions. During the 1962 Cuban Missile Crisis, for instance, he

Robert F. Kennedy is shown here speaking in California during the 1968 presidential campaign.

helped develop the Kennedy administration's strategy to blockade Cuba instead of taking military action that could have led to nuclear war. He then negotiated with the Soviet Union on removal of the weapons.

Soon after President Kennedy's death, Robert Kennedy resigned as Attorney General and, in 1964, ran successfully for the United States Senate from New York. His opponent, incumbent Republican Senator Kenneth Keating, labeled Kennedy a "carpetbagger" during the closely contested campaign. Kennedy responded to the attacks with humor. "I have [had] really two choices over the period of the last ten months," he said at Columbia University. "I could have stayed in—I could have retired. [Laughter.] And

I—my father has done very well and I could have lived off him. [Laughter and applause.] … I tell you frankly I don't need this title because I [could] be called General, I understand, for the rest of my life. [Laughter and applause.] And I don't need the money and I don't need the office space…. [Laughter.] … Frank as it is— and maybe it's difficult to believe in the state of New York—I'd like to just be a good United States Senator. I'd like to serve." Kennedy waged an effective statewide campaign and, aided by President Lyndon Johnson's landslide, won the November election by 719,000 votes. As New York's Senator, he initiated a number of projects in the state, including assistance to underprivileged children and students with disabilities and the establishment of the Bedford-Stuyvesant Restoration Corporation to improve living conditions and employment opportunities in depressed areas of Brooklyn.

Since 1967, the program has been a model for communities all across the nation. These programs were part of a larger effort to address the needs of the dispossessed and powerless in America—the poor, the young, racial minorities and Native Americans. He sought to bring the facts about poverty to the conscience of the American people, journeying into urban ghettos, Appalachia, the Mississippi Delta and migrant workers' camps. "There are children in the Mississippi Delta," he said, "whose bellies are swollen with hunger…. Many of them cannot go to school because they have no clothes or shoes. These conditions are not confined to rural Mississippi. They exist in dark tenements in Washington, DC, within sight of the Capitol, in Harlem, in South Side Chicago, in Watts. There are children in each of these areas who have never been to school, never seen a doctor or a dentist. There are children who have never heard conversation in their homes, never read or even seen a book." He sought to remedy the problems of poverty through legislation to encourage private industry to locate in poverty-stricken areas, thus creating jobs for the unemployed, and stressed the importance of work over welfare.

Robert F. Kennedy's run for president ended on June 5, 1968, when, after speaking to the press, he was escorted through the kitchen of the Ambassador Hotel and was intercepted by Sirhan Sirhan, who mortally wounded him.

Robert Kennedy was also committed to the advancement of human rights abroad. He traveled to Eastern Europe, Latin America and South Africa to share his belief that all people have a basic human right to participate in the political decisions that affect their lives and to criticize their government without fear of reprisal. He also believed that those who strike out against injustice show the highest form of courage. "Each time a man stands up for an ideal," he said in a 1966 speech to South African students, "or acts to improve the lot of others, or strikes out against injustice, he sends forth a tiny ripple of hope, and crossing each other from a million different centers of energy and daring, those ripples build a current that can sweep down the mightiest walls of oppression and resistance." Kennedy was also absorbed during his Senate years by a quest to end the war in Vietnam. As a new Senator, Kennedy had originally supported the Johnson administration's policies in Vietnam, but also called for a greater commitment to a negotiated settlement and a renewed emphasis on economic and political reform within South Vietnam.

As the war continued to widen and America's involvement deepened, Senator Kennedy came to have serious misgivings about President Johnson's conduct of the war. Kennedy publicly broke with the Johnson administration for the first time in February 1966, proposing participation by all sides (including the Viet Cong's political arm, the National Liberation Front) in the political life of South Vietnam. The following year, he took responsibility for his role in the Kennedy administration's policy in Southeast Asia, and urged President Johnson to cease the bombing of North Vietnam and reduce, rather than enlarge, the war effort. In his final Senate speech on Vietnam, Kennedy said, "Are we like the God of the Old Testament that we can decide, in Washington, DC, what cities, what towns, what hamlets in Vietnam are going to be destroyed?… Do we have to accept that? I do not think we have to. I think we can do something about it." On March 16, 1968, Robert Kennedy announced his candidacy for the Democratic presidential nomination. It was, in the words of Arthur Schlesinger Jr., "an uproarious campaign, filled with enthusiasm and fun…. It was also a campaign moving in its sweep and passion." Indeed, he challenged the complacent in American society and sought to bridge the great divides in American life—between the races, between the poor and the affluent, between young and old, between order and dissent. His 1968 campaign brought hope to an American people troubled by discontent and violence at home and war in Vietnam. He won critical primaries in Indiana and Nebraska and spoke to enthusiastic crowds across the nation. Robert Francis Kennedy was fatally shot on June 5, 1968 at the Ambassador Hotel in Los Angeles, California shortly after claiming victory in that state's crucial Democratic primary. He was 42 years old. Although his life was cut short, Robert Kennedy's vision and ideals live on today through the work of the Robert F. Kennedy Memorial in Washington, DC.

Now, let's see who ensured that RFK would die in just his early forties—and the reasons behind it.

Almost two months to the day after Martin Luther King Jr. was shot and killed in Memphis, Tennessee, the life of yet another formidable figure in American history was brought to a violent, bloody, and controversial end. That figure was Robert Francis Kennedy. He was better known as Bobby, the younger brother of President John F. Kennedy—himself shot and killed under suspicious circumstances in Dallas, Texas, in November 1963—and the U.S. attorney general while JFK was in power. As with the deaths of King and President Kennedy, the circumstances surrounding the shooting of RFK are steeped in mystery and present more than one version of events.

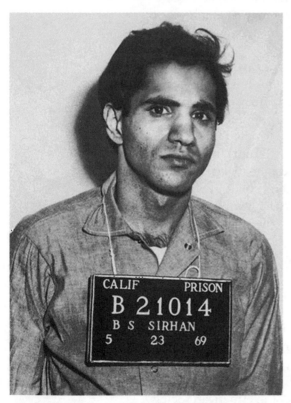

In the final verdict of the RFK assassination, it was determined that Palestinian Sirhan Sirhan acted alone to kill Robert F. Kennedy because of Kennedy's support for Israel. He now serves a life sentence at Richard J. Donovan Correctional Facility in San Diego, California.

The version that is accepted by the U.S. government is that Robert Kennedy was shot and killed in the early hours of June 5, 1968, in Los Angeles, California, by one person—Sirhan Sirhan. At the time, Kennedy was aggressively campaigning to be the Democratic nominee for president. Sirhan's actions ended that hope. Sirhan received a life sentence for murdering Kennedy, which he continues to serve to this day at the Richard J. Donovan Correctional Facility in San Diego, California.

But conspiracy claims suggest mind-controlled assassins, Manchurian candidates, and shadowy gunmen—all of whom were determined to ensure that another Kennedy never reached the White House. Let's now try to sort fact from rumor.

At the time of his killing on June 5, RFK was in a distinctly good mood. Had he not been shot, Kennedy might very well have been elected president. The time frame of the election was important, as was the run-up to the tragic events. Kennedy announced his decision to run on March 16, 1968. Significant portions of the United States were soon thereafter in states of flux as a direct result of the killing of Martin Luther King Jr. There was vehement and violent opposition to the Vietnam War, race riots were breaking out, and tens of thousands were demanding new legislation to help lessen the overwhelming amount of poverty that was blighting certain cities.

Lyndon Johnson, who was campaigning to be re-elected, realized that his time was running out, and he dropped out of the race on March 31. Vice President Hubert Humphrey jumped in and quickly became a major contender. Indeed, at the time of RFK's death, Humphrey was ahead of Kennedy with 561 delegates to Kennedy's 393. It was clear, however, that things were turning in favor of RFK, especially as a result of the California win.

An enthused RFK knew that he had to continue the tidal wave of campaigning, speaking to the voters, and getting the nation behind him if he was to make it to the White House. This involved Kennedy thanking his campaign team and followers in the Embassy Room of the Ambassador Hotel. Although the Secret Service, specifically in the wake of the assassination of JFK in November 1963, had increased its security for a U.S. president, unfortunately, the Secret Service provided *zero* protection for presidential candidates. As for Kennedy, he had just three people protecting him: three bodyguards, including William Barry, previously with the FBI.

With Kennedy now riding a distinct wave, the original plan to meet with his team and supporters was put on hold; the media demanded a statement from RFK, which, if done quickly, would allow the story to make the next morning's newspapers. Since this would continue the campaign momentum, Kennedy followed the suggestion of his aide, Fred Dutton, and agreed to speak with the media first. To reach that rapidly growing band of media, Dutton directed RFK through the hotel's kitchen, which was the most optimum route.

Kennedy gave the press what they wanted, after which there was a sudden change of plans in terms of his exit. The number of people present by now was a definitive throng. Kennedy couldn't get back to the kitchen via the original route and was forced to take another to finally make it. Kennedy and Karl Uecker, who was the hotel's maître d', increased their steps as they walked along a passageway, one in which Kennedy stopped to shake hands with a busboy named Juan Romero. At that moment, Sirhan Sirhan raced forward, letting loose with a salvo of bullets. Complete and utter chaos broke out as Sirhan's .22 caliber Iver-Johnson Cadet revolver took down Kennedy and injured a number of other people present, including one of RFK's campaign volunteers, Irwin Stroll, and *ABC News*'s William Weisel. Sirhan was quickly wrestled to the ground, but it was all to no avail. Kennedy's life was quickly ebbing away as the media looked on and captured on film the final, grim moments of his life.

RFK's wife, Ethel, was, unsurprisingly, hysterical. She knelt by her dying husband, whose final words were, "Don't lift me," as paramedics attempted to do just that, onto a stretcher. For a while, it seemed that things might be okay, despite the severe physical damage that Kennedy had suffered. His heartbeat was still strong—which was confirmed by Ethel, who had the opportunity to listen to it through a stethoscope—despite the fact that he soon passed out. For roughly half an hour, attempts were made to save his life, after which he was quickly driven to the nearby Good Samaritan Hospital.

When the medical team assigned to Kennedy carefully examined their patient, they were devastated by the damage that Sirhan's bullets had wrought: one bullet was embedded in RFK's neck. Another impacted through his right armpit and then tore out of his chest. And a third slammed into his skull at the rear of his right ear. One such injury would have been bad enough, but three practically sealed RFK's fate. He took his last breaths at 1:44 A.M., a little more than one full day after he was shot. Robert Kennedy's funeral took place on June 8. He was buried at Arlington National Cemetery near his brother, JFK. Although Hubert Humphrey won the Democratic nomination, the Republican candidate, former Vice President Richard M. Nixon, ultimately won the race for the White House.

But what of RFK's assassin, Sirhan Sirhan: was he really the solitary shooter that he was portrayed as?

Sirhan Sirhan's background is a significant part of the story: he was born in Jerusalem, was a citizen of Jordan, and was vehemently anti-Zionist. That RFK was a noted supporter of the state of Israel deeply grated on Sirhan's mind, to the point where loathing of Kennedy eventually turned into outright hatred. This can be illustrated in no greater and graphic fashion than in Sirhan's very own journal. Under the May 19, 1968, date, he wrote: "My determination to eliminate RFK is becoming more and more of an unshakable obsession. RFK must die. RFK must be killed. Robert F. Kennedy must be assassinated. Robert F. Kennedy must be assassinated before 5 June 68."

Almost certainly, these words had specific significance to Sirhan. June 5 marked the date on which the so-called Six-Day War between Israel and its opponents in the Middle East (Syria, Jordan, and Egypt) began one year earlier.

On April 17, 1969, Sirhan was found guilty of the murder of Robert Kennedy. He received a sentence of death, but that was later changed to life imprisonment. But was the evidence against him solid? To some, no.

Doubts about Sirhan's guilt surfaced very soon after he was found guilty of killing RFK. While Sirhan was interviewed in the San Quentin prison in 1969, he was interviewed by Dr. Eduard Simson-Kallas, a hypnosis expert who believed Sirhan had been subjected to some form of subliminal mind-control programming. In addition, the coroner in the RFK case, Thomas Noguchi, concluded that the bullet that entered the senator's skull, behind his right ear, had been fired at a distance of barely one inch. That suggests that even if Sirhan *was* a hypnotically controlled assassin, he must have had an accomplice, since he was most definitely further away than one inch when he shot Kennedy.

What was without doubt the biggest development in the saga of who really shot RFK surfaced in 2011, when papers were filed in federal court maintaining that Sirhan Sirhan was manipulated by a seductive girl in a mind-control plot to shoot Senator Robert F. Kennedy.

The papers, noted the media, "point to a mysterious girl in a polka-dot dress as the controller who led Sirhan to fire a gun in the pantry of the Ambassador Hotel. But the documents suggest a second person shot and killed Kennedy while using Sirhan as a diversion."

> Sirhan said, while under hypnosis, he received a specific cue from the polka-dotted girl and went into "range mode," believing he was at a firing range and seeing circles with targets in front of his very eyes.

The story of the mysterious girl is not a new one, as the late Jim Keith—a leading figure in conspiracy research until his own controversial death in 1999—said: "Immediately after the Kennedy shooting a woman named Sandra Serrano saw a Caucasian woman in a white dress with black polka dots, and a young man, tentatively identified as Mexican-American, and wearing a white shirt and gold sweater, running down the stairs that provided exit from the hotel. The woman in the polka dots said, "We've shot him! We've shot him!" Serrano asked, 'Who did you shoot?', and the woman responded, 'We shot Senator Kennedy.'"

The 2011 revelations take the story much further, as the media noted. Sirhan said, while under hypnosis, he received a specific cue from the polka-dotted girl and went into "range mode," believing he was at a firing range and seeing circles with targets in front of his very eyes.

"I thought that I was at the range more than I was actually shooting at any person, let alone Bobby Kennedy," Sirhan was quoted as saying during interviews with Daniel Brown, a Harvard University professor and an expert in trauma memory and hypnosis.

The U.K. newspaper *Daily Mail* noted: "Sirhan's lawyers, William Pepper and Laurie Dusek, are using a defense that is eerily familiar to another Kennedy murder—that there was more than one shooter. They say the 67-year-old Christian Palestinian born in Jerusalem was hypno-programmed to divert attention from a shooter who actually killed Mr. Kennedy in 1968. They also allege he was an easy scapegoat because he is Arab."

"The public has been shielded from the darker side of the practice. The average person is unaware that hypnosis can and is used to induct antisocial conduct in humans," the 1969 papers stated. Those same papers also noted that Sirhan was "an involuntary participant in the crimes being committed because he was subjected to sophisticated, hypno-programming and memory implantation techniques which rendered him unable to consciously control his thoughts and actions at the time the crimes were being committed."

Then, in 2012, the *Huffington Post* noted: "Nina Rhodes-Hughes, a key witness to the Robert F. Kennedy assassination at the Ambassador Hotel in 1968, is making bombshell claims in a CNN interview, suggesting that convicted murderer Sirhan Sirhan didn't act alone."

In Rhodes-Hughes's own words: "What has to come out is that there was another shooter to my right. The truth has got to be told. No more cover-ups."

The *Post* added: "Rhodes-Hughes, now 78, claims the FBI 'twisted' her statements to investigators after the incident in order to come up with the conclusion that she had only heard 8 shots, an account that was used as evidence that Sirhan carried out the act without an accomplice."

The late Jim Keith referred to an odd—and, perhaps, highly revealing—discussion between Sirhan Sirhan and UCLA psychiatrist Bernard Diamond. Keith stated that when Diamond was speaking with Sirhan about certain entries in his notebooks, Diamond, asked, "Is this crazy writing?"

Sirhan chose to reply in writing, rather than verbally: "YES. YES. YES."

"Are you crazy?" the doctor pressed.

"NO. NO."

"Well, why are you writing crazy?"

"PRACTICE PRACTICE PRACTICE."

"Practice for what?"

"MIND CONTROL MIND CONTROL MIND CONTROL."

The final word goes to Charles R. McQuiston, one of the originators of Psychological Stress Evaluator (PSE) technology and a member of U.S. Army intelligence, who said of Sirhan:

"I'm convinced that Sirhan wasn't aware of what he was doing. He was in a hypnotic trance when he pulled the trigger and killed Senator Kennedy. Everything in the PSE charts tells me that someone else was involved in the assassination—and that Sirhan was programmed through hypnosis to kill RFK. What we have here is a real live 'Manchurian Candidate.'"

REMOTE VIEWER PAT PRICE SPIES ON RUSSIA

For decades, numerous nations around the world have done their utmost to try to harness the mysterious powers of the mind and utilize them as tools of espionage. Sometimes, as we shall soon see, digging into matters of the mind can get one killed. Extrasensory perception (ESP), clairvoyance, precognition, and astral projection have all been utilized by the CIA, the KGB, and British intelligence on more than a few occasions. As astonishing as it may sound, the world of psychic 007s is all too real. It's a subject that has been researched with varying degrees of success for decades. The earliest indications of serious interest on the part of the U.S. government in the field of psychic phenomena are described in a formerly classified CIA document written in 1977 by Dr. Kenneth A. Kress, then an engineer with the CIA's Office of Technical Services, and titled "Parapsychology in Intelligence." According to Kress:

> Anecdotal reports of extrasensory perception capabilities have reached U.S. national security agencies at least since World War II, when Hitler was said to rely on astrologers and seers. Suggestions for military applications of ESP continued to be received after World War II. In 1952, the Department of Defense was lectured on the possible usefulness of extrasensory perception in psychological warfare.

> In 1961, the CIA's Office of Technical Services became interested in the claims of ESP. Technical project officers soon contacted Stephen I. Abrams, the Director of the Parapsychological Laboratory, Oxford University, England. Under the auspices of Project ULTRA, Abrams prepared a review article which claimed ESP was "demonstrated but not understood or controllable."

Kress added: "The report was read with interest but produced no further action for another decade."

Indeed, it was in the early 1970s that the research began in earnest (although the FBI got involved in a strange affair in the 1950s). In April 1972, Dr. Russell Targ, a laser physicist with a personal interest in parapsychology and the power of the human mind, met with CIA personnel from the Office of Strategic Intelligence, specifically to discuss paranormal phenomena. Of paramount concern to the CIA was the fact that Targ informed them that the Soviet Union was deeply involved in researching psychic phenomena, mental telepathy, and ESP. It did not take the CIA long to realize that the purpose of the Soviet research was to determine if ESP could be used as a tool of espionage. It was this realization that galvanized the CIA into action. As the Kress report stated in 1973: "The Office of Technical Services funded a $50,000 expanded effort in parapsychology."

The initial studies utilized a variety of people who were carefully and secretly brought into the project and who demonstrated a whole range of seemingly paranormal skills. Those same skills could not be reliably replicated on every occasion, however. As evidence of this, Kenneth Kress informed his superiors that "one subject, by mental effort, apparently caused an increase in temperature; the action could not be duplicated by the second subject. The second subject was able to reproduce, with impressive accuracy, information inside sealed envelopes. Under identical conditions, the first subject could reproduce nothing."

The initial studies utilized a variety of people who were carefully and secretly brought into the project and who demonstrated a whole range of seemingly paranormal skills.

Similarly, some government-sponsored psychics in the period from 1973 to 1974 located secret missile installations in the Soviet Union, found terrorist groups in the Middle East, and successfully remote viewed the interior of the Chinese Embassy in Washington, D.C. Others, meanwhile, provided data that was sketchy and, at times, simply wrong. And it was the continuing rate of success versus the frequency of failure that led to heated debate within the CIA about the overall relevancy and validity of the project.

In "Parapsychology in Intelligence," Kenneth Kress confirmed this. After the CIA's remote viewing team attempted to broaden the range of its operation and secure extra funding in mid-1973, said Kress: "I was told not to increase the scope of the project and not to anticipate any follow-on in this area. The project was too sensitive and potentially embarrassing."

Despite this, the CIA's research continued, with many of its advances due to a skilled psychic named Pat Price, who had achieved a number of extraordinary successes in the field of ESP, including successfully remotely viewing a sensitive installation that fell under the auspices of the National Security Agency and psychically penetrating missile sites in Libya. Price's sudden and untimely death from a heart attack in 1975 indirectly led the CIA—according to the official story at least—to minimize its research into psychic espionage.

Tim Rifat, who has deeply studied the world of top-secret governmental research into psychic spying, says of Pat Price's death: "It was alleged at the time that the Soviets poisoned Price. It would have been a top priority for the KGB to eliminate Price as his phenomenal remote-viewing abilities would have posed a significant danger to the USSR's paranormal warfare buildup. He may also have been the victim of an elite group of Russian psi-warriors trained to remotely kill enemies of the Soviet Union."

Murder or just a heart attack? Soon, the whole strange story will come tumbling out, as you will see.

In his 1997 book *Remote Viewers*, Jim Schnabel told the story of the U.S. intelligence community's involvement in the controversial issue of psychic spying that largely began in the early to mid-1970s. Commenting on the skills of Price, a talented remote viewer in relation to matters of a UFO

Using ESP, remote viewer Pat Price claimed he had used his psychic abilities to detect a large presence of aliens who had created a base inside Alaska's Mount Hayes (pictured).

nature, Schnabel noted that Price was of the opinion that "Alaska's Mount Hayes, the jewel of a glacial range northeast of Anchorage, housed one of the aliens' largest bases." According to Price, the aliens that lived deep inside Mount Hayes were very human looking, differing only in their heart, lungs, blood, and eyes. Ominously, he said that the aliens use "thought transfer for motor control of us." Price added: "The site has also been responsible for strange activity and malfunction of U.S. and Soviet space objects." Rather notably, despite the controversial nature of this story, we find that the U.S. military took a great deal of interest in tales of UFO activity in Alaska in the formative years of the subject. For example, formerly classified FBI files tell of startling UFO encounters in Alaska in the period 1947–1950.

In August 1947, a highly impressive account of a UFO incident involving two serving members of the military was supplied to the FBI at Anchorage. The report began: "This is to advise that two army officers reported to the Office of the Director of Intelligence Headquarters Alaskan Department, at Fort Richardson, Alaska, that they had witnessed an object passing through the air at a tremendous rate of speed which could not be judged as to miles per hour."

According to the official report, the UFO was initially sighted by only one of the two officers, but he soon alerted his colleague to the strange sight. "The object appeared to be shaped like a sphere and did not give the impression of being saucer-like or comparable to a disk. The first officer stated that it would be impossible to give minute details concerning the object, but that it appeared to be approximately two or three feet in diameter and did not leave any vapor trail in the sky."

Experienced officer that he was, in his first attempt to gauge the altitude of the object from a comparison with cloud formations in the area, he determined that whatever the nature of the mystery sphere, it was cruising at a height of more than ten thousand feet. And it should be noted that to be at such a height and still be visible, in all probability, the UFO must have exceeded by a wide margin the initial size estimate of "two or three feet."

When questioned, the second officer gave a substantially similar account, the only marked difference being that, in his opinion, he considered the object to have been approximately ten feet in diameter and compared it to "half the size of a full moon on an ordinary night." This discrepancy in size was apparently due to the fact that the second officer believed the UFO was more likely to have been at a height of three to four thousand feet, rather than at an altitude of ten thousand feet as had been suggested by his colleague.

The difference of opinion over the altitude and size of the object may or may not have been significant; the important factor, however, was that both officers agreed that some type of anomalous object had most definitely been seen. And as the report concluded: "the second officer pointed out that one of the remarkable features of this report was that it was definitely traveling against the wind."

Shortly afterward, the FBI Office at Anchorage reported to Bureau director J. Edgar Hoover that "we have been able to locate a flyer [who] observed some flying object near Bethel, Alaska in July 1947." The report to Hoover continued: "[The pilot] related that the occasion of seeing the flying object near Bethel was on a July day when the sky was completely clear of clouds, and it being during the early part, it is daylight the entire night. The time of his sighting [of] this flying object was about 10 PM and the sun had just dropped beyond the horizon. Flying weather was extremely good and he was coming into the Bethel Airport with a DC-3."

On approaching the airport, the pilot was amazed to see to his left an unidentified craft "the size of a C-54 without any fuselage," which seemed to resemble a "flying wing." As a result of its unique shape, the pilot was initially unable to determine whether the object was heading toward his aircraft or away from it, and he elected to make a forty-five--degree turn in an attempt to diffuse any possible chance of collision. The FBI noted that the pilot was certain that the craft was free of any external power source, such as a propeller-driven engine, and exhibited no exhaust as it flew by.

The document added: "He called on his radio to the Civil Aeronautics Administration station at Bethel, asking what aircraft was in the vicinity and they had no reports of any aircraft. The object he sighted was some five or ten miles from the airport before his arrival and [he] stated that the path did not go directly across the airport. He, of course, could not tell whether the object was making any noise and stated that it was flying at a thousand foot altitude and estimated travel at 300 miles per hour.

"It was traveling in the direction from Bethel to Nome, which is in a northwesterly direction. He noted no radio interference and is unable to describe the color other than it appeared dark but of definite shape and did not blend into the sky but had a definite, concise outline. [He] clearly observed the object at this time."

As the 1940s drew to a close and a new decade dawned, the FBI continued to receive and log high-quality UFO reports on a regular basis. Of those, one of the more credible related to a noteworthy series of encounters that occurred in Alaskan airspace over the course of two days in early 1950. Forwarded to the FBI by an official U.S. Navy source, the confidential, three-page intelligence report paints a startling picture of multiple UFO encounters involving the military. Titled "Unidentified Phenomena in Vicinity of Kodiak, Alaska," it concerns "a report of sightings of unidentified airborne objects, by various naval personnel, on 22 and 23 January 1950."

In January of 1950, UFOs were spotted close to Coast Guard Air Station Kodiak (shown here) by two U.S. patrol plane officers.

The author of the report noted: "at 220240W January Lt. Smith, USN, patrol plane commander of P2V3 No. 4 of Patrol Squadron One reported an unidentified radar contact 20 miles north of the Naval Air Station, Kodiak, Alaska. When this contact was first made, Lt. Smith was flying the Kodiak Security Patrol. At 0243W, 8 minutes later a radar contact was made on an object 10 miles southeast of NAS Kodiak. Lt. Smith checked with the control tower to determine known traffic in the area, and was informed that there was none. During this period, the radar operator, Gaskey, ALC, USN, reported intermittent radar interference of a type never before experienced. Contact was lost at this time, but intermittent interference continued."

Smith and Gaskey were not the only two to report that unidentified vehicles had intruded into Alaskan airspace. At the time of these encounters, the USS *Tilbrook* was anchored in the vicinity of "buoy 19" in the nearby man ship channel. Onboard the *Tilbrook* was a seaman named Morgan (first name unknown) who was standing watch. At some point between 0200 and 0300 hours, Morgan reported that a "very fast moving red light, which appeared to be of exhaust nature seemed to come from the southeast, moved clockwise in a large circle in the direction of, and around Kodiak and returned out in a generally southeast direction."

Perhaps not quite believing what he was seeing, Morgan alerted one of his shipmates, Carver, to the strange spectacle, and both watched as the UFO made a "return flight." According to the testimony of Morgan and Carver: "The object was in sight for an estimated 30 seconds. No odor or sound was detected, and the object was described to have the appearance of a ball of fire about one foot in diameter."

The report then records yet another encounter with the mystery visitor: "At 220440W, conducting routine Kodiak security patrol, Lt. Smith reported a visual sighting of an unidentified airborne object at a range of 5 miles, on the starboard bow. This object showed indications of great speed on the radar scope. The trailing edge of the blip gave a tail like indication."

Lieutenant Smith quickly advised the rest of the crew of the PV23 No. 24 that the UFO was in sight, and all watched fascinated as the strange vehicle soared overhead at a speed estimated to have been around 1,800 miles per hour. Smith climbed to intercept the UFO and vainly tried to circle it. Needless to say, its high speed and remarkable maneuverability ensured that Smith's actions were futile. However, neither Lieutenant Smith nor his crew was quite prepared for what happened next.

"Subsequently the object seemed to be opening the range," the official report reads, "and Smith attempted to close the range. The UFO was observed to open out somewhat, then to turn to the left and come up on Smith's quarter. Smith considered this to be a highly threatening gesture and turned out all lights in the aircraft. Four minutes later the object disappeared from view in a southeasterly direction."

At 0435 hours on the following day, Lieutenants Barco and Causer of Patrol Squadron One were conducting the Kodiak Security Patrol when they, too, sighted an unidentified aerial vehicle. At the time of their encounter, the aircraft in which the officers were flying was approximately sixty-two miles south of Kodiak. For ten minutes, Barco and Causer, along with the pilot, Captain Paulson, watched stunned as the mysterious object twisted and turned in the Alaskan sky. An assessment of these reports read thus:

1. To Lt. Smith and crew it appeared as two orange lights rotating about a common center, 'like two jet aircraft making slow rolls in tight formation.' It had a wide speed range. 2. To Morgan and Carver, it appeared as a reddish orange ball of fire about one foot in diameter, traveling at a high rate of speed. 3. To Causer, Barco and Paulson, it appeared to be a pulsating orange yellow projectile shaped flame, with regular periods of pulsation on 3 to 5 seconds. Later, as the object increased the range, the pulsations appeared to increase to on 7 or 8 seconds and off 7 to 8 seconds.

The final comment on the encounters reads: "In view of the fact that no weather balloons were known to have been released within a reasonable time before the sightings, it appears that the object or objects were not balloons. If not balloons the objects must be regarded as phenomena (possibly meteorites), the exact nature of which could not be determined by this office."

The "meteorite" theory for this series of encounters is particularly puzzling. It goes without saying that meteorites do not stay in sight for "an estimated 30 seconds," meteorites do not close in on military aircraft in what is deemed to be a "highly threatening gesture," and they do not appear as "two orange lights rotating about a common center."

In other words, it seems safe to conclude that genuinely anomalous phenomena were indeed witnessed by experienced military personnel at Kodiak, Alaska, in January 1950.

Does any of this prove that there really is an alien base deep within Alaska's Mount Hayes, as Pat Price suggested? No, of course not. But in view of all the above, perhaps it's time someone took a closer look at Price's claims. You know … just in case.

Far more pressing, however, is the still controversial death of Price, which we will come to right now.

REMOTE VIEWER PAT PRICE IS KILLED BY RUSSIA

Such were Pat Price's skills when it came to the matter of remote viewing that in 1973, he was brought into an elite fold, one that was overseen by the CIA. He was specifically brought into the Office of Technical Services and its Office of Research and Development. The goal was to have Price do his utmost to try to penetrate some of the most guarded secrets of the former Soviet Union. If Price could access top-secret files, papers, and documents created by the Russian government and military, in theory, the U.S. government might be able to dispense of its "secret agents" and, instead, have a near-army of psychic spies—watching the enemy via the power of the human mind. One of the CIA's first operations was to have Price try to remote a domestic target—namely, a classified installation run by the National Security Agency. Such were Price's powers, he quickly identified the facility exactly for what it was. In the immediate wake of the successful operation, the CIA prepared the following summary not just for itself but for the NSA's staff, too.

The CIA stated: "Pat Price, who had no military or intelligence background, provided a list of project titles associated with current and past activities including one of extreme sensitivity. Also, the codename of the site was provided. Other information concerning the physical layout of the site was accurate."

It wasn't long at all before Price found himself engaged in a number of perilous situations and investigations of overseas agencies and intelligence- and military-based operations for the CIA. For example, on a number of occasions, Price was ordered to target various Soviet embassies and military bases of Libya. In 1974, there was an unforeseen, but amazing, development in the life and secret career of Pat Price. He was given the task of remote viewing Alaska's Mount Hayes. Given the fact that the CIA's remote-viewing project was designed to spy on foreign, and potentially dangerous, overseas nations, one has to wonder why the CIA would be spying on the United States. There was actually a very good reason as to why the CIA initiated this particular project. It was an incredible reason, too.

Upon remote viewing the huge Mount Hayes, Price "saw" something incredible and mind-blowing: a huge installation buried deep within the heart of the mountain, run by a vast, extraterrestrial race. Not only that, the aliens looked very much like us. The only differences were that the eyes of the E.T.s were slightly different to ours, as were their internal organs. The fact that the CIA had ordered Price to remote view Mount Hayes suggests that agency spies had prior knowledge of what was going on deep within the massive mountain. How, precisely, the CIA knew what was afoot is a matter that has never been resolved. The CIA keeps its secrets close to its chest, which is perfectly understandable. Now, we come to the most disturbing aspect of this particular *X-Files*-type situation: namely, that as Price dug deeper into the heart of the mountain, so to speak, he became more obsessed by the secret presence of this extraterrestrial race, and he began to suspect that the aliens had the ability to manipulate us by what he described as "thought transfer for motor control of us." In other words, mind control. Matters didn't end there, though. To his concern and fascination, Price told his CIA handlers that he had uncovered three more extraterrestrial bases hidden in mountainous locations. They were Australia's Mount Ziel, Spain's Mount Perdido in the Pyrenees Mountains, and Zimbabwe's Mount Inyangani (now known as Mount Nyangani). Quite understandably, this was all deeply concerning to the CIA. The stark reality seemed to be that potentially dangerous aliens were living under the surface of our planet and were manipulating our minds for reasons that the CIA had yet to fathom. The whole thing worried Price and his colleagues in the CIA.

> The fact that the CIA had ordered Price to remote view Mount Hayes suggests that agency spies had prior knowledge of what was going on deep within the massive mountain.

There is little doubt that Price would have continued with his research into the matter of these underground E.T.s and their sinister agenda. Unfortunately, something unforeseen stepped in and brought things to a shuddering, terrible end: death. Price passed away on July 14, 1975. It was the nature of his death that was so disturbing. Just a few days before his untimely death, Price had a number of covert rendezvous with a variety of agents from the National Security Agency and the Office of Naval Intelligence. The meetings were initiated to determine if Price would be willing to undertake remote-viewing operations for both agencies. Price agreed to both projects. In no time at all, the operations began.

Just a few days after the meetings, Price flew out of Washington, D.C. He was to fly to Salt Lake City and then to Las Vegas. We may never know for sure if Price suspected that his life was in danger. The fact is, however, that with all of this top-secret work being undertaken for U.S. intelligence, Price became concerned about his safety to at least a certain degree, so he gave important, sensitive documents to a friend in case anything were to happen to him. On the afternoon of July 13, Price arrived at the Stardust Hotel in Las Vegas. As he approached the desk to check in, a man walked straight into Price. It was a violent collision. He felt a shooting pain in his leg, as if he had been hit with a needle. With hindsight, that may very well have been what happened. Very quickly, Price started to feel ill and decided to lie down and take a nap.

A few hours later, and still not feeling well, Price met with several friends for dinner. There was something on his mind. Not only did Price tell them about the collision in the lobby just a few hours earlier, but he also confided in them that while he was in Washington, D.C., just a little more than a day earlier, he had seen someone slip something in his coffee. Having seen this chilling, covert action occur, Price left the coffee alone and exited the restaurant quickly. Price cut the dinner meeting short and went back to his room.

Around 5:00 A.M. the next day, Price woke up in significant physical distress. His breathing was not right. He had severe cramps in his back and stomach and was sweating profusely. He called the friend who had the important papers, who quickly raced to Price's room. A doctor was about to be called when Price began to convulse. Then, he went into cardiac arrest. Despite the best efforts of paramedics, who were quickly on the scene and managed to briefly kick-start his heart, it was all to no avail. Price was soon dead. It is a fact that Price had heart disease. With that in mind, his death could have been due to wholly natural causes and nothing else at all. But we should not forget the fact that Price had seen someone surreptitiously slip something into his coffee just a couple of days earlier. Then there was the matter of the potentially suspicious collision in the hotel lobby. To this day, the death of Pat Price is still discussed in hushed tones where the conspiratorial lurk.

Now, let's take a look at an eerily similar case to that of Pat Price that occurred in the United Kingdom just a few years later. As you'll soon see, it all very much sounds like the script for an adventure-filled spy movie. It is, however, all too morbidly and disturbingly real.

DEATH IN LONDON BY A POISONED UMBRELLA

Just a few years after the highly suspicious death of remote viewer Pat Price, there was a very similar and equally disturbing incident that provoked a great deal of alarm within the highest echelons of the U.K. government. It occurred on a bustling street in the heart of London. The victim was a man named Georgi Markov, a Bulgarian writer who went on to incur the wrath of Bulgaria's intelligence service. As a dissident, Markov was almost inevitably destined to cross paths with the dark side of Bulgaria's government. And he did. His life was quickly snuffed out after a strange and deadly encounter. Before we get to the matter of Markov's death, let's first take a look at his life. After all, it was his career and actions that led to his end.

Markov was born in 1929 in southern Bulgaria; his goal was to work in the field of chemistry, which he eventually did. As a nineteen-year-old university student, he took a job as a chemical engineer. Fate, however, stepped in and ensured that there would be big changes for Markov. In the same year that Markov was immersed in the arena of chemical engineering, he was struck with tuberculosis, an infectious disease that can cause severe damage to the lungs. His serious condition brought his chemical engineering work to a quick halt. While he was bedridden, Markov decided to change careers and become a writer. Before the 1950s were over, Markov had written two novels, *The Ajax Winners* and *The Night of Caesium*. His profile as a respected writer increased in 1962 when his third full-length novel, *Man*, was published. There was more to come: Markov took a position with Bulgaria's Narodna Mladezh publishing company. More books appeared from Markov, as did short story collections and stage plays. All was going well for Markov.

Author Georgi Markov, whose books were not always flattering to the leadership of his native Bulgaria, fled his country for fear of retaliation. Unfortunately, someone caught up with him and murdered him.

Since 1991, the Republic of Bulgaria has had a democratic government and been part of NATO. The welcome change resulted from widespread revolutionary activity in Bulgaria in 1989: as in the former East Germany and the Soviet Union, communism was falling. Things were very different for the people of Bulgaria, however, in that pre-1989 period. During that time, Bulgaria was part of the communist Soviet Union. Writers who published somewhat inflammatory material—as Markov most definitely did—had to keep a lookout for their health.

By the 1960s, some of Markov's work was outright banned in Bulgaria chiefly because of the dissident-type approach that Markov took to his work. It most assuredly did not go down well with Bulgarian authorities. Things got worse when the Bulgarian Secret Service opened a surveillance file on him. Markov was referred to by those in the government who were watching him as "The Wanderer." With the heat on him, Markov chose to leave Bulgaria and travel to Italy, the home of Markov's brother. Markov felt relieved that he was no longer in his home country of Bulgaria. But he felt that it was a tragedy that to get his work to a larger audience, he had to flee to Italy. When he experienced passport problems, Markov left for the United Kingdom, fearful of the possibility that Bulgarian authorities would seize his passport and haul him back home. So Markov defected. Outraged, the Bulgarian government sentenced him to six and a half years in jail. Luckily for Markov, the United Kingdom welcomed him, and the Bulgarians were unable to detain him.

Markov quickly made a home for himself in London and took a job with the BBC World Service. This job allowed Markov to safely express his negative views of Bulgaria's regime. From the mid-1970s onward, life was good for Markov: he married, and he and his wife, Annabel Dilke, had a child, Alexandra-Raina. During this period, Markov intensified his criticism of the Bulgarian government and its communist regime. The time finally came when the Bulgarian Secret Service decided to do something about Markov once and for all: they had him killed.

Georgi Markov died on September 11, 1978, at the age of forty-nine. The buildup to the end went as follows: four days earlier, on September 7,

Markov was crossing Waterloo Bridge, famous for the view it provides of London's long and winding River Thames. After crossing the bridge, Markov headed to a nearby bus stop, which would take him close to his place of work: the studios of the BBC. While Markov waited for the bus, his killer quickly moved in. Suddenly, Markov jumped; he was hit by sudden, piercing pain in his right thigh. It felt like a needle or a pin had quickly entered his leg, which is exactly what happened. Markov turned around to see a man behind him picking up an umbrella. The mysterious figure hailed a cab and was quickly lost in the bustling crowds of London.

By the time Markov arrived at the BBC World Service, the pain was still bothering him. On his leg, he saw a circular area of redness, not unlike that of an insect bite or sting. But this felt far worse. A few hours later, Markov began to experience flulike symptoms. As the evening progressed, Markov's condition worsened. He was taken to St James' Hospital, where he spiraled into a serious condition and died. Markov's autopsy revealed that he had been hit by a pellet filled with deadly ricin, which is produced in the seeds of the castor oil plant. The Metropolitan Police quickly initiated an investigation. While they concluded that a Bulgarian assassin—or, at least, someone hired by the Bulgarians—was responsible for the murder, the matter remained a mystery for years. However, one man claimed to know the truth. His name was Oleg Gordievsky.

Oleg Gordievsky was born in Moscow, Russia, in 1938 and received training with the People's Commissariat for Internal Affairs (NKVD). In 1963, he joined the KGB, achieving the rank of colonel. Gordievsky was soon posted to the Soviet Embassy in Copenhagen, Denmark. While he was stationed there, Gordievsky became very disillusioned by his time spent in the KGB; he decided there was only one cause of action he could take: he carefully planned on secretly working for the other side, the West. The Danish Security Intelligence Service took deep note of Gordievsky. They wasted no time in contacting their counterparts in MI6. Staff members at MI6 were informed that Gordievsky just might be willing to switch sides, albeit with him still appearing to be faithful to his controllers in the KGB. MI6 was quick to react. Until the mid-1980s, Gordievsky played the role of dutiful KGB office, but all the while, he was leaking important classified material to British intelligence.

With the help of Oleg Gordievsky (pictured), a defecting Soviet KGB agent, the secret of who killed Markov soon came to light.

It didn't last, though. In 1985, Gordievsky's cover was finally blown. He was soon back in Moscow, going through brutal interrogation. The future looked bleak, but in July 1985 Gordievsky was smuggled out of Russia, into Finland, and then into the United Kingdom via Norway. It would be more than half a decade before Gordievsky's family could follow him. All of which brings us back to the controversies surrounding Georgi Markov.

According to Gordievsky, while the assassin was Bulgarian, the hit itself was planned by the Soviet Union's ruthless KGB. The story was not over, however.

On March 23, 2013, the United Kingdom's *Telegraph* ran an article titled "Prime suspect in Georgi Markov 'umbrella poison' murder tracked down to Austria." In part, it stated the following: "The writer, who was living in the capital, was assassinated on the orders of the Bulgarian secret service as he waited for a bus on Waterloo Bridge in September 1978. While his killers have never been found, a suspect in the case has emerged: a spy known in Bulgarian files as Agent Piccadilly. He was named in Bulgaria eight years ago as Francesco Gullino, a Danish national of Italian origin, who worked for the then Communist regime using his business as an antiques dealer as a cover. Mr. Gullino's whereabouts have remained unknown. But, finally, he has been tracked down to an obscure Austrian town where he has admitted working for the Bulgarian secret service, Darzhavna Sigurnost (DS), but denied any involvement in Mr. Markov's murder. Now that he has been located, Scotland Yard, whose file on the Markov murder remains open, are likely to want to question Mr. Gullino."

Detectives from Scotland Yard were indeed very interested in following up on this revelation. In fact, the story had been told before, as far back as the early 2000s. What made the story big news was the fact that Gullino had, in 2013, been tracked down. Despite this new data, no one has ever been charged with Markov's murder. His remains are buried in a twelfth-century church in the small village of Whitchurch Canonicorum in the county of Dorset, England. In 2000, the Bulgarian government commended Markov for the important work he did for "Bulgarian literature, drama and non-fiction and for exceptional civic position and frontation to the Communist regime."

KILLING A ROCK STAR

The countdown to the murder of rock music legend and former Beatle John Lennon arguably began hours before it actually occurred, which was at 10:50 P.M. on December 8, 1980. During the afternoon of Lennon's last day alive, he and Yoko Ono were photographed at their apartment in New York City's Dakota hotel by Annie Leibowitz, who was there to secure pictures for a *Rolling Stone* magazine story. When the shoot was over, Lennon did a radio interview with San Francisco host Dave Sholin. Somewhat eerily, Lennon said during the interview: "I still believe in love, peace. I still believe in positive thinking. And I consider that my work won't be finished until I'm dead and buried, and I hope that's a long, long time." Lennon did not know it, but the end was getting closer by the minute.

With the interview complete, John and Yoko left the hotel and headed to a waiting limousine, which was to take them to the nearby Plant Studio. As they strolled toward the vehicle, Lennon was approached by a young, bespectacled man who said absolutely nothing whatsoever. It was Mark David Chapman, whose only action was to push a copy of Lennon's *Double Fantasy* album into the hands of the former Beatle. Lennon, always willing to meet with fans, signed the album, which seemingly satisfied Chapman, who went on his way—as did John and Yoko.

Shortly before 11:00 P.M., the pair returned to the Dakota hotel. Chapman was still there, hanging around since Lennon gave him an autograph just a few hours earlier. Yoko exited the limousine first, and John followed. Tragedy was only mere moments away. As Lennon passed Chapman—and apparently recognized him from earlier—the words "Mr. Lennon!" rang out. Lennon turned in time to see Chapman assuming a combat-style position and gripping a pistol with both hands. It was all too late, however.

Chapman—who later said that, at that very moment, he heard a voice in his head say "Do it, do it, do it!"—fired on Lennon. Two bullets slammed into his back and two more into his left shoulder. Chapman had chosen his method of killing Lennon carefully. Chapman's pistol was loaded with hollow-tipped bullets, which are designed to cause maximum, pulverizing damage. They did exactly that. Lennon, covered in blood and fatally injured, managed to stagger up the steps of the hotel, collapsing as he uttered the words, "I'm shot." For his part, Chapman simply removed his hat and coat and sat down on the sidewalk.

It became clear to all those present—which included the Dakota's concierge, Jay Hastings, and the doorman, José Sanjenís Perdomo, formerly an agent of both Cuba's secret police and the CIA—that Lennon needed immediate emergency attention. There wasn't even a second to lose. Police officers James Moran and Bill Gamble were quickly on the scene and raced Lennon to St. Luke's Roosevelt Hospital Center. Although Lennon was initially vaguely conscious in the back of the pair's car, he soon slipped into complete unconsciousness.

Despite the very best efforts of the responding doctors and nurses, Lennon could not be saved. The sheer level of destruction to his internal organs, arteries, and blood vessels sealed his fate back at the Dakota. As for Chapman, although a battery of psychologists deemed him psychotic (five of whom stated he was suffering from full-blown schizophrenia), he was perceived as able to stand trial. He pleaded guilty to the murder of John Lennon and received a sentence of twenty-five years to life. Chapman remains incarcerated to this day, despite having had seven parole hearings—all of which ended in denials. And now we come to the most controversial aspect of the shooting of John Lennon.

The *Atomic Poet* website notes: "After Mark David Chapman shot and killed John Lennon, he calmly opened up *Catcher in the Rye* and proceeded to read it—before being apprehended. John Hinckley, the man who attempted to kill Ronald Reagan, also was in possession of the book. It is also alleged that Lee Harvey Oswald was quite fond of the book, though this is disputed. *Catcher in the Rye* has sold 65 million copies. Of the millions who have enjoyed the book, perhaps three have become well-known assassins. Still, we should ask: is there any merit to the book being an assassination trigger?"

Writer Aidan Doyle says: "There are enough rumors about murders linked to J. D. Salinger's classic that the unwitting assassins in the Mel Gibson film *Conspiracy Theory* are portrayed as being brainwashed with the urge to buy the novel. John Lennon's murderer, Mark David Chapman, was famously

Shown here just moments before he was shot by John Hinckley Jr., President Ronald Reagan leaves the Washington Hilton Hotel after a speaking engagement. Just behind him on the left is Press Secretary James Brady, who was shot in the head and seriously wounded.

obsessed with *The Catcher in the Rye*. Chapman wanted to change his name to Holden Caulfield and once wrote in a copy of the book 'This is my statement,' and signed the protagonist's name. He had a copy of the book in his possession when the police arrested him."

But why, exactly, should the book have any bearing on Chapman's crazed killing of John Lennon? Conspiracy theorists maintain that trained, mind-controlled assassins born out of the CIA's controversial MKUltra program are "switched on" by certain key "trigger words" that appear in the text of *The Catcher in the Rye*. Lawrence Wilson, MD, notes that a "hypnotist can implant the suggestion that when the phone rings twice, or when the doorbell rings, a post-hypnotic suggestion such as to kill whomever is in the room, even if it is your wife, will go into effect. This is used by some foreign police agencies to train hypnotized assassins." Hence the theory that Chapman may have been a victim of deep hypnosis on the part of MKUltra operatives. But rather than relying on a phone or doorbell ringing, they used segments of *The Catcher in the Rye* as the trigger that turned Chapman into a ruthless killer, one who had no control over his deadly actions on December 8, 1980.

After the breakup of the Beatles, John Lennon (pictured) and his wife moved to the Dakota Apartments in New York, where the beloved musician met his end.

The blog *CIA Killed Lennon* states: "While a teenager in Decatur, Georgia, Chapman did a lot of LSD, then found Jesus, and devoted his life to working with the YMCA, which, according to Philip Agee (*CIA Diary*, 1975), was prime recruiting grounds for CIA stations in Latin America. Chapman's YMCA employment records are missing. In June 1975, Chapman volunteered to work in the YMCA office in Beirut, Lebanon, as the civil war erupted. Returning to the U.S., Chapman was sent to work with newly resettled Vietnamese refugees (and CIA assets) in Fort Chaffee, Arkansas, run by World Vision, an evangelical organization accused of CIA collaboration in Honduras and El Salvador."

Let's not forget, too, that the doorman at the Dakota hotel, José Sanjenís Perdomo, had worked with both Cuba's secret police and the CIA. On the matter of Perdomo, *Rumor Mill News* stated in 2004:

Newly discovered information about doorman José Perdomo suggests he may have been John Lennon's true assassin and Mark David Chapman was merely a patsy who confessed to the crime while under the spell of relentless mind control techniques such as hypnosis, drug abuse, shock treatment, sleep deprivation, and so on. Perdomo was tasked to provide security for Lennon at the rock star's upscale apartment complex, the Dakota, the night of the murder. Records reveal a "José Joaquín Sanjenis Perdomo" (aliases: "Joaquín Sanjenis" and "Sam Jenis") was an anti-Castro Cuban exile and member of Brigade 2506 during the Bay of Pigs Invasion in 1961, a failed CIA operation to overthrow Fidel Castro.

To understand why someone may have wished to see John Lennon terminated, we have to turn to the writings of British conspiracy theorist Jon King:

In his book *Who Killed John Lennon?* author Fenton Bresler presents evidence that the former Beatle's death was not the work of a 'lone nut', but that Mark David Chapman was a CIA asset and that the CIA itself—or a faction within it—was behind the assassination. Bresler cites Lennon's political activism as a primary motive.

In support of his claim, Bresler quotes late radio host, Mae Brussell, who broke the Watergate scandal, along with *Washington Post* reporters Bob Woodward and Carl Bernstein.

"It was a conspiracy," Brussell affirmed. "Reagan had just won the election. They knew what kind of president he was going to be. There was only one man who could bring out a million people on demonstration in protest at his policies—and that was Lennon."

Indeed, a year after Lennon's death, CIA-backed forces famously massacred more than a thousand civilians in El Salvador, where America was busy fighting a particularly dirty war.

Lennon was opposed to that war, and word is the White House feared he may have spoilt the party had he remained alive and resumed his role as a political activist—which, according to those closest to him, he was planning to do.

Now declassified FBI surveillance files on John Lennon make it very clear that the man was not at all approved of in official quarters. Both the Bureau and President Richard M. Nixon viewed Lennon as a troublesome agitator. As a result, and as the papers that have surfaced through the Freedom of Information Act show, a number of attempts were made to try to find substantial dirt on Lennon that would allow the government to send him back to England. One area of investigation that was followed revolved around various financial donations that Lennon had made to left-wing groups in the United States. This angered the FBI but was not seen as something strong enough to have Lennon deported. Drug-based charges certainly would have worked, but the Bureau was never in a position to firmly pin anything on Lennon.

One issue that was of particular concern to the FBI was the fact that in 1972, Lennon had donated money to a group called the Election Year Strategy Information Center (EYSIC). The FBI noted in its files: "The Election Year Strategy Information Center has been formed to direct movement activities during coming election year to culminate with demonstrations at Republican National Convention, August next. Sources advise John Lennon, former member of The Beatles singing group, has contributed seventy-five thousand dollars to assist in formation of EYSIC."

The FBI shared this data with the Immigration and Naturalization Service, as the following 1972 memo demonstrates: "EYSIC, apparently dedicated to creating dis-

The Imagine Memorial in New York's Central Park is dedicated to John Lennon.

ruptions during Republican National Convention, obviously being heavily influenced by John Lennon, British citizen who is currently in U.S. attempting to obtain U.S. citizenship. Inasmuch as he is attempting to stay permanently in U.S., it is anticipated pertinent information concerning him will be disseminated to State and INS."

The battle to have Lennon deported continued.

On March 16, 1972, the following was prepared by the FBI's Communications Section: "On March 16th Mr Vincent Schiano, Chief Trial Attorney, Immigration and Naturalization Service, New York City advised that John Lennon and his wife Yoko Ono appeared at INS, NYC, this date for deportation proceedings. Both individuals thru their attorney won delays on hearings. Lennon requested delay while he attempted to fight a narcotics conviction in England. Yoko Ono requested delay on basis of child custody case in which she is involved. Mr Schiano advised that new hearings would be held on April 18 next. If Lennon wins overthrow of British narcotic conviction, INS will reconsider their attempts to deport Lennon and wife."

Three days later, the FBI reported: "Lennon and his wife might be preparing for lengthy delaying tactics to avert their deportation in the near future…. Careful attention should be given to reports that he is a heavy narcotics user and any information developed in this regard should be furnished to narcotics authorities and immediately furnished to Bureau."

It was all to no avail, however. In 1974, the FBI finally relented—in the face of no direct, incriminating evidence of outright criminal activity on the part of Lennon—and the legendary Beatle was allowed to stay in the States. Sadly, as we have seen, Lennon's stay was not for long.

For those who cannot bring themselves to accept that Chapman's actions were due to subliminal programming, it's worth noting the 1942 words of Dr. George Estabrooks, Ph.D., chairman of the Department of Psychology at Colgate University: "I can hypnotize a man, without his knowledge or consent, into committing treason against the United States."

If a person could be hypnotized into committing treason against the United States at the dawning of the 1940s, then hypnotizing someone into a similar state four decades later—and having them kill a famous rock star known for his political activism and his ability to influence the mindset of millions—seems not so unlikely after all.

SCIENTISTS WHO DROPPED LIKE FLIES

To many, it might sound like the ultimate plotline of a conspiracy thriller: dozens of scientists and technicians, all working on highly classified programs and linked to one company, dead under controversial and unusual circumstances. But these real-life events occurred from the early 1970s to 1991 and remain unresolved to this very day. The deaths center around the top-secret work of Marconi Electronic Systems, which today is part of BAE Systems Electronics Limited. Its work includes the development of futuristic weaponry and spy-satellite technology.

As far as can be ascertained, the first to die was Robert Wilson, who, by 1971, had carved for himself a successful career with Marconi, specifically at its facility in Chelmsford, England. By that time, however, Wilson was ready to move on and take his work to a new level and to a new company. This decision may have spelled his doom. One Sunday afternoon the following year, as Wilson was tidying up his attic, he stumbled upon a stash of files from his old employer. He could not imagine how they got there and, deeply worried, contacted Marconi. A major investigation was quickly launched.

Although Marconi's security staff members were seemingly satisfied that this was simply a case of Wilson having misplaced the files and forgotten about them, the story was about to quickly turn both tragic and sinister. Less than twenty-four hours later, Wilson put a bullet into his chest. He was cleaning a loaded gun when it accidentally discharged. Luckily for Wilson, the bullet missed his heart and vital arteries, and he survived. But a year later, Wilson's body was found in his garage, the result of carbon-monoxide poisoning.

Wilson's death was quickly followed by the passing of yet another employee of the same Chelmsford facility, Jack Darlow. Whereas Wilson had shot himself in the chest, Darlow had stabbed himself with a long, sharp blade. Death came quickly. There was then a lull in the deaths, but by 1982, they returned with a vengeance.

In March 1982, Professor Keith Bowden, whose computer expertise made him a valuable employee of Marconi, lost his life in a car accident. His vehicle left a three-lane highway at high speed and slammed into a railway line. Death was instantaneous. In March 1985, Roger Hill, a draughtsman with Marconi, died of a shotgun blast. His death was ruled a suicide. Just months later, the body of Jonathan Wash, an employee of a department within British Telecom that had extensive links to Marconi, was found dead on the sidewalk of an Abidjan, Ivory Coast, hotel. Wash had fallen, or was pushed, from the balcony of his room. Wash had told friends and family he believed someone was watching and following him, and he suspected his life was in danger, adding to the suspicions that his death was not due to accident or suicide.

In 1986, the death toll increased dramatically. On August 4, a highly regarded young man named Vimal Bhagvangi Dajibhai jumped to his death from England's Clifton Suspension Bridge into the deep waters below. Dajibhai held a secret clearance with Marconi Underwater Systems, a subsidiary of the main company. Approximately eight weeks later, one of the most grisly of all the Marconi scientist deaths occurred. The victim was computer programmer Arshad Sharif. The terrible and bizarre nature of Sharif's death even made the news thousands of miles away in the United States. The *Los Angeles Times* reported that Sharif "died in macabre circumstances … when he apparently tied one end of a rope around a tree and the other around his neck, then got into his car and stepped on the accelerator. An inquest ruled suicide."

Marconi stock was very valuable during the growth of the company and the new technology it developed during World War II, but things changed when the SDI Program ("Star Wars") was developed. Marconi's talent pool was decimated by a mysterious series of employee deaths.

The coroner in the Sharif case, Donald Hawkins, commented wryly on the fact that Marconi was experiencing an extraordinary number of odd deaths: "As James Bond would say—this is beyond coincidence."

As the months progressed, so did the deaths. The case of Dr. John Brittan was particularly disturbing, since he had *two* run-ins with death, the second of which he did not survive. On Christmas 1986, Brittan ended up in a ditch after his car violently and inexplicably lurched across the road. He was lucky to survive. Sadly, though, this was merely a respite. Less than two weeks into January 1987 (and immediately after Brittan returned to the United Kingdom from the States, where he had been on official, secret business), Brittan's body was found in his garage. He was the unfortunate victim of the effects of deadly carbon monoxide.

Also dead in January 1987 was Richard Pugh, a computer expert who had done work for Marconi and whose death the Ministry of Defense dismissed with the following words: "We have heard about him but he had nothing to do with us."

Then there is the extremely weird saga of Avtar Singh-Gida. An employee of the British Ministry of Defense who worked on a number of Marconi programs, he vanished from his home in Loughborough, England, around the same time that Brittan had died. His family feared the worst. Fortunately, Singh-Gida did not turn up dead. He was found, bafflingly, in Paris fifteen weeks later. He had no memory of where he had been or what he had done during that period.

The deaths of Brittan, Dajibhai, and Sharif—coupled with the odd case of Singh-Gida—prompted a member of Parliament, John Cartwright, to state authoritatively that the deaths "stretch the possibility of mere coincidence too far."

Cartwright's words proved to be eerily prophetic.

On February 22, 1987, Peter Peapell, a lecturer at the Royal College of Military Science, who had been consulted by Marconi on various projects, was yet another figure whose death was due to carbon monoxide poisoning in his own garage. In the same month, David Skeels, a Marconi engineer, was found dead under *identical* circumstances. Victor Moore was attached to Marconi Space and Defense Systems at the time of his February 1987 death, reportedly of a drug overdose. At the time, he was said to be under investigation by MI5, the British equivalent of the FBI.

One month later, in March 1987, David Sands killed himself under truly horrific circumstances. He was in the employ of Elliott Automation Space and Advanced Military Systems Ltd., which had a working relationship with Marconi at the time. Sands, whose family and colleagues said he was exhibiting no signs of stress or strain, loaded his car with containers of gasoline and drove—at "high voltage," as the police worded it—into an empty restaurant. A fiery death was inevitable.

In April 1987, there was yet another death, this time of an employee of the Royal College of Military Science. Stuart Gooding's car slammed head-on into a truck on the island of Cyprus. Colleagues of Gooding expressed doubt at the accidental death verdict. On the very same day that Gooding died, David Greenhalgh died after falling (or being pushed) off a railway bridge at Maidenhead, Berkshire. Greenhalgh just happened to be working on the same program as David Sands.

Just seven days after Greenhalgh and Gooding died, and only a short distance away, Shani Warren took her last breaths. Warren worked for Micro Scope, a company taken over by Marconi just weeks later. Despite being found in just a foot and a half of water and with a gag in her mouth, her feet bound, and her hands tied behind her back, the incredible official verdict was suicide.

On May 3, 1987, Michael Baker was killed in a car "accident" in Dorset, England. He worked on classified programs for Plessey. Twelve years later, Plessey became a part of British Aerospace when the latter combined with Marconi. Ten months after, Trevor Knight, who worked for Marconi Space and Defense Systems in Stanmore, Middlesex, England, died—as had so many others—from carbon monoxide poisoning in his garage. There were other unexplained deaths in 1988: midway through the year, Brigadier Peter Ferry (a business-development manager with Marconi) and Plessey's Alistair Beckham both killed themselves via electrocution. And finally, there was the mysterious 1991 death of Malcolm Puddy. He had told his bosses at Marconi he had stumbled on something amazing. What that was, no one knows. Within twenty-four hours, Puddy was dead. His body was hauled out of a canal near his home.

So, what was the cause of such a huge catalog of mysterious and sinister deaths? Here is where we reach decidedly controversial territory.

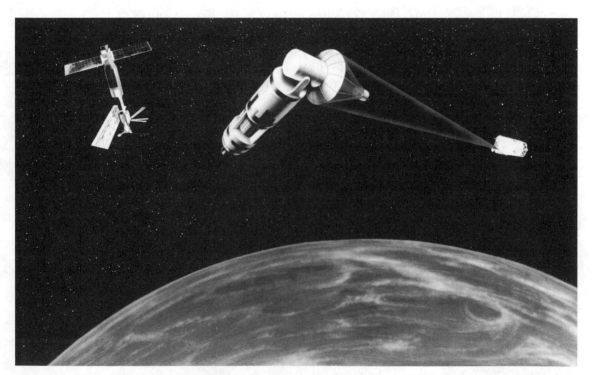

This is a 1984 concept drawing of how the SDI system would use lasers to deter nuclear attacks from enemies such as the USSR.

It's an undeniable fact that many of those who met untimely ends were working with the U.S.-based Strategic Defense Initiative (SDI) program championed by President Ronald Reagan. (It famously became known as "Star Wars.") Even those who weren't directly allied to SDI were employed on issues that were tangential to the project, such as advanced laser-based technologies, and outer space-based operations for the British Ministry of Defense.

The Department of Defense's Missile Defense Agency (MDA) notes of "Star Wars" that "by the early eighties, a number of strategic analysts had begun to worry that the Soviets had achieved a first strike capability that would allow them to cripple U.S. strategic forces and still retain enough nuclear weapons to destroy America's cities. In February 1983, this situation led the Joint Chiefs of Staff to recommend to President Ronald Reagan that the U.S. begin to place greater emphasis in its strategic plans on developing missile defenses.

"President Reagan was highly receptive to this recommendation. In a nationally televised speech on March 23, 1983, the president announced his decision to initiate an expanded research and development program to see if strategic defenses were feasible.

"In April 1984, following a year of technical and strategic studies to determine how best to pursue the president's goal, the Defense Department established the Strategic Defense Initiative Organization (SDIO) under the leadership of its first director, Lieutenant General James A. Abrahamson of the U.S. Air Force. This organization was to carry out the SDI program of research and development (R&D) to resolve the feasibility issue. After two and a half years of R&D, at the end of 1986 the President and Secretary of Defense decided to enter a missile defense system into the defense acquisition process. SDIO began to develop defenses against widespread missile attacks."

Thus was born the Strategic Defense Initiative. Things did not work out quite as well as President Reagan had hoped, however. Overly ambitious and lacking in adequate technologies to bring it to fruition, it was placed on the back burner, ultimately mutating into the Clinton-era Ballistic Missile Defense Organization, which has since been reorganized as the aforementioned Missile Defense Agency.

Conspiracy theorists suggest that at the height of SDI research, the former Soviet Union became deeply concerned by the distinct possibility that its entire nuclear arsenal might very well be rendered useless by an orbiting armada of laser-based weapons. In this scenario, the Soviets made a deadly and controversial decision: they decided to assassinate just about as many people as conceivably possible who were linked to the SDI program—from those directly involved to those only tangentially attached. But how could such a thing have been achieved? How could so many seemingly tragic suicides actually be murder? What of those car crashes? How were the Russians able to engineer such events? The answer may lie in the field of mind control.

Whistle-blowers have suggested the answers to the deaths of the Marconi personnel can be found in the pages of a formerly classified U.S. Defense Intelligence Agency document, dated March 1976: "Biological Effects of Electromagnetic Radiation (Radiowaves and Microwaves)"—Eurasian Communist Countries. Written by Ronald L. Adams and Dr. R. A. Williams of the U.S. Army (and specifically of the Medical Intelligence and Information Agency), it notes in part:

"The Eurasian Communist countries are actively involved in evaluation of the biological significance of radio-waves and microwaves. Most of the research being conducted involves animals or in vitro evaluations, but active programs of a retrospective nature designed to elucidate the effects on humans are also being conducted."

Of deep concern to the United States was the incredible revelation that the Soviets had developed technology that allowed them to beam "messages" into the minds of targeted individuals. Rather notably, the DIA and the Army concluded that such messages might direct a person to commit suicide. Even if the person was not depressed, said Adams and Williams, the technology could be utilized to plunge them into sudden states of "irritability, agitation, tension, drowsiness, sleeplessness, depression, anxiety, forgetfulness, and lack of concentration."

The authors added: "Sounds and possibly even words which appear to be originating intracranially can be induced by signal modulation at very low average-power densities."

They concluded: "The Soviets will continue to investigate the nature of internal sound perception. Their research will include studies on perceptual distortion and other psycho-physiological effects. The results of these investigations could have military applications if the Soviets develop methods for disrupting or disturbing human behavior."

Were the Marconi personnel wiped out by a Soviet hit squad, one that was determined to do its absolute utmost to ensure the SDI program failed? As incredible and as sci-fi-like as it seems, that just might have been *exactly* what happened.

THE MARCONI MYSTERY GROWS

We now come to what is undeniably the weirdest story in the saga of the Strategic Defense Initiative and mysterious deaths in the defense industry, specifically those connected to Marconi. It's a tale that came from Gordon Creighton, who moved effortlessly in the fields of UFOs and U.K. government secrecy. Indeed, when he retired from the government, his interests in UFOs expanded massively, to the point that he became the editor of the long-running publication *Flying Saucer Review*. When Creighton died in 2003, the United Kingdom's prestigious newspaper *The Times*, published a notable obituary, which, in part, read as follows:

> Government service occupied most of the working life of Gordon Creighton, but he perhaps made his greatest mark as an authority on unidentified flying objects. His conviction that extraterrestrials were visiting Earth seemed oddly at variance with the more orthodox worlds of diplomacy and Whitehall.... His expertise took him into government research on maps in oriental and other languages with the Permanent Committee on Geographical Names, and he spent eight years as an intelligence officer on Russian and Chinese affairs at the Ministry of Defense. It is said that in the intelligence post he worked directly below the secret Whitehall department where the Air Ministry and the RAF were studying information on UFOs.

When Creighton first immersed himself in the subject of UFOs in the 1940s, he believed that the phenomenon was extraterrestrial in nature. Over time, however, his views on the subject began to change to a radical and incredible degree. Certainly by the late 1970s, Creighton was convinced that the phenomenon had supernatural origins. Specifically, he came to believe that the mystery had its origins in the world of the Middle Eastern Djinn, from which the term "genie" is taken.

Rosemary Ellen Guiley, who died in July 2019, was an expert in the field of the Djinn and its history. She said: "In Arabian lore, djinn (also spelled jinn) are a race of supernaturally empowered beings who have the ability to intervene in the affairs of people. Like the Greek daimones, djinn are self-propagating and can be either good or evil. They can be conjured in magical rites to perform various tasks and services. A djinni (singular) appears as a wish-granting 'genie' in folk tales such as in The Book of 1001 Nights collection of folk tales."

She added: "In Western lore djinn are sometimes equated with demons, but they are not the same. They are often portrayed as having a demonic-like appearance, but they can also appear in beautiful, seductive forms. The djinn are masterful shape-shifters, and their favored forms are snakes and black dogs. They also can masquerade as anything: humans, animals, ghosts, cryptids, *and other entities such as extraterrestrials* [italics mine], demons, shadow people, fairies, angels and more."

There is also this from Guiley: "[They] are born of smokeless fire (which in modern terms could be plasma). They live very long lives but they are not immortal. According to some accounts, they live with other supernatural beings in the Kaf, a mythical range of emerald mountains that encircles the Earth. In modern terms, they live in a parallel dimension."

All of this brings us directly back to Gordon Creighton.

An F-4J Phantom II carries a target vehicle near Holloman Air Force Base in New Mexico as part of the Flexible Lightweight Agile Guided Experiment Project, which would later be incorporated into the SDI program. This image was taken in 1986 and represents a part of Reagan's Strategic Defense Initiative.

When the controversy surrounding the Marconi deaths was at its peak—and the subject of considerable media attention in the United Kingdom—Creighton made tantalizing allusions to the matter of the deaths and his suspicions that they were the work of deadly Djinn. Their purpose: to derail Reagan's Strategic Defense Initiative—"Star Wars." When Creighton came out with his controversial theories, I contacted him, as I had been following the Marconi saga, too. He had quite a tale to tell, which is putting matters mildly.

Creighton was of the belief that many of the deaths of Marconi personnel in the 1980s were the results of suicides. But as Creighton also saw things, they were not what one could call normal suicides. By that, he meant that deadly Djinn were mind-controlling the victims and forcing them to commit suicide as a means to slow down the progress on the Star Wars program. We're talking about a Djinn-based version of the CIA's MKUltra: a plan to enslave the minds of their targets and force them to take their own lives. Compounding things more, Creighton suspected that it wasn't just the Djinn who were hunting down the Marconi people but rather Russian assassination squads. In light of that, and if true, it's no wonder so many Marconi employees died in such a short time and under bizarre circumstances.

But if the Djinn are supernatural entities that live in other dimensions and are plasma-based, rather than being of flesh and blood, then how could the technology planned for the Strategic Defense Initiative affect them? Creighton had formulated a theory, based on what he claimed was information provided by three Marconi whistleblowers who had spent time at Area 51 in the early 1980s, working secretly with their American colleagues. While Creighton's revelations on this particular issue are limited in content—which he said was a result of his desire to protect his whistleblowers—they are still highly thought provoking. Creighton said that his shadowy informants had told him that one of the weapons being designed to destroy the Djinn presence on Earth by using weaponry designed for SDI could—as Creighton worded it—"disrupt the Djinn's [plasma-based] form."

The weirdness didn't end there. It had barely begun.

Things got even stranger. Creighton asserted that elements of British intelligence, at the height of SDI research in the 1980s, secretly consulted with experts on the Djinn. This allegedly led to contact with such creatures and a sort of "Faustian pact" between powerful figures here on Earth and the Djinn. The plan was to try to ensure a truce—albeit, probably, an uneasy truce—between the western world's military and the Djinn. The Djinn would agree to hold off on unleashing a "worldwide deception" and a "planetary invasion" if an agreement was made that SDI would not proceed. Western governments grudgingly agreed and were also forced to turn a blind eye to such things as Djinn-driven "alien abductions" and "cattle mutilations," added Creighton.

If you think things could not get any weirder, then you're wrong. Creighton made the astonishing claim that at least some of the Marconi deaths were the work of malevolent Djinn and also of British intelligence—both seeking to ensure that the aims of the "pact" (the end of SDI) were achieved. Yes, it's quite a story, one involving Russian assassins, U.K. assassins, and even Djinn assassins! It's no wonder that years after I interviewed Creighton, I still ponder on his story.

But pondering on it doesn't mean it's the absolute truth. Or even anywhere near it. For example, assuming that Djinn are real, all-powerful, and manipulators of the human race, why would they even need to enter into some kind of Faustian agreement in the first place? Why not simply wipe out the SDI people directly and avoid any kind of "negotiation" with government officials? And, of course, the idea of Djinn and government officials "negotiating" on the SDI program sounds beyond surreal. And I remain puzzled with regard to Creighton's claim that the ultimately ill-fated SDI program had the ability to wipe out plasma-based entities from some completely different realm of existence.

In conclusion, I would have to say that Gordon Creighton clearly believed that the UFO phenomenon was Djinn based. And I believe that Creighton had insider sources in Marconi who spent time at Area 51 in the early 1980s. I have no doubt of that. To what extent his theories concerning SDI, the Marconi deaths, and the Djinn had any merit, however, is anyone's guess. The whole thing lacks verification, and the bulk of the story came from Creighton himself and from certain unnamed "sources." Maybe it was just a theory on his part and nothing else.

On the other hand, could there be a nugget or several of truth in Creighton's thoughts and conclusions? Yes, there certainly could be. Creighton was no fool. He did move in high and influential circles in the military and intelligence services of the United Kingdom. Is the big secret concerning UFOs that they're not extraterrestrial but supernatural?

DEATH ON THE SPACE SHUTTLE

At 11:39 A.M. EST on January 28, 1986, the space shuttle *Challenger* suffered an unmitigated disaster only seventy-three seconds into its flight, disintegrated over the Atlantic Ocean, and led to the tragic deaths of its seven crew members: commander Dick Scobee, pilot Michael J. Smith, mission specialists Ronald McNair, Judith Resnik, and Ellison Onizuka, and payload specialists Gregory Jarvis and Christa McAuliffe. As NASA's investigation concluded, the disintegration of the shuttle began when an O-ring seal in its right solid rocket booster failed at the moment of liftoff and caused a breach in the joint that it sealed, thus allowing pressurized hot gas from within the solid rocket motor to reach the outside and impinge upon the external fuel tank. This, in turn, led to the structural failure of the same external tank, and unstoppable and inevitable tragedy and death were the only possible outcomes.

Not everyone was convinced the event was an accident, however, as the Freedom of Information Act has now demonstrated. In the immediate wake of the affair, the FBI's Washington Field Office found itself embroiled in a very curious saga relative to the destruction of the shuttle.

The story is a truly odd one, indeed, involving psychic phenomena and the presence of a distinctly shadowy and all-powerful Japanese terrorist group. Interestingly, several extracts from the FBI file on this particularly odd affair have been summarily blacked out for reasons specifically relative to the national security of the United States. And with that all outlined, now read on.

According to the heavily redacted documentation that the FBI has been willing to release into the public domain, a source of some standing, one that was apparently very well known to Bureau agents, had come into contact with a woman—whose name the FBI has been extremely careful to completely delete from the available papers—who "claims to be in contact with certain psychic forces that provide her with higher information on selected subjects. She refers to these forces as 'Source' and when providing information from Source she often speaks in the collective 'we.' [The woman] claimed that she had come to Washington, D.C. to provide information concerning the *Challenger* Space Shuttle explosion on 1/28/86."

The FBI continued:

On 2/24/86, [the woman] was debriefed concerning the information she wished to reveal. The enclosed audio tape [Note: which the FBI has not yet declassified] is a record of that entire session and is self-explanatory. The following points are emphasized during the course of the briefing:

(A) The Space Shuttle explosion was not the result of a technical malfunction. Rather, it was an act of sabotage perpetrated by a terrorist organization.

(B) There were three saboteurs on the scene at Cape Canaveral. These included two ground crewmen and one of the astronauts who died in the explosion.

(C) The terrorist organization is a Japanese based fanatical group with an ancestral lineage and a deep seated hatred toward the United States. Its motivation in destroying the Shuttle was to embarrass and discredit the United States and to impede the progress of the space program.

(D) The three saboteurs were all of oriental heritage. They were apparently recruited by the terrorist organization after their employment by NASA.

(E) The explosion was effected by a device placed inside the external fuel tank of the Shuttle. An individual whose description seems to match that of an engineer or technician placed this charge. The charge was triggered by a second saboteur using a hand-held transmitter while standing in the crowds watching the Shuttle liftoff. The individual matches the description of a guard or security person.

(F) The astronaut saboteur chose to die in the explosion as a sort of ritual death or "cleansing".

(G) The descriptions of the saboteurs provided by [source] are probably complete enough to pinpoint the individuals. Although names and addresses are not available, in the case of the "guard" [source] pinpointed his residence on a 1:24,000 scale topographical map of an area of Florida near

Cape Canaveral. She also provided a description of his physical appearance as well as his life style. While actual names are difficult for source to acquire [source] claims she could easily identify the saboteurs from a list of names if NASA could provide one.

(H) Source's motivation in revealing this information is to assure the United States that its space program is a safe undertaking and that there is no major technical flaw in the Shuttle equipment.... Source is concerned about possible lengthy delays in the progress of the space program that will allow other nations to surge ahead. [Source] predicted that wreckage of the Shuttle will be found within the next several days that will support the sabotage allegation.

In essence, that is the extent of the declassified material on this particularly unusual, highly controversial, and probably unique conspiracy theory;

The quiet before the storm as the ill-fated space shuttle Challenger is slowly moved into position prior to launch on January 28, 1986.

but even though most may scoff at its contents, it's notable that the FBI has admitted to withholding in their entirety, in the specific name of national security, twenty-six pages of secret documentation on this weird saga. Is this notable food for thought or merely the result of overwhelming bureaucracy? Some might say the jury is still out. Why? Well, there's another death attached to all of this. Yet again, it's a weird story that may have conspiratorial overtones attached to it.

Born into an Air Force family in the town of Roswell, New Mexico, in 1943, Henry John Deutschendorf Jr. gained worldwide fame as singer–guitarist John Denver, who is perhaps best known for his hits "Take Me Home, Country Roads"; "Rocky Mountain High"; "Thank God, I'm a Country Boy"; and "Leaving on a Jet Plane," the latter having been recorded by Peter, Paul and Mary, which reached number one on the charts. As Denver's popularity grew in the 1970s, so did his passion for politics and pressing social and humanitarian issues. This passion led the world of officialdom to take note of the man's activities, as a May 22, 1975, document generated as a result of interagency interest in Denver makes abundantly clear. According to the document, a "Dump the War Rally" took place at the Metropolitan Sports Arena in Bloomington, Minnesota, on May 23, 1971. Among those listed as speakers were U.S. representative Paul McCloskey, former U.S. representative Allard Lowenstein, former U.S. senator Eugene J. McCarthy, U.S. representative Donald Riegle, and former Navy lieutenant (and, later, U.S. senator, presidential candidate, and secretary of state) John Kerry.

An article had appeared in the May 3, 1971, issue of the *Minneapolis Star* that quoted the rally sponsors denying that "the antiwar rally is part of a 'dump Nixon movement.'" Nevertheless, government files reveal that "Wheelock Whitney, a Republican leader, would not endorse this rally because he considers it a 'dump Nixon effort.'"

Official papers further noted that a spokesman for the Bipartisan Caucus to End the War had said "We're not waiting for November 1972" and that the same spokesman had informed the *Minneapolis Star* that it wanted to "persuade the political animal who holds the presidency to change his course of action before the election."

In this case, officialdom took no action, beyond filing the data for potential future reference, and the "Denver File" (which ultimately ran to thirty-three pages) seems to have remained largely inactive until December 1979, when the FBI reported that threats had been made to kill the singer: "Approximately seventeen threatening phone calls directed at singer John Denver have been received in Los Angeles since December 1, 1979. A female, speaking German and English has called daily from Germany demanding first to speak to Denver and then stating that her mother's boyfriend is coming to

Los Angeles to kill Denver. John Denver, who is presently at his home in Aspen, Colorado, is aware of the threats."

Aside from politics and humanitarian issues, Denver's other big passion was outer space. He even took, and notably passed, NASA's physical and mental examination to determine if he was fit enough to cope with the extreme rigors of a journey into space. As a result, he almost made it onto the *Challenger* space shuttle. Denver was ultimately not selected, which prevented him from joining the ill-fated January 1986 mission that ended in utter disaster. This event led to an FBI investigation of the accident that ran to 170 pages.

There is a genuinely weird saga in the life and career of John Denver that touches upon official secrecy and that deserves to be mentioned. One of those aboard the tragic *Challenger* space shuttle flight that Denver

The late country/western singer John Denver received a number of death threats, according to an FBI file, because of his positions on social and humanitarian issues.

almost got to travel on was astronaut Ellison Onizuka. He had told his close friend Chris Coffey that, while serving in the Air Force at McClelland Air Force Base in 1973, Onizuka had viewed a piece of black-and-white film footage that showed alien bodies on slabs. They were alien bodies not unlike those supposedly recovered from a crashed UFO by the military in 1947 at Roswell, New Mexico, Denver's hometown. Denver was rumored to have been told of the "aliens on the slab" story by a NASA insider in the summer of 1997. Denver died on October 12, 1997, a few months after hearing about those dead aliens, when his private plane plunged into the ocean near Pacific Grove, California. A curious set of coincidences, to say the least.

Similarly, in his report "UFO Crash/Retrievals: Is the Coverup Lid Lifting?", Leonard Stringfield wrote: "In 1985, Chris Coffey, of Cincinnati, who was a close friend of astronaut Ellison Onizuka, revealed to me that she had asked him when they met after one of his visits to Wright-Patterson AFB, about his interest in UFOs. He admitted he kept an open mind on the subject and added that his curiosity was aroused when he and a select group of air force pilots, at McClelland AFB in 1973, were shown a black-and-white movie film featuring 'alien bodies on a slab.'"

Stringfield continued: "In his state of shock, he said he remembered saying aloud, 'Oh, my God!' Chris, knowing my work in C/R [Crash/Retrievals], had arranged for me to meet Onizuka to discuss UFOs after his scheduled flight on the space shuttle Challenger. As it turned out, fate intervened when the shuttle exploded."

The presidential commission on the tragic Challenger disaster concluded as follows:

> The consensus of the Commission and participating investigative agencies is that the loss of the Space Shuttle *Challenger* was caused by a failure in the joint between the two lower segments of the right Solid Rocket Motor. The specific failure was the destruction of the seals that are intended to prevent hot gases from leaking through the joint during the propellant burn of the rocket motor. The evidence assembled by the Commission indicates that no other element of the Space Shuttle system contributed to this failure.

> In arriving at this conclusion, the Commission reviewed in detail all available data, reports and records; directed and supervised numerous tests, analyses, and experiments by NASA, civilian contractors and various government agencies; and then developed specific failure scenarios and the range of most probable causative factors. The sections that follow discuss the results of the investigation.

> The results of the accident investigation and analysis will be presented in this and the following sections. Throughout the investigation three critical questions were central to the inquiry, namely:

> • What were the circumstances surrounding mission 51-L that contributed to the catastrophic termination of that flight in contrast to 24 successful flights preceding it?

> • What evidence pointed to the right Solid Rocket Booster as the source of the accident as opposed to other elements of the Space Shuttle?

> • Finally, what was the mechanism of failure?

> Using mission data, subsequently completed tests and analyses, and recovered wreckage, the Commission identified all possible faults that could originate in the respective flight elements of the Space Shuttle which might have the potential to lead to loss of the *Challenger*. Potential contributors to the accident examined by the Commission were the launch pad (exonerated in Chapter IX of this report), the External Tank, the Space Shuttle Main Engines, the Orbiter and related equipment, payload/Orbiter interfaces, the payload, Solid Rocket Boosters and Solid Rocket Motors.

In a parallel effort, the question of sabotage was examined in detail and reviewed by the Commission in executive session. There is no evidence of sabotage, either at the launch pad or during other processes prior to or during launch.

On January 29, 1986, a formerly secret document was dispatched to the then-director of the FBI, William H. Webster, by a special agent who was based at the Bureau's Boston, Massachusetts, office that told an extraordinary and controversial story. Two days before the destruction of NASA's Challenger space shuttle on January 28, declassified FBI files now reflect, the newsroom at Boston's Channel 7 television station received a very worrying call from an unnamed source that had a direct bearing on the space shuttle explosion.

It was at 8:35 on the night at issue, recorded the FBI, when "the caller indicated that he was part of a group of three people who were going to sabotage the Shuttle, causing it to blow up and kill all aboard." The FBI—astutely realizing that even if the call was a hoax or fantasy of very bad-taste proportions, it simply could not afford to ignore the matter—quickly ordered a number of its special agents to descend upon Channel 7 with the utmost haste and to speak with the particular person at the station who had taken the call.

The FBI agents extensively interviewed staff members at the station and were told that the mysterious caller said that a series of "horrible, horrible things were going to happen" and that "at least five people are going to be killed" by a secret group that was said to consist of three individuals. The space shuttle Challenger, the caller had starkly claimed to the news channel, was about to fly its very last mission—and it was a mission that was going to end in death and complete tragedy, no less, for all of those who were onboard.

Despite the problematic fact that the man chose to leave no name, the FBI actually had a very good idea of who he might have been, as is clearly evidenced by the following that is extracted from the FBI's files on this particular matter: "During briefing of SAC [Special Agent in Charge], ASAC [Assistant Special Agent in Charge], and appropriate supervisory personnel relative to aforementioned and employment of agent personnel, it was recalled that in September of 1985, a walk in complainant, of questionable mentality, had intimated that he had been responsible for the delay of previous Shuttles, plane crashes and other catastrophic events."

In this photo of the 1986 Challenger catastrophe, the cabin where the astronauts are confined is visible.

The FBI quickly set about trying to find the man—and, luckily, they soon did so. He was found nonchalantly eating dinner at a nearby Frank's Steak House, where he was duly apprehended and arrested. It was noted immediately, and diplomatically, too, by the FBI agents present at the scene, however, that the man was clearly "not in possession of full faculties." As a result, he was released into the specific care of an unnamed, local medical unit for a "five-day mental evaluation." Ultimately, due to his emotional condition, no prosecution was ever brought against the still unidentified individual.

It is ironic that although the man in question was clearly mentally disturbed to a very significant degree, had no real intention of ever blowing up Challenger or any of NASA's other space shuttles and had made similar, previous threats and claims to the effect that one of the shuttles was going to be destroyed (none of which had ever occurred), on this occasion, he got it practically spot-on: shortly after the man's call to the newsroom of Channel 7, the shuttle tragedy occurred.

Sometimes, truth actually is stranger than the wildest of all science-fiction scenarios. Synchronicity? Coincidence? Paranormal prophecy? A conspiracy yet to be unraveled? The jury remains out.

The final word on this particular matter went to the FBI, who recorded, somewhat wearily and warily, one strongly suspects: "It is entirely feasible, and in all probability likely, that [the man] will make similar calls prior to departure of future Space Shuttles." Currently available FBI files, however, do not reflect any evidence that the man at issue crossed paths with agents of the Bureau ever again.

Thus a very strange and once secret saga of the doomed Challenger space shuttle came to a quiet close.

FROM DEVILISH TO DEAD

From 2007 to 2010, I investigated the strange story of a U.S. government think-tank-style group nicknamed the Collins Elite, a story that has its origins in 1991. Its belief is that the UFO phenomenon has demonic origins and that the extraterrestrial angle is merely an ingenious, deceptive ruse employed by Satan. The goal: to further allow his minions to get their claws into us all and lead us down a distinctly dark pathway before Judgment Day and the final countdown begins. As someone who holds no particular views on the nature of religion or life after death, I have no real opinion on the validity of the beliefs of the Collins Elite aside from the fact that I find it fascinating that such a think-tank group actually exists. But what interests me most of all is that a certain theme runs through much of this story that can also be found elsewhere at an official level, and it's one I find somewhat disturbing. It's the matter of strange and suspicious deaths.

I was put on the trail of the Collins Elite by Ray Boeche, an Anglican priest and former state director for Nebraska with the Mutual UFO Network (MUFON). In a truly fascinating interview with Ray in 2007, he told me how he had been clandestinely approached in 1991 by two Department of Defense (DoD) physicists working on a classified program to try to contact what were described to Ray as nonhuman entities (NHEs).

In ufological terms, we would call these entities the diminutive, black-eyed "Grays." For the people on the DoD project, they may very well have begun with that view, too, but ultimately they came around to the notion that this was merely a terrible ruse. Like the Collins Elite, Ray's ufological Deep Throat-like sources finally accepted that the entities at issue were demonic. But there was an interesting and disturbing further aspect to this revelation: there

It was former MUFON state director Ray Boeche who suggested that the Grays (aliens like those illustrated above) were demonic, not extraterrestrial, in origin.

were those on the project who believed that engaging the NHEs in some form of "Faustian pact," as a means to understand and harness their extraordinary and potentially lethal powers, could actually aid in the development of occult-based weapons of war, such as the ability to provoke psychic assassinations.

Ray Boeche believes that the UFO phenomenon has demonic, rather than extraterrestrial, origins. In November 2001, Boeche met two physicists working on a classified program buried deep in the heart of the Department of Defense. The story told to Boeche revolved around attempts on part of the people in that same program to contact NHEs. Some of us might call them aliens. Others, though, might suggest they are demons. I interviewed Boeche extensively about the story. If the story is true, and Boeche was not the subject of a disinformation program, it's mind-blowing and horrifying. He said:

> I found it interesting because they had contacted me at work; and I have no idea how they tracked me down there. But they wanted to know if we could get together and have lunch to discuss something important. I met them for a brief period of time on that first meeting, and then they said: "We'd like to get together and have a longer conversation." I arranged a time and it was quite a lengthy discussion, probably three and a half hours. And that's how it all came about.

> After both meetings, when I was able to verify that the men held the degrees they claimed to hold, and were apparently who they claimed to be, I was intrigued and excited at the possibility of having stumbled on a more or less untouched area which could be researched. But I was also cautious in terms of "why me?"

> I had no way of knowing before our face-to-face meeting if there was any legitimacy to this at all. I wasn't given any information at all before our meeting, just the indication that they were involved in areas of research I would find interesting, and that they had some concerns they wished to discuss with me. Both men were physicists. I'd guess they were probably in their early to mid-fifties, and they were in a real moral dilemma. Both of them were Christians and were working on a Department of Defense project that involved trying to contact the NHEs. In

fact, this was described to me as an "obsessive effort." And part of this effort was to try and control the NHEs and use their powers in military weapons applications and in intelligence areas, such as remote-viewing and psychotronic weapons.

They came to believe that the NHEs were not extraterrestrial at all; they believed they were some sort of demonic entities. And that regardless of how benevolent or beneficial any of the contact they had with these entities *seemed* to be, it always ended up being tainted, for lack of a better term, with something that ultimately turned out to be bad. There was ultimately *nothing* positive from the interaction with the NHE entities. They felt it really fell more under the category of some vast spiritual deception instead of UFOs and aliens. In the course of the whole discussion, it was clear that they really viewed this as having a demonic origin that was there to simply try and confuse the issue in terms of who they were, what they wanted, and what the source of the ultimate truth is. If you extrapolate from their take that these are demons in the biblical sense of the word, then what they would be doing here is trying to create a spiritual deception to fool as many people as possible.

From what they told me, it seemed like someone had invoked something and it opened a doorway to let these things in. That's certainly the impression they gave me. I was never able to get an exact point of origin of these sorts of experiments, or of their involvement, and when they got started. But I did get the impression that because of what they knew and the information that they presented, they had been involved for at least several years, even if the project had gone on for much longer. They were concerned that they had undertaken this initially with the best of intentions, but then as things developed they saw a very negative side to it that wasn't apparent earlier. So, that's what leads me to think they had a relatively lengthy involvement.

Most of it was related to psychotronic weaponry and remote viewing and even deaths by what were supposed to be psychic methods. The project personnel were allowed to assume they had somehow technologically mastered the ability to do what the NHEs could do: remote-viewing and psychotronics. But, in actuality, it was these entities doing it all the time, or allowing it to happen, for purposes that suited their deception. With both psychotronic weapons and remote-viewing, I was told that the DoD had not really mastered a technology to do that at all; they were allowed by the NHEs to think that this is what they had done. But the NHEs were always the causal factor.

They showed me a dozen photos of three different people—four photos of each person, *who had apparently been killed by these experiments* [italics mine]. These were all post-mortem photographs, taken in-situ, after the experiments. The areas shown in all of the photographs were like a dentist's chair or a barber's chair, and the bodies were still in those positions, sitting in the chairs. Still there, with EEG and EKG leads coming off of them. They were all wired. It was a very clinical setting, and there was no indication of who they were. It was a very disturbing sort of thing. And I'm thinking in the back of my mind: if these are real, who would they have gotten for these experiments? Were they volunteers? Were they some sort of prisoners? I have no idea. Were they American? Were they foreign? There was no way to tell.

They had read some of my stuff, and they knew that I'd become a pastor and that I had a Christian viewpoint from which I could examine these things. And they were concerned morally and ethically that they had allowed themselves to be duped into doing this research, and it had taken such a turn. My concern was always that: why come to me? Who am I? I can't do anything for you. I'm happy to evaluate it as best I can, but if you have this concern, why not go to a Christian leader with a lot more clout and public visibility than I've got? But that was their reason: they were aware of the research I had done on a lot of things, that I could approach it from a Christian viewpoint, and that it was more of a moral dilemma for them. They wanted the information out there. But, to me, I have to think: is any of this accurate? On one hand, is this a way to throw disinformation out? But, on the other hand, I think that even if they wanted to just spread disinformation, they could have done it with someone a lot more influential than me.

I've been involved in this since 1965 and this is the most bizarre stuff I've ever run across. I didn't know what to make of it then and I don't know what to make of it now.

Of particular interest are some of Ray Boeche's very own notes made during the period he was liaising with elements of the U.S. Department of Defense. From my own perspective, what follows next may amount to nothing less than attempts to kill powerful figures in the governments of both the United States and the then-Soviet Union via the means of mind manipulation and control. Boeche's papers state:

1972—President Nixon, on his visit to the USSR complained of 'unusual feelings.' His physician, and others in the party also displayed inappropriate behavior, including unaccountable weeping. 1979—President Carter visits Soviet embassy while in Vienna to sign SALT II. Carter began to display bizarre behavior on his return to Washington; cancelling a major speech on energy policy, and suddenly leaving Camp David, where he invited a number of experts for consultation, then suddenly took off for visits with a PA machinist, and a retired Marine in West Virginia. In both instances, intelligence specialists with a knowledge of Soviet psychotronics speculated that both Presidents may have undergone "psychic tampering."

Ray Boeche's notes also reveal the following: "During a speech given by Brezhnev at the Chkalov aircraft factory in Tashkent, a scaffolding which Brezhnev was standing near suddenly collapsed, sending him to the ground.... U.S. intelligence assets in the USSR reported that the scaffolding collapse was an assassination attempt which had been achieved psychotronically."

Now, whether the entities really were demonic, to this day, I truthfully don't know. But I do know that history is absolutely littered with examples where people have dabbled in the realm of the occult as part of a concerted effort to contact entities from beyond the veil, only for things to come crashing down around them. Ill health (both mental and physical), extraordinary long runs of bad luck, disaster and misfortune, utter madness, and even death are all signs of what many term "psychic backlash." And, it seems from what Ray Boeche was told, this was precisely what the DoD project was experiencing—which is why it had major concerns about continuing with such research.

But since the publication of *Final Events*, I have uncovered further, disturbing data suggesting these Faustian pacts are still going on—and have been for a long time. One such story came from a man formerly attached to a U.S. military group known as the Night Stalkers, who maintained that the real purpose behind the cattle-mutilation phenomenon was to appease occult-based entities, with

Soviet leader Leonid Brezhnev was almost killed by falling scaffolding at an aircraft factory, an incident Boeche claimed was a psychotronic assassination attempt.

whom elements of the official world were desperately trying to engage and work. In essence, his story is that the removal of vital organs, and particularly so the blood, from mutilated cattle is not the work of aliens at all—as many within ufology believe is the case. Rather, my source maintained, the culprit is the military itself. The reason, I am told, is so that the the blood and organs may be utilized in ancient, sacrificial appeasement rites to incredibly old deities of a type that can offer something in return: supernatural powers of a type that, if understood and harnessed, may even be weaponized.

This, clearly, is very similar to the central theme of the story provided to Ray Boeche in 1991: namely, making deals with the denizens of a very dark realm as a means to achieve some near-unique military advantage over your potential foes. We see something here that fits right in with Boeche's account and with the cattle-mutilation affair: namely, making a deal with paranormal entities where there is a perceived gain to be made from a military perspective.

I admit that I hold no firm beliefs on the specific nature of other realms of existence, only that I am sure they most assuredly do exist, and they appear to be the domains of entities who do not have our best interests at heart. And as a result, I see absolutely no good at all coming out of a situation where military and government forces have the arrogance to believe they can actually deal with, take on, and exploit these same entities—and, ultimately, achieve something that, from officialdom's perspective, is considered worthwhile: the development and deployment of fantastic, supernatural weaponry.

There is only ever one inevitable, positive outcome of a Faustian pact with supernatural life forms. The problem, however, is that the outcome is only ever positive for *them*, never for *us*. I'll leave you with the words of Ray Boeche, which get to the crux of this very issue: "In an effort to establish contact with non-human entities, every avenue is being explored. *Satanic rituals involving human sacrifice have been performed* [italics mine]."

It should be noted that from the 1960s to the 1970s, a top-secret group similar in nature and scope to the Collins Elite existed. It was code named Operation Often. "During the late 1960s, the CIA experimented with mediums in an attempt to contact and possibly debrief dead CIA agents. These attempts, according to Victor Marchetti, a former high-ranking CIA official, were part of a larger effort to harness psychic powers for various intelligence-related missions that included utilizing clairvoyants to divine the intentions of the Kremlin leadership," wrote Dr. Nelson Pacheco and Tommy Blann in their book *Unmasking the Enemy*. It was also as a result of this series of CIA experiments with mediums, a CIA man named Robert Manners told me, that a shocking and terrifying discovery was made, one that supported the beliefs and theories of the Collins Elite and that also saw its operational abilities and scope increased. Manners pointed out that it is critical to be aware of the time frame of this new development: within the shadowy world of espionage, very strange things of a truly occult-like and demonic nature were pressing ahead during the late 1960s and early 1970s. And to understand and appreciate the precise nature of the matter, Manners said, it's necessary to delve into the world of Dr. Sidney Gottlieb.

In March 1960, under the Cuban Project, a CIA plan approved by President Eisenhower and overseen by the CIA's directorate for plans, Richard M. Bissell, Gottlieb suggested spraying Fidel Castro's television studio with LSD and saturating his shoes with thallium so that his beard would fall out. Gottlieb also hatched schemes to assassinate Castro that would have made the character Q from the James Bond novels and movies proud, including the use of a poisoned cigar, a poisoned wetsuit, an exploding conch shell, and a poisonous fountain pen. History has shown, of course, that all the attempts failed.

U.S. president Dwight Eisenhower approved a CIA plan to spray a Cuban television station with LSD.

But Gottlieb was not finished with assassination attempts. He also worked on a project to have Iraq's General Abd al-Karim Qasim's handkerchief contaminated with botulinum, and he played a role in the CIA's attempt to assassinate Prime Minister Patrice Lumumba of the Republic of the Congo. In the summer of 1960, Gottlieb himself secretly transported certain "toxic biological materials" to the CIA's field station in the Congo. As fate would have it, however, a military coup deposed the prime minister before agents were able to unleash the deadly virus. Almost a decade later, Gottlieb began delving into far darker areas.

In 1969, Robert Manners revealed to me, a unit of scientists attached to the CIA's Office of Research and Development dared to follow the path the TSS had taken a decade and a half earlier in the field of mind control. But the scientists had other, far more controversial plans, several of which involved trying to invade, understand, and harness demonic powers as tools of espionage.

To ensure that the project stood some chance of achieving its unusual aims, Gottlieb approached Richard Helms, the CIA director from 1966 to 1973, and secured a $150,000 grant for the new project, which became known as Operation Often. The curiously named study took its title from the fact that Gottlieb was well known for reminding his colleagues that "*often* we are very close to our goals then we pull back" and "*often* we forget that the only scientific way forward is to learn from the past."

Investigative writer Gordon Thomas said: "Operation Often's roots could be traced back to the research Dr. [Donald Ewen] Cameron had approved in trying to establish links between eye coloring, soil conditions and mental illness." Thomas also noted that when he was given access to Cameron's research and notes after Cameron's death in 1967, Gottlieb was struck by the fact that "Dr. Cameron could have been on the verge of a breakthrough in exploring the paranormal. Operation Often was intended to take over the unfinished work, and go beyond—to explore the world of black magic and the supernatural." And thus, the stage was set for the next act in the U.S. government's involvement in, and understanding of, what they perceived to be the true nature of the UFO presence on Earth.

But who exactly was Dr. Cameron? A Scottish American psychiatrist from Bridge of Allan, Scotland, who graduated from the University of Glasgow in 1924, he later moved to Albany, New York, and—like the Black Sorcerer himself, Dr. Sidney Gottlieb—became involved in the controversial MKUltra. After being recruited by the CIA, Cameron commuted to Montreal, Canada, every week, where he worked at the Allan Memorial Institute of McGill University and was paid $69,000 from 1957 to 1964 to secretly undertake experimentation on specific behalf of MKUltra. It is not surprising, therefore, that Gottlieb picked up some of the strands of Cameron's work after his death in 1967.

As Operation Often progressed, the project began to immerse itself in uncharted waters, and the staff ultimately spent more time mingling with fairground fortune-tellers, palmists, clairvoyants, demonologists, and mediums than they did with fellow agency personnel. By May 1971, the operation even had three astrologers on the payroll—each of whom was paid the tidy sum of $350 per week plus expenses—to regularly review copies of newly published magazines and newspapers in the hope that they might be "psychically alerted" to something of a defense or intelligence nature. And things got even more controversial.

In April 1972, in an effort to understand more about demonology and to ascertain if the subject held any meaningful intelligence applications, two Operation Often operatives clandestinely approached the monsignor in charge of exorcisms for New York's Catholic diocese. He quickly sent them packing, utterly refusing to get involved in the project in any manner. No wonder: the matter of psychic assassinations reared its ugly head during the meeting and, hardly surprisingly, the monsignor was having none of it.

DARING TO TANGLE WITH DEADLY TENTACLES

On August 1, 1991, the body of a middle-aged man was discovered in a shower in a room at the Sheraton Inn in Martinsburg, West Virginia. It was a grim sight for the maid who made the discovery. The man, it seemed, had committed suicide: his wrists were cut deep. Hotel staff soon identified the victim as Danny Casolaro, a freelance investigative journalist.

Was Casolaro's death really just the suicide that it appeared to be? The investigation continued to grow—to the point where it wasn't just the local police looking into the death but also conspiracy theorists. The latter group had a very good reason for looking into Casolaro's sudden death. For about a year and a half leading up to his reported suicide, Casolaro had been looking into a powerful group of people who sound very much like candidates for a New World Order. Casolaro termed this group "The Octopus." Appropriately, but unfortunately and tragically, the Octopus soon got its tentacles into Casolaro and dragged him down to an untimely death.

Casolaro's investigations started as a result of his interactions with William Hamilton, a retired computer software expert from the National Security Agency. As part of his work, Hamilton devised a highly sophisticated program designed to help the U.S. Department of Justice chase down criminals. For a while, all went well. The time came, though, when the Department of Justice stunned Hamilton by informing him that he had been overcharging the department for his technology, known as PROMIS. A huge legal feud followed; Hamilton lost. His software program, however, survived; its widespread surveillance and tracking abilities promised a great deal.

It wasn't long at all before entire swathes of the U.S. intelligence community began bootlegging Hamilton's software. But with a difference: the

United States sold copies to numerous nations, including Iran and Israel. These versions included a program that contained what, in computer-speak, is known as a backdoor. In simple terms, when the relevant nations downloaded the program, it allowed the United States to secretly spy on them. It allowed the United States to see what these nations—many of which were not current or potential enemies—were doing with the program. It was a story that fascinated Danny Casolaro, who decided to dig into the matter further. The investigation turned into an obsession for Casolaro.

What Casolaro found was that the Octopus did not operate out of one specific facility—of the types that apply to the likes of the CIA, NSA, and FBI. Rather, they were a loose-knit collection of powerful people all around the world who would come together for clandestine meetings and try to determine how best to manipulate the human race in the years ahead—all for the benefit of the Octopus, of course.

The more Casolaro dug, the more he found that the Octopus had played major roles in major, historic, world-altering events. The long list included the Cuban Missile Crisis of 1962; Watergate, which led to the resignation of President Richard M. Nixon; and the December 1988 destruction of a Boeing 747 jumbo jet over the town of Lockerbie, Scotland.

If that was not enough, the Octopus also had significant input into what was afoot at the world's most well-known secret base: Area 51. Casolaro learned that a top-secret program was afoot at Area 51 to create lethal viruses that were so powerful they had the ability, if released en masse, to wipe out massive percentages of the human race. Rumors reached Casolaro to the effect that this particular program was part of an ongoing plan to, one day, depopulate the planet and have the surviving population placed under unrelenting control of a powerful elite.

U.S. president Richard Nixon (shown here giving his resignation speech in 1974) was brought down by the Watergate scandal, which may have been the work of the Octopus.

The Area 51 story got even more controversial. Casolaro was told that a secret group, known as Majestic 12, oversaw at Area 51 the wreckage and alien bodies said to have been found in Roswell, New Mexico, in the summer of 1947. For the record, the Majestic 12 issue has been an integral one to the field of ufology for decades. For some UFO investigators, Majestic 12 is the real deal. For others, though, it's nothing but government disinformation designed to confuse the Roswell incident even further.

It was while Casolaro was looking into the UFO connections to the Octopus that he came across Michael Riconosciuto. He had an uncanny ability to worm his way into the domains of U.S. intelligence, espionage, classified programs, and the UFO phenomenon—as well as the world of highly classified vehicles that may have looked like alien spacecraft but which, in reality, were highly classified prototype aircraft of the military, tested and flown within the perimeters of Area 51. By now, Casolaro's head was spinning—which is hardly surprising.

Unfortunately, Casolaro did not live to see the truth of the Octopus unveiled—by himself, he hoped. While Casolaro's death *could* have been due to suicide—certainly, that's what it looked like—there were solid and valid reasons to suggest that his death was due to something very different. At the time of his passing, Casolaro was not in a state of woe or depression. It was the exact opposite: he was energized by new leads and new revelations in his quest to find the truth of the Octopus, its activities, and its motivations.

Barely twenty-four hours before he died, Casolaro met with William Turner, one of his sources for information on the Octopus. By all accounts, the meeting was a profitable one for Casolaro. Other people at the hotel happened to have brief chats with Casolaro, and no one described him as appearing depressed, stressed, or worried. That did not take away the fact, though, that the authorities went with the suicide conclusion. There were problems with that, too. One of the most glaring problems related to the matter of Casolaro's slashed wrists. The gashes were very deep. Inflicting one such deep wound would not be a problem. It's a little-known fact, though, that severing the ulnar artery causes that same hand to, essentially, become useless, similar to what it feels like to fall asleep on one's arm: the blood is restricted, and overwhelming numbness sets in. So, yes, Casolaro could have slashed one wrist to such a deep degree, but that same hand would largely be unable to inflict so much major damage to the other wrist.

It's no surprise that, taking into consideration all the controversy surrounding Casolaro's life, investigations, and death, that other researchers began to look into his story. Two of those were Kenn Thomas and Jim Keith, who, in 1996, penned a book on the whole affair titled *The Octopus*. In late 1999, things turned ominous. Keith found that his computer had been hacked into and that someone was reading his every written word. Soon thereafter, Keith died in a Reno hospital under questionable circumstances. Then, in 2001, Ron Bonds, the publisher of *The Octopus*, died under equally controversial circumstances. The Octopus, it seems, is determined to ensure that no one gets too close to the truth of its world-manipulating activities, no matter what the cost.

It's worth noting that, according to his notes, Casolaro had a source within the Wackenhut Corporation, which had been contracted on many occasions to undertake security-based work at Area 51. G4S Secure Solutions (USA) is an American security services company and a wholly owned subsidiary of G4S plc. It was founded in 1954 in Coral Gables, Florida, by George Wackenhut and three partners (all of them former FBI agents). In 2002, the company was acquired for $570 million by Danish corporation Group 4 Falck (itself then merged to form a British company, G4S, in 2004). In 2010, G4S Wackenhut changed its name to G4S Secure Solutions (USA) to reflect the new business model. The G4S Americas Region headquarters is in Jupiter, Florida.

After early struggles (including a fistfight between George Wackenhut and one of his partners), Wackenhut took sole control of his company in 1958, then choosing to name it after himself. By 1964, he had contracts to guard the Kennedy Space Center and the U.S. Atomic Energy Commission's

> The Octopus, it seems, is determined to ensure that no one gets too close to the truth of its world-manipulating activities, no matter what the cost.

nuclear test site in Nevada, which included Area 51. The following year, Wackenhut took his company public. In the mid-1960s, Florida governor Claude Kirk commissioned the Wackenhut Corporation to help fight a "war on organized crime," awarding the company a $500,000 contract. The commission lasted about a year but led to more than eighty criminal indictments, including many for local politicians and government employees. Following the murder of a British tourist at a rest stop in 1993, Florida contracted with Wackenhut to provide security at all state rest stops.

The company's work includes permanent guarding service, security officers, manned security, disaster response, emergency services, control-room monitoring, armed security, unarmed security, special event security, security patrols, reception/concierge service, access control, emergency medical technicians (EMT) service, and ambassador service. Like other security companies, G4S targets specific sectors: energy, utilities, chemical/petrochemical, financial institutions, government, hospitals and healthcare facilities, major corporations, construction, ports and airports, residential communities, retail and commercial real estate, and transit systems.

Having expanded into providing food services for U.S. prisons in the 1960s, in 1984, Wackenhut launched a subsidiary to design and manage jails and detention centers for the burgeoning private prison market. Wackenhut then became the nation's second-largest for-profit prison operator. In April 1999, the state of Louisiana took over the running of Wackenhut's fifteen-month-old juvenile prison after the U.S. Justice Department accused Wackenhut of subjecting its young inmates to "excessive abuse and neglect."

U.S. journalist Greg Palast commented on the case: "New Mexico's privately operated prisons are filled with America's impoverished, violent outcasts—and those are the guards."

The GEO Group, Inc. now runs former Wackenhut facilities in fourteen states as well as in South Africa and Australia. Some facilities, such as the Wackenhut Corrections Centers in New York, retain the Wackenhut name, despite no longer having any open connection with the company. Frequent rumors that the company was in the employ of the Central Intelligence Agency, particularly in the 1960s, were never substantiated; however, George Wackenhut, who was obsessive about high-tech security gadgets in his private life, never denied the rumors.

DROWNED BY ACCIDENT OR MURDER?

On April 27, 1959, Richard Condon's classic novel, *The Manchurian Candidate*, was published. It's an absorbing story of how the human mind can be controlled, enslaved, and, as a result, primed to perform just about any act, good or bad. In the book, it's mostly bad. The story is set in 1952, much of it during the Korean War. The primary character in *The Manchurian Candidate* is Sergeant Raymond Shaw. He and his team are captured by a Soviet outfit and are subjected to ruthless brainwashing and hypnosis. The reason: to warp minds and create the ultimate assassin. In this case, it's Shaw. The Russian controllers successfully turn Shaw into a killing machine, one who follows orders without question. So-called "trigger words" are used to turn Shaw "on" and to ensure he wipes out whomever the Soviets want gone. As the story progresses, we learn that the goal is to affect the result of the looming presidential election, with Shaw's mother playing an integral role in the outcome—an outcome that will see the United States turned into what we might call a police state, with the Russians calling many of the prime shots.

Acclaimed film critic Roger Ebert said of the movie: "The title of 'The Manchurian Candidate' has entered everyday speech as shorthand for a brainwashed sleeper, a subject who has been hypnotized and instructed to act when his controllers pull the psychological trigger. In the movie, an American patrol is captured by Chinese communists during the Korean War, and one soldier is programmed to become an assassin; two years later, he's ordered to kill a presidential candidate. That such programming is impossible has not prevented it from being absorbed as fact; this movie, released in 1962, has influenced American history by forever coloring speculation about Lee Harvey Oswald.

William Colby, the tenth director of the CIA, died in 1996 while on a solo canoe trip. Was his death accidental? A suicide? Or something more sinister?

Would the speculation about Oswald's background and motives have been as fevered without the film as a template?"

The Manchurian Candidate was remade in 2004, with significant changes from both Condon's original novel and the 1962 movie. Notably, in the 2004 version, we see Shaw kill a key figure in the story by drowning him as he paddles his kayak. It's made to look like a tragic accident. It's not. It should be noted that this "death by kayak" angle was almost certainly inspired by the 1996 death of former CIA director William Colby. Fact and fiction blending in eye-opening fashion? There's no doubt about it. Let's take a look at the life and still controversial death of Colby—a death that many researchers believe was cold-blooded murder.

Before we get to the matter of William Colby's death, let's begin with his life. Staff at the Arlington National Cemetery, where Colby is buried, state:

In 1945 Colby married Barbara Heinzen; they had four children. He obtained a law degree from Columbia University in 1947, the same year that Congress approved the formation of the Central Intelligence Agency (CIA). After working for a short time in a law firm, Colby in 1949 joined the new agency. He served in Stockholm (1951–1953) and then in Rome (1953–1958), where he helped to arrange the secret subsidization of political parties to prevent communist electoral victories. Most of the recipients were centrist or slightly left of center, a political alignment that proved effective in combating communism but gave Colby the reputation of having endorsed the "opening to the Left."

As for the specifics of Colby's work with, and status in, the CIA, there is the following, also from staff at the cemetery:

Colby was CIA station chief in Saigon from 1959 to 1962 and headed the agency's Far East division from 1962 to 1967. Then from 1968 to 1971 he directed the Phoenix program in South Vietnam, which sought to identify and eliminate communist activists (the Viet Cong) at the village level. Colby felt that the program was superior to the use of military force, which he believed was too blunt an instrument and alienated the Vietnamese. Nevertheless, estimates of the number killed under Phoenix range as high as sixty thousand people. (Colby put the number at 20,587.) Phoenix has also been defended on relativist grounds—the Viet Cong assassinated nearly forty thousand of their enemies in the period from 1957 to 1972. But none of these arguments could prevent the program from becoming a focal point of the antiwar movement. Although Colby maintained that the deaths characteristically arose in combat and not as a result of cold-blooded murder, critics of Phoenix labeled it an assassination program and a crime against humanity.

After Phoenix, Colby rose within the CIA's Washington bureaucracy, and on 4 September 1973 President Richard Nixon appointed him director of the agency. During his tenure the press and Congress turned on the CIA, accusing it of crimes and misdemeanors ranging from assassination plots to espionage against Americans at home. When in 1975 both houses of Congress set up inquiries into the activities of the intelligence community, Colby offered significant if limited cooperation. For example, he handed over to the Senate committee chaired by Idaho Democrat Frank Church details of the CIA's recent operations against the left-leaning government in Chile. The agency's attempts to sabotage the Chilean economy had contributed to the downfall of South America's oldest democracy and to the installation of a vicious dictatorship. Colby's candor on such matters shocked colleagues in the CIA, some of whom never forgave him for opening up the activities of what was, after all, a secret agency. His only daughter, Catherine, had died after a painful illness in April 1973, and colleagues speculated that the tragedy unlocked what some regarded as Colby's already overdeveloped Christian conscience. Though he strenuously denied that his daughter had opposed Phoenix, perhaps Colby did want to atone for his part in the program. It is also clear that he disapproved of certain of the CIA's activities that he called "deplorable" and "wrong" and wanted them stopped. In any case, he realized that a display of flexibility in his dealings with Congress would increase the agency's chances of survival.

With CIA morale at a low ebb, Colby's enemies began to line up. On the Left, a coalition of muckraking journalists, Vietnam War critics, and ambitious legislators refused to give him credit for attempting to open up the agency. On the Right, conservatives such as Barry Goldwater disliked Colby's liberalism and concessions to the Church committee. Colby had become politically vulnerable, and on 30 January 1976 President Gerald Ford replaced him with George H. W. Bush. Colby had introduced some significant reforms, such as the prohibition of assassination as an instrument of national policy and the practice of informing select members of Congress about the CIA's activities, but his intelligence career was over.

And in conclusion, there is this, also from the archives of the Arlington National Cemetery:

Colby's life continued to be eventful. In 1978 he published his memoir, *Honorable Men*, in which he defended himself against the Left over Phoenix and against the Right over his decision to clear the air while director of the CIA. In 1982, following the enactment of stringent secrecy legislation in the administration of President Ronald Reagan, the U.S. government began proceedings against Colby for making unauthorized disclosures, in the French-language edition of his memoir, about American

The torch was passed to President Gerald Ford after President Nixon resigned. Here he is holding a meeting of the NSA with William Colby (far left) addressing the agency.

efforts to retrieve secret codes from a sunken Soviet submarine. His agreement to pay a $10,000 fine in an out-of-court settlement barely covered the cracks between Colby and his enemies on the Right.

In 1984 Colby divorced his first wife and married a former diplomat, Sally Shelton. He had resumed legal practice and lectured widely, taking up a new cause—the campaign for a freeze on nuclear arms. On a spring day in 1996, Colby went down to the waterfront near his weekend home in Rock Point, Maryland, and launched his canoe into a stiff breeze. Until his body was found several days later with no evident signs of foul play, the press had one more chance to speculate about the fate of a man whose manner of death seemed to conjure up the enigma of his life.

And speaking of Colby's death....

On May 7, 1996, the *Chicago Tribune* reported the following: "The body of former Central Intelligence Director William Colby was discovered Monday along the shoreline of Maryland's Wicomico River, not far from where the 76-year-old retired spymaster disappeared April 27 while canoeing. Colby's remains were identified by his wife, Sally Shelton-Colby, at the site, some 60 miles southeast of Washington. She had held out hope he was alive and only injured, waiting for rescue in the surrounding marshland. His death was presumed to have been due to hypothermia and drowning. 'There is nothing unusual about this case at all,' said Lt. Mark Sanders of the Maryland Department of Natural Resources, which took a leading role in the weeklong search for Colby. The Federal Bureau of Investigation's Maryland headquarters in Baltimore confirmed that no evidence had been uncovered that would warrant a bureau investigation."

Not everyone agreed with that "no evidence" comment.

On February 21, 2010, the *American Chronicle* website ran an article titled "Who Killed William Colby?" The article largely focused on the in-depth research of journalist Zalin Grant. As the article states:

Colby's body was found nine days after his disappearance. After a quick autopsy on May 6, 1996, by David R. Fowler, assistant medical examiner for John Smialek, Maryland's chief medical examiner, declared death by heart attack—a declaration having the salutary effect of dispersing the news media. Unfortunately, there was no evidence for such a conclusion. Grant was told different stories about the cause of death depending upon whom he asked and the time of day. As Grant pulled together other details of the murder, he was able to determine that a squad of 3–5 assassins in two groups engineered the murder. One group grabbed Colby whom they demanded to empty all of his pockets and then took by car to the murder location. The other team commandeered his boat and brought it to the location where [nearby resident Kevin] Akers found it. The location was required because it had the sand needed to secure the boat in place. The place was needed because it was the only location with an accessible road to the water and out of view of potential witnesses. After the killers murdered Colby, they allowed his body to decompose for 9 days in order to make it impossible to determine the cause of death. So, the internal organs rotted while the exterior retained excellent composure. Thus, they assumed correctly that the coroners would rule accidental drowning. When they dumped the body at the crime scene the killers had not counted on the currents which would drift the body to a location other than where the boat was found. This detail would help solidify the case for murder.

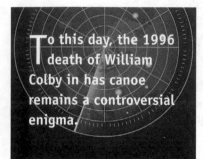

To this day, the 1996 death of William Colby in has canoe remains a controversial enigma.

On September 22, 2011, *Vanity Fair*'s Maureen Orth penned an article titled "Former CIA Director William Colby: The Man Nobody Knew." Orth wrote: "In an effort to explain his father, Carl Colby's new documentary, *The Man Nobody Knew,* which premieres tomorrow, offers a Who's Who parade of former top-level C.I.A. and government officials as well as some of the most knowledgeable journalists who cover the agency—from Robert Gates and Donald Rumsfeld to Sy Hersh and David Ignatius. As they opine on the institution and William Colby's influence, the film gives viewers a true sense of what it is to live a lie day after day and to hobnob at the highest levels in other countries—all while seeking to advance U.S. interests by whatever means necessary."

Carl Colby said of his father: "His death was ruled an accident—a stroke or a heart attack—but I think he was done. He didn't have a lot left to live for. And he never wanted to grow old. He always refused the 'senior discount.' One day I told him that his old college buddy had been found sitting under a bridge suffering from advanced Alzheimer's. And my dad said, 'That will never happen to me. One day you'll hear I'm walking along a goat path on a Greek island and I just fell into the sea.'"

To this day, the 1996 death of William Colby in his canoe remains a controversial enigma.

One final thing: if William Colby was murdered—drowned in his own canoe—then just maybe, a similar murder might have been successfully achieved long before. Another case of murder in deep waters? This takes us to the matter of the mysterious death of Australian prime minister Harold Holt, who vanished on December 17, 1967. The National Film and Sound Archive of Australia says of Holt's weird disappearance:

> With Australia at war in Vietnam in 1967, suddenly Prime Minister Harold Holt disappeared without a trace—an event unparalleled in the history of western democracy. The nation was in shock and disbelief at the shattering news, hoping for a miracle for the man who famously declared it was 'all the way with LBJ'. Police led a 'softly softly' investigation and concluded accidental drowning. But at the height of Cold War paranoia, persistent doubts about his disappearance fueled rumor and wild speculation. Why did Holt go into such violent surf that day? Had he chosen a bizarre way out of a difficult situation? Why were police withholding crucial facts? What had they overlooked?

Gilbert King, writing for *Smithsonian.com*, said:

On the gusty afternoon of December 17, 1967, a group of five adults arrived at Cheviot Beach, near Portsea, Victoria, and strolled along the Bass Strait beneath the warm Australian sun. Harold Holt was eager for a swim, and after stepping behind a rock outcrop in the sand dunes, he emerged wearing a pair of blue swim trunks. Marjorie Gillespie and her daughter, Vyner, both in bikinis, turned to the water and noticed that the surf, at high tide, was higher than they'd ever seen it.

"I know this beach like the back of my hand," Holt replied, and walked into the surf without breaking his stride. Immediately, he began swimming away from the beach. Martin Simpson, Vyner's boyfriend, followed but stopped when he was knee-deep in the surf. "There was a fairly strong undercurrent," he said, "so I just splashed around without going in too far." The third man in the group, Alan Stewart, told the others, "If Mr. Holt can take it, I had better go in too." But he stopped quickly when he felt a tremendous undertow swirling around his legs. He watched Holt swim out into what he

Harold Holt, shown here in 1963, was the Australian prime minister and head of the Liberal Party when he mysteriously drowned in 1967.

considered "dangerous turbulence." Marjorie Gillespie had kept an eye on Holt as he swam further away, drifting from them until the water seemed to boil around him and he disappeared.

The National Archives of Australia veers to an unfortunate explanation for what happened on that day:

Harold Holt disappeared while swimming at Cheviot Beach near Portsea, Victoria on 17 December, 1967. His body was never recovered. Without determining the cause of Holt's death, a joint report by Commonwealth and Victoria Police, submitted in January 1968, concluded that "there has been no indication that the disappearance of the late Mr. Holt was anything other" than a tragic accident. The report found that his last movements followed a routine domestic pattern, his demeanor had been normal and despite his knowledge of the beach, the turbulent conditions (high winds, rough seas and rip tides) overcame him. The explanations put forward for a failure to find the body included an attack by marine life, the body being carried out to sea by tides or becoming wedged in rock crevices. While a variety of theories have been expounded about Holt's disappearance, the Commonwealth Government did not deem a formal inquiry necessary, accepting the conclusions of the Police report.

On August 24, 2005, journalist Bernard O'Riordan wrote of the then-latest development in the matter:

A copy of the police report, now housed at the National Archives of Australia, made no mention of how Holt may have died or the whereabouts of his body. In the fevered cold war climate this simply fueled the conspiracy theories and provided Australians with their own home-grown version of the John F Kennedy assassination intrigue. Holt had been prime minister for 22 months when he disappeared, prompting claims that he may have committed suicide because of political pressures, or run off with a mistress.

In 1983, a former Australian naval officer, Ronald Titcombe, persuaded the British novelist Anthony Grey that Holt had been a Chinese spy since the early 1930s. He claimed that Holt, fearing detection by Australian intelligence officers, had sought political asylum in a Chinese midget submarine waiting off Portsea, near Melbourne. Holt's widow, the fashion designer Zara Holt, dismissed this conspiracy theory several years later when she said: "Harry? Chinese submarine? He didn't even like Chinese cooking." Others believed the CIA killed Holt because they thought he was about to take Australia out of Vietnam, given the strong opposition to the war by many Australians. The CIA theory was equally fanciful, given that Holt had pledged during a visit to the White House in 1966 to go 'all the way with LBJ', referring to the then American president, Lyndon Johnson.

On September 3, 2005, Nick Squires of the United Kingdom's *Telegraph* wrote of Holt:

> His disappearance was variously blamed on suicide, a shark attack, a Chinese submarine or a CIA assassination plot. But the mystery surrounding the fate of a former Australian prime minister was finally laid to rest yesterday. Authorities concluded that Harold Holt, who vanished while swimming off the coast of Victoria nearly 40 years ago, simply died from drowning. He disappeared on Dec 17, 1967 but his body was never found. Victoria's state coroner, Graeme Johnstone, said in a formal ruling yesterday that Holt, 59, drowned in heavy surf south of Melbourne and all the other theories were fanciful. "Mr. Holt took an unnecessary risk and drowned in rough water off Cheviot Beach," he said. "Perhaps, in hindsight, there should have been an inquiry as it may have avoided the development of some of the unsubstantiated rumors and unusual theories."

Just like the death of William Colby in the waters of the Wicomico River in 1996, the vanishing of Henry Holt in the waters off of Victoria continues to provoke intrigue and wonder.

THE DEATH OF A PRINCESS

When Diana, Princess of Wales, was killed in a car crash in Paris, France, on August 31, 1997, the world was shocked. But was Diana's death nothing more than a tragic accident? Not everyone is quite so sure. Indeed, there is a wealth of material linking Diana's death to the secret activities of certain clandestine, powerful groups. *Vigilant Citizen* provides the following:

> Similarly to the Virgin Mary, Diana had (and still has) legions of followers, worshiping her giving nature and her maternal energy. In other words, she seems to fulfill the almost inherent need in human beings to worship a female goddess, giver of life and filled with compassion. The media has been a key actor in the creation of this icon by documenting every detail of her fairytale wedding, her troubled marriage, her humanitarian activities and, finally, her untimely death. Was Diana picked and groomed to become a sort of a "modern day Goddess" to ultimately be sacrificed, in accordance with ancient pagan practices? This might sound preposterous to the average *National Inquirer* reader, but not to the connoisseur of the occult practices of the world elite. Furthermore, numerous clues and symbols have been placed by this group to subtly commemorate the occult nature of Lady Di's death.

Vigilant Citizen continues: "The city of Paris was built by the Merovingians, a medieval dynasty which ruled France for numerous generations. Before converting to Christianity, the Merovingian religion was a mysterious brand of paganism. The Pont D'Alma Tunnel was a sacred site dedicated to the Moon Goddess Diana, where they used to practice ritual sacrifices. During those ceremonies, it was of an utmost importance that the sacrificed victim died inside the underground temple. The assassination of Diana was a reenactment of this ancient pagan tradition."

As for who, exactly, the Merovingians were, historian James Wiener provides this: "Mythologized and circumscribed for over 1500 years, the Merovingians were a powerful Frankish dynasty, which exercised control over much of modern-day France, Germany, Switzerland, Austria, and the Low Countries. During the Early Middle Ages, the Merovingian kingdoms were arguably the most powerful and most important polities to emerge after the collapse of the Western Roman Empire, blending Gallo-Roman institutions with Germanic Frankish customs."

IlluminatiWatcher expands on this issue: "The Merovingian dynasty worshiped the goddess Diana, and the murder of Princess Diana is a ritual sacrifice to the goddess Diana. To believe this, we must believe that the Merovingian dynasty secretly retained power up to present day, which isn't too far of a stretch. If the British Royal Family can continue to hold a position of power over the citizens simply because they have a 'superior' blood, perhaps France has Merovingian bloodlines in positions of power unknown to the citizens."

Intriguing words, to say the very least. Now, let's look at one of the strangest affairs in the matter of the death of Princess Diana.

Many mysteries surround the death of Diana, Princess of Wales.

Agencies such as the FBI, the CIA, and the State Department have declassified a wealth of documents on numerous celebrity figures. There can be no doubt, however, that those same agencies, and many more, continue to withhold materials on other famous individuals, most notably on the late Diana, Princess of Wales. Along with her lover, Dodi Fayed, and driver Henri Paul, Diana was killed in a horrific car crash in Paris, France, on August 31, 1997. And while it is certainly true that secret files on Diana are known to exist within the archives of various departments and official bodies, the exact circumstances surrounding her untimely death are massively confused by other files, namely, unofficially released files that many view firmly as nothing more than hoaxed material but that some believe may be real.

In December 1998, the United States's supersecret National Security Agency admitted that it was holding more than a thousand pages of classified documents on the princess. The fact that many view Diana's death as highly suspicious has roused major concern and interest on a worldwide basis about what those documents actually contain. And the fact that the NSA has flatly refused to declassify its files on Diana has made the story even more intriguing in the eyes of both the press and the public.

British tabloids reported extensively and sometimes sensationally on the revelations at the time they first surfaced: "America's spy chiefs admitted last night they snooped on Princess Diana for years—and learned some of her most intimate love secrets," the *Daily Mirror* loudly proclaimed, while the *Daily Record* stated that the NSA's surveillance had continued "right until she died in the Paris car crash with Dodi Fayed." The *Washington Post* took the view that "the truth" was likely to be less "lurid," however, and cited the comments of a "U.S. intelligence official" who asserted that the references contained within the files to Diana were merely "incidental." The *Post* added, "In denying the request, the NSA disclosed existence of a 1,056-page Diana file and reported that Fort Meade, where the agency is located, had produced 39 'NSA-originated and NSA-controlled documents,' totaling 124 pages."

These documents, the NSA explained, were being withheld "because their disclosure could reasonably be expected to cause exceptionally grave damage to the national security" and, if released, would potentially disclose "sources and methods" utilized by the U.S. intelligence-gathering network. But as the *Post* also reported: "The giant spy agency, Maryland's largest employer, has been the subject of intense controversy in Britain and across Europe since a report released in January by the European Parliament concluded that 'within Europe, all e-mail, telephone and fax communications are routinely intercepted by the United States National Security Agency.'"

The NSA is not the only agency known to be holding files on the dead royal. According to an NSA Freedom of Information officer, the CIA also has at least two classified documents on file that relate to the princess. And the Defense Intelligence Agency (DIA) has admitted that it possessed both "information" and "product" on Diana. When asked why the DIA would have a classified document mentioning Diana, Lt. Col. James McNeil, a spokesman for the DIA, admitted that he had "no idea why. All of our stuff is on military. Obviously she wasn't in the military." Diana *was*, however, a major player in the long and drawn-out battle to have landmines outlawed, which *would* have been of prime concern to the military as well as to the defense contractors of numerous nations.

Interestingly, in 1999, Britain's *Guardian* learned that at least *some* of the material held by the NSA originated with the British intelligence services MI5 and MI6, portions of which were officially classified Top Secret. "The documents on the dead princess seem to have arisen because of the company she kept rather than through any attempt to target her," said the *Guardian*, "and the agency goes out of its way to say that it did not compile any of the spy reports itself."

The *Guardian* also noted that the NSA had stressed that its policy did not involve targeting "British subjects" as a part of its "foreign intelligence mission." However, it was also reported that the NSA did admit that "other countries could communicate about these subjects; therefore, this agency could acquire intelligence concerning British subjects."

And there can be little doubt that at least some of that classified documentation surely must relate to the data that was collected by Mohamed Al-Fayed, the father of Diana's lover, Dodi Fayed, and the subsequent lawsuit filed by Al-Fayed in 2000 in the U.S. District Court for the District of Columbia. The lawsuit in question, which was bravely designed to force numerous agencies to relinquish their files on Diana, but that has unfortunately failed thus far, began as follows:

> This is an action under the Freedom of Information Act ... for the expedited processing and disclosure of agency records pertaining to the deaths of Princess Diana and Dodi Fayed, and events and individuals associated with the tragedy, that were improperly withheld from plaintiffs Mohammed Al Fayed and Punch Limited by defendants Central Intelligence Agency, the National Security Agency, the Defense Intelligence Agency, the United States Departments of Defense, Justice and State, the Federal Bureau of Investigation, the Executive Office of United States Attorneys, the Immigration and Naturalization Service and the United States Secret Service.

In a section titled "Background," an outline was provided of the fatal crash that killed Diana and Dodi:

> On August 31, 1997, at approximately 12:25 A.M. local time, an automobile carrying Diana Francis Spencer, Princess of Wales, and Dodi Al Fayed crashed into the thirteenth pillar in the tunnel under the Place d'Alma in Paris, France. Princess Diana and Dodi Al Fayed were killed along with the automobile's driver, Henri Paul, a French security officer at the Ritz Hotel. Bodyguard Trevor Rees-Jones was the sole survivor. Shortly after the tragedy, Premier Juge d'instruction Herv Stephan, a French investigating magistrate, instituted an investigation. On or about January 29, 1999, it was announced that the investigation had ended and concluded that the tragedy was caused by drunk driving by Henri Paul, excessive speed and a dangerous stretch of road. Nine photographers and a press motorcyclist were placed under formal investigation— a step immediately before being formally charged—for man-

The Alma Tunnel in Paris is where Henri Paul, Princess Diana, and Dodi Fayed were killed in a traffic accident. They were being pursued by the paparazzi and crashed into the tunnel wall. The bodyguard for Princess Diana, Trevor Rees-Jones, was the sole survivor.

slaughter and failing to render aid to accident victims. On or about September 3, 1999, Judge Stephan dismissed all charges against the photographers and motorcyclist. The decision to formally end the investigation is presently under appeal by Al Fayed, and judicial proceedings are scheduled for September 2001.

The document then focused its attention upon the revelations of a British government agent, Richard Tomlinson:

Richard Tomlinson, 37, is a former MI6 (British foreign intelligence service) officer who served from September 1991 through April 1995. On or about August 28, 1998, Tomlinson informed investigating magistrate Herv Stephan that Henri Paul, the chauffeur killed in the tragedy, had been on the MI6 payroll for at least three years. He also revealed that the death crash resembled a MI6 plot to kill Yugoslavian President Slobodan Milosevic in Geneva. A copy of the affidavit Tomlinson provided to Judge Stephan is available at www.alfayed.com/dianaanddodi/tomlinson.html.

In or around September 1998, Tomlinson traveled to the United States on board a Swiss Air Flight in order to appear on an NBC television program to discuss his recent revelations. Upon arrival at John F. Kennedy International Airport in New York, Tomlinson was escorted off the plane by United States government officials and detained for several hours. He was never permitted to enter the United States, and instead was placed back on a plane to Europe.

Upon information and belief, the United States government prevented Tomlinson from entering the United States at the request of MI6 or other British government officials.

Oswald LeWinter ("LeWinter"), 70, has claimed to be a former United States intelligence operative for more than two decades. He has been linked to several high profile controversies here in the United States and Europe, all of which involved allegations of intelligence connections and specifically the CIA. These controversies have included LeWinter providing what apparently turned out to be disinformation regarding "October Surprise," which involved allegations that individuals associated with Ronald Reagan's presidential campaign delayed the release of American hostages in Iran in order to defeat President Jimmy Carter; claims by LeWinter that the CIA was involved in the 1986 assassination of former Swedish Prime Minister Olof Palme; his appearance in a 1994 documentary on the bombing of Pan Am Flight 103 entitled *The Maltese Double Cross* in which LeWinter claimed that the CIA knew that Libya was not responsible for the terrorist attack; and a 1998 attempt, more fully described below, to sell fraudulent CIA documents concerning the deaths of Princess Diana and Dodi Al Fayed.

In his book *October Surprise* (1991), Professor Gary Sick describes LeWinter as an "intelligence operative," who was a "graduate of University of California at Berkeley and had a master's degree in English literature from San Francisco State." "He spoke German and English, but he had also acquired a working knowledge of Hebrew, Persian, and French, and some Urdu." Sick stated LeWinter "had served with U.S. forces in Vietnam and also claimed long experience with various U.S. and Israeli intelligence agencies."

Upon information and belief, LeWinter previously formally maintained a relationship with the CIA, at least to the extent he provided information to the Agency during the 1970s. The CIA presently maintains in its possession records that confirm a relationship, as well as information pertaining to the fraud attempt described below.

In a lengthy section of the document titled "The Effort to Defraud Mohamed Al Fayed," the strange story is told of a series of controversial documents that surfaced not long after the death of the Princess of Wales, documents that were purported to be official leaked U.S. government documents about the secret surveillance of Diana:

In late 1997 or early 1998, Keith Fleer ("Fleer"), a prominent California attorney, George Williamson ("Williamson"), an independent journalist, Pat Macmillan ("Macmillan") and LeWinter—the latter two are both alleged former CIA agents—participated in an enterprise to sell forged documents purportedly stolen from the CIA that indicated MI6—the British foreign intelligence agency—had plotted to murder Princess Diana and

This is one of the two memorials set up in Harrods department store by Mohamed Al-Fayed to honor Princess Diana and his son, Dodi Fayed.

Dodi Al Fayed. Other individuals who are alleged to have played a role in the scheme include Linda Tumulty, who is tied to the late film producer Alan Francovich, and another former CIA operative named Thompson.

LeWinter, Macmillan, and other associates apparently forged the documents and planned to misrepresent them as genuine to induce potential buyers to purchase the documents. Along with Williamson, who was also aware that the documents to be sold were not authentic, LeWinter, Macmillan, and their colleagues agreed that a sale of the forged documents to a tabloid newspaper should be arranged. The participants in the scheme anticipated a sale price of over $1 million.

Upon information and belief, at the suggestion of Gaby Leon (phonetic), an individual who allegedly formerly worked for the Argentine Secret Service, Williamson was advised to contact Fleer, an entertainment attorney in Los Angeles, for advice on the sale of the documents and to serve as a broker for their sale.

In their course of discussions, Fleer noted that Al-Fayed had offered a reward of up to $20 million for information concerning the deaths of his son and Princess Diana, and he suggested that they should approach Al-Fayed in lieu of a tabloid and offer him the information for $20 million. Fleer stated that he knew one of Al-Fayed's attorneys in Washington, D.C., and would make the necessary approaches to him. Upon information and belief, Fleer was to receive 5 percent of any monies obtained through the sale of the alleged CIA documents.

On or about March 24, 1998, Fleer contacted Douglas Marvin ("Marvin"), Al Fayed's legal representative in Washington. Marvin, in turn, put Fleer in contact with John Macnamara ("Macnamara"), Al Fayed's chief of security. In a series of telephone conversations over the first two weeks of April 1998, between Fleer and Macnamara, Fleer stated that he had been approached by reliable individuals with credible information that the deaths of Dodi Al Fayed and Princess Diana were not accidental but in fact were the product of a carefully planned assassination carried out at the behest of British intelligence with the knowledge and acquiescence of Buckingham Palace. Fleer indicated that his immediate contact was Williamson, an investigative reporter, and that several "principals" were also involved.

According to Fleer, Williamson had connections with CIA sources who had been reliable in the past. Those CIA employees, Fleer stated, would be prepared to disclose their information concerning the deaths of Dodi Al Fayed and the Princess, provided that Al Fayed would provide them with the financial security and assistance to "take measures to protect themselves"—a price of $20 million. Fleer indicated that, while it was unlikely that the CIA employees would agree to testify in any manner, they could provide authentic and sufficiently detailed CIA documentary evidence to prove the involvement of British intelligence agencies in the assassination plot. Fleer also stated that the CIA sources knew that a CIA operative in Europe had been contacted by someone within the British intelligence agency MI6. The British agent indicated that an assassination team was being compiled and asked for assistance. The CIA employee subsequently cabled for instructions and received in return a telex indicating that the CIA was not to become involved directly but that the agent could give British intelligence the name of a contact with a Mossad-affiliated "K team" operating out of Switzerland.

In addition to the telexes from and to the CIA operative, Fleer indicated that the CIA sources could and would supply Al Fayed with a relevant intelligence collection report and a medical document indicating that the Princess was pregnant at the time of her death. Fleer also indicated that there was a report of the results of an internal CIA investigation into the agency's involvement with the assassination of Dodi Al Fayed and Princess Diana, but that this document could only be obtained through a "seven figure" cash payment.

On or about April 8, 1998, Fleer requested that Macnamara arrange for the wire transfer of $25,000 "expense money" so that Al Fayed's representatives and the "principals" could meet in a foreign country to arrange for the inspection of the CIA documents and their subsequent sale to Al Fayed.

Given that alleged classified information was being offered for sale, on or about April 13, 1998, Al Fayed's representatives contacted and began cooperating with officials from the FBI and the CIA. From here on, all actions taken by Al Fayed's representatives were done so with the approval and supervision of law enforcement and intelligence officials of the United States government.

On or about April 13, 1998, Fleer requested that Macnamara send the $25,000 via wire transfer to the account of Garland and Loman, Inc., a New Mexico company with an affiliate in Juarez, Mexico, at the Western Bank, 201 North Church Street, Las Cruces, New Mexico 88001. Fleer explained in a subsequent call to Macnamara that the Western Bank would contact Williamson when the funds were received. The FBI directed Al Fayed's representatives to wire the money from a bank in the District of Columbia so that criminal jurisdiction would lie with the United States Attorney's Office for the District of Columbia. Macnamara was told that at the very least the transmittal and receipt of the funds would constitute wire fraud, even if nothing else came of the intended transaction to sell the documents.

On or about April 14, 1998, with the approval of U.S. law enforcement authorities, Marvin ordered the wire transfer of $25,000 from a NationsBank branch in Washington, D.C. to the Garland & Loman account. FBI, CIA and EOUSA officials were all aware of the ongoing events.

Upon information and belief, Williamson traveled to the Garland and Loman premises in New Mexico to withdraw the $25,000 wire transfer with the intent to use those funds to

Nothing better shows just how beloved Princess Diana was by the world than this outpouring of flowers for her funeral.

finance and further the sale of the forged documents to Al Fayed. Williamson subsequently traveled to London, England and disbursed some or all of the $25,000 to his co-conspirators; including, but not limited to, LeWinter.

On or about April 14, 1998, following confirmation from Williamson that the $25,000 wire transfer had been received, Fleer informed Macnamara that the meeting to exchange the documents for payment was to take place in Vienna, Austria. Fleer stated that in Austria, Al Fayed's representatives would meet with four "principals," who would offer for sale two CIA telexes and a doctor's certificate that Princess Diana was pregnant at the time of her death. Fleer emphasized that the internal CIA investigative report on the circumstances of the crash would not, however, be provided at the Vienna meeting because "they" had yet to procure it.

With the intent to render the proceeds of the sale difficult or impossible to trace, and in an effort to conceal their source, Fleer instructed Macnamara during their conversation on or about April 14, 2000, that he should arrange to have the $15 million negotiated purchase price (having been reduced from $20 million) for the documents deposited at the Austrian bank Kredit Anstalt in a Sparbuch, an anonymous, bearer passbook account. Fleer stated that the passbook was to be handed over to the "principals" at the Vienna meeting as payment for the documents.

On or about April 20, 1998, Macnamara received a telephone call in Austria from Williamson, who stated that he was at the Hilton Hotel, New York City. Williamson confirmed that he dealt regularly with the "principals" supplying the documents and that he served as their go-between. He also stated that the "principals" would be present in Vienna and that at least one of them, whose identity remains unknown, had traveled from the United States to meet with Al Fayed's representatives. At an initial meeting, Al Fayed's representatives would be shown at least one of the CIA telexes dealing with the assassination of Dodi Fayed and Princess Diana, and that a serving member of the CIA would be on hand to authenticate the document. Additionally, Williamson also stated that the $25,000 wired by Macnamara had been spent and that "nobody's cheating on you."

Following additional negotiations concerning the time, place, and format of the Vienna meeting, Macnamara received two telephone calls from an unknown individual on his mobile phone discussing the mechanics of the document exchange and setting a meeting for April 22, 1998, 2:00 P.M. at the Hotel Ambassador, 1010 Vienna, Neuer Markt 5. Macnamara was to sit on the Kartner Strabe side, where he would be approached by one of the "principals." With the approval of United States and Austrian law enforcement authorities, Macnamara followed the instructions that had been given to him regarding the planned rendezvous.

At approximately 2:30 P.M. local time, a man (later identified as LeWinter) approached Macnamara and identified himself as an ex-CIA agent who was in Vienna with six CIA and Mossad agents to deal with "the business." LeWinter spoke to Macnamara for approximately one half hour, briefing him on the provenance of the CIA documents, and indicated that there had been a meeting in London between an MI6 operative named Spelding and a CIA agent named Harrison, who was attached to the United States Embassy in London. At that meeting, Spelding asked Harrison for the CIA's assistance in assassinating Dodi Al Fayed, who had formed a close relationship with Princess Diana. Harrison allegedly cabled CIA headquarters in Langley, Virginia for instructions and was informed via telex that the CIA would not become involved but could refer the British to the Mossad "K team" in Geneva. LeWinter indicated to Macnamara that these two telexes were for sale, and he also gave a brief description of the CIA investigative report that could be obtained, including a reference in that report to Princess Diana's pregnancy.

At the conclusion of their meeting at the Hotel Ambassador, LeWinter provided a telephone number and requested Macnamara to call him there under the name George Mearah at 5:00 P.M. Law enforcement personnel working with Macnamara traced the telephone number to the Hotel Stadt Bamberg, where they confirmed that the hotel had as a guest an American named Oswald LeWinter who matched Mearah's description.

By arrangement, and with the approval of United States and Austrian authorities, Macnamara met with LeWinter later that afternoon at the Ambassador Hotel. Following further discussions with Macnamara, LeWinter was taken into custody at the Ambassador Hotel by Austrian law enforcement officials. On information and belief, two associates (one of which has apparently been identified as Thompson) of LeWinter who were nearby evaded capture. In fact, it turns out that one of the individuals who assisted LeWinter during his time in Vienna was Karl Koecher, a Czechoslovakian intelligence operative who had infiltrated the CIA as a "sleeper" agent during the 1970s. After more than a decade of spying on the United States, Koecher was arrested and ultimately exchanged in a spy trade for Soviet dissident Anatoly Shcharansky on February 11, 1986. Upon information and belief, Koecher and LeWinter became acquainted while serving in prison together in New York State.

There can be little doubt that even if the documents were faked, a great deal of thought had certainly gone into their content, as can be seen from the text of one of the documents contained within the collection that was circulated to the British media. Indeed, the lead-in to one of the documents, dated June 17, 1997, looked very impressive. It was headed "DOMESTIC COLLECTION DIVISION Foreign Intelligence Information Report Directorate of Intelligence WARNING NOTICE—INTELLIGENCE SOURCES AND METHODS INVOLVED REPORT CLASS: TOP SECRET" and read:

1. Relationship initiated between Diana POW and Dodi aF according to reliable intel sources in November 1996. Intimacy begins shortly after they meet. (Report filed).

2. Reliable source reports Palace seriously disturbed by liaison. PM considers any al Fayed relationship politically disastrous. [The Duke of] Edinburgh sees serious threat to dynasty should relationship endure. Quote reported: "Such an affair is racially and morally repugnant and no son of a Bedouin camel trader is fit for the mother of a future king," Edinburgh. (Report filed).

3. Request from highest circles to DEA attaché UK for 6 on Dodi re: Cocaine. See File forwarded to UK embassy DC. (Copy filed).

4. US liaison to MI6 requested by David Spedding for assistance in providing permanent solution to Dodi problem. Blessing of Palace secured (Twiz filed).

5. WHuse [White House] denies Spedding request. Harrison authorized only to arrange meeting for MI6 representative with K-Team Geneva. (Twiz on file).

6. Meeting in Geneva reportedly successful (Report filed).

7. al Fayed Mercedes Limo stolen and returned with electronics missing. Reliable intel source confirms K-team involved. Source reports car rebuilt to respond to external radio controls. (Report filed).

8. COBGeneva reports that on May 28, 1997 heavily weighted Fiat Turbo.

And there, the document ends. In an intriguing twist, a July 23, 1999, article titled "Fayed, the spies and the $20m plot to show Palace was behind Diana's death," written by journalists Stuart Millar and Duncan Campbell, reported that "Le Winter has since claimed, during two meetings with the Harrods head of security, that although the papers shown to Mr. Fayed were forgeries, they were copies of real documents held by the CIA." No wonder then that the death of Diana, Princess of Wales, continues to provoke intense controversy more than two decades after her untimely demise.

A JOURNALIST LOSES HER LIFE

As we have seen, working in the field of investigative journalism can be dicey. Even deadly, no less. The untimely and suspicious deaths of Dorothy Kilgallen in 1965, Georgi Markov in 1978, and Danny Casolaro in 1991 are perfect examples. The list does not end there, however. Another case, which shook the United Kingdom in 1999, is that of the BBC's Jill Dando. To put things into perspective, Dando was on a par in the United Kingdom with the likes of CNN's Erin Burnett in terms of her quality of work, her visibility, and her connection to the viewers. That all came to a terrible end, however, when Dando's life was snuffed out on April 26, 1999. What was first reported to have been a murder soon became something else: a full-blown assassination. Before we get to the death of Jill Dando, let's first take a look at her life and her career.

Born on November 9, 1961, Dando began her career in the media working for a regional U.K.-based newspaper, the *Western Mercury*. Dando most assuredly had her sights on greater things. She achieved them, too. In 1985 Dando's first position was with *BBC Radio Devon* (in the southwest of England). Two years later, she took a position with *Spotlight South West*, which was followed in 1987 by *BBC Spotlight*. Things really took off for Dando in 1988, when she was offered a prestigious position reading the news in London. In the years ahead, Dando became a regular and familiar face on *Breakfast Time*, the *BBC One O'Clock News*, and the *BBC Six O'Clock News*. It was, however, the BBC's *Crimewatch* that most people associated Dando with. The longtime show investigated open murder cases and had a huge following. In a terrible state of irony, Dando's death became the subject of an episode of the very show she fronted. The big questions were: Who killed Jill Dando? And why? As the investigation developed, matters became strange and conspiratorial.

What we know for sure is that Jill Dando was killed early on the morning of April 26, 1999. She had spent the night with her boyfriend, Alan Farthing, at his home in Chiswick (a district of west London) and drove back to her own home in Fulham, southwest London. Dando reached her home around 11:30 A.M.; seconds later, she would be dead. Extensive forensic investigations made it clear that Dando got out of her car of her own volition and walked to the front door of her home. She took out her keys to open the door but was suddenly seized from behind by a still unknown assailant, who violently slammed her to the ground, with her face pushed against the tiled floor. The killer pumped a single bullet into the left side of Dando's head; the bullet cut through her skull, exiting on the right side. She was dead in the blink of an eye.

Incredibly, all of this occurred with no one realizing right away what had happened. Dando's neighbor, Helen Doble, found Dando's body around fifteen minutes after the shooting took place, but another neighbor, Richard Hughes, heard a "cry" outside but failed to hear the gunshot that took Dando's life. Indeed, he was completely unaware that Dando's body lay outside of her home. Hughes was, however, able to see the killer: he was described as being middle-aged, white, and around six feet tall. According to Hughes, the man walked away, rather than running. It was only when Doble found Dando's body that Hughes realized she had been murdered and that he had seen the killer.

Given the fact that this was not just a terrible murder but an extremely high profile one, too, both the media and the United Kingdom's Metropolitan Police did their absolute utmost to try to solve the shocking crime. Indeed, the police launched a huge operation to get to the bottom of it all. The name of the operation was Operation Oxborough. As *Vice's* James McMahon reported: "A former detective who worked on the case would only talk to me on the condition of anonymity. He talks of how 191 CCTV cameras conclusively proved Dando wasn't followed the morning of her death. How the number of people put forth as potentially being involved in the murder exceeds 2,100. Additionally, it is known that more than 5,000 people were interviewed with over 2,500 statements taken. All 486 people in Dando's Filofax were investigated and over 14,000 emails were examined. 'Other than terror-related enquiries, I know of no other investigation with anything like the volume,' he says."

Such was Jill Dando's popularity as BBC newscaster that, upon her death, a Japanese fan and botanist, T. Kiya, cultivated a beautiful, red shrub flower and named it after the news announcer.

The investigation left no stones unturned as people questioned thousands of people. The team determined that a 9mm-caliber, semi-automatic pistol was the weapon that killed Dando. Despite the extensive and professional investigation, very few leads came to the fore. There was, however, one name that kept cropping up—Barry George, who lived very close to Dando. After a period of intense surveillance, George was finally arrested. He was convicted and, on July 2, 2001, was sentenced to life in prison. That was not the end of the situation, however. Not everyone was convinced that George was the culprit. As a result, and after a pair of failed appeals, George was finally acquitted on August 1, 2008. It should be noted, too, that George received significant monetary payments from two U.K. newspapers—*The News of the World* and *The Sun*—as a result of public statements made by the press about George's character.

> It wasn't long before questions and observations of a very strange and unforeseen nature surfaced. They went down a highly conspiratorial road, too.

The *Independent* also waded into the controversy, noting the following: "Mr. George had previous convictions for attempted rape and indecent assault. On one occasion in the early 1980s he was found hiding in the bushes at Kensington Palace, wearing khaki, carrying a knife and a length of rope.... He also had some experience with firearms: he spent nearly a year in the Territorial Army before being discharged in November 1982, being taught how to maintain and shoot assault rifles and machine guns. Women complained that he had stalked them. When police searched Mr. George's flat, they found many photographs of local women, and no fewer than four copies of the Jill Dando memorial issue of the BBC's in-house magazine *Ariel*."

In the wake of Barry George's acquittal, the race was on to try to find the real killer. It was suggested that Dando's work on the BBC's *Crimewatch* show might have enraged an unknown criminal who then hired an assassin to end Dando's life. As plausible as this theory was, it led nowhere. Dando's boyfriends were interviewed; nothing at all suggested any kind of connection to her death. Then, there was the strangest theory of all—one that might very well lead us to the heart of the matter.

It wasn't long before questions and observations of a very strange and unforeseen nature surfaced. They went down a highly conspiratorial road, too. They revolved around NATO, Serbia, and a deadly, hired assassin. It's important here to note the time frame: Jill Dando was killed on April 26, 1999. Just three days earlier, on April 23, sixteen employees of the Radio Television of Serbia were killed by NATO forces, specifically by carefully targeted bombs. The theory went that the killing of Dando—a major media figure—was ordered by Željko Ražnatović, a ruthless Serbian warlord wanted by numerous intelligence groups and law-enforcement agencies, including Interpol. In this scenario, Dando was murdered in retaliation for the killing of the sixteen staff members of the Radio Television of Serbia. It's intriguing to note that Barry George's defense brought up this very issue as they sought to get him off the hook. Ironically, in January 2000, Ražnatović himself was assassinated. His killer remains unknown, although rumors suggest that the culprit was attached to U.S. intelligence.

The death of Jill Dando still provokes a great deal of controversy and debate. For example, when the twentieth anniversary of Dando's death came around in 2019, there were new developments. On April 25, 2019, the United Kingdom's *Standard* ran an article titled "Jill Dando murder: ITV documentary reveals details of Serbia assassination theory." As journalist Rebecca Speare-Cole wrote: "A new ITV documentary has uncovered compelling new ground in the 20-year-old unsolved murder of Jill Dando with a theory that the BBC presenter was a revenge hit for NATO bombings in Serbia."

Speare-Cole continued with regard to a documentary titled *Jill Dando— The 20 Year Mystery* that aired in the United Kingdom on April 25, 2019: "The documentary uncovers what appears to be a potentially significant flaw in the investigation into her death [known as] Operation Oxborough. Met Police said the case remains open so they cannot comment other than to say detectives will explore any new information that becomes available. The Serbian population are still to this day outraged by the attack, a local man telling reporter Julie Etchingham: 'It would be the same if Moscow hit the BBC with a nuclear missile.' According to the documentary, the police files contain intelligence reports stating Ms. Dando was murdered in revenge for the bombing but the Met Police investigation did not think the Serbia theory was credible. The National Criminal Service, known then as Britain's FBI, even released an intelligence report to investigators which alleged that Ms. Dando was murdered in revenge of the RTS bombing. Compelling evidence shows that a man appeared to have made a series of calls to the BBC, citing the murder as revenge for the bombing of the state radio and television service."

The controversy—and attendant conspiracy theory—surrounding Jill Dando's death show no sign of going away anytime soon.

POST-9/11 ASSASSINATIONS

From the final months of 2001 to mid-2005, near-countless people employed in the elite field of microbiology—the study of organisms that are too small to be seen with the naked eye, such as bacteria and viruses—died under circumstances that some within the media and government came to view as highly suspicious and deeply disturbing. Many of the deaths appeared at first glance to have reasonable explanations. But even those who were skeptical of the notion that the deaths were suspicious in nature could not deny one overriding and important factor: many of those dead microbiologists had secret links to worldwide intelligence services, including the United States' CIA, Britain's MI5 and MI6, and Israel's Mossad.

Inevitably, this mysterious collection of deaths, in such a tightly knit area of cutting-edge research, has led to a proliferation of theories in an attempt to resolve the matter. Some believe that a cell of deep-cover terrorists from the Middle East wiped out the leading names within the field of microbiology as part of a plot to prevent Western nations from developing the ultimate bioweapon. A darker theory suggests that this same weapon has *already* been developed, and, with their work complete, the microbiologists were systematically killed by Western intelligence in an effort to prevent them from being kidnapped by terrorists who may then have forced them to work for the other side.

The controversy largely began on November 12, 2001, when Dr. Benito Que, a cell biologist working on infectious diseases, including HIV, was found dead outside of his laboratory at the Miami Medical School, Florida. The *Miami Herald* stated that his death occurred as he headed for his car, a white Ford Explorer, parked on Northwest 10th Avenue. Police said that he was possibly the victim of a mugger.

According to later developments uncovered by the media, however, the new word on the street was that Dr. Que had been attacked by four men equipped with baseball bats. This was later recanted, however, and officials stated that Que had died from cardiac arrest. And with that final statement in the public domain, police refused to comment any further on Que's death, rather intriguingly.

Eleven days later, Dr. Vladimir Pasechnik, a former microbiologist for Biopreparat, a bioweapon production facility that existed in Russia prior to the collapse of the Soviet Union, was found dead near his home in the county of Wiltshire, England. His defection to Britain in 1989 revealed to the West for the first time the incredible scale of the Soviet Union's clandestine biological warfare program.

> His defection to Britain in 1989 revealed to the West for the first time the incredible scale of the Soviet Union's clandestine biological warfare program.

And his revelations about the scale of the Soviet Union's production of biological agents including anthrax, plague, tularemia, and smallpox provided an inside account of one of the best-kept secrets of the Cold War. According to British intelligence, Pasechnik passed away from effects of a massive stroke and nothing more.

Then, on November 24, 2001, the FBI announced that it was monitoring an investigation into the disappearance of a Harvard biologist because of "his research into potentially lethal viruses," including Ebola. Dr. Don C. Wiley, 57, had last been seen in Memphis, Tennessee, where he attended the annual meeting of the Scientific Advisory Board of the St. Jude Children's Research Hospital. His rented car was found at 4:00 A.M. on November 16 on a bridge over the Mississippi River with a full fuel tank and the key still in the ignition.

Wiley had left the Peabody Hotel just four hours earlier. He was due to meet his wife and two children later that same day in Cambridge, Massachusetts. FBI agents took an interest in Wiley's disappearance because of his expertise and as a direct result of "our state of affairs post-September 11," said Memphis-based FBI agent William Woerner.

Wiley was a Harvard biochemistry and biophysics professor and was considered a national expert on Ebola, HIV, herpes, and influenza. In 1999, Wiley and another Harvard professor, Dr. Jack Strominger, won the Japan Prize for their discoveries of how the immune system protects humans from infection.

Notably, on the same day that authorities were diligently searching for Wiley, three more microbiologists were killed when a Swissair flight from Berlin to Zurich crashed during its landing approach. Altogether, twenty-two people died, and nine survived. Among the dead were Dr. Yaakov Matzner, 54, dean of the Hebrew University School of Medicine; Amiramp Eldor, 59, who ran the

Hematology Department at Ichilov Hospital in Tel Aviv and was a world-recognized expert in blood clotting; and Avishai Berkman, 50, director of the Tel Aviv Public Health Department.

On December 12, 2001, it was revealed that a leading researcher on DNA sequencing analysis had been found dead in the secluded northern Virginian farmhouse where he lived alone. The body of Robert M. Schwartz was discovered by neighbors, two days earlier, after coworkers at his place of employment reported he had seemingly skipped work and had missed a meeting.

"We're all stunned," said Anne Armstrong, president of the Virginia Center for Innovative Technology, a nonprofit agency where Schwartz worked. "We don't know anything. What we're assuming is maybe he walked in on something." Schwartz was a founding member of the Virginia Biotechnology Association, worked at the center for almost fifteen years, and served as the executive director of research and development and university relations. He also worked on the first national online database of DNA sequence information.

Robert A. Schwartz, a leading DNA researcher, was among the many Americans who mysteriously passed away during a short period of time.

On the other side of the world, forty-eight-hours later, equally disturbing events were occurring. Set Van Nguyen was a microbiologist at the Commonwealth Scientific and Industrial Research Organization's Animal Diseases Establishment at Geelong, Australia. He had been employed there for fifteen years when his end came far too suspiciously soon.

Police in Victoria, Australia, stated: "Set Van Nguyen, 44, appeared to have died after entering an airlock into a storage laboratory filled with nitrogen. His body was found when his wife became worried after he failed to return from work. He was killed after entering a low temperature storage area where biological samples were kept. He did not know the room was full of deadly gas which had leaked from a liquid nitrogen cooling system. Unable to breathe, Mr. Nguyen collapsed and died."

Also on the same day, much publicity was given to a story that appeared in the United Kingdom's *Times* newspaper that discussed how Israel was working on a biological weapon designed to kill specific types of people.

The *Times* reported that "the intention is to use the ability of viruses and certain bacteria to alter the DNA inside their host's living cells. The scientists are trying to engineer deadly microorganisms that attack only those bearing the distinctive genes." It was a highly controversial plan to provoke death by racial profiling, in other words.

On December 15, 2001, a formal announcement was made that three people had been charged with murder in the case of the aforementioned Robert M. Schwartz. Police revealed that he had been killed with a two-foot sword in a "planned assassination" and that an "X" had been carved into his back. "I have no idea what this means," said the prosecutor, Robert Anderson. Police in Maryland arrested Kyle Hulbert, 18, Michael Pfohl, 21, and Katherine Inglis, 19.

Reuters news service stated that Wiley's death had "triggered alarm bells," due to the "current bio-warfare fears" and the nature of his work....

The next day, an intriguing revelation surfaced to the effect that Inglis, in January 2001, had reported to the Naval Recruit Training Command Center in Great Lakes, Illinois. Navy officials stated that she had been trained to work "in aviation" but had suddenly, and inexplicably, left on May 28. One of the other suspects, Pfohl, had, very shortly before Schwartz's death, expressed an interest in joining the elite, deadly, and covert world of Special Forces.

Four days on, police announced they had located the remains of missing Harvard University scientist Don C. Wiley. A body carrying identification was found on December 18 near a hydroelectric plant in the Mississippi River, about three hundred miles from where Wiley was last seen. Police Lt. Joe Scott said that a positive identification was planned when the body was returned to Memphis for an autopsy.

A number of scientific organizations, including St. Jude Children's Research Hospital, where Wiley worked, put up rewards totaling $26,000 for information leading to the arrest and charge of anyone responsible for Wiley's disappearance. "As soon as the body gets in our morgue, the medical examiner will begin the autopsy to help answer a lot of questions," said Memphis police director Walter Crews.

Interestingly, Reuters news service stated that Wiley's death had "triggered alarm bells" due to the "current bio-warfare fears" and the nature of his work but did not elaborate as to who, exactly, the alarm bells had been triggered with. The FBI stated that it was leaving the investigation of Wiley's death in the hands of the police. Friends and family of Wiley, meanwhile, stated vocally and publicly that he would not commit suicide under any circumstances.

And still controversial deaths continued to occur, this time in Russia. On January 28, 2002, a microbiologist and a member of the Russian Academy of Science, Alexi Brushlinski, died as the result of what was blamed on a "bandit attack" in Moscow. Then, two weeks later, Victor Korshunov, 56, also a noted microbiologist, was hit over the head and killed at the entrance to his home in Moscow, Russia. He was the head of the microbiology subfaculty at Russian State Medical University.

Four days after that revelation, a similar story surfaced out of England. Detectives were busily trying to unravel the circumstances that led to the death of a leading university research scientist, Ian Langford, 40, a senior fellow at the University of East Anglia's Center for Social and Economic Research. His work began in 1993 after he gained his Ph.D. in childhood leukemia and infection following a first-class honors degree in environmental sciences. He had worked most recently as a senior researcher assessing risk to the environment.

Professor Kerry Turner, director of the center, said: "We are all very shocked by this appalling news. Ian was without doubt one of Europe's leading experts on environmental risk, specializing in links between human health and environmental risk."

On March 24, 2002, Denver car dealer Kent Rickenbaugh, his wife, Caroline, and their son, Bart, were killed in a plane crash near Centennial Airport. The pilot, Dr. Steven Mostow, was also killed. It transpires that Mostow, 63, was one of the United States' leading infectious disease experts and the associate dean at the University of Colorado's Health Sciences Center. Mostow was a crusader for better health, an early advocate for widespread flu vaccinations, and more recently had been deep in talks with U.S. intelligence officials on the threat of bioterrorism.

On the same day that Dr. Mostow was killed, another life ended—in England again—when fifty-five-year-old microbiologist David Wynn-Williams was hit by a car while jogging near his home in Cambridge. He was an astrobiologist with the Antarctic Astrobiology Project and the NASA Ames Research Center and was studying how microbes, of a potentially hostile nature, adapt to living in extreme environments.

On July 18, 2003, the British press reported that David Kelly, a British biological weapons expert, had slashed his own wrists while walking in the woods near his home. Kelly was the British Ministry of Defense's chief scientific officer and the senior adviser to the proliferation and arms control secretariat and the Foreign Office's Non-Proliferation Department. The senior adviser on biological weapons to the UN biological weapons inspections teams (Unscom) from 1994 to 1999, Kelly was also viewed as preeminent in his field worldwide. Almost four months to the day later, scientist Robert Leslie Burghoff, 45, was killed by a hit-and-run driver who jumped the sidewalk and ploughed into him in the South Braeswood neighborhood of Houston, Texas. At the time, he was studying outbreaks of viruses onboard cruise ships and their potential links to terrorist activity.

Moving into 2004, during the first week of May, a Russian scientist at a former Soviet biological weapons laboratory in Siberia died after an alleged accident with a needle laced with Ebola. Officials said the incident raised concerns about safety and secrecy at the State Research Center of Virology and Biotechnology, known as Vector, which in Soviet times specialized in turning deadly viruses into biological weapons.

On July 3, 2004, Dr. Paul Norman, 52, of Salisbury, Wiltshire, England, was killed when the single-engine Cessna 206 aircraft he was piloting crashed in the county of Devon. He was married with a fourteen-year-old son and a twenty-year-old daughter. Norman was the chief scientist for chemical and biological defense at the British Ministry of Defense's laboratory at Porton Down, Wiltshire. The crash site was sealed off and examined by officials from the Air Accidents Investigation Branch, and the wreckage of the aircraft was removed from the site to the AAIB base at Farnborough, England. The tragedy was firmly ruled accidental and nothing else.

Another doctor and scientist who died mysteriously was Dr. Anthony John Clark, who was part of the team that created the sheep clone named Dolly.

In August 2004, six weeks after Norman's death, Professor John Clark, head of the science laboratory that created Dolly the "cloned" sheep, was found hanging in his holiday home. Clark led the Roslin Institute in Midlothian, Scotland, one of the world's leading animal biotechnology research centers, and he played a crucial role in creating the transgenic sheep that earned the institute worldwide fame. Professor Clark also founded three spin-off firms from Roslin: PPL Therapeutics, Rosgen, and Roslin BioMed.

As a new year dawned, the deaths continued to increase. On January 7, 2005, Korean Jeong H. Im, a retired research assistant professor at the University of Missouri and primarily a protein chemist, died of multiple stab wounds to the chest before firefighters found his body in the trunk of a burning car on the third level of the Maryland Avenue Garage in Columbia. A person of interest, described as a male 6' to 6' 2" wearing some type of mask, was seen acting in a suspicious fashion in the garage. He was never caught.

Then, in May 2005, Australian scientist David Banks, a fifty-five-year-old who was the principal scientist with Biosecurity Australia, a company described as being a "quarantine authority," was killed in an aircraft crash at Queensland. At the time, he was undertaking a "survey for the Northern Australia quarantine strategy." Officials ruled it a tragic accident.

Were the deaths of so many microbiologists in such a clearly delineated period simply a bizarre and collective coincidence? Or was something stranger afoot? In today's climate of near-surreal uncertainty, it should, of course, be recognized that any suspicious deaths in the fields of microbiology, bacteriological warfare, or lethal viruses—especially where many of the victims had links to the covert intelligence services of a number of countries—might be an indication that powerful figures were at work in at least *some* of the deaths, if not indeed all of them. Microbiology is a dangerous game at the best of times. Between 2001 and 2005, however, it became downright deadly.

Although the vast majority of controversial deaths in the field of microbiology occurred between 2001 and 2005, they still continue. *Healthy Protocols* noted in 2013:

> The death of Andrew Moulden is shrouded in mystery. Some sources say he had a heart attack and others say he committed suicide. A colleague of Dr. Moulden who wishes to remain anonymous reported to *Health Impact News* that he/she had contact with him two weeks before he died in 2013. Dr. Moulden told our source and a small number of trusted colleagues in October of 2013 that he was about to break his silence and would be releasing new information that would be a major challenge to the vaccine business of big pharma. He was ready to come back. Even though he had been silent, he had never stopped his research. Then, two weeks later, Dr. Moulden suddenly died. Dr. Moulden was about to release a body of research and treatments, which could have destroyed the vaccine model of disease management, destroyed a major source of funding for the pharmaceutical industry, and at the same time seriously damaged the foundation of the germ theory of disease.

In 2014, the *Telegraph* reported:

> A Cambridge Professor has made the astonishing claim that three scientists investigating the melting of Arctic ice may have been assassinated within the space of a few months. Professor Peter Wadhams said he feared being labelled a "looney" over his suspicion that the deaths of the scientists were more than just an "extraordinary" coincidence. But he insisted the trio could have been murdered and hinted that the oil industry or else sinister

government forces might be implicated. The three scientists he identified—Seymour Laxon and Katharine Giles, both climate change scientists at University College London, and Tim Boyd of the Scottish Association for Marine Science—all died within the space of a few months in early 2013. Professor Laxon fell down a flight of stairs at a New Year's Eve party at a house in Essex while Dr Giles died when she was in collision with a lorry when cycling to work in London. Dr Boyd is thought to have been struck by lightning while walking in Scotland. Prof Wadhams said that in the weeks after Prof Laxon's death he believed he was targeted by a lorry which tried to force him off the road. He reported the incident to the police.

Interestingly, microbial matters at the Arctic were areas that all three were working on. The *Investment Watch* blog, in August 2014, revealed the following:

> Glenn Thomas, a leading consultant in Geneva, an expert in AIDS and, above all, Ebola Virus, was on board the Boeing 777 Malaysia Airlines cut down on the border between Ukraine and Russia. Glenn Thomas was also the coordinator of the media and was involved in the investigations that were bringing to light the issue of trial operations of Ebola virus in the laboratory of biological weapons at the hospital in Kenema. Now that this workshop was closed by order of the Government of Sierra Leone, more details emerge about the interests that were hidden behind its management. Bill and Melinda Gates have connections with biological weapons labs located in Kenema, the epicenter of the epidemic of Ebola, developed from the hospital where they were going for clinical trials in humans for the development of its vaccine, and now, following the opening of an informal survey, it appears the name of George Soros, through its Foundation, is funding the laboratory of biological weapons.

Steve Quayle, who has carefully studied the mysterious wave of deaths that has occurred in the last decade and a half, posted this story in 2015 about yet another death:

> Alberto Behar, Robotics expert NASA at the JPL, died instantly when his single-engine plane nosedived shortly after takeoff Friday from Van Nuys Airport. He worked on two Mars missions and spent years researching how robots work in harsh environments like volcanoes and underwater. As part of the NASA team exploring Mars with the *Curiosity* rover, Behar was respon-

sible for a device that detected hydrogen on the planet's surface as the rover moved.

[Forty-seven]-year-old NASA Scientist Alberto Behar helped to prove that there had once been water on Mars according to the *Daily Mail* story published to announce his recent death in a plane crash that happened on Friday in LA, California. While plane crashes do happen and scientists do die, Behar's name has now been added to a very long list of scientists and astronomers who have met their untimely ends prematurely, leading us to ask, did Behar know something that "they" don't want the rest of society to find out?

AIDS, SARIN, AND ANTHRAX

Did a secret U.S. group, buried deep in the heart of the military, create the AIDS virus as a means to assassinate people on a gigantic scale? No. But in the 1980s, the then-Soviet Union's KGB was determined to spread just such a controversial rumor. A January 2005 U.S. Department of State document titled "AIDS as a Biological Weapon" and declassified under the terms of the Freedom of Information Act reveals the strange story of how the rumors began and were ultimately quashed. The document begins:

"When the AIDS disease was first recognized in the early 1980s, its origins were a mystery. A deadly new disease had suddenly appeared, with no obvious explanation of what had caused it. In such a situation, false rumors and misinformation naturally arose, and Soviet disinformation specialists exploited this situation as well as the musings of conspiracy theorists to help shape their brief but highly effective disinformation campaign on this issue."

The Department of State continued: "In March 1992, then-Russian intelligence chief and later Russian Prime Minister Yevgeni Primakov admitted that the disinformation service of the Soviet KGB had concocted the false story that the AIDS virus had been created in a US military laboratory as a biological weapon. The Russian newspaper *Izvestiya* reported on March 19, 1992: '[Primakov] mentioned the well-known articles printed a few years ago in our central newspapers about AIDS supposedly originating from secret Pentagon laboratories.'

"According to Yevgeni Primakov, the articles exposing US scientists' 'crafty' plots were fabricated in KGB offices. The Soviets eventually abandoned the AIDS disinformation campaign in their media under pressure from the U.S. government in August 1987."

It was not just the KGB, however, who were spreading rumors of a secret U.S. group creating the AIDS virus, as the Department of State knew all too well:

"In addition to the Soviet disinformation specialists, a tiny handful of fringe-group conspiracy theorists also espoused the false charge that the AIDS virus had been created as a biological weapon. One of them was Mr. Theodore Strecker, an attorney in the United States, who had a brother, Robert, who was a physician in Los Angeles. Theodore wrote a manifesto, 'This is a Bio-Attack Alert' on March 28, 1986. He imagined that traitorous American doctors, United Nations bureaucrats, and Soviet officials were involved in a gigantic conspiracy to destroy the United States with biological warfare. He wrote, 'We have allowed the United Nations World Health Organization to combine with traitors in the United States National Institute of Health to start a Soviet Union attack.'"

The document continues: "Mr. Strecker claimed that the 'War on Cancer' led by the U.S. National Institutes of Health (NIH) was a cover for developing AIDS. He wrote, 'the virologists of WHO [the World Health Organization], NCI [the U.S. National Institute of Cancer], and the NIH, have written in plain English their plan for conquest of America and are presently executing it disguised as cancer research.'"

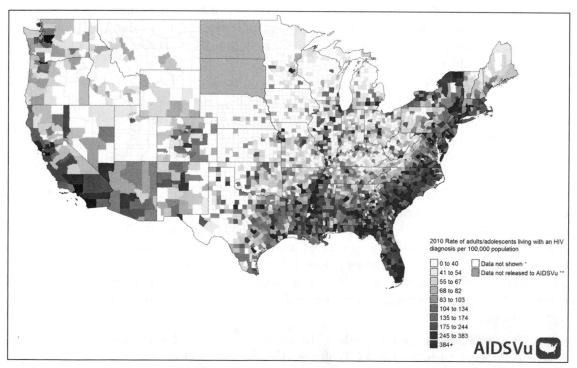

2010 Rate of adults/adolescents living with an HIV
diagnosis per 100,000 population

- 0 to 40
- 41 to 54
- 55 to 67
- 68 to 82
- 83 to 103
- 104 to 134
- 135 to 174
- 175 to 244
- 245 to 383
- 384+
- Data not shown *
- Data not released to AIDSVu **

AIDSVu

While there have been medical advancements in the treatment of AIDS and HIV, the virus is still widespread in the United States, as this 2010 map illustrates.

"Mr. Strecker," said the Department of State, "saw the Soviet Union at the heart of this alleged conspiracy."

Indeed, Strecker himself said: "This is an attempt to exhaust America with hatred, struggle, want, confusion, and inoculation of disease. The enemy intends to control our population with disease, make us dependent upon their remedies, engineer each birth, and reduce America to a servant of the Supreme Soviet."

The Department of State added: "Mr. Strecker sent his manifesto to the president and vice president of the United States, governors of several states, and various U.S. government departments, urging them to ' retake the virus labs using force if necessary' and other dramatic emergency measures. It did not have the galvanizing effect he had hoped."

As for the real origins of AIDS, the Department of State said: "In the mid-1980s, there was still considerable confusion about how AIDS had developed, although scientists universally agreed that it was a naturally occurring disease, not one that was man-made. In the intervening years, science has done much to solve this mystery. There is now strong scientific evidence that the AIDS virus originated as a subspecies of a virus that commonly infects the western equatorial African chimpanzee."

In 1995, terrorists wreaked havoc and death in Tokyo, Japan. They were members of a group known as Aum Shinrikyo. The U.S. Department of State prepared an extensive report on the catastrophic event, the summary of which outlines the shocking series of events:

"Aum Shinrikyo (Aum) was designated as a Foreign Terrorist Organization on October 8, 1997. Jailed leader Shoko Asahara established Aum in 1987, and the organization received legal status in Japan as a religious entity in 1989. The Japanese government revoked its recognition of Aum as a religious organization following Aum's deadly sarin gas attack in Tokyo in March 1995. Despite claims of renunciation of violence and Asahara's teachings, members of the group continue to adhere to the violent and apocalyptic teachings of its founder."

In March 1995, Aum members simultaneously released the chemical nerve agent sarin on several Tokyo subway trains, killing twelve people and causing up to six thousand to seek medical treatment. Subsequent investigations by the Japanese government revealed the group was responsible for other mysterious chemical incidents in Japan in 1994, including a sarin gas attack on a residential neighborhood in Matsumoto that killed seven and hospitalized approximately five hundred. Japanese police arrested Asahara in May 1995; in February 2004, authorities sentenced him to death for his role in the 1995 attacks. In September 2006, Asahara lost his final appeal against the death penalty, and the Japanese Supreme Court upheld the decision in October 2007.

Gas-masked Japanese police aid victims of the sarin gas attack of 1966.

In February 2010, the death sentence for senior Aum member Tomomitsu Miimi was finalized by Japan's Supreme Court. In 2011, the death sentences of Masami Tsuchiya, Tomomasa Nakagawa, and Seiichi Endo were affirmed by Japanese courts, bringing the number of Aum members on death row to thirteen.

Since 1997, the group has recruited new members, engaged in commercial enterprises, and acquired property, although it scaled back these activities significantly in 2001 in response to a public outcry. In July 2001, Russian authorities arrested a group of Russian Aum followers who had planned to detonate bombs near the Imperial Palace in Tokyo as part of an operation to free Asahara from jail and smuggle him to Russia.

Although Aum has not conducted a terrorist attack since 1995, concerns remain regarding its continued adherence to the violent teachings of founder Asahara that led Aum to carry out the 1995 sarin gas attack. According to a study by the Japanese government issued in December 2009, Aum Shinrikyo/Aleph membership in Japan is approximately fifteen hundred with another two hundred in Russia. As of November 2011, Aum continues to maintain thirty-two facilities in fifteen prefectures in Japan and may continue to possess a few facilities in Russia. At the time of the Tokyo subway attack, the group claimed to have as many as forty thousand members worldwide, including nine thousand in Japan and thirty thousand in Russia. Aum's principal membership is located in Japan; a residual branch of about two hundred followers live in Russia.

Exactly one week after the September 11, 2001, terrorist attacks, the United States was plunged into another equally fraught and fear-filled situation. It became known as Amerithrax, the official title of the subsequent FBI investigation into the affair, in which anonymously mailed envelopes, containing deadly anthrax spores, were sent to prominent politicians and members of the media: assassination via deadly bacteria.

It was an affair of deeply conspiratorial proportions that, curiously, began the night of September 11. Vice President Dick Cheney and members of his staff were given an antibiotic called Ciprofloxacin. It has the ability to treat and offer protection from a wide body of bacterial infections and conditions, including anthrax.

On September 18, five letters sent by sources then unknown arrived at the offices of *NBC News*, *ABC News*, the *National Enquirer*, *CBS News*, and the *New York Post*. Or, rather, it's *presumed* that is the case. While the letters sent to *NBC News* and the *New York Post* certainly were found and recovered for forensic analysis by the FBI, the remaining three were never found. Staff at *ABC News*, *CBS News*, and the *National Enquirer* were quickly infected by anthrax, leading to the assumption that letters were the source. Although that's a logical assumption, it is still unproven.

On October 9, events escalated to an entirely new level when two Democratic senators—Tom Daschle of South Dakota and Patrick Leahy of Vermont—were also the recipients of envelopes containing potentially deadly anthrax spores. As a result, the U.S. government briefly shut down its own mail service. Ultimately, approximately two dozen people were infected and five died as a result of the series of letters mailed between September 18 and October 9, 2001. As for where exactly the letters were mailed from, the most likely location was a box situated just a short distance from Princeton University. The hunt was immediately on for the culprit or culprits.

History and investigative journalism has shown that great steps were taken to try to prove—and convince the mainstream media and the entire populace—that the source of the anthrax was Iraq's iron-fisted leader, Saddam Hussein. The media quickly bought the story. One example occurred less than three weeks after the targeting of Daschle and Leahy. *ABC News*'s Brian Ross stated: "Sources tell ABC News the anthrax in the tainted letter sent to Senate Majority Leader Tom Daschle was laced with bentonite. The potent additive is known to have been used by only one country in producing biochemical weapons—Iraq."

It turned out that while Hussein had used bentonite (a form of clay) in his bioweapons program, the claim that it was found in the anthrax spores was false. How such an incorrect claim became fact in the minds of many remains a matter of deep debate.

Notably, it wasn't just Saddam Hussein who was being blamed for the attacks. Fingers were also pointed in the direction of al-Qaeda and Osama bin Laden. Indeed, senior figures in the White House did their absolute utmost to have FBI director Robert Mueller confirm this as a fact. He did not, which reportedly led to members of the presidential administration expressing their unhappiness with him. The FBI was not happy, either. FBI personnel, by now heavily involved in the investigation of the attacks, had already concluded that the kind of anthrax used was highly unlikely to have been concocted by, as one agent memorably worded it, "some guy in a cave."

As the months progressed, and with no meaningful data pointing in the direction of

A photo taken by the FBI shows the anthrax-loaded letter sent to infect members of the U.S. government. It is addressed to Senator Tom Daschle (D-SD).

Iraq or Afghanistan, the FBI began looking in what many considered to be an even more controversial direction: the very heart of the United States itself. One of those who the FBI had major concerns about was Steven Jay Hatfill, an undeniable expert in the field of germ warfare. From 1997 to 1999, Hatfill was employed at the U.S. Army Medical Research Institute of Infectious Diseases. USAMRIID is, essentially, the Department of Defense's primary research facility in the field of biological weapons and is housed at Fort Detrick, Maryland.

In 1941, President Franklin D. Roosevelt secretly ordered the establishment of what came to be officially known as the U.S. Biological Warfare Program. As a result of Roosevelt's historic move, in 1943, the newly designated Camp Detrick in Maryland was assigned to the Army Chemical Warfare Service for the specific development of a center dedicated to biological warfare issues. Twelve months later, Camp Detrick was established as an installation focused on the research and diligent development of both offensive and defensive biological warfare techniques and agents.

In 1956, the name of the installation was changed from Camp Detrick to Fort Detrick, although its workload remained very much the same. Then, on April 1, 1972, following the official closure of offensive biological warfare studies in the United States, the control of Fort Detrick was transferred from the U.S. Army Materiel Command to the Office of the Surgeon General, Department of the Army. One year later, Fort Detrick was assigned to the newly created U.S. Army Health Services Command. And in 1995, the HSC was itself reorganized into the U.S. Army Medical Command.

Ironically, the FBI was put on the trail of Hatfill not by its own agents but by media sources and activists. Falling into the former category was Nicholas Donabet Kristof. Commencing in 2002, the Pulitzer Prize-winning journalist with the *Washington Post* and *New York Times* wrote a number of articles that suggested Hatfill was possibly the guilty party in the anthrax attacks. Molecular biologist Barbara Hatch Rosenberg also suggested a homegrown terrorist as the probable source, one acting with the "unwitting assistance of a sophisticated government program."

The FBI was soon digging deeply into Hatfill's background. His home was extensively searched (in July and August 2002), and the FBI admitted that Hatfill was considered a person of interest in its anthrax investigation. It turned out that Hatfill was innocent of any and all involvement. Justifiably outraged, he sued the U.S. government and was awarded almost $6 million in damages. The FBI moved on to another suspect.

The final person on the FBI's list of suspects was Dr. Bruce Edwards Ivins. He was a microbiologist who had been employed at the Fort Detrick-based USAMRIID for almost two decades. Although Hatfill had been targeted by the FBI as far back as 2002, it wasn't until 2007 that Ivins found himself in the Bureau's sights.

For the FBI's investigative team, there was a valid reason why Ivins was now considered its chief suspect: the strain of anthrax used in the attacks was taken in 1981 from a cow in Sarita, South Texas. It was then sent to USAM-RIID for analysis. Despite all the efforts to put the blame on Saddam Hussein and Osama bin Laden, the trail actually led to Fort Detrick.

Rather ironically, Ivins played a significant role in analyzing the very anthrax samples that had caused so much chaos and death in late 2001. They were analyses that Ivins conducted for the FBI, no less. Such was the respect that Ivins had achieved among his colleagues in 2003 that he received the Decoration for Exceptional Civilian Service Award from the Department of Defense. It is presently the highest award that the DoD can give to a civilian employee.

By 2007, the FBI was watching Ivins closely. Ivins's home was raided, the FBI indicated he was now their primary suspect, threats of the death penalty for a guilty verdict were discussed, and he began to suffer from depression, stress, and anxiety. He was subsequently hospitalized in March 2008.

By 2007, the FBI was watching Ivins closely. Ivins's home was raided, the FBI indicated he was now their primary suspect....

The FBI noted: "At a group therapy session on July 9, 2008, Dr. Ivins was particularly upset. He revealed to the counselor and psychologist leading the group, and other members of the group, that he was a suspect in the anthrax investigation and that he was angry at the investigators, the government, and the system in general. He said he was not going to face the death penalty, but instead had a plan to 'take out' co-workers and other individuals who had wronged him. He noted that it was possible, with a plan, to commit murder and not make a mess. He stated that he had a bullet-proof vest, and a list of co-workers who had wronged him, and said that he was going to obtain a Glock firearm from his son within the next day, because federal agents were watching him and he could not obtain a weapon on his own. He added that he was going to 'go out in a blaze of glory.'"

Three months later, the FBI advised Ivins that he was very likely going to be charged with committing one of the worst terrorist attacks in American history. It did not happen, however. On July 27, 2008, Ivins committed suicide. His weapon of choice was a significant and deadly amount of Tylenol, which took its fatal toll on his kidneys and liver. The FBI closed its case on Ivins. It may not have gotten its man, so to speak, but the verdict was that Ivins was almost certainly the guilty party. Not everyone agreed with the FBI, however.

One of those who stood up in support of Ivins was Dr. Henry S. Heine, who worked with Ivins at USAMRIID. Heine very vocally rejected the idea that Ivins could have perfected such a strain of anthrax and avoided detection in the process. He also maintained that within USAMRIID, and "among the senior scientists," absolutely "no one believes" that Ivins was responsible.

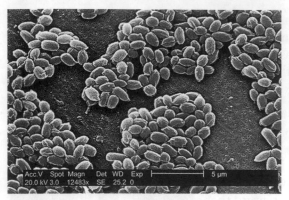

Shown magnified by an electron microscope, anthrax spores can survive in a dormant state for many years and still infect a host.

There was far more damning data to follow. Having scrupulously studied the FBI's investigation of Ivins, the National Academy of Sciences, in April 2010, came to a controversial conclusion that placed the Bureau in a distinctly uncomfortable light. The NAS said that the FBI had "overstated the strength of genetic analysis linking the mailed anthrax to a supply kept by Bruce E. Ivins."

Not only that, the NAS added that it was "impossible to reach any definitive conclusion about the origins of the anthrax in the letters, based solely on the available scientific evidence."

Democratic senator Patrick Leahy—one of the very people targeted by the attacker—had his say on the matter of Ivins's supposed involvement. His words were not well received by the FBI or the Bush Administration: "If [Ivins] is the one who sent the letter, I do not believe in any way, shape or manner that he is the only person involved in this attack on Congress and the American people. I do not believe that at all."

Then there was Dr. Meryl Nass, a noted expert on anthrax and its effects. While it was indeed quite possible to link a particular strain of anthrax to one particular facility, said Nass, further linking that same strain to one person, such as Ivins, was nearly impossible to achieve.

The words of Heine, the NAS, Leahy, and Nass mattered very little to the FBI. It shut down its investigation on February 19, 2010, still perceiving Ivins as the brains behind the attacks. Perhaps the FBI was right and Ivins was the man, after all. But what if he wasn't? What if the FBI got it catastrophically wrong?

If not Saddam Hussein, Osama bin Laden, Dr. Bruce Edwards Ivins, or Steven Jay Hatfill, then who, exactly, was the guilty party? A highly disturbing theory—one supported by conspiracists—offered a distinctly alarming scenario: that the events of September 18 to October 9, 2001, were orchestrated by powerful figures within, or attached to, the White House. The purpose behind their deranged plot: to place the blame for the anthrax attacks on Iraq or al-Qaeda, as a means to engineer further support for the War on Terror and the eventual annexing and control of the entire Middle East.

Some conspiracy theorists point to another factor that is highly suggestive of the Bush Administration playing at least some role in the anthrax affair, whether officially or off the record. It revolves around Democratic senators Tom Daschle and Patrick Leahy. It's important to note the time frame when the anthrax attacks occurred: late 2001. This was when President Bush was pushing to have the Patriot Act passed.

Neither Daschle nor Leahy had much love for the controversial act. Daschle, the Senate majority leader, did not believe they should rush the bill through without giving all of its many and varied implications deep thought and study. As the Senate majority leader, Daschle held significant sway over the amount of time the act would likely take to pass.

Moving on to Senator Leahy, only five days before Amerithrax erupted, he openly accused the Bush presidency of reneging on a certain agreement contained in the bill. Just like Daschle, Leahy had the ability to slow down the passing of the Patriot Act. However, on October 24, the Patriot Act was passed, and all without the Senate actually reading it.

Some conspiracy theorists point to another factor that is highly suggestive of the Bush Administration playing at least some role in the anthrax affair....

Republican representative Ron Paul noted: "It's my understanding the bill wasn't printed before the vote—at least I couldn't get it. They played all kinds of games, kept the House in session all night, and it was a very complicated bill. Maybe a handful of staffers actually read it, but the bill definitely was not available to members before the vote."

Forty-eight hours later, President Bush signed the necessary paperwork that made the Patriot Act law. That the anthrax attacks directly hastened the passing of the act is not in doubt.

And finally, of potential support for this same "the government did it" theory is the fact that the type of anthrax used in the 2001 mailings also goes by the name of "militarized anthrax." It was the brainchild of William C. Patrick III. He had a prestigious career, which culminated in 1986 with him becoming the programs analysis officer at Fort Detrick's USAMRIID.

Patrick, who died in 2010—the same year the FBI closed its file on Ivins—near-singlehandedly created a system by which anthrax spores could be concentrated at a level of one trillion spores per gram. And what was the level of concentration in the spores found in all the anthrax letters of 2001? You guessed it: one trillion spores per gram. To date, the United States is the only nation on the planet that has succeeded in achieving such a specific level of concentration.

DOCTORS, BANKERS, AND UNTIMELY DEATHS

In 2016, the *Free Thought Project* informed its readers: "In 2015 there was a popular 'conspiracy theory' floating around the internet after a rash of mysterious 'suicides' by high profile banking professions. What once looked like wild speculation is now beginning to resemble a vast criminal conspiracy connected to the Libor, interest-rigging scandal. Over forty international bankers allegedly killed themselves over a two-year period in the wake of a major international scandal that implicated financial firms across the globe. However, three of these seemingly unrelated suicides seem to share common threads related to their connections to Deutsche Bank. These three banker suicides, in New York, London, and Siena, Italy, took place within 17 months of each other in 2013/14 in what investigators labeled as a series of unrelated suicides."

Free Thought Project continued: "Financial regulators in both Europe and the U.S. in 2013 began a probe that would ultimately become known as the Libor scandal, in which London bankers conspired to rig the London Interbank Offered Rate, which determines the interest banks charged on mortgages, personal and auto loans. The scandal rocked the financial world and cost a consortium of international banks, including Deutsche Bank, about $20 billion in fines."

One of those who died under unusual circumstances, in March 2013, was David Rossi, a fifty-one-year-old communications director at the world's oldest bank, Italian Monte dei Paschi di Siena. It was on the verge of disaster as a result of massive losses in the financial crisis of 2008. Rossi fell to his death on March 6, 2013. *The New York Times* said of his death:

"A devastating security video shows Rossi landing on the pavement on his back, facing the building—an odd position more likely to occur when a body

Three suicides had one thing in common: a connection to Deutsche Bank.

is pushed from a window. The footage shows the three-story fall didn't kill Rossi instantly. For almost 20 minutes, the banker lay on the dimly lit cobblestones, occasionally moving an arm and leg. As he lay dying, two murky figures appear. Two men appear and one walks over to gaze at the banker. He offers no aid or comfort and doesn't call for help before turning around and calmly walking out of the alley. About an hour later, a co-worker discovered Rossi's body. The arms were bruised and he sustained a head wound that, according to the local medical examiner's report, suggested there might have been a struggle prior to his fall."

And there is this from *Wall Street on Parade* from April 2014: "It doesn't get any more Orwellian than this: Wall Street mega banks crash the U.S. financial system in 2008. Hundreds of thousands of financial industry workers lose their jobs. Then, beginning late last year, a rash of suspicious deaths start to occur among current and former bank employees. Next we learn that four of the Wall Street mega banks likely hold over $680 billion face amount of life insurance on their workers, payable to the banks, not the families. We ask their Federal regulator for the details of this life insurance under a Freedom of Information Act request and we're told the information constitutes 'trade secrets.'"

Clearly, powerful figures do not want the media too close to uncovering the truth of this dark and deadly aspect of the banking business. Powerful figures within the New World Order? Who else?

On July 18, 2003, it was widely reported in the media that Dr. David Kelly, a British biological weapons expert, had slashed his own wrists while walking in the woods near his home. Kelly was the British Ministry of Defence's chief scientific officer and the senior adviser to the proliferation and arms control secretariat, and to the Foreign Office's Non-Proliferation Department. The senior adviser on biological weapons to the UN biological weapons inspections teams (Unscom) from 1994 to 1999, Kelly was also, in the opinion of his peers, preeminent in his field, not only in the United Kingdom but in the world, too.

Kelly also had grave doubts about the claims being made that Saddam Hussein possessed significant numbers of weapons of mass destruction (WMD). Of course, the WMD issue was an integral part of the New World Order's plans to justify an invasion of the Middle East. That Kelly was a prominent figure, and to the NWO a troublesome figure, meant that something had to be done to quash his stance and words. Fortunately for the New World Order, Kelly's "suicide" conveniently paved the way for the U.K. government of Tony Blair to endorse the plans of the Bush Administration to launch a full-blown invasion. But was Kelly's death really caused by suicide? Many suggest not. And many of them are notable figures, too.

Ten years after Kelly's death, the *Guardian* ran an article that made it very clear many were far from happy with the explanation that Kelly took his own life. The *Guardian* said:

> Kelly's death led not to an inquest, but a public inquiry by Lord Hutton, which brought a rare glimpse into the secret worlds of Whitehall, British intelligence, the low arts of high politics, and the workings of the BBC....

> The inquiry found that Kelly died after cutting an artery, had taken an overdose of painkillers and had heart disease which left his arteries "significantly narrowed." Thus, said experts, less blood loss may have killed the scientist than that needed to kill a healthy man. Among those who have called for an inquest or have doubts it was a suicide are former Tory leader Michael Howard, and Liberal Democrat minister Norman Baker, who wrote a book saying Kelly was most likely murdered. A group of doctors say Hutton's findings should be discarded and a new inquest held. Dr. Stephen Frost said: "We have lots of evidence.... No coroner in the land would reach a verdict of suicide as Lord Hutton did."

Saddam Hussein, who was president of Iraq from 1979 to 2003, was accused by the U.S. government of building weapons of mass destruction, a claim later shown to be false.

Norman Baker, a member of the U.K. Parliament, made the following statement: "My investigations have since convinced me that it is nigh on clinically impossible for Dr. Kelly to have died by his own hand and that both his personality and the other circumstantial evidence strongly militate against suicide.... British diplomat David Broucher told the Hutton inquiry that, some months before Dr. Kelly's death, he had asked him what would happen if Iraq were invaded. Rather chillingly, Dr. Kelly replied that he 'would probably be found dead in the woods.' At the inquiry, this was construed as meaning that he had already had suicidal thoughts. That, of course, is patently absurd. Nobody can seriously suggest that he was suicidal at the time the meeting took place—yet Lord Hutton seems to have made his mind up about the way in which Dr. Kelly died before the inquiry even began. The result is a series of gaping, unresolved anomalies. Crucially, in his report, Hutton declared that the principal cause of death was bleeding from a self-inflicted knife wound on Dr. Kelly's left wrist. Yet Dr. Nicholas Hunt, the pathologist who carried out the post-mortem examination on Dr. Kelly, stated that he had cut only one blood vessel—the ulnar artery.

"Since the arteries in the wrist are of matchstick thickness, severing just one of them does not lead to life-threatening blood loss, especially if it is cut crossways, the method apparently adopted by Dr. Kelly, rather than along its length. The artery simply retracts and stops bleeding. As a scientist who would have known more about human anatomy than most, Dr. Kelly was particularly unlikely to have targeted the ulnar artery. Buried deep in the wrist, it can only be accessed through the extremely painful process of cutting through nerves and tendons. It is not common for those who commit suicide to wish to inflict significant pain on themselves as part of the process. In Dr. Kelly's case, the unlikelihood is compounded by the suggestion that his chosen instrument was a blunt pruning knife."

So convinced was Norman Baker that Dr. David Kelly was murdered, he wrote a book on the subject, *The Strange Death of David Kelly*. Nigel Jones, writing for the *Telegraph*, said: "If Baker's meticulous account is to be believed, what happened on that gentle English hillside was murder most foul, carelessly dressed up to look like suicide."

Jones continues: "Baker fills in the political background to Kelly's death—the duplicities and deceptions advanced to justify the Iraq war; then ticks off the likely suspects for Kelly's death, starting with the nuttiest—no, it wasn't a ritualized pagan killing on a ley line; nor were the Russians guilty.

Iraqi politicians Ayad Allawi (left) and Ahmed Abdel Hadi Chalabi (right) were considered dissidents by the United States. Allawi was vice president of Iraq from 2014 to 2015, and Chalabi founded the Iraqi National Congress and was prime minister as well.

Reluctantly, he even acquits MI6 and the CIA of direct responsibility, while making it clear that both had the capability to carry out the killing and concluding that both probably were aware that it would happen and covered up the fact that it had."

Jones makes it clear, however, that Baker believes that figures powerful enough to influence and change nations were most assuredly involved: "followers of the exiled CIA- and MI6-backed 'dissidents' Ahmed Chalabi and Iyad Allawi, cousins both hoping to be installed in power in the wake of a successful Anglo-American invasion."

Jones added: "As Baker rightly comments, proponents of 'conspiracy theories' tend to be dismissed as nutters. His own courageous and well-publicized probing into Kelly's death has been dismissed with the usual 'we don't do that kind of thing, old boy.' But, as this disquieting book makes very clear—unfortunately, we do."

On July 29, 2015, *Health Impact News* ran an article titled "Is the U.S. Medical Mafia Murdering Alternative Health Doctors Who Have Real Cures Not Approved by the FDA?" It stated: "On June 19, 2015, Dr. [Jeffrey] Bradstreet reportedly shot himself in the chest after his offices were raided by U.S. FDA agents and State of Georgia law enforcement agents. Three days before his death, agents exercised a search warrant to gather information about the use of GcMAF with autistic patients in his clinic. Human GcMAF holds great promise in the treatment of various illnesses including cancer, autism, chronic fatigue and possibly Parkinson's. Since 1990, 59 research papers have been published on GcMAF, 20 of these pertaining to the treatment of cancer."

Freedom Outpost, in October 2015, offered the following from writer Tim Brown: "Back in July, I reported that five holistic doctors had met untimely and suspicious deaths within 30 days and that five more were still missing. Within days of that report, two more doctors were also found dead under suspicious circumstances, which made 7 inside of a month. Now, within the span of 90 days, eleven doctors have been found dead under suspicious circumstances, and just prior to the writing of this article a twelfth holistic doctor, Marie Paas was found dead due to an apparent suicide."

In February 2016, *Natural News* posted a news story titled "Wave of holistic doctor deaths continues, as Florida chiropractor suddenly dies despite being 'hearty and healthy.'" The following is an extract from the article, written by Julie Wilson: "A wave of mysterious deaths continues to plague practitioners in the field of holistic medicine, including chiropractors, herbalists and other alternative healers, with the latest fatality involving a licensed chiropractor who also worked as a full-time teacher. Dr. Rod Floyd, Associate Professor and Faculty-Clinician with the Palmer College of Chiropractic at the Port Orange, Fla. campus, had just celebrated he and his wife's 37th wedding anniversary, when he abruptly passed away in his home late last month."

"50 Holistic Doctors Have Mysteriously Died In The Last Year, But What's Being Done About It?" That was the eye-catching title of an article that appeared at *Truth Theory* in June 2016. The story was intriguing and highlighted thirty-four deaths within the previous year. They said: "We'll let you be the judge on whether or not the untimely demise of many of these practitioners is fate or suspect. What matters most is that if these doctors were killed because they're practicing true medicine, the injustice is uncovered and the parties responsible pay for their crimes."

Snopes.com took a different approach and stated: "As of March 2015, there was an estimated range of 897,000 to just over 1,000,000 doctors in the

United States, and per every 100,000 people (of all vocations) each year, approximately 821 die. Going by those numbers alone, between 6,500 and 8,200 medical doctors will statistically die of myriad causes in any given year."

Are we seeing the sinister murder of holistic doctors on a large scale by a ruthless New World Order? That may be exactly what is happening.

STOPPING THE HUMAN HEART

For decades, numerous nations around the world have done their utmost to try to harness the mysterious powers of the mind and utilize them as tools of espionage. Extrasensory perception (ESP), clairvoyance, precognition, and astral projection have all been utilized by the CIA, the KGB, and British intelligence on more than a few occasions. As astonishing as it may sound, the world of psychic 007s is all too real. The subject has been researched with varying degrees of success for decades.

The earliest indication of serious interest on the part of the U.S. government in the field of psychic phenomena can be found in a formerly classified CIA document written in 1977 by Dr. Kenneth A. Kress, then an engineer with the CIA's Office of Technical Services, titled "Parapsychology in Intelligence." According to Kress: "Anecdotal reports of extrasensory perception capabilities have reached U.S. national security agencies at least since World War II, when Hitler was said to rely on astrologers and seers. Suggestions for military applications of ESP continued to be received after World War II. In 1952, the Department of Defense was lectured on the possible usefulness of extrasensory perception in psychological warfare.

"In 1961, the CIA's Office of Technical Services became interested in the claims of ESP. Technical project officers soon contacted Stephen I. Abrams, the Director of the Parapsychological Laboratory, Oxford University, England. Under the auspices of Project ULTRA, Abrams prepared a review article which claimed ESP was demonstrated but not understood or controllable."

Kress added: "The report was read with interest but produced no further action for another decade."

Indeed, it was in the early 1970s that the research began in earnest. In April 1972, Dr. Russell Targ, a laser physicist with a personal interest in parapsychology and the power of the human mind, met with CIA personnel from the Office of Strategic Intelligence, specifically to discuss paranormal phenomena.

Of paramount concern to the CIA was the fact that Targ informed it that the Soviet Union was deeply involved in researching psychic phenomena, mental telepathy, and ESP. It did not take the CIA long to realize that the purpose of the Soviet research was to determine if ESP could be used as a tool of espionage. As one CIA agent said: "Can you imagine if a bunch of psychic 007's from Russia could focus their minds to short-circuit our missile systems or our satellite surveillance equipment and get access to classified information in this way? The possibilities—if it worked—would be disastrous."

This realization galvanized the CIA into action. As the Kress report stated in 1973: "The Office of Technical Services funded a $50,000 expanded effort in parapsychology."

The initial studies utilized a variety of people who were carefully and secretly brought into the project and who demonstrated a whole range of seemingly paranormal skills. Those same skills could not be reliably replicated on every occasion, however.

Russell Targ met with the CIA Office of Strategic Intelligence for a discussion on parapsychology and how it can play a role in protecting U.S. interests.

Some government-sponsored psychics in the period from 1973 to 1974 located secret missile installations in the Soviet Union, found terrorist groups in the Middle East, and successfully remote viewed the interior of the Chinese Embassy in Washington, D.C. Others, meanwhile, provided data that was sketchy and, at times, simply wrong.

And it was the continuing rate of success versus the frequency of failure that led to heated debate within the CIA about the overall relevancy and validity of the project.

In "Parapsychology in Intelligence," Kenneth Kress confirmed this. After the CIA's remote-viewing team attempted to broaden the range of its operation and secure extra funding in mid-1973, said Kress: "I was told not to increase the scope of the project and not to anticipate any follow-on in this area. The project was too sensitive and potentially embarrassing."

Despite this, the CIA's research continued, with many of its advances due to a skilled psychic named Pat Price, who had achieved a number of extraordinary successes in the field of ESP, including successfully remotely viewing a sensitive installation that fell under the auspices of the National Security Agency and psychically penetrating missile sites in Libya.

Price's sudden and untimely death from a heart attack in 1975 indirectly led the CIA—according to the official story, at least—to minimize its research into psychic espionage.

Tim Rifat, who has deeply studied the world of top-secret, governmental research into psychic spying, says of Price's death: "It was alleged at the time that the Soviets poisoned Price. It would have been a top priority for the KGB to eliminate Price as his phenomenal remote-viewing abilities would have posed a significant danger to the USSR's paranormal warfare buildup. He may also have been the victim of an elite group of Russian psi-warriors trained to remotely kill enemies of the Soviet Union."

> In essence, the report stated that from an espionage and intelligence-gathering perspective, remote viewing and related phenomena were largely useless.

The scenario of research being minimized in the aftermath of Price's potentially suspicious passing was reinforced when, in 1995, a CIA-sponsored report, titled "An Evaluation of the Remote-Viewing Program—Research and Operational Applications," was produced by the American Institutes for Research (AIR). In essence, the report stated that from an espionage and intelligence-gathering perspective, remote viewing and related phenomena were largely useless.

Not everyone agreed with that conclusion, however, including W. Adam Mandelbaum, author of *The Psychic Battlefield* and a former U.S. intelligence officer, who said: "The AIR report was US-intelligence-purchased disinformation intentionally formatted to misrepresent the true states of remote-viewing research, and the true operational utility of the phenomenon."

Regardless of whether or not the CIA's role in remote-viewing operations was downsized, terminated, or simply hidden from prying eyes, it is a matter of fact that additional agencies within the U.S. government, military, and intelligence community took—and continue to take—a deep interest in psychic espionage.

The Defense Intelligence Agency (DIA), for example, has had long-standing involvement and interest in understanding and using paranormal powers both on the battlefield and in the cloak-and-dagger world of espionage. As an illustration of this, a DIA report from 1972 titled "Controlled Offensive Behavior—USSR" made an astonishing claim: "Before the end of the 1970s, Soviet diplomats will be able to sit in their foreign embassies and use ESP to steal the secrets of their enemies. A spy would be hypnotized, then his invisible 'spirit' would be ordered to leave his body, travel across barriers of space and time to a foreign government's security facility, and there read top-secret documents and relay back their information.

"The Soviets," the report continued, "are at least 25 years ahead of the U.S. in psychic research and have realized the immense military advantage of the psychic ability known as astral projection (out of the body travel)."

Similarly, in 1973 and 1975, the DIA commissioned two lengthy reports that delved deep into the heart of Soviet research of psychic phenomena and included details of one extraordinary experiment undertaken by the Russian military in the 1950s.

A somewhat disturbing extract from the DIA's files on this particular experiment states: "Dr. Pavel Naumov conducted animal bio-communication studies between a submerged Soviet Navy submarine and a shore research station. These tests involved a mother rabbit and her newborn litter and occurred around 1956."

The author of the report continued: "According to Naumov, Soviet scientists placed the baby rabbits aboard the submarine. They kept the mother rabbit in a laboratory on shore where they implanted electrodes in her brain. When the submarine was submerged, assistants killed the rabbits one by one. At each precise moment of death, the mother rabbit's brain produced detectable and record-able reactions."

It was also noted by the DIA that "as late as 1970 the precise protocol and results of this test described were believed to be classified."

Russian scientists placed rabbits into a Soviet submarine like this one. When they killed the rabbits, they were able to record how the mothers of the rabbits that were in a lab on shore reacted to the deaths.

Nevertheless, the DIA was able to determine that the Soviets' reasoning behind such experimentation was to try to understand the nature of ESP, astral projection, and the power of the mind—and even the existence of a soul—in animals such as dogs, rabbits, and primates. And if eventually understood in the animal kingdom, said the DIA, the Soviets' next step would be to focus on human beings and the way in which those same phenomena might be used as a weapon of war and espionage.

In the United Kingdom, the situation was broadly similar: at the height of the Second World War, formerly classified files at the National Archives, Kew, reveal elements of the British Police Force occasionally and stealthily employed the use of dowsers—normally associated with underground searches for water—to locate victims buried under the rubble of inner-city destruction wrought by Nazi bomber pilots.

Such was the controversy surrounding this unique brand of psychic police work that even the government's wartime Ministry of Home Security became embroiled in the affair, urging caution in endorsing "support for the mysterious" at such a "particularly dangerous time"—this despite the apparent success of its "dowsing detectives."

Still on the matter of Britain's secret spies, there is the matter of a "novel" titled *The Psychic Spy*. Written by Irene Allen-Block in 2013, it contains the following endorsement from me:

> In late 1970s London, a young woman is secretly recruited to work for British intelligence. Her world soon becomes dominated by psychic-spying, enemy agents, assassinations, and suspicious deaths. Add to the mix, the Lockerbie tragedy, the Falklands War, and the classified world of MI6, and you have a great story filled with adventure, intrigue and shadowy characters. As Irene Allen-Block skillfully shows, the mind is a mysterious and dangerous tool.

The publisher of the book, Glannant Ty, notes:

> *The Psychic Spy* tells the story of Eileen Evans, a beautiful young woman and talented psychic who is unwittingly recruited by MI6 to join their new top secret Remote Viewing program 'Blue Star' during the heart of the Cold War in the 1970's and 80's. Eileen quickly finds herself embroiled in excitement and danger as she quickly becomes a 'psychic spy' for British intelligence. Finding forbidden love with another agent, Eileen descends into a dark world filled with political intrigue, danger and death. Not only must she cope with the possibility of losing her life, she must also struggle with the very real threat of losing her soul.

> Smart, sexy and filled with humor and peril, *The Psychic Spy* is a thrilling adventure that explores a little-known but very real world where governments use actual psychics to spy on their enemies, and in some cases, even their allies! Using her own real-life experiences as a remote viewer, Irene Allen-Block has created a powerful tale that should entertain and educate readers on a piece of history that has been hidden in the shadows.

The Psychic Spy is made all the more intriguing by the fact that the book is actually a thinly veiled version of the *real-life* exploits of the aut while, from the late 1970s onward, she was in the secret employ of Bri intelligence, in the field of psychic spying.

What of today's world? Are psychic spies engaged in helping to end the War on Terror? In November 2001, the media reported that the FBI had quietly approached private remote-viewing companies with a view to predicting likely targets of future terrorist attacks. As Lyn Buchanan, the author of *The Seventh Sense*—a book that examines Buchanan's personal role in the U.S. government's remote-viewing story—says on this specific subject: "We want the message to get to terrorists everywhere that no one attacks our country and kills our people and gets away with it. We can, and we will, find you."

> In November 2001, the media reported that the FBI had quietly approached private remote-viewing companies with a view to predicting likely targets of future terrorist attacks.

Decades after official research began into remote viewing and ESP, it seems that the worlds of the psychic and the spy continue to cross paths.

"Biological Effects of Electromagnetic Radiation (Radiowaves and Microwaves)—Eurasian Communist Countries" is a 1976 document that was prepared for the U.S. Defense Intelligence Agency. It was written by Ronald L. Adams and Dr. R. A. Williams of the U.S. Army's Medical Intelligence and Information Agency. The document was declassified via the terms of the Freedom of Information Act many years ago, but the contents of the document still have the ability to provoke deep controversy. One particular segment of the Adams–Williams report stands out. It is titled "Cardiovascular System." The pair stated the following:

> Heavy emphasis has been placed on investigations involving electromagnetic radiation on the cardiovascular system. Effects on hemodynamics include blood pressure variations and cardiac arrhythmias. Comparison of a group of engineers and administrative officials who were exposed to microwaves for a period of years and an unexposed group revealed a significantly higher incidence of coronary disease. Exposure may, therefore, promote an earlier onset of cardiovascular disease in susceptible individuals.

It should be noted that interest in how, and under what specific circumstances, the human heart can be affected was not exclusively the interest of the U.S. Army's Medical Intelligence and Information Agency. For example, staff members who were employed in the Foreign Technology Division of Wright-Patterson Air Force Base in Dayton, Ohio, also dug deeply into this particularly controversial area. We know this because—as was the case with the Adams-Williams paper—Wright-Patterson AFB's files on the matter have now been declassified into the public domain. In 1978, the U.S. Air Force published a report titled "Paraphysics R&D—Warsaw Pact." As was the case the 1976 document, the 1978 Air Force report was also prepared for personnel within the Defense Intelligence Agency. This document, however, was somewhat more alternative in nature and scope. The authors of the report focused much of their time on how the heart could be affected by supernatural skills in a potentially dangerous way. The papers make it clear that people could even be killed in a fashion that would look like a normal, tragic death but that in reality would be caused by psychic phenomena.

Extrasensory perception (ESP), mind reading, and psychic phenomena were all studied when it came to the extent to which the human heart could be damaged—even involving murder, which was what the United States had deep concerns about: namely, Russian assassins trying to kill U.S. citizens via mind power. Staff at Wright-Patterson Air Force Base were particularly concerned by the extent to which the Russians were working in this particular field. The document demonstrates that the one person, far more than any other, that the Air Force had concerns about was Dr. Gennadiy Aleksandrovich Sergeyev. The doctor worked in the field of "technical services" at the Leningrad-based Institute of Physiology.

According to the work and results of Sergeyev's controversy-filled research, one of his particularly skilled psychics in this field was a woman named Nina Kulagina. In 1970 Sergeyev came to see just how dangerous Kulagina's abilities could be. Members of the Foreign Technology Staff at Wright-Patterson Air Force Base reported that one day, "Kulagina attempted to increase the heart rate of a skeptical physician." Matters did not end there, however. Air Force personnel advised the Defense Intelligence Agency that "electroencephalogram, electrocardiogram, and other parameters were measured" and that "within 1 minute after the experiment began," the heart of the same physician "reached dangerous levels, and the experiment was terminated." For the U.S. Air Force, the whole matter was deemed to be a very "serious intelligence problem."

What all of this potentially suggests is that the Russians, at the height of the Cold War, *may* have succeeded in carrying out what we might term "psychic assassinations" or "murder by microwaves." And doing so by fatally affecting the hearts of the targeted individuals. While many people of a skeptical nature might dismiss such admittedly highly controversial notions, the fact is that the U.S Air Force, the U.S. Army's Medical Intelligence and Information Agency, and the Defense Intelligence remained concerned and worried about such strange possibilities. Another important issue is worth noting: the research and the documents that I have referred to in this particular article date back to 1976 and to 1978. This inevitably begs important questions for all of us to ponder: four decades further down the line, just how far has the research progressed? Can people now be targeted and assassinated in a way that appears innocent but which, in reality, is sinister? These are questions that we should seriously think about.

ASSASSINATION, SACRIFICE, AND THE OCCULT

Let us now take a look at one of the most alternative ways to assassinate someone. It's by using the powers of the world of the occult. As incredible as it may sound, such killings have occurred time and time again. February 14, 1945, was the date of a still unresolved murder in rural England that bore all the hallmarks of death at the hands of a secret society. Some suggested a band of witches were the culprits, while others thought a secret sect of druids. The victim was a farmworker, seventy-four-year-old Charles Walton, found dead with a pitchfork sticking out of his chest. He was a resident of a small, picturesque village in Warwickshire, England, called Lower Quinton. Walton had lived in the village all his life in a pleasant, old cottage that stood across from the local church. It was a scene not unlike what one might expect to see on *Downton Abbey* or in the pages of a Jane Austen novel. Until, that is, murder, mayhem, and a secret cult came to Lower Quinton.

So far as can be ascertained, no one in the village had a grudge against Walton: he was known to all of the locals. He was an affable but quiet sort and, somewhat intriguingly, had the ability to entice wild birds to eat seeds from his hands. He was also said to have the power to reduce a wild, aggressive dog to a man's best friend simply by speaking to it. On top of that, he had expert knowledge of local folklore and legend. Rumors suggest that perhaps, Walton's slightly uncanny "powers" had ensured him a place in a secret witchcraft cult, which he ultimately fell out of favor with, and, as a result, paid with his life.

What is known for sure is that on the day in question, Valentine's Day, Walton was busily trimming hedges on what was known as Hillground, a large field at the foot of the Meon Hill. His tools were a hook and a pitchfork. While working on the hedges, someone stealthily intervened and took Walton's life in savage fashion. When his body was stumbled on by a shocked local, all hell broke loose in the small village. He was lying dead on the grassy ground, with the pitchfork pinning him to the ground, the hook pierced into his throat, and a large cross cut into his chest.

For centuries, Meon Hill has been associated with supernatural activity: sightings of blazing-eyed black dogs—not unlike the terrible beast in Sir Arthur Conan Doyle's *The Hound of the Baskervilles*—have been reported. Satan himself is said to have kicked a large rock from the top of the hill to the bottom of it with the intention of flattening Evesham Abbey.

Such was the strange and sinister nature of Walton's death that the investigation wasn't just left in the hands of the local "bobbies." None other than Scotland Yard's finest detectives were soon on the case, with the entire investigation under the control of Detective Inspector Robert Fabian. Despite an extensive investigation and suspicions that the guilty party was a man named Albert Potter—who was employing Walton on the day he met his grisly end—the matter was never resolved to the satisfaction of the police, and the crime remained a mystery.

Meon Hill, known as England's most haunted hill, and Lower Quinton near Warwickshire, England, is the location of the unsolved murder of Charles Walton.

Detective Inspector Fabian later said of his investigation: "One of my most memorable murder cases was at the village of Lower Quinton, near the stone Druid circle of the Whispering Knights. There a man had been killed by a reproduction of a Druidical ceremony on St. Valentine's Eve."

He also offered the following memorable words: "I advise anybody who is tempted at any time to venture into Black Magic, witchcraft, Shamanism—call it what you will—to remember Charles Walton and to think of his death, which was clearly the ghastly climax of a pagan rite. There is no stronger argument for keeping as far away as possible from the villains with their swords, incense and mumbo-jumbo. It is prudence on which your future peace of mind and even your life could depend."

Village folk from Lower Quinton are still reluctant to speak about the decades-old affair. Tony Smith, the landlord of the village's College Arms pub, told the BBC: "I can't talk to you about that. After 17 years of running this place I know there are some things we don't talk about. Talking about it would upset people and there's no sense in alienating people in a small village like this. There are no relatives of Charles Walton left in the village and people that might have known what happened are all dead or gone."

A Lower Quinton resident, Mrs. Wakelon, who ran the village store, was equally reluctant to say much to the BBC: "People don't talk about it; it's a closed subject. Those that know about it are gone, except one who's in hospital and another that's in a nursing home. All the others have gone or passed away."

The manager of the local post office, referred to by the BBC as Joyce, spoke in a similar vein and tones: "No one will talk to you about it. The family have all gone now, anyway. There are none of the Walton family left here now. I have no answers to your questions."

Death by pitchfork, rumors of a witchcraft cult, and a village still living in uneasy and closed-mouth fashion. The memories of the murder of Charles Walton show no signs of fading away anytime soon.

The summer of 1969 was a strange period in the quest for the truth behind the legend of the Loch Ness Monster. It was a decidedly alternative period, too, given that information surfaced on a secret "dragon cult" operating in the vicinity of the huge loch that was said to have been killing people and using their bodies in diabolical rituals. In early June, three American students travelled to Loch Ness to visit Boleskine House, an old hunting lodge (which burned down in 2015) that had once been owned by one of the key players in the world of secret societies, the legendary "Great Beast," the occultist and magician Aleister Crowley.

While walking around a centuries-old cemetery that stands close to where Boleskine House stood, the students came across a strangely decorated piece of tapestry. It was roughly four feet by five feet and was wrapped like a large sea-snail shell. It was covered in artwork of snakes and words that were soon shown to have been written in Turkish. One of the words translated as "serpent," which was a most apt description for the beast of Loch Ness. Rather notably, Turkey has its very own lake monster, which is said to dwell in the waters of Lake Van. The tapestry was also adorned with images of lotus flowers. In ancient Chinese folklore, dragons had a particular taste for lotus flowers—to the extent that in lakes where dragons were said to reside, the people of China would leave such flowers on the shores as a means to appease the violent beasts.

Of the several other people who had the opportunity to see and examine the tapestry in June 1969, one was a near-full-time Nessie seeker named Frederick "Ted" Holiday. He couldn't fail to make a connection between the Loch Ness Monster and the dragon- and serpent-based imagery. On top of that, the matter of the lotus flowers led Holiday to conclude that all of this was evidence of some kind of clandestine "dragon cult" operating in the area. Holiday knew all too well that Aleister Crowley was linked to all manner of secret societies, so Holiday suspected the presence of a dragon cult in the area.

Aleister Crowley, a mysterious man suspected to be involved in many secret societies, was known for teaching and writing about the occult.

As he began to dig even further into the story, Holiday uncovered rumors of alleged human sacrifice and assassination in the wooded areas surrounding Loch Ness, as well as attempts by the secret group to try to "invoke" supernatural serpents from the dark waters of the loch.

The mysterious group in question, Holiday believed, was said to worship Tiamat, a terrifying Babylonian snake goddess, or sea dragon, that was revered and feared chiefly because of her murderous, homicidal ways. She mated with Abzu, the god of freshwater, to create a number of supernatural dragon- and serpent-like offspring. Then there were the dreaded Scorpion Men, equally hideous offspring of Tiamat that were, as their name suggests, a horrific combination of humans and giant arachnids. According to legend, Abzu planned to secretly kill his children but was thwarted from doing so when they rose up and slayed him instead. Likewise, Tiamat was ultimately slaughtered by the god of storms, the four-eyed giant known as Marduk.

If, however, one knew the ways of the ancients, one could still call upon the power and essence of Tiamat—despite her death—as a means to achieve power, wealth, influence, and sex. Such rituals were definitively Faustian in nature, however (as they almost always are), and the conjurer had to take great heed when summoning the spirit form of Tiamat, lest violent, deadly forces might be unleashed. It was highly possible, thought Holiday, that the monsters seen at Loch Ness were manifestations of Tiamat, in some latter-day incarnation, specifically provoked to manifest by that aforementioned cult. Nothing was ever conclusively proved, but the entire situation left a bad taste in Holiday's mouth, made him deeply worried for his own safety, and eventually convinced him that the legendary creature of Loch Ness was itself supernatural in nature.

On August 31, 2000, a year before I moved to the United States, a man named Rob Lea telephoned me, and, in somewhat excited, but also distinctly worried, tones, informed me that for a number of years, he had been near-obsessively pursuing an elite and powerful body of people engaged in the mutilation and sacrifice of both people and animals in the United Kingdom, via ancient rite and ritual no less, for purposes relative to personal wealth, incredible power, and even cold-blooded, heartless murder. Needless to say, I wanted, and needed, to hear more. Two days later, I drove to an old pub in the picturesque English village of Milford to meet with my concerned informant. Rob had seen my photograph in a recent edition of the local *Chase Post* newspaper, in which I had referenced the animal-mutilation controversy, which specifically prompted him to contact me.

It was very clear to see that Rob was a firm devotee of all things Gothic. He was dressed in black jeans; big black boots; and a knee-length, shiny, black, leather coat, through which could be seen an old T-shirt emblazoned with a photograph of Siouxsie from the band Siouxsie and the Banshees, and a badge that displayed Charles Manson's face was fastened tightly to the collar of his jacket.

The near-emaciated and pale Rob viewed himself as something akin to a modern-day Sherlock Holmes, and after taking in his dark and disturbing story, I could only concur. Either that, or he was an insane fantasist of truly infinite proportions. However, the fact that his story dovetailed so eerily and closely with those of so many other people who came my way led me to believe that he was speaking both truthfully and earnestly.

As I sat and listened intently, Rob advised me that as a direct result of a horrific incident that had taken place in 1989 on a farm in Newport, England, that was owned by his family at the time, he began to develop a deep and personal interest in animal-mutilation incidents.

Notably, Rob was not an over-the-top, paranoid *X-Files* junkie seeking to validate stories that alien entities from some far-off world were stealthily extracting bovine body parts and clandestinely transferring them to a James

In 1989, Rob Lea's father found five of his sheep slaughtered on his farm, their organs placed in a pile in what appeared to be the result of some satanic ceremony.

Bond-style, secret underground installation deep in the heart of New Mexico for distinctly out-of-this-world reasons. No: Rob's quest had taken him down a very different road, one that was as dangerous and terrifying as it was winding and shadowy.

Matters all began, said Rob, in late August 1989, when his father rose early one morning to the unforgettable sight of five of his sheep, all dead, lying in a rough circle in a field that sat directly behind the family's home. All of the animals had been slaughtered: their throats had been carefully cut by what bore all the hallmarks of being a sharp instrument, and several of their major internal organs had been piled high, in a bloody mountainous mess, in the middle of the circle.

Not without significant justification, thoughts of devil worship, satanic sacrifice, and occult activities overwhelmed the frantic mind of Rob's father. Unsurprisingly, the family quickly telephoned the local police, who were quickly on the scene. An official report was filed, amid urgings from the two officers who attended that the Lea family should refrain from giving the incident any publicity.

Unfortunately, absolutely no clues or answers were ever forthcoming from the police, and the unsettling incident was never repeated. But that didn't stop it from leaving a deep and undeniable impression on the then-teenage Rob. Indeed, there was much more to come. Rob smiled and carefully placed a black briefcase on the top of the table. As he flipped its brass-colored locks, I moved the glasses and the ashtray aside to allow for more room and sat back, admittedly intrigued to see what would develop. I was both surprised and amazed, to say the least.

Rob pulled out of a large, padded envelope seven 6 x 4, 35mm, color photographs that clearly and graphically showed the scene of complete carnage at his family's farm eleven years earlier. He continued, with a slightly detectable degree of nerves in his voice, and admitted to me that when he first began digging into the animal-mutilation mystery, he was a firm adherent of the theory that deadly extraterrestrials just might have been behind the predatory attacks. As time progressed, however, and as Rob delved ever deeper into the heart of the puzzle, he found that, in many ways, something much more disturbing than alien visitations was firmly afoot.

By the late 1990s, said Rob, he had quietly and carefully traveled the length and breadth of the British Isles in pursuit of the answers to the conundrum and had inadvertently stumbled upon a sinister, and possibly deadly, group of people based near Bristol—grandly dubbed by Rob as the Cult of the Moon Beast—that, he asserted, were using slaughtered farm animals, and even household pets, in ancient rites and archaic rituals of a sacrificial nature.

The purpose, said Rob, was to use the sacrificed unfortunates as a means of conjuring up monstrous entities from some vile netherworld that would then be dispatched to commit atrocities on behalf of their masters in the Cult of the Moon Beast.

Rob had been stealthily watching the activities of the Cult of the Moon Beast—which, he stressed, was merely a term that he had applied to this closely knit group of approximately fifteen individuals—for approximately seven years by the time we met. He admitted he had no firm idea of the group's real name or even if it actually had a designated moniker. Although the cult was firmly based in Bristol, said Rob, its members were spread both far and wide, with at least four hailing from the East Coast town of Ipswich; two from the Staffordshire town of Cannock; two from the city of Exeter; one from Tavistock, Devonshire; and five from Bromley, in the county of Kent.

> According to Rob, the Cult of the Moon Beast was engaged in occult-drive rites designed to summon up unholy beasts that originated within a realm or dimension that co-existed with ours.

Rob said he had clandestinely and doggedly tracked the movements of the group and had personally—albeit stealthily—viewed three of their dark practices: one of which, he said, had occurred in early 2000 near the Ingestre Park Golf Club, deep in the heart of the Cannock Chase woods in Staffordshire, which had been the site of numerous encounters with a veritable menagerie of mysterious beasts, including werewolves; Bigfoot-type entities; ghostly, black dogs; and huge, marauding cats.

"And what exactly is this group doing?" I asked.

According to Rob, the Cult of the Moon Beast was engaged in occult-drive rites designed to summon up unholy beasts that originated within a realm or dimension that coexisted with ours. He added that certain locales around the country—and, indeed, across the globe—allowed for a doorway or portal to be opened to order, if one followed the correct, ancient rites, rituals, and "rules of animal sacrifice," of which the Cult of the Moon Beast seemingly had a deep and profound knowledge and awareness. Numerous such portals existed in Devon, Cornwall, and Staffordshire, Rob assured me in an earnest fashion.

"Yes, but again, why are they doing this? What's the purpose?" I pressed.

Rob looked me square in the face and, after a moment or two of deafening silence, uttered one word: "Murder."

"Murder," I repeated in a tone that was a statement rather than a question.

Rob nodded eagerly and related to me that the beasts in question were not physical, flesh-and-blood-style beings—at least, not in the way that we, mere mortals, understand things. Rather, they were a form of nonphysical intelligence that could take on the appearance of whatever was in the mind's eye of the beholder—more often than not, that of a large, black cat.

"Okay," I said. "What you're saying does make some sense to me, at least, as I've heard things similar to this several times before. But if these things aren't actually physically real animals, then how are they killing people?"

Rob leaned back in the seat and replied matter-of-factly: "Mind power: fright, suggestion. They'll stop your heart in a beat with fear. You want someone dead, you kill them through fear—fear of the unknown, fear of anything. That's much better than risking taking someone out with a gun or a knife; there's less of a chance of getting caught."

"Right; I understand that. But what is so special about this group that it needs so many people dead?"

Rob continued further that the Cult of the Moon Beast was linked with some very influential people and that, when needed, the cult was "hired for its services"—and paid very handsomely—by the highest echelons of private industry and even by the intelligence services of the British government.

As he explained it to me: "You want someone dead, then you give them a heart attack by having a monster appear in their bedroom at night. Or you drive them to suicide by making them think they are going mad if they are seeing werewolves."

An ancient cult, working and killing in stealth? Death by conjured-up, monstrous entities? A conspiracy that reached the heart of the British government? Yes, this is what Rob Lea claimed. Even today, years after Rob told his tale, it still provokes a sense of menace and all things macabre and mysterious.

Filey Brigg is an impressively sized, rocky peninsula that juts out from the coast of the Yorkshire, England, town of Filey. Local folklore suggests that the rocks are actually the remains of the bones of an ancient sea dragon. Unlikely, to say the least. But the story may have at least a basis in reality. In all likelihood, the story takes its inspiration from centuries-old sightings of giant monsters of the sea that called the crashing waters off Filey Brigg their home. One person who was able to attest to this was Wilkinson Herbert, a coast guard who in February 1934 had a traumatic encounter with just such a sea dragon at Filey Brigg. It was a dark, cloudy, and windy night when Herbert's life was turned upside down.

The first indication that something foul and supernatural was afoot came when Herbert heard the terrifying growling of what sounded like a dozen or more vicious hounds. The growling, however, was coming from something else entirely. As he looked out at the harsh, cold waves, Herbert saw—to his

The rocks at Filey Brigg in North Yorkshire, England, are, according to locals, actually the bones of an ancient sea dragon.

terror—a large beast around thirty feet in length and equipped with a muscular, humped back and four legs that extended into flippers. For a heart-stopping instant, the bright, glowing eyes of the beast locked onto Herbert's eyes. Not surprisingly, he said: "It was a most gruesome and thrilling experience. I have seen big animals abroad, but nothing like this."

Further up the same stretch of coastland is the county of Tyne and Wear. And in the vicinity of the county's South Shields is Marsden Bay, an area overflowing with rich tales of magic, mystery, witchcraft, and supernatural, ghostly activity. Legend tells of a man named Jack Bates (a.k.a. "Jack the Blaster") who, with his wife, Jessie, moved to the area in 1782. Instead of setting up home in the village of Marsden itself, however, the Bates family decided that they would blast a sizeable amount of rock out of Marsden Bay and create for themselves a kind of grotto-style home.

It wasn't long before local smugglers saw Jack's cavelike environment as the ideal place to store their goods, which led Jack to become one of their

Dragons and other monstrous creatures were an important part of Viking mythology, as evidenced in the carvings on their famous longships.

number. It was a secret working arrangement that existed until the year of Jack the Blaster's death in 1792. The caves were later extended, to the point where they housed, rather astonishingly, a fifteen-room mansion. Today, the caves are home to the Marsden Grotto, one of the very few "cave pubs" in Europe.

Mike Hallowell is a local author–researcher who has uncovered evidence of a secret cult in the area whose controversial and dangerous activities extend back centuries. It all began with the Viking invasion of the United Kingdom in the ninth century and their beliefs in a violent, marauding sea monster known as the Shoney. Since the Shoney's hunting ground ranged from the coast of England to the waters of Scandinavia, and the monster had a reputation for ferociousness, the Vikings did all they could to placate it. That primarily meant providing the beast with *human* offerings.

The process of deciding who would be the creature's victim was a grim one: the crews of the Viking ships would draw straws, and he who drew the shortest straw would be doomed to a terrible fate. He would first be bound by hand and foot. Then, unable to move, he would have his throat violently slashed. After which, the body of the unfortunate soul would be tossed into the churning waters with the hope that the Shoney would be satisfied and would not attack the Vikings' longships, as they were known. Sometimes, the bodies were never seen again. On other occasions, they washed up on the shore of Marsden, hideously mutilated and savagely torn to pieces.

Incredibly, however, this was not a practice strictly limited to the time when the Vikings roamed and pillaged in marauding fashion. Mike Hallowell was able to determine that belief in the Shoney never actually died out. As a result, the last such sacrifice was rumored to have occurred in 1928. Hallowell's sources also told him that the grotto's caves regularly and secretly acted as morgues for the bodies of the dead that the Shoney tossed back onto the beach following each sacrifice.

And now the story becomes even more disturbing: as a dedicated researcher of the unknown, Hallowell began to dig ever deeper into the enigma of Marsden's dragon cult and even contacted local police authorities to try to determine the truth of the matter. At the height of his research, Hallowell received a number of anonymous phone calls sternly and darkly warning him to keep away from Marsden and its tale of a "serpent sacrifice cult" and verbally threatening him as to what might happen if he didn't. To his credit, Hallowell pushed on, undeterred by the threats. While much of his data is circumstantial, Hallowell has made a strong case that such a cult still continues its dark activities there—and possibly in other parts of the United Kingdom, too.

Now, it's time to take a look at the way in which the world of assignation blends horrifically and easily with the world of the occult. In September 2001, an investigation began into one of the United Kingdom's most mysterious and still unresolved murders. It revolved around the shocking killing of a young boy who was suspected of being the victim of a mysterious and deadly cult. On September 21, the body of a child was found in London's River Thames near the reconstruction of Shakespeare's Globe theater. But all that was recovered was the poor child's torso: his arms, legs, and head were missing—and his body was drained of blood. The police wasted no time in trying to get to the bottom of the mystery, which caught the attention of practically the entire U.K. population and the media.

> **W**ithin West African witchcraft cults, it is not at all uncommon for the victims' amputated limbs to be used as a form of medicine.

It quickly became clear to the police that this was not a common case of murder but rather a disturbing example of full-blown sacrifice. All of the child's limbs had been removed with what was obviously surgical expertise, and his stomach contents included the calabar bean, which is native to Africa. If ingested, the calabar bean can provoke seizures, respiratory failure, and even death. Oddly, the boy's stomach also contained clay particles that were peppered with gold dust. The shocking story was widely reported in the media amid rumors that perhaps an African secret society had killed the young boy, who the police dubbed Adam.

Forensic analysis of Adam's remains revealed that they contained close to three times higher-than-normal levels of lead and copper, which suggested Adam originated in West Africa, almost certainly Nigeria. That theory was bolstered when it was determined that the calabar bean particles found in Adam's stomach were of a kind that were only found in Nigeria's Edo State. Detective Constable Will O'Reilly and Commander Andy Baker led the investigation. Soon, they were able to determine that the shorts attached to Adam's waist were only available in Austria and Germany. In addition, the investigators determined that this was indeed a case of human sacrifice.

One of those brought into the investigation was Dr. Richard Hoskins of Bath University, an authority on African voodoo cults and their practices. He said: "Adam's body was drained of blood, as an offering to whatever god his murderer believed in. The gold flecks in his intestine were used to make the sacrifice more appealing to that god. The sacrifice of animals happens throughout sub-Saharan Africa and is used to empower people, often as a form of protection from the wrath of the gods. Human sacrifice is believed to be the most 'empowering' form of sacrifice—and offering up a child is the most extreme form of all."

Within West African witchcraft cults, it is not at all uncommon for the victims' amputated limbs to be used as a form of medicine. The eyes, fingers, and sexual organs are also utilized as magical charms.

Despite the overwhelming mystery surrounding the case, a breakthrough was finally made. It revolved around a Nigerian woman named Joyce Osagiede. She was detained at Scotland's Glasgow Airport by immigration officers partly because she was acting in a highly erratic fashion. Significantly, she claimed knowledge of "extreme religious ceremonies" that her husband was involved in. Detective Constable O'Reilly and Commander Baker wasted no time in checking out the woman's story. They discovered something notable.

Osagiede and her children were temporarily housed in a Glasgow apartment, where the team found a pair of shorts identical to those that Adam was wearing at the time of his death. Osagiede was also found to have lived for a while in Germany, where such shorts, the police had confirmed, were available. However, it was also discovered that Osagiede was in Hamburg, Germany, at the time of Adam's murder. So although she may very well have known something of the grisly affair, she couldn't have been the murderer. British authorities quickly deported her back to Nigeria. That was not the end of the matter, however.

Years later, Osagiede decided to come clean on what she claimed she knew. According to Osagiede, while living in Germany, she took care of a young, Nigerian boy whose mother was about to be sent back home after German authorities had refused to give her permission to stay. Osagiede said she later handed the boy, who she called Ikpomwosa, over to a man only known as Bawa, who was prepared to take him to London, England. She was certain that whatever cult Bawa was attached to, "They used [Ikpomwosa] for a ritual in the water."

There are, however, problems with this story. Osagiede has also claimed that the boy's name was Patrick Erhabor. And she later maintained that Bawa was actually Kingsley Ojo, a bogus asylum seeker who arrived in the United Kingdom in 1997. Ojo denies any involvement in the death of the child, and the police have found nothing that might suggest any involvement on his part. Nevertheless, as the BBC noted:

"Ojo, who used three different identities, was arrested in London in 2002 by officers investigating the Adam case. In his flat they found in a plastic bag, a mixture of bone, sand and flecks of gold very similar to a concoction found in the dead boy's stomach. There was also a video marked 'rituals' which showed a B-movie in which an actor cuts off the head of a man. Ojo said the video and mixture belonged to other people in the house and detectives could not establish a link between him and the Adam case. In 2004, he was sentenced to four-and-a-half years in prison for people smuggling. While in prison he contacted officers and offered to help with the inquiry. But investigators concluded he was wasting police time and he was deported to Nigeria."

The police's latest word on this horrific saga: "The investigation remains ongoing and any new information provided to the team will be thoroughly investigated."

A CATALOG OF VERY WEIRD KILLINGS

In the summer of 2006, a large crop circle appeared in a field practically right next door to Chartley Castle, a centuries-old construction in the English county of Staffordshire. Strewn around the fringes of the crop circle was a large pile of colorful peacock feathers. While the presence of the peacock feathers at the site of the circle was interesting and odd, it wasn't necessarily connected to the circle. Or, maybe it was; according to one person, at least. *The Dictionary of Phrase and Fable* recorded that:

> The peacock's tail is the emblem of an Evil Eye, or an ever-vigilant traitor. The tale is this: Argus was the chief Minister of Osiris, King of Egypt. When the king started on his Indian expedition, he left his queen, Isis, regent, and Argus was to be her chief adviser. Argus, with one hundred spies (called eyes), soon made himself so powerful and formidable that he shut up the queen-regent in a strong castle, and proclaimed himself king. Mercury marched against him, took him prisoner, and cut off his head; whereupon Juno metamorphosed Argus into a peacock, and set his eyes in its tale.

And with that information now digested, I will acquaint you with the the odd saga of the Chartley Castle ape-man. Jane Adams is a devotee of Wicca who I first met in a Wiltshire crop circle in August 1997. She has an intriguing theory to account for the presence of those out-of-place feathers. She is of the opinion that the presence of the feathers at Chartley Castle is evidence that the people she believes are guilty of making the formations in the crops use the peacock's "Evil Eye" in what she describes as "black ceremonies."

Adams further claims that these very same ceremonies have been conducted—under the camouflage of darkness and on a number of occasions—within British-based crop circles and within ancient stone circles, too. And she adds that those responsible were endeavoring to create "negativity" and invoke bizarre, life-threatening creatures from darkened realms that coexist with ours, including some that would fit the image of a Bigfoot-type beast seen at Chartley Castle by a man named Mick Dodds and his wife in September 1986. As for the reason why, Adams claims the goal is to harness the beasts and then make use of them in, as she describes it, "psychic assassinations" of people who might be opposed to the activities of the group.

And there was much more to come. Adams also revealed to me that she possessed "personal knowledge" that these same people had engaged in sacrificing animals "near a stone circle in Devon, England some time ago." The purpose? To try to conjure up, from some ethereal netherworld, both "a black cat" and a creature that would most certainly fit the description of a British Bigfoot, which would then duly perform the group's dark bidding: a form of supernatural assassination via coordinated heart attacks.

Many people with an interest in powerful, secret societies will be familiar with the likes of the Bilderbergers, the Illuminati, and the Freemasons. Very few, however, will be conversant with an equally powerful body of people called the Taigheirm. Like so many other secret societies, the Taigheirm is populated by people who crave absolute power, massive wealth, and elite standing in society. It is, however, the way that the members of the Taigheirm achieve their goals that place them in their own near-unique category.

Located in the Staffordshire area of the United Kingdom, the ruins of Chartley Castle are where a crop circle was found, along with an unexplained scattering of peacock feathers.

This centuries-old cult, which has existed and operated in stealth in the highlands of Scotland since at least the seventeenth century, uses ancient sacrificial rituals to get just about anything and everything it desires. It is rumored that numerous Scottish politicians, police officers, bankers, actors, doctors, judges, and landowners are just some of the Taigheirm's many and varied members.

Merrily Harpur is a British researcher who has carefully and deeply studied the history of the Taigheirm. She says that key to the success of the members is "an infernal magical sacrifice of cats in rites dedicated to the subterranean gods of pagan times, from whom particular gifts and benefits were solicited. They were called in the Highlands and the Western Isles of Scotland, the black-cat spirits."

The process of sacrifice was, and still is, gruesome in the extreme. Isolated and lonely places high in the mountains of Scotland are chosen chiefly to ensure privacy. Secrecy is paramount. Members arrive, in black cloaks and pointed hats, at the chosen spot in the dead of night, determined at all times to protect their identities and presence from outsiders. Then comes the main event. Huge spits are built, upon which cats are slowly roasted while still alive for up to four days and nights, during which the operator of the spit is denied sleep or nourishment, aside from an occasional sip of water. Supposedly, when the ritual is at its height, from the paranormal ether terrifying, huge, black cats with glowing, red eyes appear before the conjurer, demanding to know what it is that he or she wishes to have bestowed on them: money, influence, or something else. In return, and in a fashion befitting the likes of Faust, on his or her death, the conjurer agrees to turn over his or her soul to those ancient, mighty gods worshipped by the Taigheirm.

Without doubt, the one person, more than any other, who was conversant with the terrible rituals of the Taigheirm was J. Y. W. Lloyd, who penned an acclaimed 1881 book, *The History of the Prince, the Lord's Marcher, and the Ancient Nobility of Powys Fadog and the Ancient Lords of Arwystli, Cedewen, and Meirionydd*. Lloyd became fascinated by the Taigheirm after reading Horst's *Deuteroscopy*, which was the first published work to expose the actions of this heartless group. Lloyd recorded: "The midnight hour, between Friday and Saturday, was the authentic time for these horrible practices and invocations."

Horst, himself, presented a terrible image: "After the cats were dedicated to all the devils, and put into a magico-sympathetic condition, by the shameful things done to them, and the agony occasioned to them, one of them was at once put alive upon the spit, and amid terrific howlings, roasted before a slow fire. The moment that the howls of one tortured cat ceased in death, another was put upon the spit, for a minute of interval must not take place if they would control hell; and this continued for the four entire days

Sir Allan Maclean, 4th Baronet of Morvern in Scotland, was an eighteenth-century clan chief who performed one of the last rituals of the Taigheirm.

and nights. If the exorcist could hold it out still longer, and even till his physical powers were absolutely exhausted, he must do so."

After that four-day period, said Horst, "infernal spirits appeared in the shape of black cats. There came continually more and more of these cats; and their howlings, mingled with those roasting on the spit, were terrific. Finally, appeared a cat of a monstrous size, with dreadful menaces. When the Taigheirm was complete, the sacrificer [sic] demanded of the spirits the reward of his offering, which consisted of various things; as riches, children, food, and clothing. The gift of second sight, which they had not had before, was, however, the usual recompense; and they retained it to the day of their death."

As the nineteenth century reached its end, Lloyd came to believe that while the legend and cruel and cold reputation of the Taigheirm still existed, the group, as a fully functioning entity, no longer did. He recorded that one of the very last Taigheirm rituals was held on the Scottish island of Mull in the early 1800s. Lloyd added that the folk of Mull "still show the place where Allan Maclean, at that time the incantor, and sacrificial priest, stood with his assistant, Lachlain Maclean, both men of a determined and unbending character."

Theirs was reportedly a frightening ritual held on a cold winter's night under a full moon. Lloyd noted: "Allan Maclean continued his sacrifice to the fourth day, when he was exhausted both in body and mind, and sunk in a swoon; but, from this day he received the second-sight to the time of his death, as also did his assistant. In the people, the belief was unshaken, that the second-sight was the natural consequence of celebrating the Taigheirm."

There is, however, intriguing data strongly suggesting that the Taigheirm are still with us, lurking in the shadows and still extending their power and influence. In 1922, Carl Van Vechten commented on post-nineteenth-century Taigheirm activity in a footnote contained in his book *The Tiger in the House*. It reads: "The night of the day I first learned of the Taigheirm I dined with some friends who were also entertaining Seumas, Chief of Clann Fhearghuis of Stra-chur. He informed me that to the best of his knowledge the Taigheirm is *still* celebrated in the Highlands of Scotland."

Then there is the account of Donald Johnson, born and bred in Scotland but who, just like his late father, worked as a butler for a powerful and rich family that had its roots in the ancient English county of Staffordshire. According to Johnson, his father was invited by his employers to join an English offshoot of the Taigheirm in the winter of 1982—providing that he was willing to leave his old life and friends behind him and fully embrace the Taigheirm and its horrific teachings. Johnson Sr. was ready to do so until he witnessed one of the monstrous sacrifices deep in the heart of England's Cannock Chase woods, and on the proverbial dark and stormy night, no less.

Johnson Sr.'s decision to quickly walk away was not at all appreciated by the Taigheirm, who reportedly made explicit threats about what might happen to him if he ever dared to go public with what he knew and had seen. Such was his fear, he stayed completely and utterly silent on the matter until he told his son, Donald, in 2010, who went public with the story in December of that year out of fear for his own safety. Notably, Johnson claimed that it wasn't just animals that were used in the sacrifices: it was people, too; their lives were taken from them in the name of power, influence, and wealth. These were assassinations.

In early 2008, rumors circulated to the effect that a U.S.-based equivalent of the ancient Scottish order of the Taigheirm was operating in Dallas, Texas. As was the case with the original Scottish members, those tied to this Texas group were using the rites and rituals to achieve two things: power and wealth. While such rumors were never conclusively proved to be real, the fact is that from 2008 to 2011, there were numerous cases of cat mutilation in Dallas. And they clearly weren't the work of coyotes or bobcats. There was method in the grisly, citywide madness.

It all began in the summer of 2008, when a pair of cats was found "dissected"—according to local media—in the city's Lover's Lane. Almost one year later, a cat was found dead with organs removed with surgical precision in Dallas's Lakewood Heights. The unfortunate man who stumbled on the remains of the poor animal said: "The cat was literally cut in half at its midsection. There was no blood on our front lawn, so it appears that the mutilation probably occurred elsewhere and the remains were dumped on our lawn by the perpetrator."

Two more cats were found within days, also mutilated in fashions that suggested the culprits were all too human. As a result, the Dallas Society for the Protection of Cruelty to Animals offered a $5,000 reward for anyone who could help solve the disturbing mystery, but there was not even a single taker. A couple of weeks later, Dallas's Midway Hollow was targeted. The local police said: "We used to think it was a juvenile up to no good. But now we think it might be an older guy who lives nearby, snatches these cats, mutilates them, then takes them back to where he finds them."

Then, in August, the local NBC affiliate reported on the discovery of six dead and mutilated cats in the northwest part of Dallas.

Although 2009 and 2010 were quiet, 2011 was anything but. It all began again in April of that year, when a "surgically mutilated" cat was stumbled on in Wilshire Heights, Dallas. Yet again, a substantial reward was on offer. There was, however, nothing but silence and not a single lead in sight.

Without a doubt, the most controversial theory surfaced in May 2011. The story, from a local conspiracy theorist, Bob Small, was that the Taigheirm group was allied to the far more well-known Skull and Bones group, which was founded in 1832 at Yale University in New Haven, Connecticut. Yet again, there were local rumors of human sacrifice to appease ancient deities—all in the name of money, sex, and power.

> Yet again, there were local rumors of human sacrifice to appease ancient deities—all in the name of money, sex, and power.

"In the spiritual beliefs of many African tribes," said the late Brad Steiger, "the leopard is a totem animal that guides the spirits of the dead to rest. For many centuries there has existed a leopard cult in West Africa, particularly in Nigeria and Sierra Leone, whose members kill as does the leopard, by slashing, gashing, and mauling their human prey with steel claws and knives. Once a victim has been chosen and the date and time of the killing agreed upon, the executioner, known as the Bati Yeli, is selected. The Bati Yeli wears the ritual leopard mask and a leopardskin robe. Preferably, the human sacrifice is performed at one of the leopard cult's jungle shrines. After the cult has killed their victim, they drink the blood and eat the flesh. The cultists believe that a magical elixir known as borfima, which they brew from their victim's intestines, grants them superhuman powers and enables them to transform into leopards."

Pat O'Dwyer, the assistant district commissioner at Port Loko, Sierra Leone, stumbled upon such a secret cult of the killing kind in the 1930s in Makeni, Sierra Leone. O'Dwyer said: "I had not been alone in charge of the station for long before a dead body was brought in from the country very much disintegrating. You can imagine that a dead body would not last long in the tropics. The chief's messenger, who brought it, said that the chief's view was that the man had been the victim of a secret society and that it was murder. The body had obviously been clawed about and the first thing for me to find out was what the doctor thought about the body's injuries.

"The corpse was taken, therefore, to the doctor who said that it was so decomposed that he could not really tell. However, the claw marks could be those of a leopard, or they could be imposed by metal claws and inflicted by man. I held an enquiry and the most feasible thing seemed to me to return a verdict of accidental death. I concluded that the man, who was a farmer living far out in the bush in a hut on the edge of the forest, had been the victim of a real leopard's attack and had thus met his death.

"After the verdict I heard murmurings by the Court Messengers to the effect that really he had been murdered by a secret society. Well, this is where the African's mind becomes very confused. There is no doubt that secret societies did exist, which were really murder societies: the Leopard Society, the Alligator Society and the Baboon Society. The allegations were that members of each of these societies took very secret and binding vows and associating themselves with these animals, simulated their methods of killing their selected victims.

"Thus, the Leopard Society would dress themselves in leopard skins and attach to their hands and feet metal claws. They would then lay in wait for their victim and pounce on him, clawing him to death. The Alligator Society would similarly attire themselves and wait by the water side and drown their victims and the Baboon Society would batter their victims to death. It was well known that these animals would also attack human beings and kill them, particularly children, out in the bush.

"A further possibility which the Africans believed in was that a member of these societies had the power to direct his soul into the body of a leopard, alligator or baboon and conduct that animal to attack the victim of his choice. A little while after this time there was trouble in the Kenema district where members of the baboon society were put on trial for murder. The evidence against them was very strong, and the accused themselves added evidence to prove their own guilt. They were found guilty and sentenced to death for murder and the sentence was carried out."

A particularly harrowing story came from Dr. Werner Junge, a German who traveled to Liberia in 1930 and stayed for approximately ten years. He said of his discovery of someone who had fallen victim to the Leopard Society:

There, on a mat in a house, I found the horribly mutilated body of a fifteen-year-old girl. The neck was torn to ribbons by the teeth and claws of the animal, the intestines were torn out, the pelvis shattered, and one thigh was missing. A part of the thigh, gnawed to the bone, and a piece of the shin-bone lay near the body. It seemed at first glance that only a beast of prey could

A leopard cult existed in Africa in which members used metal hooks to simulate the big cat's claws when killing their victims.

have treated the girl's body in this way, but closer investigation brought certain particularities to light which did not fit in with the picture. I observed, for example, that the skin at the edge of the undamaged part of the chest was torn by strangely regular gashes about an inch long. Also the liver had been removed from the body with a clean cut no beast could make. I was struck, too, by a piece of intestine the ends of which appeared to have been smoothly cut off, and, lastly, there was the fracture of the thigh—a classic example of fracture by bending.

Edward Lansdale was a man highly skilled in the field of what is known, in military circles, as psychological warfare. Back in the early 1950s, Lansdale—who rose to prominence during the Second World War while working with the Office of Strategic Services, a forerunner of the CIA—spread rumors throughout the Philippines that a deadly vampire was wildly on the loose. Its name was the Aswang, a blood-sucking monstrosity, of which the people of the Philippines lived in complete dread. The reason for Lansdale's actions was bizarre and simple.

In 1952, the Philippines were in turmoil as a result of an uprising by the Hukbalahap, or Huks. They were vehemently antigovernment rebels and did their very best to oust the president of the Philippines, Elpidio Rivera Quirino,

Major General Edward Lansdale knew the value of the local mythology with the local natives and turned their fear of a creature known as Aswang to his advantage in a plan to defeat the Huks.

with whom Lansdale was friends. When Quirino asked the major general to help end the reign of terror that the Hukbalahap had generated, he quickly came onboard.

One of the first things that Lansdale noted was that the rebels were deathly afraid of the vampiric Aswang and its nocturnal, blood-drinking activities. As the major general recalled: "To the superstitious, the Huk battleground was a haunted place filled with ghosts and eerie creatures. A combat psywar squad was brought in. It planted stories among town residents of an Aswang living on the hill where the Huks were based. Two nights later, after giving the stories time to make their way up to the hill camp, the psywar squad set up an ambush along the trail used by the Huks."

That same psywar squad then did something that was very alternative but which proved to be extremely effective. They silently grabbed one of the Hukbalahap rebels, snapped his neck, and used a specially created metallic device that left two deep, vicious-looking puncture marks on the neck of the man. But that was barely the start of things: they then quietly tied a rope around the man's ankles, hung his body from a nearby tree, and let just about as much blood as possible drain out of his body. After several hours, the corpse was lowered to the ground and left close to the Hukbalahap camp, specifically to ensure it was found by his comrades. They *did* find it.

The result, as Lansdale noted, was overwhelmingly positive from the perspective of the Philippine government: "When the Huks returned to look for the missing man and found their bloodless comrade, every member of the patrol believed that the Aswang had got him and that one of them would be next if they remained on that hill. When daylight came, the whole Huk squadron moved out of the vicinity."

It was an ingenious and spectacularly successful tactic, which was reportedly utilized on more than fifteen occasions to take back strategic ground from the Hukbalahap soldiers. A vampire of legend was now one of reality—or so the rebels believed.

Martin J. Clemens says that "located in West Sussex, England, Clapham Wood stands to the north of the small village of Clapham. Historically, Clapham has been an archetypal English village, one that's been around, likely, since Saxon times. Over the last 300 years, it has remained largely hidden from the outside world, except, that is, for the last four decades."

The "four decades" comment is a very apt one. Since the early 1970s, Clapham Wood has been associated with murder, mystery, and a secret society called the Friends of Hecate. The mystery began in 1972. That June, a police constable named Peter Goldsmith disappeared while walking through the woods. His body was not found until December 13. What makes this even more intriguing is the fact that two months before Goldsmith vanished, he had been investigating the death of a woman who had been murdered in the very same woods. Two victims were inextricably linked to one another.

And, as Martin Clemens reveals, "In July 1975, pensioner Leon Foster disappeared and was subsequently found three weeks later, by a couple who were searching for a horse in the wood, a horse that had also gone missing under mysterious circumstances. Next, on Halloween of 1978, the vicar of Clapham, the retired Reverend Harry Snelling went missing. His body was found three years later, by a Canadian tourist. Again, no cause of death could be identified."

Things were far from over. Three years later, in 1981, the body of Jillian Matthews was found in the woods. She had also been raped. Moving away from the human casualties of Clapham Wood, there's the matter of the disappearance of a number of dogs. On this matter, Clemens says:

"Three cases in particular—which were covered widely by the press—told of two dogs that went missing without a trace and a third that suffered a

Clapham Wood in West Sussex, England, is the location of more than a few unusual events, including death, rape, and the disappearance of a number of dogs.

mysterious paralyzation. The son of Peter Love, while walking their family chow in the wood, watched as his dog ran amongst thicket of trees in the forest and disappeared, never to be seen again. The following week, farmer John Cornford's collie disappeared in the same place. A third dog, a golden retriever owned by Mr. E. F. Rawlins, was found partially paralyzed after running into the woods, the cause of which was never determined and which eventually led to its being euthanized."

It's hardly surprising that Clapham Wood gained a reputation as a place filled with menace and mystery. In 1987, information surfaced suggesting that Clapham Wood was filled with something else, too: a powerful and dangerous group called the Friends of Hecate, whose membership included elements of the British government.

Of Hecate, Aaron J. Atsma says: "HEKATE (or Hecate) was the goddess of magic, witchcraft, the night, moon, ghosts and necromancy. She was the only child of the Titanes Perses and Asteria from whom she received her power over heaven, earth, and sea. Hekate assisted Demeter in her search for Persephone, guiding her through the night with flaming torches. After the mother-daughter reunion she became Persephone's minister and companion in Haides.

"Two metamorphosis myths describe the origins of her animal familiars: the black she-dog and the polecat (a mustelid house pet kept to hunt vermin). The bitch was originally the Trojan Queen Hekabe, who leapt into the sea after the fall of Troy and was transformed by the goddess into her familiar. The polecat was originally the witch Gale who was transformed into the beast to punish her for her incontinence. Others say it was Galinthias, the nurse of Alkmene, transformed by the angry Eileithyia, but received by Hekate as her animal."

The story of the Friends of Hecate first surfaced publicly in the pages of *The Demonic Connection*, a 1987 book written by Toyne Newton, Charles Walker, and Alan Brown. According to Walker, he met with one of the members of the secret group, who confirmed that the deaths of the various people—and the disappearances of the dogs—were the work of the Friends of Hecate, which has been described as "a quasi-pagan British occult order."

While the existence of the Friends of Hecate has yet to be fully confirmed, the unsettling story of dark and mysterious deaths in the heart of Clapham Wood has ensured the legend of the group survives and thrives.

ASSASSINATION ON A WORLDWIDE SCALE

Is a nefarious, secret, and deadly group hard at work to reduce the world's population—and to reduce it quickly, drastically, and to levels that will amount to nothing less than full-blown decimation? We're talking about assassinations on incredible, obscene levels. Certainly, one only has to take a look at the case of Adolf Hitler. He waged a determined war of extermination against the Jews during the Second World War. As a result, with phenomenal, horrific speed, an entire race of people came close to being systematically wiped off the face of the planet. Could such a thing happen again? If it does, will it be due to the actions of a future Hitler, a madman with lunatic delusions of grandeur? Maybe not: conspiracy theorists maintain that the assassination-driven death knell will be for *billions*, and it might come from none other than a secret cabal hidden deep within the heart of the United Nations.

Earth undoubtedly cannot adequately house an ever-growing population indefinitely. The world's weather is also changing—in ways that are seen as both hostile and suspicious—which has given rise to the likelihood that global warming is the culprit. Humankind's ever-growing need for dwindling fossil foods, combined with its near-exponentially increasing polluting of the planet's ecosystem, has almost irreversibly altered our future and has raised fears that our most precious commodity—water—will soon become scarce. As a result, perhaps billions of us will be culled to ensure the survival of the elite.

Many conspiracy theorists believe that things began on December 10, 1974, when a highly controversial report was prepared for the United States' National Security Council. The report and its attendant project and study were overseen by one of the most powerful figures in global politics, Henry Kissinger, who held such positions as U.S. secretary of state and national security advisor

Nobel Peace Prize winner Henry Kissinger had many years of experience working as politician, diplomat, and geopolitical consultant. He also authored an important paper on overpopulation in America.

to the president. The report was titled "Implications of Worldwide Population Growth for U.S. Security and Overseas Interests."

As the authors noted, in those particular countries where growth and development were far from being on par with the rest of the planet—such as Thailand, Pakistan, Brazil, Ethiopia, Egypt, Turkey, and Nigeria—there was a distinct possibility that with falling food supplies, dwindling water and fuel, and an increase of people, demands from the relevant populations for action to combat famine would soon lead to civil unrest and uncontrollable anarchy. There was another worry for Kissinger's people. If the economies of countries with exploding populations collapsed, the result might be that the United States would be unable to import from those same countries items that were essential to its own economy. In that scenario, everyone suffers. Or, maybe not: Kissinger was determined that the United States would not fall, even if other nations did. It was up to the United Nations and the United States to solve the problem.

Clearly, as the following extracts show, a great deal of thought had gone into how the rise of populations in the underdeveloped world could possibly bring the United States to its knees:

"The U.S. economy will require large and increasing amounts of minerals from abroad, especially from less developed countries. That fact gives the U.S. enhanced interest in the political, economic, and social stability of the supplying countries. Wherever a lessening of population pressures through reduced birth rates can increase the prospects for such stability, population policy becomes relevant to resource supplies and to the economic interests of the United States."

The document continues: "The location of known reserves of higher grade ores of most minerals favors increasing dependence of all industrialized regions on imports from less developed countries. The real problems of mineral supplies lie not in basic physical sufficiency, but in the politico-economic issues of access, terms for exploration and exploitation, and division of the benefits among producers, consumers, and host country governments."

Anticipating how things could turn very bad for the United States, there is the following: "Whether through government action, labor conflicts, sabotage, or civil disturbance, the smooth flow of needed materials will be jeopardized. Although population pressure is obviously not the only factor involved, these types of frustrations are much less likely under conditions of slow or zero population growth."

The brains behind the report then targeted the people themselves, their collective mindset, and how to get around increasing issues of concern. In a section titled "Populations with a High Proportion of Growth," it was noted:

"The young people, who are in much higher proportions in many LDCs [least developed countries], are likely to be more volatile, unstable, prone to extremes, alienation and violence than an older population. These young people can more readily be persuaded to attack the legal institutions of the government or real property of the 'establishment,' 'imperialists,' multinational corporations, or other—often foreign—influences blamed for their troubles."

There were words of warning in the report, too: "We must take care that our activities should not give the appearance to the LDCs of an industrialized country policy directed against the LDCs. Caution must be taken that in any approaches in this field we support in the LDCs are ones we can support within this country. 'Third World' leaders should be in the forefront and obtain the credit for successful programs. In this context it is important to demonstrate to LDC leaders that such family planning programs have worked and can work within a reasonable period of time."

The authors of the report make an interesting statement: "In these sensitive relations, however, it is important in style as well as substance to avoid the appearance of coercion."

In other words, the report does not deny that nations might be coerced, only that there is a concerted effort to "avoid the appearance" of such.

So much for the 1970s, when the program of planetary extermination, on an obscene scale, is reported to have begun. But what of today? According to some, it's out of control: "A reasonable estimate for an industrialized world society at the present North American material standard of living would be 1 billion. At the more frugal European standard of living, 2 to 3 billion would be possible," stated the United Nations' Global Diversity Assessment, in shockingly matter-of-fact fashion.

THE MAN WITH THE MISSING HANDS

For more than a decade, Lisa Hagan has done a fine job as my literary agent. She is also a good friend. Not only that: in the last few years, Lisa has had a few very strange experiences that are all too common in certain MIB-based encounters. I say "certain" ones because Lisa's encounters seem to be specifically with the government type of MIB, rather than with the clearly paranormal kind of Men in Black. Remember: John Keel was certain there were *two* groups of MIB. Maybe, there are even more factions.

On February 21, 2017, I interviewed Lisa about her many experiences, all of which, when combined, point to the fact that she has been under close surveillance for a very long time. We'll begin with my controversial 2005 book *Body Snatchers in the Desert*, which was focused on a nonalien theory for what happened near Roswell, New Mexico, in July 1947.

Virtually all of the book's research was completed by the end of 2003, and the first seven or eight months of 2004 were spent writing the manuscript for Simon & Schuster. Only days after I mailed a copy of the manuscript to the publisher, it vanished, overnight, from the publisher's offices in New York. Josh Martino and Patrick Huyghe, who both worked on the editing of the book, were perplexed—and more than a little disturbed and concerned, too. Jokes about the manuscript, probably now being held in the underground vaults of the NSA, may not have been too far from the truth, Patrick suggested.

I must confess that I had totally forgotten about this odd event until I decided to interview Lisa for this book. That was when something came flooding back into my mind, something Lisa had told me years ago that concerned links between publishing houses and the government/intelligence community. And so, this was the ideal time to finally get the story nailed. Lisa told me that

The Simon & Schuster building in New York City is where the manuscript for *Body Snatchers in the Desert* apparently just disappeared.

it's common for government agencies to take notice of books on controversial subjects that might give the author unwanted attention—even before the publication date:

> If I want to do anything that is going to blow the whistle on something that the government doesn't want out there publicly, the government can shut that down—at the publishing house. They have people on the inside. It took me a long time, after being rejected on certain projects, to finally realize that what was happening to me was the same thing that had happened to my mother: shut down by publishers on the stories the government didn't want out there.

> I still work with these publishers—they do their job; I do my job. I do know that one of the publishers I worked with in New York—this was back when all the manuscripts were printed—they had certain people who read the manuscripts *before* the editors got to them. I don't know which way it goes: maybe, they were recruited by an agency when they were already working for the company. Or, they infiltrated it. But, I do know of people in the publishing industry who have been asked to be informants—asked by people in the government. There are definitely people who have been recruited.

MIB in the book-publishing industry? Yep, that's exactly how it looked. And as someone whose books have made the front pages of the *New York Times*, *USA Today*, the *New York Times Book Review*, and the *Los Angeles Times*, Lisa should certainly know what she is talking about. We then got into something of an equally sinister—but very different—fashion. She said someone had been prowling around her property under cover of darkness:

> It's very dark where I live and there are only a few people here. It's very heavily wooded and there's a lot of farmland. And it's all dirt road, so there's not a lot of traffic. So far, it has happened to me at least three or four times. My house is a long bungalow, and my bedroom is on the end, near the car-port. And, periodically, I'll be lying there reading, with the light on. It's always been between

10:00 and 11:00 at night, and I'll hear my vehicle trunk open. Then I hear it close. I do have a picture of a handprint, in the dust on my trunk that I took after it happened one night. I kept the picture in case I wanted to do anything with it, which I did not.

If I had wanted to I could have crept up in my pajamas and intervened, but what would I do? It made me mad, though. Nothing was ever taken from the trunk. But, I did check if anything had been put in there. Those bugs are small though, so who knows?

Then there was the matter of Lisa's encounter with what sounded just like one of John Keel's "phantom photographers." Lisa told me the strange story:

It was a Sunday and I was in the kitchen making something, standing at my kitchen sink. And, I saw a flash to the left. In my yard. I looked over and there was a little white Honda. An Accord, I think; two people. There was a guy taking pictures of the side of my house. And then they drove right in front of the house and took a picture—right where I was standing in front of the kitchen window. They were only about two car-lengths from the window. They went down past my house and then came back. And then they drove off. That made me nervous and my anxiety went up. My intuition, my alarm bells, went off.

And on similar territory, there was this from Lisa:

The other story is that my aunt and I had seen a UFO on our farm. This was Christmas night, 2015. And, on the 26th she left. I called and asked friends if they wanted to come over, to look for UFOs. They were like, "No, we're already in bed." But, another friend wanted to come over and see if we might see anything. We were standing by the trunk of my vehicle—the trunk someone had been in and out of—as we had the iPads and the binoculars resting on it. It was a beautiful night and we were talking and looking around. As my friend left, he said that when he was maybe ten cars away from me, around a row of trees here, there was a black, unmarked SUV with a lot of antenna on it. Not long after that, the same friend was driving on our main road—the road that everyone lives off—and there were two of those SUVs, with men outside them with binoculars, overlooking our farm.

So just what, exactly, could have prompted someone to have placed Lisa under deep surveillance? There is an answer to that question. It revolves around the 1997 assassination of a screenwriter named Gary Devore. The story of

> It revolves around the 1997 assassination of a screenwriter named Gary Devore. The story of his life and death is filled with conspiratorial aspects....

his life and death is filled with conspiratorial aspects, including the involvement of the CIA and Russian drug barons. On this matter of Devore's life and death, Lisa said:

> One other thing that happened: I have been working on a book on Gary Devore; he's dead now, but worked with the CIA. And oddly enough, my author is dead now, too. When he would send things to me, like his manuscripts and pictures, I would go to the mailbox and some of it was opened and there was nothing in the packages. Other times just one thing would be missing. Or, the packages would have been opened, but everything was in there.

I knew only too well the story of Gary Devore. In September 2015, the United Kingdom's *Daily Mail* reported: "When the skeletal remains of Hollywood screenwriter Gary Devore were found strapped into his Ford Explorer submerged beneath the California Aqueduct in 1998 it brought an end to one of America's most high profile missing person cases. The fact that Devore was on his way to deliver a film script that promised to explain the 'real reason' why the U.S. invaded Panama, has long given rise to a slew of conspiracies surrounding the nature of his 'accidental' death."

The *Daily Mail* continued: "It didn't help that Devore's hands were missing from the crash scene, along with the script, and that investigators could offer no plausible explanation as to how a car could leave the highway and end up in the position it was found a year after he disappeared."

As the *Daily Mail* also noted: "Devore was working with the CIA in Panama and even a White House source concedes his mysterious death bears all the hallmarks of a cover-up."

But that's not all. There's far more to the story.

Vice.com noted: "Gary Devore was driving home through the Mojave Desert having just finished a film script. Devore was a successful Hollywood screenwriter, script doctor and producer, known for films like *Raw Deal,* starring Arnold Schwarzenegger, and *Dogs of War*, starring Christopher Walken. But this script wasn't like those films. It was full of allegations against the US government involving drugs and bank robbery, all set against one of the twentieth century's most controversial wars, the invasion of Panama."

They add: "Devore disappeared in 1997 and, despite an extensive search, no trace of him was found for a year. He was eventually discovered by an amateur detective who said he had "a hunch." It seemed he had hit the barriers on the California Aqueduct and flipped into the water below. Unsurprisingly, the case became popular with conspiracy theorists, with many people speculating Devore may have been murdered by anyone from Russian drug gangs to the CIA."

Matt Alford is the author of a book on the life and death of Devore. Its appropriate title is *The Writer with No Hands*. Of Alford's book, *Spy Culture* provides the following: "From 2008, Alford spent years accumulating all the news coverage, documentaries, FBI reports and other files and sources that he could in the hope of piecing together what had really happened. Wendy Devore reported how agents from the CIA, DOD, NSA and FBI, including Chase Brandon, were crawling all over the case in the initial days. Devore was also the best man at the wedding of Tommy Lee Jones—Brandon's cousin. As Wendy herself continued to dig she discovered that Devore had spent time in Panama with the CIA, seemingly confirming that Devore was in a position to know some dirty secrets that could have got him killed.

"Gary's missing hands provided one of the strangest and most tantalizing possibilities. No hands were found in the car, making it all but completely impossible that they were amputated as a result of the crash. A few hand bones were found, but in the opinion of the coroner they not only weren't Gary's, they were in fact over 200 years old. Was this a warning to other screenwriters who might consider using their hands (their writing talent) to threaten the state? The phrase 'hallmarks of a ritualistic murder' springs to mind."

The mysterious death of Gary Devore remains a mystery.

KILLING BY SOUND

Murder by sound? It may sound impossible. The reality, however, is that it isn't. Imagine the scene: you and a group of friends—concerned about the ever-increasing level of surveillance of, and spying on, the public by agencies of government, the intelligence community, and the military—decide to attend a peaceful demonstration that is being held in your hometown. In total, a couple hundred people voice their concerns that too much control is being exerted upon the population. Suddenly, however, things go awry. In no time at all, everyone in the crowd suddenly feels nauseous. Some lose their balance and fall over. Others vomit. More than a few are overwhelmed by dizziness and have to lie on the ground. Some develop the shakes. In a worst-case scenario, your heart might misfire, and you will soon be taking your last breaths. None of this is due to the hot weather, stress, or hysteria. Quite the opposite: you have been targeted, and hit by, a weapon that has disabled you via sound.

Although we give little thought to sound, it plays a massive role in our lives from varying perspectives. The sound of the voice of an old friend we haven't seen in years can make us happy. The screams of someone late at night provoke concern and worry. The sirens of fire trucks might provoke anxiety. And music can be uplifting, relaxing, or energizing, depending on the type of music one prefers. There is, however, another aspect to sound: it can be used as a weapon of control against us.

What, exactly, is sound? Apple provides a concise explanation: "All sounds are vibrations traveling through the air as sound waves. Sound waves are caused by the vibrations of objects and radiate outward from their source in all directions."

Let us now look at the ways in which sound can be used to control us, to alter our perceptions, and to even destabilize us—physically and mentally. We'll begin with something called infrasound. It is an extremely low-frequency sound that is below the 20HZ mark and is undetectable to the human ear. A number of animals use infrasound as a means to communicate with each other. The long list includes giraffes, whales, and elephants. It's a form of communication in the animal kingdom that can be highly effective for significant numbers of miles.

There is another important aspect of infrasound: when it is directed at humans, it can provoke a wealth of unsettling physical and psychological sensations as well as both audible and visual hallucinations. Death can even follow. Many are interpreted as supernatural events when, in reality, it is simply the mechanisms of the brain misfiring when hit by infrasound. Consider the following:

"Mysteriously snuffed out candles, weird sensations and shivers down the spine may not be due to the presence of ghosts in haunted houses but to very low frequency sound that is inaudible to humans," reported the Associated Press in September 2003. "British scientists have shown in a controlled experiment that the extreme bass sound known as infrasound produces a range of bizarre effects in people...."

A psychologist and professor at the University of Hertfordshire, Richard Wiseman has noted that some believe certain levels of sound provoke an odd sense in people that they are in the presence of a ghost.

"Some scientists have suggested that this level of sound may be present at some allegedly haunted sites and so cause people to have odd sensations that they attribute to a ghost—our findings support these ideas," noted Professor Richard Wiseman of the University of Hertfordshire in the United Kingdom.

Startling and disturbing information relative to how sound can be used as a tool of control and manipulation can be found in the pages of a formerly classified U.S. Defense Intelligence Agency document, dated March 1976: "Biological Effects of Electromagnetic Radiation (Radio-waves and Microwaves) Eurasian Communist Countries." Written by Ronald L. Adams and Dr. R. A. Williams of the U.S. Army (and specifically of the Medical Intelligence and Information Agency), it notes in part:

"The Eurasian Communist countries are actively involved in evaluation of the biological significance of radio-waves and microwaves.

Most of the research being conducted involves animals or in vitro evaluations, but active programs of a retrospective nature designed to elucidate the effects on humans are also being conducted."

Of deep concern to the U.S. military and intelligence community was the incredible revelation that the Soviets had developed technology that allowed them to beam "messages" into the minds of targeted individuals. Rather notably, the DIA and the Army concluded that such messages might direct a person to commit suicide. Even if the person was not depressed, said Adams and Williams, the technology could be utilized to plunge them into sudden states of "irritability, agitation, tension, drowsiness, sleeplessness, depression, anxiety, forgetfulness, and lack of concentration."

The authors added: "Sounds and possibly even words which appear to be originating intra-cranially can be induced by signal modulation at very low average-power densities."

They concluded: "The Soviets will continue to investigate the nature of internal sound perception. Their research will include studies on perceptual distortion and other psycho-physiological effects. The results of these investigations could have military applications if the Soviets develop methods for disrupting or disturbing human behavior."

When, in the mid-1980s, plans were formulated by the iron-fist regime of then-Prime Minister Margaret Thatcher to base nuclear "cruise" missiles at strategic military bases in the British Isles, it provoked massive demonstrations on the part of the general public—particularly at the Royal Air Force Greenham Common, a now closed-down military installation in Berkshire, England.

As a result of the planned placement of missiles at Greenham Common, a large group of female peace protesters set up camp outside the base. It wasn't long, however, before many of the women began to experience a series of disturbing symptoms, including deep depression; overwhelming anxiety attacks; intense, migrainelike headaches; alarming losses of short-term memory; and mind-destabilizing effects.

As a direct result of this alarming and highly suspicious development, theories began to quickly develop and circulate to the effect that the women were being specifically targeted with electromagnetic weaponry as part of an intensive effort to bring their demonstrations—which had generated a large amount of support—to an abrupt and permanent end.

This was no wide-eyed conspiracy theory, either: even Britain's highly respected *Guardian* ran a story in a March 10, 1986, article titled "Peace Women Fear Electronic Zapping at Base." It reported that the military possessed "an intruder detection system called BISS, Base Installation Security System, which operates on a sufficiently high frequency to bounce radar waves off a human body moving in the vicinity of a perimeter fence."

As the research into what was afoot at Greenham Common continued, a further theory surfaced: that the women who were protesting were targeted by extremely low-frequency weapons. This begs an important question: how effective is such technology? The answer is simple and disturbing: it is extremely effective. It has been suggested by conspiracy theorists that at least some of this technology was secretly tested in the early 1990s in and around the area of Taos, New Mexico.

Live Science notes of the hum that it "seems to have first been reported in the early 1990s. Joe Mullins, a professor emeritus of engineering at the University of New Mexico, conducted research into the Taos Hum. Based on a survey of residents, about 2 percent of the general population was believed to be 'hearers,' those who claimed to detect the hum. Sensitive equipment was set up in the homes of several of the 'hearers,' measuring sounds and vibrations, but after extensive testing nothing unusual was detected."

In more recent years, such hums have been heard all around the world. In 2015, the United Kingdom's *Independent* reported: "In Britain, the most famous example was the 'Bristol hum' that made the news in the late 1970s. One newspaper asked readers in the city: 'Have you heard the Hum?' and at least eight hundred people said they had. Alarmingly, it was revealed that when the humming was at its absolute height, people were affected by intense migraines and even nosebleeds. When the humming stopped, so did the side-effects. As for the specific sound, it was likened to a car engine which was 'idling,' some distance away from the people affected."

> This begs an important question: how effective is such technology? The answer is simple and disturbing: it is extremely effective.

In a 2016 article titled "A Maddening Sound," writer Colin Dickey detailed a number of such examples, including this one:

"Sue Taylor first started hearing it at night in 2009. A retired psychiatric nurse, Taylor lives in Roslin, Scotland, a small village seven miles outside of Edinburgh. 'A thick, low hum,' is how she described it, something 'permeating the entire house,' keeping her awake."

Taylor's initial thought was that perhaps the annoying—almost destabilizing—noise was coming from a factory close by. Maybe a generator. As a result, Taylor decided to do a bit of detective work, checking out the surrounding area and even hanging out outside the homes of her friends and neighbors in an effort to resolve the mystery. Unfortunately, although the hum was clearly a real phenomenon, she failed to crack the mystery. Things proceeded to get worse: the hum plagued her during the night—to the extent that she even had her ears examined by a doctor, who could find no problems at all. She began to suffer from a cross between vertigo and dizziness, which made her sick. Even the house felt as if it was shaking slightly.

In 2011, Andrew Liszewski wrote an article for *Gizmodo* with an eye-catching title: "Future Riot Shields Will Suffocate Protestors with Low Frequency Speakers." Sci-fi, this was not. It was all too disturbingly real. Liszewski said: "It's not the first crowd control tool to use sound waves, but Raytheon's patent for a new type of riot shield that produces low frequency sound waves to disrupt the respiratory tract and hinder breathing, sounds a little scary."

Liszewski was not wrong. He revealed that the "LRAD sound cannon," as it is known, is one such device; it provokes migraines and sickness specifically by targeting people with incredibly loud noises that rattle people's heads to a point where they become pretty much destabilized. Liszewski noted that Raytheon's new device was a far more disturbing one. The so-called "non-lethal pressure shield" creates what is known as a "pulsed pressure wave" that targets the parts of the body that regulate breathing and specifically scrambles those same parts of the body. In other words, the targeted individual finds one's self briefly unable to breathe or even catch their breath. The result is that the person under attack will temporarily

Infrasound can be used as a weapon that causes non-lethal deterrent, as is the case of the LRAD 500X, which is shown here being used by NYPD officers to fend off protestors at an Occupy Wall Street demonstration.

faint, or become light-headed, due to the lack of oxygen to the brain, effectively rendering him or her unable to do pretty much anything until he or she comes around, which is generally a couple of minutes later.

Raytheon doesn't shy away from confirming that it has created such technology, and it admits that its destabilizing technology would be the perfect tool for enforcement officials. Raytheon states: "Since the early 1990s there has been an increasing interest—mainly in the U.S.—in so-called non-lethal weapons (NLW) which are intended to disable equipment or personnel while avoiding or minimizing permanent and severe damage to humans. NLW are thought to provide new, additional options to apply military force under post-Cold War conditions, but they may also be used in a police context."

Raytheon sees the day coming when its acoustic weapons will be utilized regularly in warfare, in "riots," in "hostage-taking," and in what are termed "peace-keeping operations." The latter category may simply be normal, everyday citizens exercising their right to demonstrate against things they see as inherently wrong. Should those of us who choose to take to the streets and make our feelings known to our government one day find ourselves effectively "zapped" by such technologies, it will be a very dark and disturbing day for freedom of speech, to be sure.

Journalist Lily Hay Newman revealed that such technology was utilized during the unrest that took place on August 9, 2014, in Ferguson, Missouri, following the shooting of Michael Brown by police officer Darren Wilson. Newman revealed that the specific devices were long-range acoustic device (LRAD) cannons. She added: "The idea … was to create acoustic technology that could clearly transmit sound, like verbal directions, over a long distance. The devices also began to employ intense sound as a deterring weapon against pirates at sea."

Newman also notes that LRAD cannons might be utilized against "protesters," such as those allied to Occupy Wall Street, a protest movement established to campaign against economic inequality. Newman notes that LRAD cannons would cause Occupy Wall Street supporters to "flee from painful sound waves." Some believe that targeting U.S. citizens who are exercising their outrage against the government can be perceived as one of the first steps to a slippery slide into a full-blown police state.

Global Security tells us the following: "High-intensity low-frequency sound may cause … organs to resonate, causing a number of physiological results, *possibly including death* [italics mine]. Acoustic weapons pose the hazard of being indiscriminate weapons, potentially imposing the same damage on friendly forces and noncombatants as on enemy combatants or other targets."

They also note that it's not just people who can be affected by such technologies but that when directed at vehicles, they, too, can be affected, specifically when targeted with low-frequencies, such as the aforementioned infrasound technology.

These so-called "non-lethal technologies" (at least, they are *supposed* to be nonlethal) are not just being deployed in areas where crowd control is needed or when Big Brother types want to break up peaceful protesters. The technology can also be targeted at specific individuals. The list of side effects that can result from direct exposure from sound-based weaponry can be grim. According to Ronald L. Adams and Dr. R. A. Williams of the U.S. Army's Medical Intelligence and Information Agency, symptons include "headache, fatigue, perspiring, dizziness, menstrual disorders, irritability, agitation, tension, drowsiness, sleeplessness, depression, anxiety, forgetfulness, and lack of concentration."

I say it is anyone's guess because most of the post-1970s government documents on the topic of sound-based weaponry and when and where it has been used remains hidden.

A startling development in the saga of acoustic weapons in August 2017 provoked worldwide commentary. It was revealed that going back to

Staff at the U.S. Embassy in Cuba were subjected to an acoustic attack in 2016 that caused symptoms ranging from headaches and confusion to memory loss and deafness.

2016, U.S. Embassy staff stationed on the island of Cuba started to become sick. Symptoms included deafness, confusion, memory loss, lack of focus, tingling in the fingers, and vertigo. Although the events began in 2016, the story did not surface publicly until a year later—demonstrating the undeniable secrecy surrounding the events. When staff at the embassy were interviewed by intelligence agents, a pattern was established that showed that people became sick when they were in government buildings, not when they were at home. Someone was directly and specifically targeting the employees of the U.S. Embassy.

The CIA, the Defense Intelligence Agency, and the U.S. Army were all secretly contacted to determine if an answer could be found. The agencies quickly theorized that in all probability, the source of all the problems was acoustic weapons—highly advanced versions of the kinds of technology that have been studied and used for decades.

There were significant doubts on the part of the U.S. intelligence community and the military that this was the work of the Cubans alone. No one within the Department of Defense believed that the Cubans possessed such sophisticated technology or had the ability to implement it on a large, ongoing scale. The overwhelming conclusion was that given the close links between the governments of Cuba and Russia, the Russians had probably supplied the Cuban government with the technology, who then chose to use it against the United States. Speculation was rife that this new acoustic technology was probably still in its infancy and that as a result, the staff at the U.S. Embassy amounted to the first wave of guinea pigs.

As the story grew and more revelations surfaced, it was revealed that both the Department of State and the FBI were also caught up in the controversy as they attempted to figure out who was behind the acoustic attacks. Predictably, the Cuban government, via the Cuban Ministry of Foreign Affairs, denied it was testing or using any kind of acoustic weapon on anyone. It also denied collusion with the Russians on this particular issue. The Russians remained silent. At the time of this writing, that is where things stand.

Acoustic weapons: coming to a peaceful rally near you soon. And, eventually, to everywhere.

THE FALSE FLAG PHENOMENON

Now, it's time to look at how we may be being controlled as a result of care-fully planned and executed operations known as false flag events. They include the assassinations and sacrifices of thousands of people. *The Atlantic* describes a false flag as follows: "The term originates with naval warfare. For centuries, ships have sailed under a flag identifying their nationality. During times of war, ships would sometimes change the national flag they flew in order to fool other vessels that they sought to attack or escape from. They would fly, in other words, a 'false flag.' The term then expanded to mean any scenario under which a military attack was undertaken by a person or organi-zation pretending to be something else."

Is it possible that at least some terrible events that have occurred in recent history could actually not have been the work of terrorists? Might they, instead, have been false flags (also known as inside jobs)?

There is nothing new about false flags; they have a long and controver-sial history. One of the earliest such events occurred in 1788. A high-ranking official in the Swedish government quietly and carefully contacted a senior tailor within the Royal Swedish Opera asking if he could create a significant number of uniforms. He didn't want the uniforms to represent the Swedish military, though. Rather, he wanted the tailor to create Russian uniforms. There was a method to this oddness. It revolved around manipulation and conspiracy. Not only that, it was a coldhearted plan on the part of the Swedes.

The tailor agreed to quickly make the uniforms, even though he had no idea why the Swedish military would want to dress like Russians. Today, we know exactly why. On June 27, 1788, dressed in their Russian outfits, a team of Swedish soldiers descended on a Swedish military facility in Puumala, a municipality in Finland. The soldiers then attacked their very own installation—to make it appear as if the Imperial Russian Army were the culprits. The reason?

Prior to the attack, the Swedish government was deeply against engaging in hostilities with the Russians. After the attack, though, it was a very different situation: there was now a significant call for retribution. The faked attack was so highly classified that not even the highest echelons of the Swedish National Assembly—known as the Riksdag of the Estates—knew anything about it: it was all the work of a well-hidden cabal. In no time at all, King Gustav II took immediate steps to wage war on Russia. The Russo-Swedish War raged from June 1788 to August 1790. Close to forty thousand troops were killed in a war that resolved nothing between the two powers.

Now, let's take a trip to Japan and then on to Poland.

On September 18, 1931, the Chinese region of Manchuria was attacked by the Japanese military. The possibility of war breaking out had been bubbling for a while. All the Japanese needed was a reason to invade. They got one. Or, rather, they created it. The Japanese military came up with an idea to launch a false flag on its own soil and place the blame on the Chinese. The target was a stretch of railway on Japan's South Manchuria Railway. Lieutenant Suemori Kawamoto steered the operation to success. A tiny amount of explosives was secretly placed close to the track but not on it: the Japanese wanted to make a point, but they didn't want to cause any serious damage to their own territory or people. So, they made sure that the explosion that soon followed was limited. No one was hurt, and the track wasn't even affected. But by claiming that the attack was the work of the Chinese, it was seen as enough of a reason to go to war with China. As a result, the Second Sino-Japanese War began, and the invasion of Manchuria went ahead. All as a result of a fabricated false flag affair.

A famous false flag incident preceding the start of World War II was when the Japanese decided to fake an attack against themselves as an excuse to go to war with the Chinese.

In the lead-up to the start of the Second World War in September 1939, the German military came up with its very own false flag, which has become known as the Gleiwitz Incident. Seven members of the much-feared SS, attired in Polish military uniforms, attacked the German radio station Sender Gleiwitz in Upper Silesia. The plan was to have it appear to be the work of the Poles, which Hitler and his cronies hoped would create outrage on the part of the public and call for war against Poland.

Journalist Bob Graham says: "The audacity of the raid and the brazen manner in which it was exploited by Hitler is still astounding. It was shortly before 8 pm that SS-Sturmbannführer Alfred Naujocks and his elite six-man team drove into the radio station. In one of the cars was Franciszek Honiok, a 43-year-old unmarried Catholic farmer. He had been arrested by the SS in the village of Polomia on August 30, and ruthlessly selected as the person who would provide the 'proof' of Polish aggression against Germany."

As a result, World War II began on September 1, 1939. Only two months later, another false flag incident took place. The Soviet military launched an attack on the small Russian village of Mainila, close to the border of Finland. The attack was blamed on Finland—which allowed the Russians to plan an invasion of Finland.

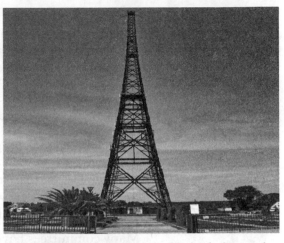

A prelude to the Nazi invasion of Poland, the attack at Gleiwitz Radio Tower was a classic "false flag" operation and ultimately gave Hitler a reason to invade Poland.

One of the most controversial claims to have come out of the Second World War is the suggestion that the terrible events at Pearl Harbor, Hawaii, on December 7, 1941, amounted to a false flag. This is not to suggest that the U.S. government was responsible for Pearl Harbor; it certainly was not. The Japanese were clearly the attacking force. The theory is that the U.S. government allowed Pearl Harbor to happen to justify America entering the Second World War—and with the U.S. public fully in favor as a result of the shocking events at Pearl Harbor. A second, and similar, theory suggests that the British government had advance knowledge of the attack on Pearl Harbor and chose to keep that information from the U.S. government—also as a means to get America into the war. Are these theories really feasible? Was there a plan to control public opinion as a result of a coldly manipulated attack on American soil? Let's see what we know for sure about Pearl Harbor—and let's review some false theories.

Just like September 11, 2001, December 7, 1941, is a date that will forever remain in the minds of not just Americans but also citizens around the world. There is no doubt that the American military, based at the U.S. Naval Base in Pearl Harbor, was caught off guard. Hundreds of Japanese fighter planes and bombers swarmed the skies. The Japanese launched torpedoes, which led to the catastrophic sinking of the United States' most valuable warships at the time. Hundreds of U.S.-built fighter planes were destroyed in the early morning attack. Close to 2,500 Americans died on that terrible day. Incredibly, so surprised was the military that the Japanese losses were minor: only sixty-four Japanese personnel were killed. Whereas America lost 394 aircraft, the Japanese toll was just twenty-nine. The Japanese lost five submarines; the United States lost thirty destroyers, eight battleships, and eight cruisers. Shock waves spread all around the world. There was no doubt about what was to follow: the United States quickly declared war on Japan and Nazi Germany. The Second World War, which had been raging since September 1939, now had a new player on the scene: the United States. Now, let's take a look at the false flag angle of Pearl Harbor.

No one wants to believe that either the U.S. or British governments—or possibly some secret combination/cabal of both—allowed the Japanese attack to occur. But in this particular saga, it's unfortunate and distressing that some data does suggest there was more to the attack than meets the eye—and certainly more than most would prefer to accept.

Many committees have been established to try to determine the full and unexpurgated facts surrounding the Pearl Harbor attack. In the 1940s alone, there were nine such inquiries. The most recent one took place in 1995, fifty-four years after the attack.

Is it really possible that U.S. and U.K. officials knew what was on the horizon and made a dark and disturbing collective decision to say nothing and permit the attack to go forward? Let's see.

Although the United States was not an active player in the Second World War until December 1941, behind the scenes, it was doing top-secret, sterling work in the field of code breaking. The Japanese were experts in creating codes that were extremely sophisticated and baffled some of the finest minds in the field of code making and code breaking. Both the United States and the United Kingdom had multiple teams working day and night to solve the riddle of what the Japanese military were saying to each other—and, more importantly, what they were planning. In the United States, the bulk of the work in this particular arena was undertaken by the Office of Naval Intelligence (ONI) and the U.S. Army's elite Signal Intelligence Service. And this is where things start to get controversial and conspiratorial.

The Japanese government's most powerful and intricate code was given the code name of Purple in the United States. There is little doubt that Purple would have been the code that the Japanese used when discussing the plans for the attack on Pearl Harbor in 1941. Here's where things get problematic and complicated. History has shown that America's code breakers had solved the Purple code—although, the Japanese had no awareness of that. Those same code breakers—as well as the intelligence personnel whose work was dictated by what the code breakers had uncovered—did not detect any chatter, significant or otherwise, that gave even a modicum of evidence that a specific attack on the United States was imminent. A variation on this suggests that the code breakers did pick up confirmations that an attack was coming quickly but that

The Japanese attack on Pearl Harbor is not an example of a "false flag" attack since there is no evidence that the United States had knowledge in advance, but there are theories that speculate that England may have known but did not warn the Americans as a way of getting them to enter World War II.

the deciphered messages were summarily and deliberately ignored by the intelligence world. Why? To provide a reason to get America into the war.

Those who are unable to accept that some element of the government may have decided to let Pearl Harbor go ahead without any interference might say that relatively small teams of code breakers did not pick up incriminating Japanese messages. The problem, though, is that the United States had in excess of seven hundred code breakers, all determined to learn what the Japanese military's plans were. Is it feasible that not one of those hundreds of people caught even a small whisper of the carnage that was to come? This question has led many conspiracy theorists to suggest that Pearl Harbor was given the green light by either the U.S. government or the U.K. government.

Moving away from the world of code breaking, there is the strange saga of the SS *Lurline*, a huge liner that was unveiled in 1932. When the Pearl Harbor attacks were almost literally on the horizon, the *Lurline* was en route to Hawaii, having left San Francisco. As the *Lurline*'s crew took the massive ship to its destination, the crew began to pick up a number of curious Morse code messages. Leslie Grogan, a man skilled in Morse code who was onboard the ship, checked the messages and determined that they were Japanese in nature. Whomever was broadcasting them was heading in an easterly direction—toward Pearl Harbor.

> If the issues sur-
> rounding code break-
> ing and a missing
> document were all that
> we had to make a case
> of conspiracy, then it
> would be a fairly shaky
> case. But there are
> other issues as well.

There are rumors that Grogan and the rest of the crew hastily contacted the U.S. military—at Pearl Harbor and elsewhere—but when they told the authorities of what they heard, they were dismissed. Such a dismissal—of highly important data that would clearly have had a major bearing upon national security issues—could only have been authorized at a high level up the chain of command. There is a good reason why all of this remains at rumor level after more than seventy-five years. Surely the matter could have been resolved by now? But there is one big problem: an official report, written by Grogan and dispatched to the 14th Naval District on Honolulu, has gone missing. Is this evidence of something sinister? Clearly, Grogan's report was hidden or destroyed for a reason. Perhaps it's because Grogan's words may have provided confirmation that the U.S. military knew the attack on Pearl Harbor was about to happen but decided to say or do nothing at all. Not a pleasant thought, to be sure.

For the record, the Japanese denied, when the war ended in 1945, that they made any kinds of broadcasts—Morse code based or otherwise: "In order to keep strict radio silence, steps such as taking off fuses in the circuit, and holding and sealing the keys were taken. During the operation, the strict radio silence was perfectly carried out. The Kido Butai used the radio instruments for the first time on the day of the attack since they had been fixed at the base approximately twenty days before and proved they worked well. Paper flaps had been inserted between key points of some transmitters on board Akagi to keep the strictest radio silence."

Attempts to locate the missing Grogan material at the National Archives, in the archives of the U.S. Navy, and at a variety of presidential libraries have failed.

If the issues surrounding code breaking and a missing document were all that we had to make a case of conspiracy, then it would be a fairly shaky case. But there are other issues as well. It's now time to turn our attention to a highly respected figure, Vice Admiral Frank E. Beatty. As a result of his duty to his country, Beatty, who died in 1976 at the age of eighty-two, was awarded the Bronze Star Medal, the Navy Cross, and the Legion of Merit. From 1941 to 1943, he served as an aide to Secretary of the Navy William Franklin Knox. Beatty went on to captain the USS *Columbia*, a light cruiser, which saw battle in the Pacific arena. Here's what Vice Admiral Beatty had to say about the events at Pearl Harbor:

> Prior to December 7, it was evident even to me that we were pushing Japan into a corner. I believed that it was the desire of President Roosevelt and Prime Minister Churchill that we get into the war, as they felt the Allies could not win without us and all our efforts to cause the Germans to declare war on us failed; the conditions we imposed upon Japan—to get out of China, for example—were so severe that we knew that nation could not accept them. We were forcing her so severely that we could have known that she would react toward the United States. All her preparations in a military way—and we knew their overall import—pointed that way.

As Beatty's words show, the United States and the United Kingdom were clearly goading the Japanese, determined to find a way to have the Japanese enter the war.

An even more startling statement was made in a document prepared in October 1940, a little more than a year before the Pearl Harbor disaster took place. The U.S. Office of Naval Intelligence quoted the words of Lieutenant Commander Arthur H. McCollum, a highly regarded military figure whose positions included director of Allied Naval Intelligence, Southwest Pacific; assistant chief of staff for intelligence, Seventh Fleet; and commanding officer of the Seventh Fleet Intelligence Center. He believed a way had to be found to get Japan into the war. He said, "If by these means Japan could be led to commit an overt act of war, so much the better."

The final words, though, go to Jonathan Daniels, President Roosevelt's administrative assistant and White House press secretary. Discussing his knowledge of the president's thoughts on Pearl Harbor, Daniels said, "The blow was heavier than he had hoped it would necessarily be. But the risks paid off; even the loss was worth the price."

Would the families of those men and women who lost their lives on December 7, 1941, agree?

BLOOD AND DEATH

One of the most macabre stories told to me on my 2004 trek around Puerto Rico with the SyFy Channel came from a woman—I'll call her Julia—who lived in Ponce. She claimed to know a great deal about the secret society that was at the heart of this controversy because her ex-husband was a member of the group. He was also a powerful figure on the island, specifically in the real estate business. He had been invited into the group in 1999, about a year before he and Julia married. His connections to the group led to their divorce less than a year after they married. When Julia's husband finally confided in her the details of his secret life, Julia was outraged—not just because he had kept his other life from her but also because of what, exactly, he was involved in.

Julia's husband told her that it was due to certain supernatural pacts between the group and the paranormal denizens of realms beyond ours that he now had so much prestige, power, and money. There was, however, a price to pay—as there always is when one does a deal with malignant, supernatural things from other dimensional planes. That price revolved around human blood. We're talking about assassinations, about killing and sacrificing people in the name of power, political agendas, money, and sex. Julia sat and listened—both horrified and terrified by what she was hearing—as her husband outlined what was going on. It was no coincidence, he said, that his life had massively altered for the better in 1999. It was all down to that invitation and his willingness to do whatever needed to be done to ensure wealth and influence.

Julia's husband had been present at a particular ritual that was held at the spacious home of a Puerto Rican drug baron, who *also* attained "success" from the same secret society. The story got even more controversial. Julia admitted that she couldn't prove any of what she was telling us back in 2004,

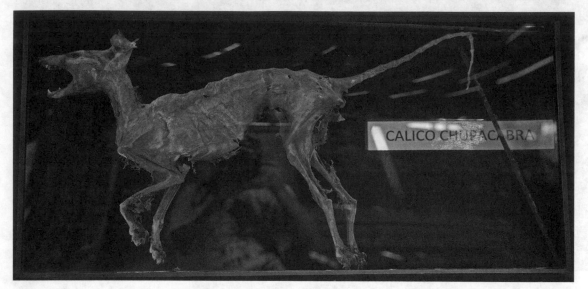

A supernatural pact was needed from those wanting both wealth and influence from the chupacabra (photo is from a display in Calico, California). The belief was that if they willingly provided their human blood to renew the spirit, they would be rewarded.

but she claimed to have been told of three people on the island who had been paid well to provide the group with supplies of their own blood and to discuss it with no one. The people were reportedly taken to the location of the meeting, which was high in the hills of the El Yunque rain forest, and the blood was taken by a local doctor—who was also well paid for his actions and his silence.

The two women and one man were placed on an ornate, large altar, where the blood was removed. Then, with the doctor and the three "donors" driven back to their respective homes (after being warned to never discuss with anyone what had happened), the blood was used in a complex ritual to conjure up and manifest a chupacabra. Julia claimed that her husband assured her that the ritual worked well: the group of several dozen—all dressed in cloaks—focused their minds on having the chupacabra appear before them, which is exactly what is said to have happened.

It was a hellish situation: the lights in the house flickered, and the room was filled with a nauseating odor of sulfur. In seconds, the air shimmered—like a heat haze on the road on a hot summer's day—and the creature slowly came into being, staring at the group malevolently and hunching over. Even long-term members of the group were shocked by what they were seeing. They were counting on its appearance, but actually seeing the monster close up was something else entirely.

One and all were quietly told to remain as calm as possible, despite the fraught and fantastic nature of the events. There was one thing that none of the members of the group could avoid seeing: the chupacabra was semitransparent. It was far more spectral than it was physical. That is, however, until the monster placed its clawed paws into a large bowl, in which substantial amounts of blood had been poured.

Within seconds of the creature doing so, its transparency was no more, and it was suddenly a completely physical entity. Julia's husband was unable to explain the process, mainly because no one seemed to understand the full scope of what it was they were dealing with. He did, however, state that the magical nature of human blood—when ingested in large amounts—not only fed the chupacabra but also gave it physical substance in our world, which was in marked difference to the ethereal form it had in its own realm. When the creature was apparently sated and fed, it vanished in a bright blue flash that affected the eyes of one and all present for up to several minutes.

Julia listened further as she was told that several other such rituals had taken place in the 1990s, the first one of which, allegedly, had led to the beginning of the chupacabra phenomenon in 1995. Julia sat back, appalled and frightened, by what she had heard, not knowing whether to believe it or not. It was, however, the undeniable fear in her husband's eyes that finally convinced her he was telling the truth—a truth that revolved around how the chupacabra needs to feast on our blood to maintain a foothold in our world. No wonder that Julia chose to leave her marriage behind her.

On my third expedition to Puerto Rico just a few years later, I heard a somewhat similar story. There were differences, but the basic plot of a connection between the chupacabra and human blood was the same. The source was a rancher whose controversial story involved the FBI, which has an office in San Juan, the capital of Puerto Rico. This was actually not the first time I had heard of an FBI–chupacabra connection. In September 2005, when I traveled to Puerto Rico with a team from Canada's Red Star Films, our guide was a local man named Orlando Pla. He told me that a couple of years earlier, the local FBI office had opened a file on the chupacabra. It was not a file on the beast itself, though. Rather, as Pla told me, the FBI was investigating the theory that the attacks on farm animals were not the work of the chupacabra but of occultists who were using the chupacabra phenomenon as a cover for their own clandestine, sacrificial activities. In some respects, this sounds *very* much like the same group that Julia told Jon Downes and me about back in 2004.

Jorge was the rancher who revealed what he knew of all this. I first met him in 2004, but he didn't want to speak out in front of the cameras and have his identity revealed. And who could blame him for that? Jorge was, however, fine about his first name and his hometown being used, but that was about all. Clearly, he had concerns about his safety, which I detected.

Jorge, like Julia, had heard of "a secret cult," as he worded it, that had strands and tentacles all across the island, specifically in the domain of big business—which *also* echoes Julia's words. Jorge's animals had been attacked by what was assumed to have been a chupacabra, and he wasted no time in calling the police. Oddly, though, a pair of FBI agents, rather than Puerto Rico's local authorities, responded and turned up to investigate. When Jorge, confused by the fact that the FBI would be interested in the killing of five of his farm animals, asked what was going on, he was quietly told that there were suspicions—which mirrored the story told to me in 2005 by Orlando Pla— that the attacks may have been the work of "cultists." The pair had a look around Jorge's property, took a few photos, thanked him, and went on their way. That was not the end of the matter, though.

Several days later, an elderly man dressed in an expensive suit arrived at Jorge's home, insisting that he talk with Jorge. It turned out that, somehow, the group that the FBI suspected was using the chupacabra issue as a cover had learned of the visit by two Bureau agents to Jorge's home. The old man—who Jorge said looked pale and sickly—warned Jorge of the perils of even *thinking* about speaking with the FBI again. For someone who seemingly wanted to keep everything under wraps, it was odd that the old man was so talkative, informing Jorge that human blood was at the heart of the chupacabra manifestations and that "blood sacrifice" was integral to the success of "the program."

Jorge's use of the word "sacrifice" was controversial, since it suggested that perhaps some of the people used in these rituals did not just offer a safe amount of their blood but lost their very lives in the name of the chupacabra. Try as I might, Jorge would not expand on this matter, and I did not learn anything else that might have suggested a line had been crossed to a terrible, unforgivable degree.

Yes, the chupacabra was all too real, Jorge was told, but the deadly beast could not exist in our world without human blood. The chupacabra did not live on human blood as a vampire bat might. Rather, it needed "blood energy." Ending the conversation, the old, withered man left and was driven away in a large, black car. Four months later, Jorge had one more attack on his property, but he chose not to report it to anyone. Except for me, when we finally caught up again.

ATTEMPTING TO KILL IN THE NAME OF THE SLENDERMAN

The Slenderman is a fictional character created in June 2009 by Eric Knudsen (using the alias of Victor Surge in the forum section of the *Something Awful* website), who took his inspiration from the world of horror fiction. The Slenderman is a creepy creature: tall; thin; long arms; a blank, faceless expression; and wearing a dark suit. It sounds almost like a nightmarish version of the Men in Black. While there is no doubt that Knudsen was the creator of what quickly became a definitive, viral meme, people have since claimed to have seen the Slenderman in the real world.

It's a case of believing in the existence of the Slenderman and, as a result, causing it to actually exist—which is similar to the phenomenon of the Tulpa or thought form. An entity is envisaged in the mind, and the imagery becomes so powerful and intense that it causes that same mind-based imagery to emerge into the real world with some degree of independent existence and self-awareness. Such a scenario may well explain why people are now seeing something that began as a piece of fiction.

In a January 24, 2015, article in the *Birmingham Mail* (titled "Spooky Slender Men Spotted in Cannock"), Mike Lockley wrote: "A paranormal probe has been launched in the Midlands following FOUR sightings of Slender Men—long, stick thin specters feared around the world. Each of the chilling close encounters took place in the Cannock area, and now investigator Lee Brickley is trying to fathom why the ghoul has descended on the Staffordshire mining town. Slender Men have been a part of global folklore for centuries. They may be known by different names, but their harrowing, elongated appearance remains the same around the world."

In the words of the witness: "This character was tall, with very thin arms and legs, dressed in what I presumed were grey trousers and a tight long-sleeved shirt of the same color. His hairless head was elongated and neck spindly, and his arms reached practically past his knees; I could not discern a facial feature. I realized he was around three meters tall."

Writer "Red Pill Junkie" notes that in 2014, "the creepy avatar took a much more sinister and serious spin when news broke about two teenage girls from southeastern Wisconsin [Morgan Geyser and Anissa Weier] who lured one of their 'friends' deep into the woods, stabbed her 19 times, and left her for dead. The heinous crime the teens confessed to the authorities once their victim miraculously managed to pull herself out of the forest had been planned as a ritual sacrifice to win the favor of Slenderman, with which they had acquired a disturbing obsession."

Before we get to the matter of that near-fatal stabbing, it's very important to note just how magnet-like the Slenderman phenomenon really is. To

Graffiti in an abandoned cabin is testimony to the interest in Slenderman, particularly among teenagers.

understand the issue, we'll turn our attentions to a man named Olav Phillips. He is the publisher of *Paranoia Magazine*. As you might deduce, this publication focuses on cover-ups and conspiracies, including assassinations. In 2014, *Paranoia Magazine* featured several articles on the Slenderman: "Slenderman: Proof of a Modern Tulpa" by Clyde Lewis, Loren and Jenny Coleman's "Slenderman Becomes Too Real," and David Weatherly's "The Tendrils of the Slenderman."

The reason Phillips has been interested in—and disturbed by—the Slenderman issue revolves around his son. He says:

> I remember speaking to my son and asked him if he had ever heard of the Slenderman—this was when I got into it, which was just a few years ago. He was about eight at the time and he gets real scared and he just says: 'What?' He asked me: 'Where did you hear about that?' I said, 'On the Net.' He was asking really softly, almost secretly, like it was something for him and his friends, but not for the grown-ups. It was *their* secret; *their* little club. Not mine.

> In my son's elementary school, Slenderman was like their version of Bloody Mary. They were fascinated by it, but scared and mortified, too. Even in Grades two and three, my son said the kids were consumed by the Slenderman thing; *completely* consumed by it. With my son and his friends, there's a lot of secrecy and paranoia with the Slenderman; you can't tell people about this. They feel comfortable about talking about it with each other, because that's their cohort. But when I come in—and I'm the old guy—I'm not supposed to know about that. That's how they see it, I think.

> About a month after me and my son had that conversation was when the girls stabbed their friend. I had to investigate it; it became like an addiction. I can't sit there and do nothing about it; it was very strange. At first, I believed it was a hundred percent horseshit, just made-up stories and nothing else. But, then, after me and my son talked about it, it struck me that there was so much fear in my son's elementary school, and the beliefs they had in the Slenderman were fairly complicated. That was when I started to think it had gone from this totally made-up story to a Tulpa—manifested by millions of children across the United States and around the world.

> The imagery and the name definitely had a lot to do with it for my son, I think; even for me. When we were kids, we were all afraid of the boogeyman: the guy under the bed or in the closet. But, you didn't really have an image to go with it. I'm forty-two

now, so we didn't have anything that visually manifested for us back then, in the 1980s. And we didn't have anything like the Internet—no pictures of the boogeyman to look at. And information was much slower to spread, too. The Slenderman thing was different: It became a meme. There were stories, images online. The way my son got it, it was like how the boogeyman story was told to me, but in a bigger 21ˢᵗ century context.

All of which brings us to the terrible events of May 2014. This was not just a case of attempted murder. It was a horrific example of how two young girls did their utmost to sacrifice a former friend. Indeed, the stabbing—from the perspective of the two girls—was the only way to ensure that the Slenderman did not come after their two families and kill them. The attack caught the attention of the people of Wisconsin, Americans, and even people around the world. The grim story was covered by the likes of CNN, the *New York Times*, the *Washington Post*, and the *Guardian*.

> Anissa Weier and Morgan Geyser were two school friends who had concocted a plot to take the life of a friend named Payton Leutner.

The mayhem took place in Waukesha, a picturesque suburb of Milwaukee, Wisconsin, which was settled in the late 1800s. May 31, 2014, is the date the people of Waukesha will never forget.

Anissa Weier and Morgan Geyser were two school friends who had concocted a plot to take the life of a friend named Payton Leutner. According to the *Creepypasta* website: "Despite the fact that it is rumored [the Slenderman] kills children almost exclusively, it is difficult to say whether or not his only objective is slaughter." Whatever the truth of the matter, "slaughter" was certainly on the minds of Weier and Geyser, who were just twelve years old, as was Leutner. And there's no doubt that both Weiser and Geyser were very familiar with *Creepypasta*: following the attempted sacrifice, "Mr. Creepypasta," a key figure in the commentary that quickly surfaced after the attack, said: "I guess *Creepypasta* is dangerous to a degree if we're talking about the Slenderman stabbing…. When you're talking about entertainment, you have to understand that it's fiction. Just because it's on the Internet doesn't mean it's real. The danger here is that *Creepypasta* is entertainment largely aimed at kids and teenagers."

In January 2016, *Milwaukee* magazine published an article that caught the attention of many: "In the Woods." In part, it stated: "Unlike Morgan, Anissa experienced little in the way of hallucinations leading up to the attacks. Sometime after she began reading *Creepypasta*, she started to see a dark figure in the wooded areas that her school bus passed, a form 'in the branches.'" A local psychologist, Anthony Jurek, suggested that what Anissa had encountered was a "visual illusion," instead of a "defined hallucination."

It was these hallucinations or illusions that set the scene for what was very soon to come.

The night before the attack, Weier and Geyser showed no signs of what was going to happen the following morning. It was just like any other Friday night. The three girls were not just friends but very good friends. All three went to the local Horning Middle School. And on the evening of the thirtieth, the three even had a sleepover. They played on a computer and went skating. The following morning, the friends ate doughnuts and strawberries for breakfast. Poor Payton had no idea of what was soon to come.

The whole thing was coldly planned: early in the morning, Geyser smuggled a large knife out of the house. A suggestion was made that the three should go to the local David's Park. Of course, there was a method to this, and it had nothing to do with having a good time. The park was the place where Geyser and Weier planned to execute Leutner. They headed out to the park on what was a pleasant day. The clock was ticking as they got to what turned out to be the site of the frenzied assault. All three knew the park well: the two girls decided that they should lure Leutner to a particularly wooded area near Big Bend Road. It was now only minutes before the near-unbelievable incident occurred. Even at this point, though, there was not even an inkling that normality would be completely and utterly shattered. Satisfied that the location, shrouded in trees, was the perfect place to kill Leutner in the name of the Slenderman, things were now at the point of no return.

Fortunately for Leutner, at the final moment, Weier backed out from taking part in what turned out to be the attempted killing of Leutner. Had both girls launched an attack on her, it's doubtful she would have survived. Geyser, however, had no qualms about what, as she saw it, needed to be done. She took out the knife and violently thrust it into Leutner nineteen times. Leutner's arms, legs, and body were subjected to terrible cuts. An artery was badly damaged, as was her pancreas. Weier simply stared on in a near-hypnotic fashion. It's no surprise that Leutner fell to the ground. Weier and Geyser assumed—wrongly, thankfully—that Leutner would soon be dead. Miraculously, however, she survived. Fate was about to step in and ensured that Leutner was not taken by the Slenderman, which was the deranged goal of the two friends.

Weier and Geyser quickly exited the park, racing to a nearby Wal-Mart. Then they ran to the Nicolet National Forest, where, the girls believed, the Slenderman lived in a creepy, old mansion. They were sure they would soon meet their master. It didn't work out like that, though. The girls were certain that Leutner was now dead as they made their way to the heart of the ancient forest. But fortunately, Leutner—despite all of the violent stabbings—managed to drag herself out of the wooded part of David's Park, even though her energy levels were plummeting rapidly. As she got to a sidewalk in the park, a cyclist stumbled upon her. Shocked to the core, he quickly got out his

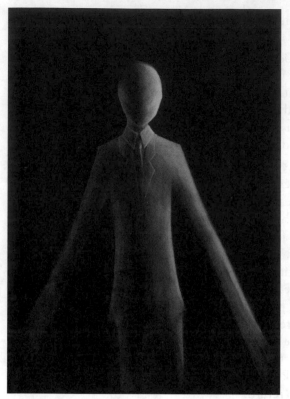

An illustration of the Slenderman captures how most witnesses have described the creature.

cell phone and told the emergency services that he had just come across a badly injured girl. Police and ambulance services were quickly on the scene. Leutner was quickly taken to the nearest hospital, at which point the sheer horrific nature of the attack became fully obvious. Even though Leutner was severely injured, she was still strong enough to whisper to the emergency services the names of her attackers: Anissa Weier and Morgan Geyser. The hunt was quickly on by the local police to find the pair.

By the time the police were on the scene, the girls had managed to travel around five miles on foot, stopping only for food and drink. At the ramp from Highway F to I-94, they were finally caught. Soon, the horrific facts came tumbling out. After apprehending the girls, the police went directly to the home of Morgan Geyser to break the terrible news to her family. Their response was one of complete devastation. Morgan's mother, Angie Geyser, revealed what happened when the family got the news from the police: "I sobbed. I ran to the bathroom and threw up. It didn't seem possible."

Sadly for all, it was bleak and grim reality. It would be no time at all before law-enforcement personnel began their investigation of the attack and their interviews with Weier and Geyser. Even for the police, this was undeniably something they had never encountered before.

What was particularly chilling for the police officers involved in the affair was Weier's apparent lack of any remorse for what had happened, albeit from the perspective of an onlooker. It was almost as if she didn't understand the gravity of what she and Geyser had planned and executed. Virtually no one on Waukesha's law-enforcement team had ever heard of the Slenderman. Weier, however, was happy to enlighten them. She described the Slenderman to a tee: his black suit, his faceless face, his spidery arms and legs, and his octopus-like tentacles. Weier also revealed to the police that the Slenderman was able to read minds and could teleport from place to place. Every portion of the surely unique interview was recorded and filmed. As for Geyser, her big concern was this: as they had failed to kill Leutner, the Slenderman just might now come after them. The Slenderman, it seems, did not stand for any kind of failure. The girls were very worried. When asked by the police if she really did think that she and her family were now under significant danger from the Slenderman, Geyser said, "Well, yeah. He's six to fourteen feet tall, has no face and always wears a red tie. I was really scared. He could kill my whole family in three seconds."

When Payton Leutner was able to talk with the authorities, she said that she understandably believed Geyser should be put behind bars for the rest of her life. She had, after all, been stabbed nineteen times by someone she thought was a very close friend. As for Weier, however, Leutner felt that, if convicted, her sentence should be significantly less—chiefly because although Weier took place in the planning of the attempted killing, she did not actually take part in the attack itself. She just looked on. Although Leutner was willing to, in essence, help Weier—and even appeared to display a degree of forgiveness—it was the seeming lack of remorse for what they had done that disturbed the detectives assigned to the case.

> As for Geyser, as a very young child she had told her mother that she encountered ghosts in her bedroom—violent entities that would tug on her hair and bite her.

As matters progressed, it appeared that there was far more to the story than had initially met the eye. For example, a lack of emotion was nothing new for Geyser. Her mother, for example, remembered how when they watched the 1942 Walt Disney movie *Bambi* together, Geyser shed not even a single tear when Bambi's mother is killed. Mrs. Geyser admitted that she found her daughter's reaction to be strange.

Further eye-opening information surfaced on the case—and the state of mind of the two girls—in a 2017 HBO documentary titled *Beware the Slenderman*. At times, it is hard to watch, chiefly because it shows how three families have suffered greatly, albeit in very different ways. The documentary also revealed some very strange aspects of the overall story. One was that Weier had nightmares of a Slenderman-type figure in her bedroom when she was just three years of age. This was almost a decade before Eric Knudsen even created the Slenderman that made him famous. As for Geyser, as a very young child, she had told her mother that she encountered ghosts in her bedroom—violent entities that would tug on her hair and bite her. One has to wonder if both girls' encounters with strange creatures in their bedrooms (and Weier's encounter being with a creature that resembled Slenderman) had at least some kind of bearing on what was to occur when the girls decided to take a life years later.

Now, it's time to take a look at the court cases that inevitably followed the attack on Payton Leutner. One of the big revelations was that Geyser was confirmed as suffering from schizophrenia. Her father, Matt Geyser, is also schizophrenic. In Morgan's case, it's known as childhood-onset schizophrenia. So badly affected was Geyser, she spent time at the Winnebago Mental Health Institute in Oshkosh, Wisconsin. Even the family could not deny Geyser's chaotic state of mind at the time. Morgan's mother, Angie, described her daughter as being "psychotic for nineteen months."

In January 2017, an illuminating feature appeared on the website of Milwaukee TV station WISN. The article, titled "Slender Man Stabbing Victim Thriving, Family Says," written by Nick Bohr, indicated that Payton Leutner was both psychologically and physically in good health. Bohr wrote: "A girl who barely survived being attacked by two friends is now thriving, taking AP classes in school and has joined her French club on a class trip to Canada, a family spokesman said.... 'There's some normalcy, after this horrific premeditated crime, and we're just very proud of her,' stated the same spokesman, Steve Lyons."

Three months later, the media brought forth the latest developments in the overall saga. On April 13, 2017, Morgan Geyser was in court for what was described as a "status conference." The purpose was to try to finalize a time for her trial to go ahead. It turned out that Geyser's trial had been pushed back for two weeks, only to allow Weier's trial to get the green light to go ahead. Geyser's attorney, Anthony Cotton, stated: "The whole idea is that she'll have a fairer jury because we'll have more information about the jurors. It probably will not speed up the process in terms of selecting a jury quicker."

In my book, *The Slenderman Mysteries*, I wrote: "It was estimated that the potential jurors would receive their questionnaires by July 2017. It's intriguing to note that Geyser's attorney put in a request that the jury specifically *not* be selected from Waukesha County—which, recall, is where the attack occurred and where all three girls were from. The reason and rationale for all of this? The huge amount of local, media publicity afforded the attack and the subsequent events, that's what. The concern was that a local jury might be influenced by all of the media coverage in their hometown—rather than taking an impartial look at the evidence in the case. Cotton also noted that the incident had been reported at a worldwide level. The judge overseeing the case stated that media-driven publicity—excessive or otherwise—was not inflammatory, was based strictly on the public record, and was not of the likes of hearsay. Geyser had a motion hearing in July, and another status conference in the latter part of August. Her trial was planned for October 16. As for Weier, on April 28, she was destined for a status conference, herself. Then, on June 8, it was revealed by the media that lawyers for the girls were seeking to determine precisely how much potential jurors might already know about the stabbing and the Slenderman controversy. Again, this was driven by legitimate concerns revolving around the extent to which knowledge of both issues might bias the jury's thoughts on the attack."

Things came to their pinnacle in August 2017 when Weier pleaded guilty to attempted second-degree homicide as a result of her mental condition. There was, however, a notable and unforeseen development, too. Even though Weier pleaded guilty, the jury did not agree and found her to be not guilty, specifically as a result of her psychological state. Geyser, for her part, pleaded to a far more serious charge, namely attempted first-degree murder.

Both girls are likely to remain in secure facilities until they are well into middle age.

MOTHMAN DEATH CURSE AND A FATAL DATE

Most people reading this will have heard of the Mothman of Point Pleasant, West Virginia. It was a winged monster that terrorized the small city and the surrounding areas between November 1966 and December 1967. Its diabolical exploits were chronicled in the 2002 hit Hollywood movie *The Mothman Prophecies*, starring Richard Gere, named after the 1975 book of the same title written by the Mothman authority John Keel. A devil-like, winged monster with red eyes, Mothman appeared quite literally out of nowhere and, some say, culminated in high tragedy and death. But how did the legend begin? To answer those questions, we have to go back to the dark night of November 12, 1966, when five gravediggers working in a cemetery in the nearby town of Clendenin were shocked to see what they described as a "brown human shape with wings" rise out of the thick, surrounding trees and soar off into the distance.

Three days later, the unearthly beast surfaced once again. It was at the highly appropriate time of the witching hour when Roger and Linda Scarberry and Steve and Mary Mallette—two young, married couples from Point Pleasant—were cruising around town in the Scarberrys' car. As they drove around an old factory, the four were puzzled to see in the shadows what looked like two red lights pointing in their direction. These were no normal lights, however. All four were shocked and horrified to discover that, in reality, the "lights" were the red eyes of a huge animal that, as Roger Scarberry would later recall, was "...shaped like a Mothman, but bigger, maybe six and a half or seven feet tall, with big wings folded against its back."

Not surprisingly, they fled the area at high speed. Unfortunately for the Scarberrys and the Mallettes, however, the beast seemingly decided to follow them: as they sped off for the safety of Point Pleasant, the winged monster took to the skies and shadowed their vehicle's every movement until it reached the city limits. The four raced to the sheriff's office and told their astounding story to Deputy Millard Halstead, who later stated: "I've known these kids all their lives. They'd never been in any trouble and they were really scared that night. I took them seriously." The mystery of the Mothman had well and truly begun. It still dominates Point Pleasant to this day.

Further encounters with the bizarre beast were reported; however, they were overshadowed by a tragic event that occurred on December 15, 1967. That day, Point Pleasant's Silver Bridge (so named after its aluminum paint), which spanned the Ohio River and connected Point Pleasant to Gallipolis, Ohio, collapsed into the river. It tragically claimed forty-six lives. While a mechanical explanation circulated—namely, a fatal flaw in a single I-bar in a suspension chain was the chief culprit—many believed the cause was linked with the ominous and brooding presence of the accursed Mothman.

In speaking with a group of friends and colleagues recently on the matter of the collapse of the bridge, I was very surprised at just how few people were aware that John Keel himself had a terrible prophecy concerning Point Pleasant. We know this, as Keel's own correspondence on the matter still exists. On November 3, 1967, Keel typed a letter to his friend Mary Hyre. As *The Demoniacal* notes: "Mary Hyre was the Point Pleasant, WV, correspondent for the Athens, OH, newspaper titled, *The Messenger*. Hyre documented strange occurrences happening in Point Pleasant in 1966–1967 and was well loved by locals due to her professional and open-minded take on the subjects. In one weekend alone, Hyre received five hundred reports of UFO sightings from locals. Hyre's fascination with flying saucers stemmed from her own sighting of a UFO, which she claimed flew over her backyard."

As for that letter Keel sent to Hyre, it included the following words, which were typed around six weeks before the bridge collapse: "Mary, I have good reasons for suspecting that [there] may soon be a disaster in the Pt. Pleasant area which will not seem to be related to the UFO mystery. A plant along the river may either blow up or burn down. Possibly the Navy installation in Pt. Pleasant will

The Mothman legend began around 1966 with reports of encounters in West Virginia. The story was made popular to a wide audience with John Keel's 1975 book *The Mothman Prophecies*.

be the center of such a disaster. A lot of people may be hurt. If this should happen, notify me as soon as you can, and write the story normally. Don't even hint to anybody anything about this."

History has shown that the Navy installation was not the "center of such a disaster." And a plant did not blow up or burn down. But it's eerie to note that Keel was clearly very unsettled by thoughts of a then-looming catastrophe in Point Pleasant. One and a half months after writing to Mary, there *was* a terrible catastrophe.

There were also strange and sinister deaths in what has become known as the Mothman Death Curse.

Jim Keith was a noted conspiracy theorist who died under extremely weird and dubious circumstances in September 1999 after attending the annual Burning Man event in the Black Rock Desert, just north of Reno, Nevada. While onstage, Keith lost his balance and fell to the ground. At first, Keith thought he had just badly bruised his leg. By the morning, though, Keith was in such agony that he had to call for paramedics, who were quickly on the scene and took him to the Washoe Medical Center in Reno. Keith was told he had fractured his tibia and that he was to be prepped for surgery, which would require him to be anesthetized. This was when things got really strange. Keith put a call through to a friend in the conspiracy field, George Pickard, and told him that one of the attendants at the hospital had the same name as someone with whom he had debated on the matter of the black helicopters a few months earlier. Coincidence? Who knows? As the time for surgery got closer, Keith got more and more anxious. He said to his nephew, Chris Davis: "I have a feeling that if they put me under I'm not coming back. I know if I get put under, I am going to die."

That's *exactly* what happened: a blood clot took Keith's life at the age of forty-nine. Conspiracy theorists were both stunned and suspicious by this untimely and tragic state of affairs, but was it an unfortunate event or a well-orchestrated murder by culprits unknown? That was the question asked most frequently in the immediate wake of Keith's death and is still asked today. UFO authority Greg Bishop says: "I would prefer to think that there was no connection to the weird computer problems," which was a reference to a series of hackings that Keith had experienced on his computer just days before he died and while he was investigating the 1997 death of Princess Diana of Wales.

Now, let's take a look at the Jim Keith–Mothman connection.

In his 1997 book *Casebook of the Men in Black*, Jim Keith focused much of his attention on the Mothman saga—as well as the timely presence in Point Pleasant of the notorious Men in Black. Some said that Keith got a little too close to the truth of the Men in Black–Mothman link and paid for it with his life. It wasn't long before Keith's publisher and buddy, Ron Bonds, was dead, too—also under controversial circumstances. Notably, back in 1991, Bonds had republished John Keel's classic 1975 book, *The Mothman Prophecies*, on the 1966–1967 events that went down in Point Pleasant. Interest in Keel's book reached stratospheric proportions in 2002 when it was turned into a big-bucks movie starring Richard Gere and Laura Linney. And that's when the deaths began to kick in big-time.

The movie hit cinemas in the United States on January 25, 2002. On that very day, the funeral of Charlie Mallette, one of the early witnesses to the Mothman, took place. Less than seven days after Mallette's death, there were five fatalities in Point Pleasant, all as a result of car accidents. Just weeks later, the executive producer of *The Mothman Prophecies*, Ted Tannebaum, died of cancer. Things got even more eerie. In much the same way that the premiere of *The Mothman Prophecies* movie in the United States was blighted by tragedy and death, exactly the same can be said about the day on which the movie hit the cinemas in Australia on May 23, 2002. On that day, a teenage boy from Fort Smith, Arkansas, named Aaron Rebsamen killed him-

self. His father was William Rebsamen, a skilled artist whose atmospheric imagery of the Mothman can be seen on the front cover of Loren Coleman's 2002 book *Mothman and Other Curious Encounters*.

A month after Rebsamen's death, Sherry Marie Yearsley was murdered; her body was dumped near an old railroad in Sparks, Nevada. She and the aforementioned Ron Bonds had dated for a while. Then, as 2002 came to its close, Mothman investigator Susan Wilcox passed away from cancer. Six months later, Jessica Kaplan, an artist hired to work on *The Mothman Prophecies* film, died in a plane crash. The acclaimed actor Alan Bates, who had a starring role in *The Mothman Prophecies*, was dead shortly before the end of 2003. Then, in July 2004, Jennifer Barrett-Pellington, wife of *The Mothman Prophecies* director Mark Pellington, died.

Now, from a deadly monster, let's take a look at a deadly date.

The Mothman has inspired fear in the populace of Point Pleasant, West Virginia, where this statue is located.

As most people with more than a passing interest in the UFO phenomenon will know, June 24, 1947, marked the beginning of the era of the flying saucer (or of the flying disk, as they were also known back then). The skies of our world were filled with strange aerial phenomena pre-1947. Take, for example, the Phantom Airships of the late 1800s, the Foo Fighters of World War II, and the 1946 wave of ghost rockets over Scandinavia. And if you're so inclined, you can dig even further into the past, with tales of such controversies as Ezekiel's Wheel, the Star of Bethlehem, and much more. But June 24, 1947, is when things got moving big-time.

June 24 is also the date on which a large number of famous figures within ufology took their last breaths. We'll begin with the matter of alleged crashed UFOs. Frank Scully was the author of a 1950 book, *Behind the Flying Saucers*. His book was a big seller and introduced UFO fans to the world of dead aliens, wrecked and recovered saucers, and the secret storage of E.T. corpses by Uncle Sam. The book has provoked a great deal of controversy in the UFO research arena. Frank Scully died on June 24, 1964.

> The story is a very weird one, encompassing what may or may not have been a genuine UFO and its occupants, as well as secret mind-altering technologies that might have led to Bryant's untimely death.

In March 2015, I wrote an article for *Mysterious Universe* titled "UFOs: Microwaved to Death?" It began as follows: "Next month, April 2015, will mark the 50th anniversary of a British UFO encounter that, while not exactly having become lost to the fog of time, is certainly no longer addressed to any significant degree. It's a classic contactee-style event that is made all the more controversial by the possibility that it may actually have had nothing to do with UFOs, after all. It may well have been a staged event, one in which the witness was led to believe he had a UFO sighting. If that has caught your attention, read on."

The article continued: "The story revolves around a man named Ernest Arthur Bryant, a resident of an old village in the English county of Devon called Scoriton. Or, as some prefer to spell it, Scorriton. As for Devon, it's an ancient and mysterious land, and which is made famous by the fact that Sir Arthur Conan Doyle set his classic Sherlock Holmes novel *The Hound of the Baskervilles* in Devon's Dartmoor National Park."

The story is a very weird one, encompassing what may or may not have been a genuine UFO and its occupants as well as secret, mind-altering technologies that might have led to Bryant's untimely death. Ernest Arthur Bryant died on June 24, 1967.

Richard Church was a young man who was active on the UFO scene in the 1960s. He had completed writing a manuscript on the connection between UFOs and the CIA. He had sent the manuscript to the publisher of Frank Edwards, author of *Flying Saucers—Here and Now!*, among others, for review. Church didn't live to see what the publisher thought of his book, however. He died on the same day as Bryant: June 24, 1967.

The aforementioned Frank Edwards's most famous book (for ufologists, at least) was *Flying Saucers—Serious Business*, which was published in 1966. Edwards died shortly before midnight on June 23, 1967. However, in U.K. time, that would have been the early morning of June 24, 1967—the very same date on which Ernest Arthur Bryant died in the United Kingdom Edwards's death was announced on June 24, 1967, at the Congress of Scientific Ufologists in New York City.

Willy Ley was a German American science writer, engineer, founder of the German Rocket Society, and someone who was very interested in UFOs and alien life. As one example of many, in 1958, he wrote an article for *Science Digest* titled "What Will 'Space People' Look Like?" NASA notes of Ley: "The German expatriate Willy Ley, had worked with some of the builders of the V-2 personally and had described his experiences, and their hopes, in his book *Rockets, Missiles, and Space Travel*. The first version, titled *Rockets*, appeared in May 1944, just months before the first firings of the V-2 as a weapon. Hence, this book proved to be very timely. His publisher, Viking Press, issued new printings repeatedly, while Ley revised it every few years, expanding both the text and the title to keep up with fast-breaking developments." Willy Ley died on June 24, 1969.

Moving on to the matter of the "ancient astronauts" controversy, one of the leading figures in that field was the late Robert Charroux. His books included *The Mysteries of the Andes*, *Masters of the World*, *The Gods Unknown*, and *Legacy of the Gods*. Charroux died on June 24, 1978.

Then there's the matter of the late comic legend Jackie Gleason. Outside of ufology, not many people know that Gleason had a long-standing interest in UFOs and had a huge and impressive library of books on the subject. There is a weird story of how Gleason was supposedly taken late one night in 1973 to Homestead Air Force Base, Florida, by President Richard M. Nixon. The two were close friends and golfing buddies. Nixon reportedly arranged for Gleason to see a number of dead aliens preserved in a freezer in a secret and secure inner sanctum at Homestead.

Rather than being excited and amazed by the sight of the dead things (which, reportedly, were far from being in good condition), Gleason was supposedly shocked and traumatized to a very significant degree. He told the story to a number of people, including his second wife, Beverly McKittrick, and Larry Warren, a U.S. airman involved in the famous UFO incident at Rendlesham Forest, England, in 1980. Gleason died on June 24, 1987.

OpenMinds states the following: "In an interview with Gleason's second wife, Beverly McKittrick, by *Esquire Magazine* about a book she was planning to write, she revealed that Gleason had told her that Nixon had shown Gleason alien bodies. The story goes that Gleason arrived home unusually late on the evening of February 19, 1973. Worried, McKittrick questioned his whereabouts. She said in the interview that his face looked 'haggard', and that he said he had been to Homestead Air Force Base and had seen alien bodies. He described them as small, 'only about two feet tall, with bald heads and disproportionately large ears.'"

And finally, the publisher of many of Frank Edwards's books on UFOs and unsolved mysteries was Lyle Stuart. He died at the age of eighty-three on June 24, 2006.

Those who are skeptical of the idea that there is some significance to these deaths and the date in question would likely have an answer to all this. They would probably say that one could check out the dates of all the deaths in ufology over the last near-seventy years and find half a dozen people who died on January 6, or on August 3, or on April 28, or on ... well, the list goes on. I don't dispute

Even comic actor Jackie Gleason had an interest in UFOs, so his golf buddy Richard M. Nixon took him down to Homestead AFB, where he got an exclusive look at some aliens on ice.

that. But it's important to remember that none of those other dates have the infamy attached to them that June 24 does. Maybe it's coincidence. Maybe it's not. Maybe there's more going on. Maybe you should take great care when the next June 24 comes around.

Just perhaps, someone is secretly assassinating people on ufology's most famous day.

NUCLEAR NIGHTMARES AND THE ASSASSINATION OF A PRESIDENT

Midway through the summer of 2017, something unforeseen and very unsettling occurred. In the second week of August, three people contacted me with eerily similar stories of atomic Armageddon. Not only that, in their nightmares, the U.S. president (not the present one…) is assassinated by North Korean agents, secretly working on behalf of Russia. When the U.S. government finds out the truth, North Korea is, in essence, turned into radioactive dust. But it doesn't end there: Russia is soon dragged in and, on the third day, nuclear weapons are used in Europe. The conflict grows and grows. In less than a week, an all-out nuclear conflict erupts. In less than a couple of hours, Europe, China, Russia, and the United States are destroyed; billions are dead, all as a result of that assassination of the U.S. president. To receive several such eerily similar accounts was, I have to admit, chilling.

Then, on August 8, I received a Facebook message from a guy named Kenny, who had a horrific dream of nuclear war two nights earlier. In Kenny's dream, the U.S. president was shot to death by a foreign agent, which led to a nuclear war. Kenny lives in San Bernardino, California, and woke up suddenly in the dead of night in a state of terror. As Kenny explained, in his dream, he was sitting in the living room of a house in a small town outside of Lubbock, Texas. Kenny had no idea of the name of the town, only that he knew it was near Lubbock—a place he has never visited. In the dream, Kenny heard a sudden and deep, rumbling sound that seemed to be coming from somewhere faraway. He went to the screen door, puzzled, and peered outside. To his horror, Kenny could see way off in the distance the one thing none of us ever wants to see: a huge, nuclear mushroom cloud looming large and ominous on the horizon.

Kenny continued that, in his dream, he was rooted to the spot, his legs shaking and his heart pounding. He could only stand and stare as the huge, radioactive cloud extended to a height of what was clearly miles. The entire sky turned black, and suddenly, a huge wave of flame and smoke—hundreds of feet high—raced across the entire landscape, completely obliterating everything in its path. In seconds, there was another explosion, again way off in the distance, but from the opposite direction. Nuclear war had begun. That was when Kenny woke up—thankful that it was all a dream but disturbed by the fact that, as Kenny told me, the dream seemed like something far more than just a regular dream. Kenny felt he had seen something that was still yet to come: a glimpse of the near future. Further dreams of nuclear nightmares came my way.

Kimberly J emailed me on August 10 and shared with me a story of disturbing proportions. She lives in Chicago, Illinois, and had a somewhat similar dream to that of Kenny but on August 9. The scenario was almost identical: a gigantic explosion destroyed her home city, killing millions and vaporizing everything for miles. A huge mushroom cloud was hanging where, only seconds earlier, there had been a bustling city of close to three million people. In this case, however, there was more: amid the carnage and the chaos, a large "birdman," as Kimberly described it, hovered over the massive cloud, "watching the end of us." The reference to the "birdman" provokes imagery of the Mothman of Point Pleasant, West Virginia, which, as we have seen, is connected to death, even to the extent of having its very own "death curse" attached to it.

The unthinkable nightmare of a mushroom cloud on the horizon has haunted many people's dreams since the Cold War.

Indeed, it very much reminded me of the dark specter of the Mothman, the sightings of which culminated in the tragic collapse of the city's Silver Bridge and led to the drownings of dozens of locals.

It just so happens that, two months before Kimberly's dream, M. J. Banias wrote an article for the *Mysterious Universe* website titled "Chicago's Current Mothman Flap 'A Warning,' Says Expert." In his article, Banias described a then-recent wave of Mothman-type sightings in and around the city. The article quoted researcher Lon Strickler, who looked into these particular cases, which led to the publication of his book on the Mothman–Chicago wave titled *Mothman Dynasty: Chicago's Winged Humanoids*. Strickler said:

"There are many opinions as to why these sightings are occurring, including a general feeling that unfortunate events may be in the city's future…. At this point, I feel that this being may be attempting to distinguish a connection between locales within the city and future events. The witnesses have been very steadfast with what they have seen, and refuse to embellish on their initial descriptions. Each witness has had a feeling of dread and foreboding, which I believe translates into a warning of some type."

Then, on August 12, I received yet another Facebook message of a similar nature; this one was from Jacob, an American who is now a resident of Mulhouse, France (coincidentally, I spent a lot of time there during my teenage years). In Jacob's dream, an emergency broadcast message appeared on his TV screen, warning people to take cover: the nukes were flying. And that was it: just a few, brief seconds of mayhem in the dream state. But it was still an undeniably nightmarish night for Jacob.

> I wondered: should we be concerned that three people had, inside one week, nightmares about nuclear war? And there was a connection to presidential assassinations?

Of course, all of this could have been as a result of the genuine growing tensions between North Korea and the United States. In fact, I'm sure that has a great deal to do with it. On August 9, the United Kingdom's *Independent* ran an article on the North Korea issue that stated, in part: "While it's unclear if North Korea can successfully target US cities like Denver *and Chicago* [italics mine] with a nuclear ICBM, it's similarly unknown if US defense systems can strike it down—adding to American anxieties." The issue of Chicago being a possible target has been mentioned in multiple news outlets. Such stories almost certainly would have been worrying to Kimberly J., who lives in the heart of the city.

I wondered: should we be concerned that three people had, inside one week, nightmares about nuclear war? And there was a connection to presidential assassinations? I thought: I wouldn't be surprised if hundreds of people around the world have had such dreams. Maybe even more. After all, the climate was hardly a stable one. It was—and still is—a time of intense anxiety. And Kimberly's sighting in her dream of a Mothman-type creature—which has been seen around Chicago in the past few months and has been linked to a possible looming disaster in the area—would likely have led some to believe that there was more to all of this than just bad dreams. There is also the fact that I got a cluster of such reports across a very short period of time, which was not exactly what I considered to be good news.

Then, there was this from Stephen Polak: "As a Chicago resident myself who has recently had a dream of being consumed [by] an enormous wall of fire, I find all of this rather disquieting…."

Five days later, the news got worse. Chris O'Brien, a well-known author of many books, including *Stalking the Herd* and *Secrets of the Mysterious Valley*, contacted me with a story to tell. It was not a good story. He said:

Back in 2005 Grandfather Martin Gashweseoma, for many decades the "Fire Clan Prophecy Tablet" holder, spent a week with Naia and I at our home in Sedona, AZ. We had met him 10 years prior and we had become friendly with the then 83 year old Traditional Elder. During one conversation about the predicted "End of the Fourth World," I asked him how the dreaded "War of the Gourd of Ashes" would end. (In 1989, Martin announced the start of the final conflict would begin within the year and it did with "Desert Storm.") He said that North Korea would send fiery birds high in the sky to the US. I pressed him for further details suggesting maybe he meant China, and he said "No, Korea will be behind this attack, possibly w/ the help (or at the behest) of China." At the time Korea had no functioning nuclear weapons program and no ICBMs. As we all know, this has changed.... Just thought I'd mention this!

The next development came on August 17 from Jason M.:

Russian troops are shown here at the Perevalne military base in Crimea, which Russia invaded and then annexed. Author Chris O'Brien asserted he had a lucid dream foretelling the event.

I also have had a very powerful, lucid dream—in which Orlando, Florida (which is about two hours from me) was hit by a massive blast followed by a tremendous fireball and mushroom cloud. The dream felt incredibly real, and I was even able to interact realistically with those around me and see and feel their fear. It was truly horrific. As someone who has had dreams that have come to pass in great detail, I took serious note of the dream, and I spoke with my wife about it moments after I woke up. The dream was also notable to me because I recall specific details and dates about the attack, because in the dream I was reading a news article about a geopolitical crisis that was rapidly spiraling out of control. It left me with an overwhelming sense.

Here is the caveat. In my dream, I knew without doubt that the attack came from Russia, and those around me expressed a similar sentiment. In the news article I had been reading, it discussed how a crisis in the Ukraine had provoked a Russian invasion and a NATO response. I had this dream in early March 2014, just days before the Russian invasion of Crimea. To say that development freaked me out is a tremendous understatement. In the dream, the attack took place in September of 2015. I have no doubt of that.

I was very apprehensive throughout 2015 and kept a close eye on news events from Ukraine. While I was relieved that nothing happened, I knew that the dream was more than just fear playing out in my unconscious mind. Since that time, I have revisited the dream many times in deep meditative states to see what more I could learn from it.

What is my point here? I know that such a dream can be horrible and terrifying. It could even conceivably foreshadow coming events. However, I suspect something else is at play. I admit that I cannot be certain, but my conclusion about my own dream is that my unconscious mind was tapping into collective awareness and fear that was about to engulf the world about that particular crisis. I think I was seeing a potential outcome that was informed by the fear and imagination of millions around the world (or would be, since the crisis had not yet happened when I had the dream), not one that was fated to happen. I suppose there is no way to know but to wait and see. But I do think it is worth cautioning that such dreams could have many potential causes other than predicting actual nuclear annihilation. At least one can hope.

Also on August 17, "Red Pill Junkie," another regular contributor to *Mysterious Universe*, waded in with his own nightmare: "I don't live in Chicago but I had a similar dream on the night of August 6th (I remember the date well because I commented upon it with a friend on FB). I was with a group of people I didn't know, and I looked outside and watched a ginormous mushroom cloud. It took a while for the thing to register but once everybody realized what we were seeing we all panicked and fled in search of refuge. I remember some tried to hide underground, but the blast buried them all alive. Then I woke up. I think this is the first time I've had a dream about nuclear Armageddon in a very long time."

On August 18, J. Griffin, commenting on the Chicago issue, said: "I'm in Chicago right now on business—the last street to my first destination was 'Nuclear Drive.' Go figure." Jacqueline Bradley sent me the following on August 21, the details of a dream that seemed to involve small, tactical nuclear weapons in a forthcoming confrontation:

> It took a while for the thing to register but once everybody realized what we were seeing we all panicked and fled in search of refuge.

A few days ago I had a dream that several nuclear events occurred—in my dream I remember the term "thermonuclear." There were several of these events popping up (appeared to be everywhere and small versions of what we would ordinarily be aware of.) No one seemed to be very perturbed by these and people were just walking around, occasionally looking around and watching these. I was aware that if you were caught up in one and died it killed off your soul or spirit too. All this was happening in broad daylight on sunny days. The dream ended where I was in some kind of alley with an old fashioned dustbin nearby. Suddenly I found myself "sinking" or evaporating and woke up. I wasn't scared by the dream, just puzzled. I too connected it with the tensions in N Korea. I've also been watching *Twin Peaks* and connected it with that, but not sure why.

One day later, Jill S. Pingleton wrote:

As a paranormal investigator and student of metaphysics, I, like many, are concerned about the prophetic potential of so many having these dreams/visions. However as a former MUFON Chief Investigator, I'm wondering if the people reporting these dreams and associations are Contactees [a reference to people in contact with extraterrestrial entities on a regular basis]?

My point is that Contactees frequently recount stories of viewing scenes of mass destruction placed in their mind's eye during encounters with ETs. I don't know if they are being given glimpses of the future or only a possible time line unless events can be changed. Like a wake-up call to Contactees to get involved and speak out for the sake of humanity. Perhaps that's also the mission of the Mothman. I wonder if any of these dreams/visions were preceded by an abduction event or if it's part of an ongoing "download" that so many Contactees experience. I think much can be learned from studying the Experiencers/Witnesses. So many questions!

Over at *Red Dirt Report*, Andrew W. Griffin commented on an August 2017 article I wrote on the matter of Mothman and nuclear nightmares. In a feature of his own titled "Riders on the storm (Strange days have tracked us down)," he said: "Clearly we are entering very troubled waters. And it seems that the collective unconscious of humanity is clueing in that we are entering a perilous period in our history. So, when I saw Nick Redfern's new post at *Mysterious Universe* —'Mothman and Nuclear Nightmares'—I took pause, as he notes that 'in the last week, three people have contacted me with eerily similar stories' involving nuclear apocalypse."

Interestingly, Andrew added that in relation to Kenny's dream of a nuclear bomb exploding near Lubbock, Texas, it was "not unlike my own dream that I wrote about on Jan. 26, 2017, which involved nuclear detonations near Joplin, Missouri. We were in a car in the vicinity of Joplin, Missouri—something I noted in my mind in that it is on that nexus of high weirdness 37 degrees north and 94 degrees west (which I recently addressed here)—and nuclear explosions, followed by menacing mushroom clouds, are going off at various intervals.... And yet as the nuclear blasts send radioactive debris through the town and infecting everything in its path, I seem to be the only one alarmed by what is happening around us. The whole experience has the feeling of a guided tour through a park or historic site...."

Then, there was a Facebook message from Andy Tomlinson of Manchester, England. In early June 2019, Andy had a dream of being in a deserted London. The city was not destroyed or in flames. It was, said Andy, "like they had all been evacuated," which is an interesting phrase to use. Well, I say the city was deserted. It was, except for two things: one was the sight of "a massive big black bird over [the Houses of] Parliament." Then, as Andy walked the streets, trying to figure out what had happened, he had that feeling of someone watching him. He turned around to see a man in a black trench coat right behind him. The man was pale, gaunt, and—as Andy worded it—"had a funny smile." Andy's description sounds very much like a certain sinister character in the saga of the Mothman—one Indrid Cold. Andy then woke up with his heart pounding, relieved that it had just been a dream. Or, was it something more than just a dream?

What was without doubt one of the most chilling stories came from Anna Jordan. On August 25, she sent me this:

Anna Jordan told the story of a dream she had twenty-five years ago in which she sees Mike Pence (pictured) long before he was vice president, announcing that a nuclear war has come.

Hi Nick, So, this dream was one I had about 25 years ago or so. Here's the dream: I was standing in the living room of the apartment I lived in at the time. I had three small kids on the floor around me playing and *Sesame Street* was on the TV. (At the time, I only had two children, but later had a third.) So, PBS is on with *Sesame Street*, but there's a break-in on the channel like when they have breaking news. It just showed like a PBS symbol and a countdown and then this man, who I knew was in the White House, came on. He was sitting at a desk, very solemn. I swear to you, it was Mike Pence. I have waited, studying White House faces for all these years waiting to see this face. The white hair, the face, the voice ... it's him, I'm sure. He just looks at the camera and says that he was very sorry, it was too late, and wished the world good luck. I don't know how, but I knew he was talking about a nuclear war. In the dream, I felt my heart drop. Then I woke up. That's about it.

Less than twenty-four hours later, Elaine Clayton sent me the following message on Facebook:

Over the decades, but more so recently, I've had dreams of hologram writings and ships in the sky. I believe some of these dreams were actually astral travels (being scanned in a space ship, etc.) and I used to be woken up by—and this is the best way to describe it—robotic forms with hologram like presence, brightly colored and with personality. I asked to stop seeing those when I could not tell who they were although they seemed benevolent. Those were visions, they happened with my eyes open sitting up. But most dreams are about space ships of magnitude often geometrically fascinating. And several have shown me that in the distance that I perceive as "in the West" atomic bombs going off although they're only more like dirty bombs, not fully atomic.

The last one went like this: I was standing looking up at a silently moving, ethereal looking space ship. It was huge and had smoke streaks coming off it toward earth. It was colorful and its structure appearing smoky, multidimensional. There was a peaceful feeling more than military or fearful. Although again it was extremely dominant and intelligent energy. I then turned to look at the landscape behind me and saw all at once about 5 or 6 bombs being dropped, immediately exploding in small mushroom clouds of fire. I registered my sense of where they landed—to the north east of Manhattan—I thought, and knew they missed their target.

But in the dream I worried about my sister knowing she was there. But then when I woke up I figured it out—my sister lives in Colorado Springs [Colorado] and very near NORAD. I believe whoever dropped the bombs dropped them from a satellite with the intention to take out NORAD. But they missed. I later learned that Kim Jong Un has a map showing his plan to bomb NORAD but his map is not smart and he'd actually be bombing Louisiana. I may post this on my own site. I am so glad you study all these things.

As August came to its close, I was contacted by an old English friend, Sally, whom I had not seen in years. She suggested that I should read *Warday*, a

A NORAD command center in Colorado, pictured here, is part of a joint U.S.–Canada effort to defend North America from missile attacks.

1984 novel written by Whitley Strieber and James Kunetka. I had actually read the book years ago, and it made for grim and disturbing reading. It's an excellently written book that tells the story of a limited nuclear attack on the United States that still kills more than sixty million people from the initial atomic blasts, famine and starvation, radiation, and a wave of out-of-control influenza. Strieber and Kunetka skillfully tell a story that could, one day, become all too real. In *Warday*, the United States is a shell of its former self, with chaos, death, and destruction rampant. *Warday* makes it very clear that had the confrontation between the United States and the old USSR escalated beyond a limited one, the result would have been unthinkable: complete and utter obliteration in the northern hemisphere.

> The story of the Mothman-type beast is only included in the book to demonstrate how, in the aftermath of the war, strange and bizarre rumors surface and spread among the survivors.

As we chatted online, I asked Sally something along the lines of: "Why should I go back and read *Warday* now?" I got a one-sentence reply: "Check out pages 213–217." Now, admittedly, it was probably in the early 1990s when I read *Warday*, so I had forgotten many of the specifics of the story beyond the crux of it. So, I checked out those pages. I found a five-page chapter on a creature not at all unlike Mothman. This issue of a Mothman-type creature being associated with a devastating attack on the United States in fictional form (*Warday*, of course) eerily parallels what people were talking about in August 2017: dreams of a nuclear event and a tie-in with Mothman.

A couple of quotes from *Warday* will give you an idea of the nature of this aspect of the story. The title of the chapter is "Rumors: Mutants and Super-Beasts." We're told, under a heading of "Rumor," that "there is a gigantic beast with bat wings and red, burning eyes that has attacked adults and carried off children. The creature stands seven feet tall and makes a soft whistling noise. It is often seen on roofs in populated areas, but only at night."

A further extract from Strieber's book concerns the testimony of an alleged eyewitness to the flying beast in California: "I had just gotten off the Glendale trolley when I heard this soft sort of cooing noise coming from the roof of a house. The sound was repeated and I turned to look toward the house. Standing on the roof was what looked like a man wrapped in a cloak. Then it spread its wings and whoosh! it was right on top of me."

It's important to note—in light of the Mothman-like references—that *Warday* is not a piece of wild science fiction. The story of the Mothman-type beast is only included in the book to demonstrate how, in the aftermath of the war, strange and bizarre rumors surface and spread among the survivors. I did, however, find it intriguing that *Warday* makes a connection between a nuclear war and "a gigantic beast with bat wings and red, burning eyes." This was, of course, what was being reported in mid-2017.

Interestingly, in 1995, Strieber himself had a graphic dream of a nuclear explosion that destroys Washington, D.C., in 2036—which sees the end of the government as we know it today and the rise, in the wake of the disaster, of a full-blown dictatorship. In his 1997 book, *The Secret School*, Strieber says of this dream (or of a brief view of what is to come via a future self) that "Washington, D.C., is in ruins. However, this isn't the center of the memory. The center of the memory is that it was suddenly and completely destroyed by an atomic bomb, and nobody knows who detonated it."

The final message on this topic came from Roger Pingleton, the wife of Jill S. Pingleton, who had contacted me a few days earlier. On August 28, Roger wrote:

> Hi Nick. My wife informed me of the subject matter of some of your recent articles and encouraged me to reach out with my experiences.
>
> Before Jill and I were married, I drove to Serpent Mound in Ohio on 11/11/2011 to meet with Jill and a group of people. I've always had weird feelings about the Ohio River valley, the mound building Indians, and the deities they worshiped there. And being that Serpent Mound is so close to Point Pleasant, I couldn't resist driving on to Point Pleasant, WV, after Serpent Mound. I slept a few hours in my pickup and drove on to Point Pleasant in the wee hours of the morning. I'd estimate my arrival to have been sometime between 3 AM and 4 AM. The best I can describe the feeling I got driving through the back roads of WV is visceral. I felt like I was being called to be there at that early hour.
>
> Driving in the back roads near the old munitions facility, I saw, up ahead, two bright circular lights above the road. My thought was that they were circular tail lights, that there was a hill up ahead and that I might catch up with the vehicle. The thing is, as I drove, I discovered there was no hill ahead of me, which freaked me out, because those two red lights were definitely higher than they should have been. Then I started thinking, "What vehicle has round tail lights these days?" A corvette maybe, but they have more than two.
>
> I couldn't help but think I had seen the eyes of the Mothman. I know it's weak evidence, but I can't come up with another plausible explanation. Not long after that, I had an apocalyptic dream. We live just south of Indianapolis. The city is on a grid and as such it's easy to tell directions. In my dream there was a giant explosion on the NW-SE diagonal axis. When I woke I worried that the city was Cincinnati, since it was to the SE of

Indy, and my sister lives there, but then I realized it could also have been Chicago, which is to the NW of Indy. I didn't put these two events together until the Mothman sightings occurred. I truly hope I am wrong about these connections.

I hoped that Roger Pingleton was wrong, too. And I hope that just about everyone else who had such dreams were wrong, too. To be sure, it was a dark and tense period, with so many people having terrifying dreams of a worldwide, disastrous nuclear war with links to the assassination of a U.S. president. So far, those nightmares have not come true. I hoped—and still hope—they never will come true.

CAN'T WE JUST DRONE THIS GUY?

Born in Australia in 1971, Julian Assange is most widely known for being the editor-in-chief of WikiLeaks, a group that has released into the public domain an untold number of official, secret documents from a wide and varied body of sources, the vast majority of which were obtained illegally as a result of computer hacking. While Assange is most assuredly associated with WikiLeaks, his involvement in hacking dates back to the 1980s. In the latter part of the decade, Assange went by the hacking name of Mendax. It was during this period that Assange hooked up with two other hackers—Prime Suspect and Trax—and created a body of hackers called the International Subversives. It is known, for sure, that the International Subversives hacked into the systems of NASA, various organizations within the U.S. Navy, the Pentagon, Stanford University, and many others.

Controversy continued to follow Assange: in the latter part of 1991, he was arrested by police authorities in Australia chiefly as a result of his online penetrations of a Canadian telecommunications company called Nortel. Assange was lucky not to have been jailed as a result given that, initially, he faced thirty-one charges. Fortunately for Assange, a plea bargain allowed him to walk away with a relatively small fine.

As the 1990s came to a close, Assange began to focus more on the secret work of the U.S. National Security Agency and established an unused online domain, *leaks.org*. In this time frame, Assange made cryptic comments about the work of the NSA and how it was undertaking widespread surveillance and spying on the public. He said, without naming the NSA—but it's clear that's who he was talking about—that "everyone's overseas phone calls are or may soon be tapped, transcribed and archived in the bowels of an unaccountable foreign spy agency."

In the mid-2000s Assange practically became a household name. It was all as a result of WikiLeaks, which Assange established in 2006. From the very beginning, WikiLeaks placed into the public domain massive numbers of pages of classified material, the subjects of which ranged from the Iraq War, the hostilities in Afghanistan, and, during the 2016 U.S. presidential election, the emails of John Podesta, Democratic candidate Hillary Clinton's campaign chair.

In 2010, the U.S. government took sizable steps to try to bring WikiLeaks revelations to a halt. Arguments were made that WikiLeaks had compromised U.S. national security, that he had placed the United States and its allies into states of jeopardy. This was soon followed by plans to have Assange extradited to Sweden, amid claims of rape. Worried that any attempt to have him arrested might see him handed over to American authorities, Assange chose to hand himself over to U.K. police in December 2010. The next development came in August 2012, when Assange was provided asylum by the government of Ecuador. To this day, Assange remains within the Embassy of Ecuador in London.

There is no doubt at all that WikiLeaks played a significant role in the plan to derail Hillary Clinton's plans to become president of the United States—Clinton, of course, being a purported major player in the New World Order and its plans to radically alter society with its iron grip. To show the extent to which Clinton viewed WikiLeaks and Assange as major threats, we have to turn our attentions in the direction of the *New York Magazine*, which, in July 2016, reported:

Computer hacking editor-in-chief of WikiLeaks, Julian Assange, is pictured here during the time he was staying in the Ecuadorian Embassy in London.

Julian Assange, the founder and head of WikiLeaks, has laid his cards on the table: He views it as his mission to do what he can to prevent Hillary Clinton from becoming president of the United States of America. And his reasons aren't just political, as Charlie Savage wrote earlier this week in the New York *Times*: In an interview with Robert Peston of ITV on June 12, Savage wrote, Assange "suggested that he not only opposed her candidacy on policy grounds, but also saw her as a personal foe."

Recently, the internet rumor mill has been circulating an enticing possibility for those rooting for an Assange takedown of Clinton: Assange says that he has, in his possession, an email or emails that will offer 'enough evidence'—that's the simple, two-word quote that is repeated over and over and over, everywhere—for authorities to indict Clinton.

That Clinton saw Assange as not just an annoying obstacle but also as a threat to her plans for the presidency is clear, as *InfoWars* noted. On October 3, 2016, Adan Salazar, writing for *InfoWars*, stated:

> Democrat presidential candidate Hillary Clinton once proposed using a military drone strike to extrajudicially assassinate Wik-ileaks founder Julian Assange, a document published by the organization states. The screenshot tweeted Monday cites a report from TruePundit.com claiming in 2010 the State Department explored ways to suppress the trouble-making Assange before he could publish damaging information on "conversations between State Dept. personnel and its foreign assets and allies."

Predator drones like this one were first used in the mid-1990s by the U.S. Air Force and the CIA. Initially, they were used solely for reconnaissance, but they were later mounted with AGM-114 Hellfire missiles, making them potentially useful for targeting political figures for assassination.

"'Can't we just drone this guy?' Clinton openly inquired, *TruePundit.com* reports. While WikiLeaks has not confirmed the veracity of the report, the *Washington Examiner* notes that during the same time, the State Department was involved in discussions on what "nonlegal" methods were available to subdue Assange. In this case, those words, "Can't we just drone this guy?" are strongly suggestive of an assassination plot. Or, at the very least, a discussion of such a thing potentially taking place.

"Emails previously released from Clinton's private server reveal Anne Marie Slaughter, a former director of policy planning at the State Department, sent an email on the same day in 2010 on the subject of possible 'nonlegal strategies' for dealing with WikiLeaks. That email also notes that a meeting was held that day to discuss WikiLeaks," reports the *Washington Examiner*.

In November 2016, in a feature titled "WikiLeaks email shows Clinton 'sealed her OWN FATE' in plot to make Donald Trump her rival," the United Kingdom's *Express's* Jon Austin told the story:

> Hillary Clinton may have paved the way for Donald Trump's victory and sealed her own fate by trying to elevate the controversial business tycoon in the press in the hope it would damage the Republicans. A camp Clinton plot to try to harm the Republican campaign by getting more press coverage for the party's more conservative candidates was revealed in an email released by Julian Assange's WikiLeaks. The email was sent in April 2015—two months before Trump announced he was going to stand and is one of tens of thousands published by Wikileaks from the apparently hacked gmail account of Clinton campaign boss John Podesta.

> The email from Marissa Astor, and assistant to Clinton campaign manager Robby Mook, to Mr. Podesta, and copied to the Democratic National Committee (DNC), suggests the campaign knew Mr. Trump was going to run for president, and believed by promoting him into the press, it could ultimately harm the Republicans. The email also suggests Hillary Clinton's team felt it would be good for Mrs. Clinton if she ran against someone like Mr. Trump, as she would have more chance of success. The memo described Donald Trump, Senator Ted Cruz, and Ben Carson as "Pied Piper candidates."

> As for what, exactly, the memo stated, it reads as follows:

> We need to be elevating the Pied Piper candidates so that they are leaders of the pack and tell the press to them seriously. Our hope is that the goal of a potential HRC campaign and the DNC would be one-in-the-same: to make whomever the Republicans

nominate unpalatable to a majority of the electorate. We have outlined three strategies to obtain our goal:

1) Force all Republican candidates to lock themselves into extreme conservative positions that will hurt them in a general election;

2) Undermine any credibility/trust Republican presidential candidates have to make inroads to our coalition or independents.

Under the heading "Pied Piper Candidates," the memo continued: "There are two ways to approach the strategies mentioned above. The first is to use the field as a whole to inflict damage on itself similar to what happened to Mitt Romney in 2012.

"The variety of candidates is a positive here, and many of the lesser known can serve as a cudgel to move the more established candidates further to the right. In this scenario, we don't want to marginalize the more extreme candidates, but make them more 'Pied Piper' candidates who actually represent the mainstream of the Republican Party. Pied Piper candidates include, but aren't limited to: Ted Cruz, Donald Trump and Ben Carson.

"Most of the more-established candidates will want to focus on building a winning general election coalition. The 'Pied Pipers' of the field will mitigate this to a degree, but more will need to be done on certain candidates to undermine their credibility among our coalition (communities of color, millennials, women) and independent voters. In this regard, the goal here would be to show that they are just the same as every other GOP candidate: extremely conservative on these issues."

As history and WikiLeaks have both shown, however, the plans of the New World Order to place Hillary Clinton in the White House failed.

KILLING ON A MASSIVE SCALE

Merriam-Webster defines assassination as "murder by sudden or secret attack often for political reasons." We almost always assume that the act of assassination is aimed at one person. What if, however, there were top-secret plans designed to take out not just one or two people but millions—also for political reasons? Maybe even billions? We're talking about a crazed and dangerous agenda, run by powerful figures and organizations, to try to lower the world's population. If you think such a thing could never happen, you would be very wrong.

There are now large numbers of global leaders who are convinced that the exploding population of the world resembles a virus or plague and that it must be combated as such. "In fact, it would be very difficult to understate just how obsessed many members of the global elite are with population control," states the website *Fourwinds10*. As it notes, the issue of population control has fallen under the scrutiny of the likes of politicians, the United Nations, and the rich and the powerful. As one might suspect, their plans to deal with the ever-growing human population are controversial in the extreme. In some cases, we're looking at plans for something akin to the extermination of millions of Jews by Nazi Germany during the Second World War. Indeed, the rich and powerful will stop at practically nothing to ensure that their agenda to wipe out not just millions of people but billions of them goes ahead without a hitch.

The Jewish analogy is an important one because it's a verifiable fact that the democratically elected Adolf Hitler systematically launched a program to ensure that the Jews would one day be no more. Thankfully, the crazed German tyrant was finally defeated. As for those claims that the Holocaust was a hoax, they are nonsense. Hitler really did try to wipe out an entire group of people. Had the Nazis won the Second World War, they would surely have continued with their murderous, barbaric scheme. I mention this because it serves to demonstrate that—based on what has come before us—history sometimes has a way of repeating itself in terrible and terrifying fashion. What happened with Hitler and the Jews in the 1940s could easily happen again, but this time, the targets will be just about everyone. The agenda is to reduce the human population by billions. They care not a bit about which races they target, just as long as they have the population at a figure they feel is manageable.

No one doubts that overpopulation is, indeed, a very serious issue, one that is an undeniable threat to our future as a species. There is only so much space and so many resources; one day, we will reach the point at which Earth can no longer adequately sustain the human population. When—rather than if—that day comes, we will very likely see worldwide chaos and anarchy as the starving, desperate millions raid stores, peoples' homes, and do just about anything and everything they can do to stay alive. So, yes, there is a problem, one that a lot of people don't even give much thought to. But some *do* give the subject a great deal of thought. Their focus is on finding a way to provoke a sudden, massive cut in the numbers. In bleak terms, they are primed and ready to cull what they term as the herd.

If you think all of this amounts to nothing but fear-mongering conspiracy fodder, you would be very wrong. There's no doubt that our future might be extremely bleak when the world's population doubles. The mainstream media is now quickly picking up on this global problem and warning of what might soon be around the corner. The United Kingdom's *Guardian* has highlighted the issues that face us, which cannot be ignored. The *Guardian* stated in 2012: "Fresh water is crucial to human society—not just for drinking, but also for farming, washing and many other activities. It is expected to become increasingly scarce in the future, and this is partly due to climate change."

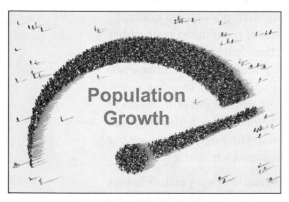

Overpopulation in the world is a reality that requires us to either find enough resources for everyone, find another planet, or decrease the population, any of which will be difficult.

The *Guardian* revealed something very disturbing: namely, that so-called regional groundwater is misunderstood in terms of how extensive and expansive its reserves of freshwater are. Or, in a worst-case scenario, are *not*. This is particularly worrying because around half of all the water used by the human race on a daily basis comes from regional groundwater. If those reserves dry up—and dry up much faster than anticipated—civilization could easily and quickly collapse upon itself. Water is the one thing we cannot live without. No water means deaths on an unimaginable level—aside, of course, for those who may be preparing for that day. They may be dicing with death, too, by hoping that a global catastrophe will allow them to radically shrink the human race.

Echoing the words of the *Guardian* are those of Melanie McDonagh, a journalist with the *Spectator*. She offers words that are grim, concerning, and extremely thought provoking. McDonagh focused her attention on the work of Anne and Paul Ehrlich. Their research into the field of worldwide disintegration led to the release of a 2013 article, which was published by the Royal Society. The title of the article was presented as an important and potentially life-changing question: "Can a Collapse of Global Civilization Be Avoided?"

The Ehrlichs pointed out that not only are we faced with massive overpopulation issues, but we are also using up precious commodities at an incredible and disturbing rate. In doing so, we are changing the environment. Global warming is a reality, regardless of what some might say otherwise. As Prince Charles put it, we are recklessly engaging in what amounts to "an act of suicide on a grand scale."

If draconian laws were put into place that limited families in every country on the planet to have just one child, even that would not have an appreciable effect on population levels for years.

There is no doubt about that. Right now, the human population is current at around seven and a half billion. If things don't change, by 2050, say the Ehrlichs, that figure will have reached around nine and a half billion. That will mean two billion more people than now will be digging ever deeper into a limited supply of essentials, such as water, oil, land, and food. The conclusion of the pair is that the only outcome will be complete collapse all across the world.

To demonstrate just how incredibly the numbers of people on the planet are growing, take note of the following: it was in the very earliest years of the nineteenth century that the world's population finally reached one billion. By around 1930, the population doubled to two billion. By the dawning of the sixties, there were three billion of us, four billion by the mid 70s, and five billion by the late eighties. As the twenty-first century began, the number was six billion. In 2013, we hit seven billion. Current estimates are that 2024 will roughly be when Earth finds itself buckling under the weight of eight billion people. By 2040, we'll be at nine billion. It's an issue that everyone should be concerned about.

It's hard to say if we can do anything about this. If draconian laws were put into place that limited families in every country on the planet to have just one child, even that would not have an appreciable effect on population levels for years. And what if people chose to have more than one child? Are millions of pregnant women going to be thrown into jail or be forced to have abortions? There are also issues pertaining to oil. One year after the Ehrlichs' report was published, *USA Today* revealed that fossil fuels, such as oil, may run out by the 2060s.

The *G2 Petroleum* website, which has been at the forefront of demonstrating why "green cars" are so important to our future survival, provide the following words on those estimates for what may occur in the 2060s: "These estimates are actually 1.1% more than last year, thanks in part to growing estimates of American shale oil. Of course, keep in mind that the oil industry is regularly growing or shrinking estimated energy reserves, with California's Monterey Shale having its reserves downgraded some 96%. There's also suspicion that countries like Saudi Arabia are outright lying about how much crude they actually have left. So yeah. Skepticism."

Gas 2 suggests that when oil disappears, some nations will be "caught flat-footed." There is no doubt that massive drops in the water supply will be bad enough. Add to that no fuel—just abandoned cars, trucks, and bikes on highways that no one else uses because they *can't* use them—and what you have is something far beyond "flat-footed." There will be a global emergency of unprecedented proportions: people will turn on one another, looting homes and killing neighbors, and all for just a few pints of water and a tank of gas. You think it couldn't happen? When matters are really down to the wire and personal survival is at stake, people will do just about anything and everything to stay alive. The end of civilization could come with rapid, astonishing speed.

Overpopulation in China was such a concern that for years, the government there mandated couples could only have one child. This led to problems, though, when parents aborted or even killed girls in favor of having boys as their only child.

All of this has led to concerns that are at the forefront of the collective minds of those who plan on doing the unthinkable: how to find a way to lower human population levels and to ensure that the collapse of society worldwide does not happen. This may sound like such people actually have an ounce of emotion in their black hearts, after all. But sadly, no; they do not. Long-term programs to try to reduce population levels in humanitarian ways are not part of their agenda. We are seen as a herd to them—*their* herd. Their plan is to find a way of wiping out billions of us in quick fashion. Only those chosen to kick-start a new world—a new society, even—will be given the life-saving antidotes to whatever kind of terrible plague they choose to unleash upon us. This may sound like science fiction, but it's not. If one looks carefully and closely, one finds strong evidence that this malignant plan is already afoot. We'll begin with the United Nations.

The UN has undertaken numerous studies that focus on the issue of the problems posed by constant, never-ending increases in population levels. In 2003, for example, a paper researched and written by the UN's Department of Economic and Social Affairs division titled "Long-range World Population Projections" revealed something shocking and scarcely possible to imagine: "If the fertility of major areas is kept constant at 1995 levels, the world population soars to 256 billion by 2150." In those terms, it's hard to comprehend what the world would look like with a population of more than 250 billion—or close to thirty times larger than today's population.

Could things be done to prevent such a calamitous future from occurring? Yes. But as noted above, it's the means by which depopulation may occur that is most concerning of all. It's hard to see how the planet and everyone and every-thing living thing on it could continue to exist in such a packed world. Undoubtedly, those pulling the strings are all too aware of that. Yes, they are coldhearted, murderous thugs who want to see an end to freedom all across the planet, but

In an incredibly outrageous piece of racism, Kissinger suggested that a plan should be put into place to target certain nations for depopulation.

they aren't stupid. They are not immortal supermen. They are keenly aware that we are limited to this planet alone. So, as they see it, if the planet is destroyed, so are they—hence their pressing desire to do something now, rather than in 2150. This brings us to the crux of this bleak agenda and the issue of how, and under what specific circumstances, the plot to wipe us out really began. It's time to take a trip back to the mid-1970s.

On December 10, 1974, a controversial, new document was circulated to the United States' National Security Council. The United States viewed the issue of overpopulation as not one of humanitarian proportions but rather one related to America's national security. The report was titled "Implications of Worldwide Population Growth for U.S. Security and Overseas Interests." The author was Henry Kissinger, whose résumé includes stints as the national securi-ty advisor to the president of the United States and the U.S. secretary of state.

Kissinger had unique and controversial plans in place to deal with the problems that overpopulation would cause. Although the problem of an ever-growing number of people was, and still is, a global one, Kissinger did not see things like that. He scarcely touched upon the western world. Instead, he suggested that only certain nations should shoulder the brunt of the problem. In an incredibly outrageous piece of racism, Kissinger suggested that a plan should be put into place to target certain nations for depopulation. They included India, Bangladesh, Pakistan, Indonesia, Thailand, the Philippines, Turkey, Nigeria, Egypt, Ethiopia, Mexico, Colombia, and Brazil. Since

Kissinger and his team had concluded that almost half of the looming increases in the world's population would be caused by the people of the aforementioned countries, it made sense from Kissinger's perspective that they should be targeted with a program to limit the number of children that a family might have. Such a program would make it punishable for people to have more than one child. Kissinger's rationale revolved around concerns that a growing population could only end in the collapse of society as the world buckles under the weight of more and more people. And there was more to come from Kissinger's team.

As studies into the issues got ever deeper, Kissinger noticed a thread that ran throughout all of the countries that he perceived as being problematic to a stable future. He informed the National Security Council that in those parts of the world where the human populations were increasing at increasing speeds, additional problems always surfaced. They almost always typically involved a lack of enough water to sustain the population, a similar lack of adequate food, and limited supplies of fuel. When those three factors were combined together, said Kissinger, this could only lead to one inevitable result: the eventual collapse of the relevant nation or nations. Kissinger saw such a situation only increasing and spreading like wildfire—if a program was not put into place to curb the growth. Kissinger's biggest concern—which, of course, was a quite natural and understandable one—was that this spiraling meltdown would eventually reach the United States, perhaps sooner than later.

Kissinger was concerned that the United States would be dragged down under the weight of those nations whose population figures were out of control.

Kissinger's additional concern was that if some of the nations on the verge of collapse—or that had already reached that point—were ones from which the United States purchased priceless and vital commodities, such as oil, then this would likely plunge the United States into a fraught and dangerous situation. He foresaw a future born out of, and constantly in a state of, chaos and anarchy. Kissinger was concerned that the United States would be dragged down under the weight of those nations whose population figures were out of control. For this reason, Kissinger felt that this pressing matter was not one just for scientists or futurists but also for those in the U.S. government, the military, and the intelligence community—in fact, Kissinger felt that it was the world of national security that should lead the fight against overpopulation. Here are a few extracts from Kissinger's document, which, having been declassified under the terms of the Freedom of Information Act, is now in the public domain:

> The U.S. economy will require large and increasing amounts of minerals from abroad, especially from less developed countries. That fact gives the U.S. enhanced interest in the political, economic, and social stability of the supplying countries. Wherever

a lessening of population pressures through reduced birth rates can increase the prospects for such stability, population policy becomes relevant to resource supplies and to the economic interests of the United States.

And then, there are these words from Kissinger's team of experts: "The location of known reserves of higher grade ores of most minerals favors increasing dependence of all industrialized regions on imports from less developed countries. The real problems of mineral supplies lie not in basic physical sufficiency, but in the politico-economic issues of access, terms for exploration and exploitation, and division of the benefits among producers, consumers, and host country governments."

It was at this point that Kissinger turned to the one angle that really worried him, to the point that he felt that action had to be taken quickly: "Whether through government action, labor conflicts, sabotage, or civil disturbance, the smooth flow of needed materials will be jeopardized. Although population pressure is obviously not the only factor involved, these types of frustrations are much less likely under conditions of slow or zero population growth."

The document adds further words to this particular aspect of the problem, again reinforcing the perceived problems that would go with declining food, water, and fuel and a huge increase in people. The section at issue is titled "Populations with a High Proportion of Growth" and most assuredly led to raised eyebrows within the highest echelons of the U.S. National Security Council: "The young people, who are in much higher proportions in many LDCs [least developed countries], are likely to be more volatile, unstable, prone to extremes, alienation and violence than an older population. These young people can more readily be persuaded to attack the legal institutions of the government or real property of the 'establishment,' 'imperialists,' multinational corporations, or other-often foreign-influences blamed for their troubles."

Kissinger and his group were far from done on the danger of overpopulation: "We must take care that our activities should not give the appearance to the LDCs of an industrialized country policy directed against the LDCs. Caution must be taken that in any approaches in this field we support in the LDCs are ones we can support within this country. 'Third World' leaders should be in the forefront and obtain the credit for successful programs. In this context it is important to demonstrate to LDC leaders that such family planning programs have worked and can work within a reasonable period of time."

Kissinger made a very eye-opening statement: "In these sensitive relations, however, it is important in style as well as substance to avoid the appearance of coercion." If we read that sentence carefully, what we see is not Kissinger avoiding using coercion, only ensuring that any actions didn't *appear* to amount to coercion—which is a very different thing. To what extent other, perhaps even more highly classified, documents on population growth remain hidden in the vaults of the National Security Council is anyone's guess. But that's not where things end. In fact, there's far more to come. Since the 1970s, much more has been done to address this potentially planet-crippling issue. And, as you will now see, the opinions and thoughts on how to achieve depopulation are getting more controversial.

"A program of sterilizing women after their second or third child, despite the relatively greater difficulty of the operation than vasectomy, might be easier to implement than trying to sterilize men. The development of a long-term sterilizing capsule that could be implanted under the skin and removed when pregnancy is desired opens additional possibilities for coercive fertility control. The capsule could be implanted at puberty and might be removable, with official permission, for a limited number of births."

Forced sterilization? Capsules "implanted" under the skin? A "program of sterilizing women"? These words are from John P. Holdren, the science advisor to the office of the president of the United States when President Barack Obama was in power.

This was not the first time that a science advisor to a U.S. president had made such a controversial statement. President George W. Bush's science advisor, Paul Ehrlich, made an equally provocative statement. He said: "Each person we add now disproportionately impacts on the environment and life-support systems of the planet." Ehrlich added: "A cancer is an uncontrolled multiplication of cells. The population explosion is an uncontrolled multiplication of people. We must shift our efforts from the treatment of the symptoms to the cutting out of the cancer. The operation will demand many apparently brutal and heartless decisions."

Yes, things are now in such a state of flux that we, the people, are being compared to cancer cells by a senior advisor to an American president.

John Holdren was the former scientific advisor to President Obama who did not hold back when describing a possible future for world populations.

Moving on, Prince Philip, the Duke of Edinburgh, the husband of Queen Elizabeth II of the United Kingdom, has stated: "If I were reincarnated I would wish to be returned to earth as a killer virus to lower human population levels." Yes, it's all very well for this old fool to make such a statement. He, after all, conveniently married into one of the wealthiest families on the planet. It's easy to pontificate in such a fashion when you're one of the elite. His words make it clear that he has no care at all for who, and how many people, might be wiped out by his theoretical "killer virus." Even more outrageous, Prince Philip openly admits that he would be happy to kill all those millions of people, albeit in the reincarnated form of a virus. That, my friends, is how we are viewed: as cancers and as people of no consequence who should be killed off by lethal viruses.

Even CNN founder Ted Turner has waded into this issue. He thinks that the world's population should be shrunk down to around three hundred million people. That's less than the population of the United States. How might Turner get rid of those seven billion people to allow just three hundred million to continue to fly the flag of the human race? There is no answer from Turner. What we can say for sure, though, is that there is no easy way to lower the population to such incredibly low levels.

The United Nations' Global Diversity Assessment states: "A reasonable estimate for an industrialized world society at the present North American material standard of living would be 1 billion. At the more frugal European standard of living, 2 to 3 billion would be possible."

Paul Joseph Watson of *Prison Planet* said in 2009: "There are still large numbers of people amongst the general public, in academia, and especially those who work for the corporate media, who are still in denial about the on-the-record stated agenda for global population reduction, as well as the consequences of this program that we already see unfolding."

Finally, there are the words of Michael Snyder, who, at *The American Dream*, wrote in 2011: "In recent years, the UN and other international organizations have become bolder about trying to push the sick population control agenda of the global elite. Most of the time organizations such as the UN will simply talk about 'stabilizing' the global population, but … there are many among the global elite that are not afraid to openly talk about a goal of reducing the population of the world to 500 million (or less)."

Trying to find a humanitarian way of slowly and carefully lowering human population levels is not actually a bad thing. After all, it is a hard fact that we cannot keep on growing in massive numbers to the point where we reach that irreversible tipping point. Something must be done. But a ruthless elite killing off billions—perhaps across a week or two or a few months—is not the answer. We fought against one ruthless dictator in the Second World War, a crazed lunatic who tried to wipe out the Jews. The last thing we need is an equivalent of Hitler—or, worse still, an entire army of them—who doesn't just want to wipe out the Jews but who wishes to see almost everyone on the planet erased.

MURDER FROM THE SKY

As we saw earlier, there are solid indications that powerful people are intent—whether now or in the future—on massively lowering human population levels on Earth. Deadly viruses are, it seems, at the forefront of this dangerous and deadly program. It may well be that the deaths of multiple microbiologists in the early 2000s were prompted by fears that at least some of those same microbiologists knew something of this planned, virus-based extermination of billions of people. There is, however, another way in which the orchestrators are hoping to ensure that their agenda goes ahead. It revolves around what are known as chemtrails—contrail-style patterns in the sky that conspiracy theorists suggest may contain deadly pathogens. This phenomenon has been around since the latter part of the 1990s. A great deal has been said and written about chemtrails. But what, exactly, are they? What are the theories? Will chemtrails provoke the end of much of the human race?

We'll start with the conventional explanation that has been put forward as a means to dismiss the phenomenon: that of contrails. Just about everyone has seen contrails; they are, of course, above us just about all the time. And there is nothing strange or sinister about them. When a plane reaches a specific height, and when the temperature has sufficiently dropped, it leads the plane's exhaust vapor to become crystalized, to the point where those crystals can be seen in the form of what are called contrails. In other words, contrails are simply the normal by-products of flying an aircraft at a high, freezing level. But are all contrails simply contrails, or are some of them chemtrails? Some believe that certain contrails are packed with killer chemicals or deadly viruses. That's when a contrail becomes a chemtrail.

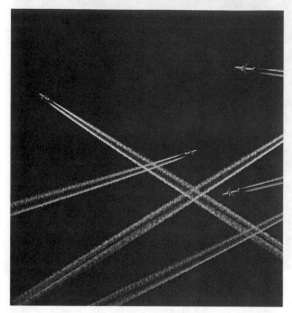

Pictured are what are most commonly known as contrails, formed from the plane's exhaust vapor freezing at high altitude. Some believe, however, that the government is using aircraft to spread viruses over unsuspecting citizens.

Although chemtrails have been discussed and debated for more than twenty years, it was not until the final year of the twentieth century that the chemtrail controversy became most visible. That was when a man named Kim Johnson got involved. At the time, Johnson was part of the New Mexicans for Science and Reason group. He was approached by the New Mexico attorney general's office, which wanted Johnson's help to try to lay to rest a growing issue in New Mexico—namely, the concern on the part of New Mexico's citizens that something ominous was going on in the skies above their heads.

Johnson studied the available data and got back to the attorney general's office swiftly. Johnson carefully looked at various photographs that, in the eyes of those who believe in the existence of chemtrails, allegedly showed planes spraying unknown agents into Earth's atmosphere. Whether chemical or biological agents, no one knew. But Johnson was determined to find the answers.

He approached Sandia National Laboratories in Albuquerque, New Mexico, whose personnel dismissed the claims as nonsense and concluded that what was seen was common contrails. Johnson also spoke with pilots who also claimed that there was no mystery to be seen. The attorney general's office was convinced there was no sinister plot and that nothing deadly was being unleashed into Earth's atmosphere for nefarious purposes. Not everyone agreed with that assessment, however. In fact, there was a steadily growing body of people who fully believed—and still do—that the skies above are being polluted on incredible, frightening levels.

Johnson stated: "That is not to say that there could not be an occasional, purposeful experimental release of, say, high altitude barium for standard wind tracking experiments. There could also be other related experiments that occur from time-to-time which release agents into the atmosphere. However, not one single picture that was presented as evidence indicates other than normal contrail formation."

One of those who has dug deep into the chemtrails issue is Ken Adachi. He has made some interesting observations on this topic. He has carefully studied those areas of the planet where reports of chemtrails have been made, and he has noticed something that, in his opinion, stands out. He believes there are some parts of the world that are being targeted and others that are being left alone. Why might that be?

Adachi believes he has an answer to that particular question. He notes that the nations that have received what he considers to be far more than their fair share of chemtrail activity include the eastern part of Europe, the United States, and Japan. He also notes that China has not reported any such activity. Adachi believes there is a specific reason for this: he concludes that there is no longer a wish to see the United States as the dominant nation on the planet. Rather, he believes that the aim is to turn China into the most powerful country on Earth—which will help spearhead the agenda of complete, worldwide control of the human race.

There is an even more disturbing angle to Adachi's work: he states that "it is being reported that people with average or below average immunity are experiencing pneumonia-like respiratory symptoms, while people with stronger immunity are only experiencing slight discomfort for a day or two or no symptoms at all." He suspects that what he terms "special bioengineered pathogens" may be being created to specifically, and only, target certain groups of people, rather than everyone.

As interest in, and concern about, the chemtrail phenomenon grew and grew, the subject leapt out of the relatively small world of conspiracy theorizing and right into the heart of the regular press. Back in 2001, *USA Today* reported something startling: "Federal bureaucracies have gotten thousands of phone calls, e-mails and letters in recent years from people demanding to know what is being sprayed and why. Some of the missives are threatening. It's impossible to tell how many supporters these ideas have attracted, but the people who believe them say they're tired of getting the brush-off from officials. And they're tired of health problems they blame on 'spraying.'"

When *USA Today* stated that government agencies had received "thousands of phone calls," they were not exaggerating. Documentation declassified under the terms of the Freedom of Information Act demonstrate that massive numbers of American citizens have contacted their local FBI offices, called the Department of Homeland Security, sent letters to the White House, and fired off concerns to the CIA.

One of those who chose to immerse himself in the chemtrail issue was longtime conspiracy theorist Jim Marrs, who died in the summer of 2017. Marrs had good reason to take a close look at the claims that something dire and dangerous was afoot. Much of Marrs's research revolved around events that occurred in Louisiana in 2007. Many researchers of the chemtrail phenomenon believe this story tipped the scales in favor of conspiracy and away from the domain of simple mistaken identity.

The man who opened the floodgates was KSLA-TV investigative journalist Jeff Ferrell. Ferrell was given the opportunity to have water analyzed that was believed to have come from a chemtrail. The results were startling. The water contained levels of barium more than three times greater than what the Environmental Protection Agency considers an acceptable level.

The U.S. government's Agency for Toxic Substances and Disease Registry states: "Eating or drinking very large amounts of barium compounds that dissolve in water or in the stomach can cause changes in heart rhythm or paralysis in humans. Some people who did not seek medical treatment soon after eating or drinking a very large amount of barium have died. Some people who eat or drink somewhat smaller amounts of barium for a short period may experience vomiting, abdominal cramps, diarrhea, difficulties in breathing, increased or decreased blood pressure, numbness around the face, and muscle weakness."

On the matter of how, and to what extent, chemtrails may be affecting us, there is this from the *Sheep Killers* site: "Our health is under attack as evidenced by the skyrocketing rates of chemtrail induced lung cancer, asthma and pulmonary/respiratory problems. Our skies are increasingly hazed over with fake barium/aluminum particulate, ethylene dibromide chemtrail clouds. Whether in the atmosphere or in the ocean, this added particulate matter is a hazard to the health of every living thing on this planet."

It was inevitable that fingers would be pointed at the U.S. government regarding the issue of chemtrails. This led to a response from the U.S. Air Force:

> The Air Force's policy is to observe and forecast the weather. The Air Force is focused on observing and forecasting the weather so the information can be used to support military operations. The Air Force is not conducting any weather modification experiments or programs and has no plans to do so in the future. The 'Chemtrail' hoax has been investigated and refuted by many established and accredited universities, scientific organizations, and major media publications.

Of course, that particular statement hardly convinced those who believed that our skies were becoming not just dangerous but outright lethal.

Mark Pilkington, the author of a book titled *Mirage Men*, which looks at how various governments have used disinformation to confuse the controversy surrounding the UFO phenomenon, has also taken a careful look at the chemtrail issue. While essentially a skeptic on the subject, he doesn't rule out every aspect of the controversy. He says:

> NASA has been carrying out genuine research into the possible effects of contrails and increased air activity on the environment. An average contrail can last for hours before evolving into cirrus clouds—the largest measured covered 2,000 square miles

(5,180 sq km) of west America. Scientists have long been concerned that, with an expected six-fold increase in plane flights, such cirrus spreads might trap heat in the Earth's atmosphere, so contributing to global warning. According to NASA research, cirrus cloud cover over America has increased five per cent since 1971, with the figure higher in the north-east.

So, yes, research into contrails is ongoing, but that doesn't prove that chemtrails are real. But it does show that where there are contrails, there are often government scientists.

Still on the matter of chemtrails and conspiracies, there is the strange story told by William Thomas, a well-known figure within the field of chemtrail research. In the early 2000s, he investigated a story from a man named Terry Stewart. Stewart was working as the manager for planning and environment at Victoria International Airport in British Columbia, Canada. On December 8, 2000, Stewart received a phone call from a man who wanted to alert the airport to "strange patterns of circles and grids being woven over the British Columbia capitol."

Stewart researched the issue and was told by personnel at the Canadian Forces Base, Comox, on Vancouver Island that a joint Canadian–American Air Force operation was in force in the skies over British Columbia. When Stewart sought more information, he was told that no further information was available. When the story broke publicly, staff at CFB Comox denied making any such statement to Stewart.

No one should be surprised to learn that the Canadian government has tried its best to have the chemtrail issues dismissed. Just like the U.S. Air Force, Canadian authorities felt the need to say something at a public level: "There is no substantiated evidence, scientific or otherwise, to support the allegation that there is high altitude spraying conducted in Canadian airspace. The term 'chemtrails' is a popularized expression, and there is no scientific evidence to support their existence. Furthermore, weather modification experiments

Mark Pilkington, in his studies of the chemtrail issue, discovered there may be an equal problem that results in more global warming.

carried out over Canadian airspace legally require that Environment Canada be notified. We have no information of any such efforts. High altitude aerial spraying of pesticides does not occur in Canada and any spraying that is currently done in Canada does not encompass the use of large military type jet aircraft."

The story of Terry Stewart was noticeably absent from the Canadian government's statement. Had it been addressed, there is a distinct possibility that there would have been a greater clamor for more information than there actually was.

> It wasn't long before the British public was clamoring for answers to what was behind the curious contrails seen over their land, too.

It wasn't long before the British public was clamoring for answers to what was behind the curious contrails seen over their land, too. And, just like the Canadians, the U.K. government chose to make a public statement. What's particularly interesting, though, is that it wasn't the public's letters that caused the government to say something. Rather, the demands came from within the government itself. In early November 2005, the chemtrails controversy was debated in the government's Houses of Parliament. Elliott Morley, the Minister of State for the Environment and Agri-Environment, provided a response. It was perhaps inevitable that Morley would play matters down. His response made it clear that despite its dismissal of the chemtrails issue, the U.K. government was most certainly aware of it:

> The Department is not researching into chemtrails from aircraft as they are not scientifically recognized phenomena. However, condensation trails (contrails) are known to exist and have been documented since the 1940s. Contrails are composed of ice crystals forming on the small particles and water vapor emitted by aircraft as the result of the combustion process, they form behind high-flying aircraft depending on the temperature and humidity of the atmosphere.

> A major scientific report, *Aviation and the Global Atmosphere*, was published in 1999 by the Intergovernmental Panel on Climate Change. The report assessed the current contribution of aviation to climate change and, based on a range of scenarios and assumptions, forecast its contribution up to 2050. It estimated that contrails covered about 0.1 per cent of the Earth's surface in 1992 and projected this cover would grow to 0.5 per cent by 2050 (on middle range assumptions). More recently this work has been updated from the results of the EU 5th Framework Project, TRADEOFF. Contrails continue to be the subject of research to help better understand both how they are formed and what effects they have on the atmosphere.

More than a decade after Morley's statement was made, the U.K. government's stance on chemtrails has not wavered.

Meanwhile, Monsanto has developed seeds that will weather the effect of the sprays, creating a tidy profit for the corporation while organics suffer. Monsanto's GMO seeds are specially designed to grow in the high presence of aluminum. Aluminum is the chemical found in chemtrails. If this poisoning continues, true organic farming may become impossible in the not-so-distant future. When aluminum pollutes soil and water, it kills crops. It collects in people and causes diseases!

Today, conspiracy theorists continue to believe that chemtrails are a worldwide menace to the health of just about all of us (the Chinese aside, we are told). On the other hand, government agencies are content in saying that the whole thing is nonsense. One side says "chemtrails!" The other cries "contrails!" The end of the contrail controversy, it seems, is nowhere in sight.

THE MOST DANGEROUS MEN OF ALL

Now, our story is at its end. As we have seen, assassinations are all around us and have been for thousands of years. While at least some assassinations are the work of the likes of hired gunmen, "secret agents," and killers for money, it may well be the case that the vast majority of such killings are the work of the dreaded Men in Black. These staples in the field of conspiracy theorizing are dangerous, ruthless, deadly figures who should be avoided at all costs. Let's see what we know about them.

Make mention of the Men in Black to most people, and it will likely provoke images of Will Smith and Tommy Lee Jones. After all, the trilogy of *Men in Black* movies were phenomenally successful and brought the subject to a huge, worldwide audience. Outside of ufology, most people assume that the Men in Black were the creations of Hollywood. This, however, is very wide of the mark: in reality, the movies were based upon a short-lived comic book series created by Lowell Cunningham in 1990. Most important of all, the comic books were based on real-life encounters with the MIB, dating back decades.

In fact, in the movies, the characters portrayed by Jones and Smith are known as J and K. There is a good reason for that: they are the initials of the late John Keel, who wrote the acclaimed book *The Mothman Prophecies* and who spent a lot of time pursuing MIB encounters, particularly in the 1960s and 1970s. In that sense, the producers of the *Men in Black* movies and comic books were paying homage to Keel. Now, let's get to the heart of the matter, namely, the real Men in Black, not those of Hollywood. Who are they? Where do they come from? What is their agenda? If there is one thing we can say for sure about the MIB, it's that they are the ultimate Controllers—they threaten, intimidate, and terrify into silence the people they visit. Let's see how the mystery all began.

In the early 1950s, Albert Bender created a UFO research group called the International Flying Saucer Bureau (IFSB). It was based out of Bender's hometown of Bridgeport, Connecticut. Bender quickly became enthused by the UFO phenomenon when it kicked off in earnest in the summer of 1947 after Kenneth Arnold's acclaimed and now legendary sighting of a squadron of UFOs over the Cascade Mountains. The world was changed, and so was Albert Bender.

As a result of the establishment of the IFSB, Bender found himself inundated with letters, phone calls, and inquiries from people wanting information about UFOs. Bender was pleased to oblige, and he created his very own newsletter, *Space Review*. The publication was regularly filled with worldwide accounts of UFO activity, alien encounters, and sightings of flying saucers. Bender's group and magazine were so popular that he found himself inundated with letters from all around the planet: communications poured in from the United Kingdom, Australia, South America, and even Russia. Bender's little journal that he typed up from his attic room of his house was suddenly a major part of ufology. It's most curious, then, that in the latter part of 1953, Bender quickly shut down the IFSB, and he ceased the publication of *Space Review*. Many of Bender's followers suspected that something was wrong, and they were right.

Albert K. Bender displays a portrait of a character known as one of the now infamous Men in Black.

When Albert Bender brought his UFO-themed work to a hasty end, a few close friends approached him to find out what was wrong. After all, right up until the time of his decision to quit, he was riding high and had a planet-wide following. So, his decision to walk away was a puzzle. One of those who wanted answers was Gray Barker, a West Virginia writer and publisher who also had a deep interest in UFOs. Barker had subscribed to *Space Review* from its very first issue and had developed a good friendship and working relationship with Bender—which was an even bigger reason for Barker to question Bender's decision.

At first, Bender was reluctant to share with Barker his reasons for backing away from the subject that had enthused him for so long, but he finally opened up. It turns out—Barker wrote in his 1956 book on the Bender affair, *They Knew Too Much about Flying Saucers*—

that Bender had been visited by a trio of men—all dressed in black—who warned him to completely drop the subject. At first, Bender chose to soldier on, which was a huge mistake. When the MIB realized that Bender had not followed their orders, they turned up the heat to an almost unbearable level. Finally, Bender got the message.

For Gray Barker, who recognized the dollar value in the story of his friend, this was great news, in a strange way, at least. The scenario of a mysterious group of men in black suits terrorizing a rising UFO researcher would make for a great book, thought Barker, which it eventually did, hence Barker's 1956 book. The problem was that although Bender somewhat reluctantly let Barker tell his story, Bender didn't tell him the whole story. Bender described the three men being dressed in black suits and confirmed the threats, but that was about all he would say. As a result, Barker assumed that the Men in Black were from the government—the FBI, the CIA, or the Air Force. Barker even mused on the possibility that the three men represented all of those agencies. When Barker's book was published, it not only caught the attention of the UFO research community, it also, for the very first time, brought the Men in Black to the attention of just about everyone involved in the UFO issue. A legend was born, which continues to this day.

While Albert Bender certainly didn't lie to Gray Barker, he most certainly did not share with him the full story. There was a good reason for that: the real story was far stranger than Barker could ever have imagined. Yes, Bender was visited by three men in black, but they were not of the kind that the U.S. government might have been expected to dispatch. Rather, they fell into the domain of the supernatural, the paranormal, and the occult.

According to Bender, late one night, after toiling away on his old typewriter in his attic, he suddenly started to feel sick. He was overwhelmed by nausea, dizziness, and a sense that he might faint; most curious of all, the room was filled with an odor of brimstone or sulfur. Both odors are associated with paranormal activity and have been for centuries. Bender lay down on the bed, fearful that he might crash to the floor if he did not. In seconds, something terrifying happened: three shadowy, ghostly, spectral beings started to materialize through the walls of Bender's room. They didn't need to knock on the door and wait for it to be opened. The silhouette-like trio then started to change: their shadowy forms became more substantial and finally took on the appearance of regular men, except for several notable differences: their eyes shone brightly, like a piece of silver reflecting the sun. Their skin was pale and sickly looking, and they were thin, to the point of almost being cadaverous. They closely resembled the deadly vampires of old, which Bender loved to read about in his spare time.

Using telepathy, rather than the spoken word, the three men warned Bender that now was the time for him to leave the UFO issue alone for good. Or else. When Bender began to shake with fear, the Men in Black realized that they had gotten their message across, and they duly departed the way they had first arrived—through the walls. For days, Bender was in a state of fear that bordered upon hysteria. Finally, though, he thought: Why should I quit ufology? After all, I've done so much work, I'm not going to stop now. So, Bender didn't stop; he decided to take on the MIB and stand up to their threats. That was a very big mistake on his part.

In the days ahead, Bender saw the MIB again. On one occasion, late on a Saturday night, Bender was sitting in his local cinema, watching a new movie, when one of the Men in Black materialized in the corner of the cinema—his blazing eyes focused on a terrified Bender. Bender immediately left the cinema. On the way home, though, Bender was plagued by the sounds of footsteps behind him, which seemed to be disembodied, as no one was in sight. In the days ahead, the MIB returned to Bender's attic, which yet again caused Bender to fall seriously ill. Finally, after another week of terror and mayhem, Bender really was done. His time in ufology was over—for the most part, anyway.

> So, Bender didn't stop, he decided to take on the MIB and stand up to their threats. That was a very big mistake on his part.

Albert Bender's story, as told in the pages of Barker's book, was substantially correct in the sense that it told of how Bender was visited, threatened, and ultimately driven to leave ufology. Through no fault of his own, though, Barker was unaware of the supernatural aspects of the story and assumed that Bender had become a victim of the U.S. government. Finally, though, Bender came clean with Barker. Far from being disappointed, Barker was overjoyed chiefly because he realized that he could spin the Bender saga into yet another book, which is exactly what happened. This time, though, Barker let Bender write the story himself. So despite being warned by the Men in Black to stay away from the flying saucer issue, Bender somewhat reluctantly reentered the scene and wrote *Flying Saucers and the Three Men*, which Barker eagerly published in 1962. Many people in ufology were put off by the overly supernatural aspects of the story and, as a result, the book was relegated to the realm of obscurity for many years.

Behind the scenes, there was another group of men in black suits—and black fedoras—who were secretly following the Bender saga: the FBI. It wanted to find out who Bender's MIB were. Thus, in a strange way, there were now two different groups of MIB: the supernatural ones encountered by Bender and the government MIB. The provisions of the Freedom of Information Act have shown that both Bender and Barker had files opened on them. Those same files make it clear that legendary FBI boss J. Edgar Hoover ordered one of his special agents to get a copy of Barker's *They Knew Too Much about Flying Saucers*.

After promoting his book, Bender yet again walked away from the UFO issue—this time for good. Bender died in March 2016 at the age of ninety-four.

In the years that followed Bender's encounters, the U.S. government would become determined to uncover the truth of the MIB. During the course of his research into the issue of the Men in Black, John Keel arranged a meeting with Colonel George P. Freeman of the U.S. Air Force. Keel's interest was driven by the fact that Colonel Freeman had circulated a memo throughout the Air Force, ordering everyone to be on guard for the Men in Black. Colonel Freeman's memo read as follows:

"Mysterious men dressed in Air Force uniforms or bearing impressive credentials from government agencies have been silencing UFO witnesses. We have checked a number of these cases, and these men are not connected to the Air Force in any way. We haven't been able to find out anything about these men. By posing as Air Force officers and government agents, they are committing a Federal offense. We would sure like to catch one—unfortunately the trail is always too cold by the time we hear about these cases, but we are still trying."

A few weeks after Colonel Freeman's memo was widely circulated, there was this one from Lieutenant General Hewitt T. Wheless, also of the U.S. Air Force: "Information, not verifiable, has reached Hq USAF that persons claiming to represent the Air Force or other Defense establishments have

The friendship that developed between Albert Bender and Gray Barker (pictured) led to the sharing of information on UFOs and Barker's *They Knew Too Much about Flying Saucers.*

contacted citizens who have sighted unidentified flying objects. In one reported case, an individual in civilian clothes, who represented himself as a member of NORAD, demanded and received photos belonging to a private citizen. In another, a person in an Air Force uniform approached local police and other citizens who had sighted a UFO, assembled them in a school room and told them that they did not see what they thought they saw and that they should not talk to anyone about the sighting. All military and civilian personnel and particularly information officers and UFO investigating officers who hear of such reports should immediately notify their local OSI offices."

It was this period of interest in the MIB on the part of the government that led to an extraordinary, and almost surreal, development.

> So the government came up with an ingenious idea: it created a group whose job it would be to keep people away from the really important parts of the UFO phenomenon. Threats, silencing, and intimidation were the orders of the day.

Although the U.S. government had no real idea of who or what the real Men in Black were, there was a realization on the part of the government that the MIB phenomenon could be used to the advantage of the likes of the NSA, the CIA, and military intelligence. It wasn't just the MIB who wanted UFO witnesses silenced: the government did, too. But the government was concerned about threatening UFO witnesses—American citizens, in other words—and being outed in the process.

So the government came up with an ingenious idea: it created a group whose job it would be to keep people away from the really important parts of the UFO phenomenon. Threats, silencing, and intimidation were the orders of the day. This was successfully achieved by having their secret agents dress and act like the real MIB who had terrorized Albert Bender and who had intruded on the life of Brad Steiger. In other words, they wore black suits, black sunglasses, and black fedoras and acted in an odd, emotionless fashion. The government really did not know (and probably still does not know) who or what the MIB really were, but that same government knew that it could exploit the phenomenon to its advantage. Dressing as the MIB would offer the government an ingenious form of camouflage. And it did. It was a case of using fear to provoke the ultimate form of control.

The two different types of MIB—government agents and something supernatural—continues in the twenty-first century.

Let's now look at some latter-day cases. In 2011, the following extraordinary account was provided to me by Tim Cowell, a British freelance videographer who has been filming professionally since 2008. He has a bachelor of arts degree with honors in film, television, and advertising from the University of Wales, Aberystwyth. His filming credits include the Fashion TV channel, corporate businesses, Wrexham Council, the education sector, and various documentaries. In addition to his freelance work, Cowell is currently studying for his second degree in creative media technology at Wrexham Glyndwr University. He also is a volunteer photographer with the Wrexham County Borough Museum and Archives.

Cowell's account demonstrates that whoever, or whatever, the Men in Black may be, they were as active in the 1990s as they were when the likes of poor Albert Bender were being terrorized back in the early 1950s. Notably, as our correspondence progressed, Tim revealed that in addition to MIB, he had experienced strange phenomena, including both ghostly and ufological encounters.

"Dear Mr. Redfern, The reason I am writing to you is with regards to a strange experience I had back in 1997 when I was 17 years old. Whether you may be able to shed light on my experience I'm not sure, but I came across your name and 'real men in black' article on the web a few moments ago and felt that your expertise on the subject might lift a nagging uncertainty that I have had for fourteen years.

"Firstly I would like to say that I have not read your "men in black" book as yet (I do intend to) but I do have an interest in the unexplained and have read many books on these subjects since I have had multiple strange experiences in my past and present. That being said, the experience I wish to convey to you has not been contaminated with any theories of others or my own.

"I am very open-minded but at the same time possess a healthy skepticism with any unexplained phenomena. However, I have not found any logical reason for what I am about to tell you (although there is always the possibility that there is one). The following account is complete truth and I have not embellished any part of it. All I hope is that you might have an explanation for what happened, be it strange or mundane, as I am uncertain as to whether this account depicts the behavior of the 'Men in Black?' At the time of the experience I was 17 years of age and was 'bunking off' [skipping class] from a college lecture to meet my then girlfriend later that afternoon....

"My Account: I was walking from my college and into town to get a coffee to while away the hour until I caught the bus to my girlfriend. I was young and newly 'in love' and walking quite happily down the main street when I had a strange feeling that I was being followed. This feeling led to an instinct of looking behind me and as I did, a few feet away, I saw a couple of men close behind. As I looked they both emitted a "blank" smile. Being young and—dare I say it—possibly naive, I had the thought that maybe they were from the college and following me because I bunked off. (On reading this whole account you will see that what happened is not the normal procedure any college would take.)

The Men in Black are known for wearing black trench coats and fedoras. Their faces often have a blank, unnerving expression.

"After I witnessed this 'blank smile' I continued to walk at my normal pace down the long main street towards my destination. I was now wondering to myself if they smiled at me because I looked at them (the old 'you look at me so I look at you' scenario). I looked behind me a second time and again they offered, in unison, that same "blank smile". I also noticed their appearance and whilst they were not wearing black suits and black fedoras, they were wearing an attire that didn't seem to fit in. Dark brown tweed suits with matching long over-coats and fedora-like hats. Without sounding clichéd (as I now know the usual nonconformity of these guys) they did appear to be from an earlier era than the ' 90s, to say the least.

"I decided to quicken my pace and noticed that their pace also quickened. Feel-ing a little paranoid I quickened my pace again; and again they also matched my speed. So now I'm almost speed walking towards the cafe to get my coffee. A third look behind me before I entered (the then) 'John Menzies' [a British store-chain] confirmed that they were still walking my way so I entered the store but waited inside a little for them to pass by. They didn't, so I ventured into the street again but they had disappeared. I immediately assumed that they had turned off or entered another shop and put it down to myself as being a paranoid college bunker.

"I re-entered the store and proceeded to walk upstairs to the cafe area. It is worth mentioning here that whilst I chose this cafe for its quietness it did always bug me that the cafe attendants rarely gave you enough time to choose what you wanted without being quickly pestered into hurrying up with your order. (The reason for this note will become apparent soon.) Having being quickly served at the counter, I found a place to sit at a table facing the cafe entrance and began to read a letter that my girlfriend had sent me (sickening I know).

"Anyway, a few moments later I looked up from the letter whilst taking a sip of my coffee and froze on the spot. The two distinguished gentlemen were a few feet away at the food counter staring at me blankly. After what seemed like an age of staring one of the men placed a large leather-like satchel that I had not noticed before on the floor. With the other man still looking at me, the other bent down, opened the satchel and pulled out a very large and old looking camera, complete with large round flash. He proceeded to point the camera directly at me and took my picture. On doing so he placed the camera back in the satchel and both men turned and slowly walked away towards the stairs.

"Completely in shock and bemused as to what just happened I was still frozen in place trying to wonder what the hell had just happened. I quickly decided to follow them (the time taken for this decision, taking into consideration the casual speed at which they exited, I calculated that they would still be going down the stairs or at least at the bottom by the time I got to them) and literally ran down the stairs. There was no sign of them so I decided to go to the store exit first and looked outside but they weren't anywhere to be seen. I then turned to look into the store again due to the fact that I might have missed them inside and that they would have had to pass me to leave. But again they were nowhere to be seen.

"One thing that was apparent to me was that whilst they were upstairs by the counter they were never attended to by the very needy cafe staff and believe me they used to pester you. To be honest, without sounding stupid it seemed like no one could see them. I know how that sounds but all I can do is explain the account in the same way I experienced it.

"Now, as a 17 year old bunking off college I was hesitant to tell my mother of this experience (not because of the ludicrous way it would have sounded—she actually took that part in her stride as she has also experienced strange phenomena in her life), but because I thought I would have been grounded for bunking off. Least to say, when I did arrive home later that day I told her the exact same thing I told you now, including why I was not in college.

"The intrigue of my experience swayed the 'grounding' and to this day I have no logical reason as why something like that would happen to me. Obviously with my interest in all things weird becoming increasingly larger over time with other experiences and the ease as to which information about ourselves can be found out via the Internet, this aspect couldn't have been the reason for this strange occurrence as I was rarely on the new 'Internet' back then.

"Anyway, what happened that day is a mystery and there could be a mundane reason for it. But there are little things that bug me. Why did I feel I was being followed only to see that I was? Why did they seem out of place in both their clothes and their blank demeanor? Why take a picture of me at all, let alone with the most old-fashioned of cameras? And how did they disappear so quickly? Is this the type of behavior that you would deem to be of 'Men in Black' origin?

"I know that account sounded a little 'wacko' but I assure you I am of sound mind. I simply have an experience that I have no answer for. Thank you for taking the time to read this long-winded email and I hope to hear from you soon. Kind regards, Tim Cowell."

I wrote back to Cowell and asked a few questions regarding the specific location, and I received the following in response:

"Hi Nick, Thanks for your reply. That experience was in my home town of Wrexham, North Wales. Like I said, it's something that I recall from time to time with a nagging uncertainty as to what it actually was and why.

"Because I have had many paranormal experiences I had wondered if there was any link between them. Most of these have been placed in the more ghostly category but there was an incident when I was even younger that myself and grandma witnessed a UFO sighting. The same night of the sighting I was sharing a bed with my cousin (we were being babysat during a weekend) and when I awoke in the morning my Gran found us 'artificially' laying in the bed ... myself lying on my back with arms crossed neatly over my chest and my cousin upside down, feet on the pillow and head under the quilt at the bottom. Not a normal way to sleep and the bed sheets were as if they had been made whilst we were already in them. Strange.

> **"I know that account sounded a little 'wacko' but I assure you I am of sound mind. I simply have an experience that I have no answer for."**

"All through my life I've seen, felt and heard 'ghosts' or whatever in my family home and even more recently encountered paranormal resistance whilst living and working in Malta which required the help of a catholic priest! I'd love to write a book about my experiences but don't know the first thing about publishing. :)

"Anyway, whilst I have and continue to experience strange things I simply had no explanation at all as to who those strange men who followed me were. The only reason I have regained interest in that strange day was thanks to a movie that I had recently watched called *The Adjustment Bureau*. In the same way that smelling a scent can transport to back to a memory I had the same jolt of surprise when I saw these 'adjustment men' in that movie as their appearance instantly reminded me of that day back in 1997. Thus thrusting me back onto the internet to try and find anyone with an answer or similar experience to mine.

"And that's when I came across your book, *The Real Men in Black*. I have to say that I do own your book *Cosmic Crashes* and because I enjoyed it and realized that you were the same author I ventured to ask you your opinion on the matter. Again, thanks for your reply and I feel better knowing that an author of your caliber and experience on the subject appreciates the weird and wonderful. Kind regards, Tim Cowell."

Denise Stoner is the director of the Florida Research Group affiliation of the UFO Research Center of Pennsylvania (UFORCOP), a MUFON

National Abduction Research Team (ART) member, a Florida MUFON field investigator, a Star Team member, and a former Florida MUFON state section director and chief investigator. She coauthored and published her first book, *The Alien Abduction Files*, which was released in May 2013.

She also holds educational forums for public and private gatherings for abduction experiencers. Her involvement in the UFO field spans more than twenty-five years. Denise has an educational background in business and psychology and is a certified hypnotist specializing in regressive hypnosis. She has taught classes in stress reduction for more than twelve years for professionals in such fields as medicine and law.

She began her research in hypnosis under Dr. Bob Romack in Denver, Colorado. They worked together for five years on pain control, smoking cessation, and past-life-regression research.

For twelve years, Denise did background investigations for the military on recruits seeking highly classified clearances for work on nuclear submarines. Prior to retirement, Denise moved to the Naval Air Warfare Center, Training Systems Division, a military research facility where she was the training coordinator for several hundred military and civilian employees.

She is a retired SCUBA instructor, cave diver, and former research member of the National Speleological Society Cave Diving Section. Her retirement from the federal government has allowed her to expand her work with UFO research and investigation. Denise has appeared on the Travel Channel, PBS, and over a hundred radio shows; and she speaks yearly at the Daytona Museum of Arts and Science and the Paranormal Investigative Association, plus other venues.

She has worked as an on-camera expert for documentaries produced in the United Kingdom. She is currently moving forward with some exciting new projects, such as her research on the commonalities among abductees, now on its second study. Her hypnotist certification came through hypnosis and regression training at the Hypnotic Research Society by Dr. Ronald P. De Vasto. Her advanced regression study was through the National Guild of Hypnotists with Donald J. Mottin.

She has been invited to become a part of the newly formed Foundation for Research into Extraterrestrial Encounters (FREE) as a member of the research team. Denise can be contacted through her website at *www.denisem stoner.com*. She says of her experiences:

"At least three times here in Florida at a particular combination health/grocery/restaurant called Whole Foods I have been observed by a strange character. This is a good place to blend as many folks who shop here are "odd characters" to begin with or 'hippie like,' gone back to nature types. So, the person who has observed me is wearing a gauzy outfit, thin hair, woven straw Panama type hat and sunglasses fits right in. His skin, hair, and clothing are all almost the same beige color.

"The difference is he has a drink in front of him, a notebook, stares at me the whole time as we eat at a table on the sidewalk. He never has food of his own nor does he touch the drink. It seems he knows when we are almost finished eating, he gets up, walks slowly past our table, rounds the corner that is clearly visible but must pass a pillar on the corner of the shopping plaza by our table. Once he goes behind that pillar, he never comes out the other side.

> "The difference is he has a drink in front of him, a notebook, stares at me the whole time as we eat at a table on the sidewalk. He never has food of his own nor does he touch the drink."

There is literally nowhere for him to go but out the other side, then down the sidewalk or out to the parking lot—but no, he is gone. I cannot get up to follow, thinking I am going to bump into him on the other side of the pillar. He lets me know in no uncertain terms that he is watching me or letting me know he is there.

"Yes, I have pondered many times what prevents me from picking up my cell phone and taking a picture of this individual. I have no answer for that. It absolutely crosses my mind the whole time the episode is taking place. Afterwards I feel foolish, know I will be made fun of in the telling of the story, and promise myself I will have the camera ready the next time. It never happens. Are we somehow prevented from having photographic evidence needed as proof?

"I do have several speaking engagements a year and have decided to add one of these odd stories each time as I feel people need to know this type of thing exists. Let them decide for themselves what they think. This is going on and that is a fact—the fact appears to be that we have some type of 'human' with unusual abilities living among the earthly beings and our only choice for now is to be observant, to watch and wait. What other options do we have?"

And Stoner has yet another account to relate....

"I would be glad to describe the situation to you as it has remained clear as crystal in my mind. As for my Mom, she knows something happened but it has gotten foggy and she doesn't know why, yet she recalls something happened that made her feel very uncomfortable.

"My Mom and I had gone to the mall on Christmas Eve for a couple of last minute stocking stuffer type gifts. We actually knew what we wanted so parked outside J.C. Penney's on the side where those goods were. We went in and immediately noticed that in late afternoon, there were only a few shoppers. We picked out our gifts and got in line at the cashier in back of two other people. We could easily see the exit door and the sun in the parking lot, we were facing that way.

"The glass doors opened and two very tall, thin women entered. They had long almost waist length blond hair parted in the middle on top and it was thin in texture. Their skin was also pale and I did not notice any make up but each had huge piercing blue eyes. Their gait was odd like they were too tall (approximately 6' 1") to walk smoothly. I was already an investigator for MUFON so was aware of oddities in people and had done background searches for the Federal Govt. so was trained to be observant.

"They were pushing one of those umbrella style strollers with no fancy attachments—just the hammock type bed, wheels, and handles. I noticed they had no purses or accessories such as a diaper bag to carry diapers or bottles, etc. The women moved slowly it seemed and drew my attention to the stroller. There was a baby blanket in the bottom portion and on top the head of a baby no bigger than a small grapefruit, pasty colored skin, no noticeable nose, a line for a mouth and huge dark eyes taking up most of the rest of this head.

"I wondered if the baby was deformed but knew this was not the case somehow. The baby appeared alert and was staring up at me. My mom bumped me with her arm to get my attention and said, 'What is wrong with that baby?' I felt I needed to tell the person in front of me because we had been talking (with her) about being slow in finishing up our shopping. When I tapped her on the shoulder I then was shocked to see not only her but the lady in front of her and the cashier were kind of frozen in place. Everything seemed to be moving in extremely slow motion around us.

> "The baby appeared alert and was staring up at me. My mom bumped me with her arm to get my attention and said, 'What is wrong with that baby?'"

"The blond women seemed to pass the thought to me that I needed to take another good look at the baby and study it. Then as if a film was put back into normal speed, they walked past me and the cash register began to work, people—the only three in the area were moving again as if nothing happened.

"I told my Mom to hold our places and I ran after the women. Just next to us was the infants' clothing department. The women had turned in to that isle. I followed and when I turned in to the isle—they disappeared. Just gone like they had never been there. I ran back the short distance to my Mom and told her they were gone. We checked out and my Mom kept saying "what was going on with that baby?" I told her no one goes shopping with a baby that tiny without taking needed supplies, bottles, diapers, clothes, etc.

"I remember asking her if she thought we had seen something alien such as a hybrid and she just shook her head as if there was no answer. We stepped out the door and that's when the experience with the men took place.

"When we exited the mall my Mom had already stepped off the curb to locate my car, I was stopped by three men who were leaning on the brick wall by the door. Wearing black suits, black hats, white shirts, sunglasses. Short in stature. The only difference from your reports was the fact that one had a briefcase—black also. I don't recall their mouths moving but it could be I was just nervous.

"One of them said, 'you will not discuss what happened inside that store, do not talk about it to anyone, do you understand?' I did not answer, stepped off the curb as I felt I was in danger and called after my Mom. Just after I stepped off the curb I turned back to discover these men were gone and there was nowhere for them to go other than in to the parking lot or further down the sidewalk as there was a brick wall where they had been and continued down the length of the building to the only door we had come out.

"We had been shown something in the store we both feel wasn't normal and were talking about it as we left to see if we were imagining things when I met these men. Does this sound typical of these types? I am too old to be abducted and used for breeding and have had a hysterectomy so that could not have been the purpose—to show me a child of mine and I felt nothing like that was going on."

From firsthand eyewitness Leighton Ward, we have a compelling story of Men in Black, thinly veiled threats, and what may have been some form of secret, underground military facility in Arizona:

"The following event took place in the spring of 1998 around 2:00 P.M. The approximate location the event occurred is about 15 miles SE of the Bill Williams Wildlife Refuge, which is a remote desert area off the Colorado River with the closest town being Parker, Arizona.

"Growing up in the small town of Lake Havasu City, you are surrounded by hundreds of miles of open desert with mountain ranges and endless dirt roads that are great for off-roading. The area this event took place is dotted with abandoned mines which we often explored. I was driving my Jeep and my buddy was behind me in his Toyota Land Cruiser.

"The road we were on was a dirt road no different than any other dirt road in the area. The area was fairly flat with a lot of low brush and creosote bushes. I pulled off the right side of the road to look around. There were no signs, no marking, no dirt piles; nothing at all out of the ordinary.

"I got out of my truck and walked about 30 feet. I came across a hole about 15 feet across, I don't know how deep it was but there was no end in sight. This hole was not visible from the road at all because of the low bushes that are all over in this area. The hole went straight down. Since I have seen a lot of mines, I had come to know what the surrounding area of a mine looks like. The area surrounding the mine is always disturbed with dirt piles from the excavation, roads to the mine and often times warning or no trespassing signs and fences.

"This particular hole had no disturbances at all. I only found it because I stumbled upon it by accident. I was surprised that there were no signs or safety fences at all. Aside from the natural camouflage of the surrounding bushes there was no attempts made to hide this hole. The only camouflage to hide the hole was the fact that there was nothing at all such as sign or roads to lead you to believe there was a hole there.

"Within a minute or two of us seeing the hole, a black suburban with dark tinted windows rolled up on us. We saw it coming up the road but by the time we saw it, it was almost to our location. I have no idea how they knew we were there so quickly. Two men, wearing all black military fatigues, with black hats and black sunglasses, got out of the driver and passenger side. Both were Caucasians about six feet tall carrying side arms. They shut their doors and simply said, 'You need to leave.'

"Being a bit of a smart ass at times and with no fences or signs showing private property or no trespassing, I figured the desert is for everyone. I simply said, 'I don't see any signs saying no trespassing.' I said it more as a joke because I really don't like to be messed around with so I wanted to see how serious they were.

"With no emotion whatsoever the driver simply said: 'I will ask you one more time to leave now.' He never took his sunglasses off or made any other movements at all. I got the point and we drove off. I really did not think too much about it back then because there are a lot of mines out there. I am now 39 and looking back and looking into similar stories, I can now say it was likely not just a mine. If it were a mine, there would have been much more security to prevent injury."

Hired guns, Men in Black, or whatever you prefer to refer them as, they are all too real. They are dangerous and deadly, menacing and murderous. And they won't hesitate to "remove" those who have been targeted for assassination. Watch out!

FURTHER READING

Albarelli, Jr., H. P. *A Terrible Mistake*. Walterville, OR: Trine Day, 2009.

"Another Dead Scientist: Composite Released in Fatal Hit and Run." *Houston Chronicle*, December 12, 2003.

Associated Press. *Biologist Disappears; FBI Interested*. November 28, 2001.

Atomic Poet. "Is Catcher in the Rye an Assassination Trigger?" AtomicPoet.com. http://atomic poet.wordpress.com/2012/01/31/is-catcher-in-the-rye-an-assassination-trigger/ (accessed January 31, 2012).

BBC News. "The Assassination of Georgi Markov." https://www.bbc.co.uk/programmes/p00p0931 (accessed March 3, 2012.)

———. "Jill Dando Murder: Brother Hopes Case Is Solved." https://www.bbc.com/news/uk-england-bristol-47779606 (accessed April 1, 2019).

BBC Radio 4. "The Murder of Georgi Markov." https://www.bbc.co.uk/programmes/b0bgblcd (accessed August 31, 2018).

Begg, Paul. *Jack the Ripper: The Uncensored Facts*. London: Robson Books, 1993.

Begg, Paul, Martin Fido, and Keith Skinner. *The Jack the Ripper A to Z*. London: Headline Book Publishing, 1991.

Bernstein, Marc D. "Ed Lansdale's Black Warfare in 1950s Vietnam." HistoryNet. http://www.historynet.com/ed-lansdales-black-warfare-in-1950s-vietnam.htm (accessed February 16, 2010).

Bowart, Walter. *Operation Mind Control*. New York: Dell Publishing, 1978.

Central Intelligence Agency. "The Bay of Pigs Invasion." https://www.cia.gov/news-informa tion/featured-story-archive/2016-featured-story-archive/the-bay-of-pigs-invasion.html (accessed April 18, 2016).

Brewda, Joseph. "Kissinger's 1974 Plan for Food Control Genocide." Executive Intelligence Review. http://www.larouchepub.com/other/1995/2249_kissinger_food.html (accessed December 8, 1995).

Brown, Tim. "12 Holistic Doctors Have Now Died within a Little Over 90 Days." Freedom Outpost. http://freedomoutpost.com/12-holistic-doctors-have-now-died-within-a-little-over-90-days/ (accessed October 13, 2015).

Collins, Tony. *Open Verdict: An Account of 25 Mysterious Deaths in the Defense Industry.* London: Sphere Books, 1990.

Conradt, Stacy. "10 Ways the CIA Tried to Kill Castro." MentalFloss.com. http://mentalfloss.com/article/30010/10-ways-cia-tried-kill-castro (accessed February 16, 2012).

Controlled Offensive Behavior—USSR. Defense Intelligence Agency, 1972.

Court TV. "Body Carrying Missing Scientist's ID Found in Mississippi River." www.courttv.com (accessed December 21, 2001).

Coppens, Philip. "Ancient Atomic Wars: Best Evidence." BibliotecaApleyades.net. http://www.bibliotecapleyades.net/ancientatomicwar/esp_ancient_atomic_07.htm (accessed January 2005).

"Daughter Charged in Slaying of Scientist." *Washington Post*, February 2, 2002.

Davidson, Michael. "A Career in Microbiology Can Be Harmful to Your Health—Especially since 9-11." Rense.com. http://www.rense.com/general20/car.htm (accessed February 15, 2002).

Davidson, Michael, and Michael C. Ruppert. "Microbiologist Death Toll Mounts as Connections to Dynocorp, Hadron, Promis Software & Disease Research Emerge." Rense.com. http://www.rense.com/general20/mic.htm (accessed March 3, 2002).

FourWinds10. "22 Shocking Population Control Quotes from the Global Elite." FourWinds10.com. http://www.fourwinds10.net/siterun_data/health/intentional_death/news.php?q=1291600521 (accessed June 12, 2014).

Garrison, Jim. *On the Trail of the Assassins.* London: Penguin Books, 1988.

Glod, Maria, and Josh White. "Va. Scientist Was Killed with Sword: Three Friends Interested in Occult and Witchcraft, Friends Say." *Washington Post*, December 14, 2001.

Gurney, Ian. "The Mystery of the Dead Scientists: Coincidence or Conspiracy?" Rense.com. http://www.rense.com/general39/death.htm (accessed July 20, 2003).

Holland, Max. "The Assassination Tapes," *Atlantic*, June 2004.

"Jack the Ripper Was Polish Immigrant Aaron Kosminski, Book Claims," *The Guardian*, September 7, 2014.

Jacobsen, Annie. *Area 51: An Uncensored History of America's Top Secret Military Base.* New York: Little, Brown, 2012.

Jones, Steve. "NWO Plans to Depopulate the Earth." Rense.com. http://rense.com/general64/pordc.htm (accessed April 13, 2005).

Keith, Jim. *Black Helicopters II.* Lilburn, GA: IllumiNet Press, 1997.

———. *Black Helicopters Over America.* Lilburn, GA: IllumiNet Press, 1994.

———. *Casebook on the Men in Black.* Lilburn, GA: IllumiNet Press, 1997.

———. *Mind Control, World Control.* Kempton, IL: Adventures Unlimited Press, 1998.

Kiger, Patrick. "The Movie That JFK Wanted Made, But Didn't Live to See." Boundary Stones. https://blogs.weta.org/boundarystones/2014/05/13/movie-jfk-wanted-made-didnt-live-see (accessed May 13, 2014).

King, Gilbert. "The Prime Minister Who Disappeared," *Smithsonian*, January 4, 2012.

Knight, Stephen. *Jack the Ripper: The Final Solution.* London: Grafton Books, 1989.

Kress, Kenneth A. *Studies in Intelligence.* Central Intelligence Agency, 1977.

Lashmar, Paul. "Pearl Harbor Conspiracy Is Bunk," *The Independent*, August 24, 1998.

Lennon, Troy. "Bulgarian Dissident Georgi Markov 'Shot' by Killer Poison Pellet from an Umbrella," *Daily Telegraph*, September 10, 2018.

Lusher, Adam. "Who Killed Jill Dando? The Main Theories behind Murder of British TV's Golden Girl," *The Independent*, April 26, 2019.

Mandelbaum, W. Adam. *The Psychic Battlefield*. New York: Thomas Dunne Books, 2000.

McDonald, Hugh. *Appointment in Dallas*. New York: Zebra, 1975.

McMahon, James. "The Unsolved Murder of Jill Dando, Britain's 90s TV Sweetheart." Vice.com. https://www.vice.com/en_ca/article/gy4ge9/unsolved-murder-jill-dando-20-year-anniversary-conspiracies (accessed April 26, 2019).

Miller Judith. "Russian Scientist Dies in Ebola Accident at Former Weapons Lab," *New York Times*, May 25, 2004.

Mitchell, Alanna, Simon Cooper, and Carolyn Abraham. "Strange Cluster of Microbiologists' Deaths under the Microscope," *Globe and Mail*, May 4, 2002.

Myers, Dale K. "The Assassination of William Greer." Secrets of a Homicide. http://jfkfiles.blogspot.com/2008/07/assassination-of-william-greer.html (accessed July 17, 2008).

Nance, Rahkia. "James Earl Ray's Brother Claims Federal Government Killed Martin Luther King," *Birmingham News*, April 1, 2008.

Newman, Alex. "Globalist Henry Kissinger Outlines 'New World Order.'" TheNewAmerican.com. http://www.thenewamerican.com/world-news/item/19030-globalist-henry-kissinger-outlines-new-world-order (accessed September 1, 2014).

———. "UN Agenda 2030." TheNewAmerican.com. http://www.thenewamerican.com/tech/environment/item/22267-un-agenda-2030-a-recipe-for-global-socialism (accessed January 6, 2016).

Organic Consumers Association. "Food for Thought—Several Dozen Microbiologists & Scientists Dead under 'Suspicious Circumstances.'" OrganicConsumers.org. http://www.organic-consumers.org/corp/suspicious012805.cfm (accessed January 27, 2005).

O'Riordan, Bernard. "Case of Missing PM to Be Reopened," *The Guardian*, August 24, 2005.

Orth, Maureen. "Former CIA Director William Colby: The Man Nobody Knew," *Vanity Fair*, September 22, 2011.

Perez, Chris. "Baffling 'Acoustic Attack' on US Embassy Workers in Cuba Causing Hearing Loss," *New York Post*, August 9, 2017.

Perloff, James. "Pearl Harbor: Hawaii Was Surprised; FDR Was Not." TheNewAmerican.com. http://www.thenewamerican.com/culture/history/item/4740-pearl-harbor-hawaii-was-surprised-fdr-was-not (accessed December 7, 2013).

Redfern, Nick. *Final Events*. San Antonio, TX: Anomalist Books, 2010.

———. Interview with Ray Boeche, January 22, 2007.

———. *The Real Men in Black*. Wayne, NJ: New Page Books, 2011.

"Report of the Presidential Commission on the Space Shuttle Challenger Accident." Washington, DC: U.S. Government Printing Office, 1986.

Rifat, Tim. *Remote Viewing*. London: Vision Paperback, 2001.

"RFK Assassination Witness Nina Rhodes-Hughes Says Sirhan Sirhan Didn't Act Alone," *Huffington Post*, April 30, 2012.

Ritter, Steve. "Wiley's Death Caused by an Accidental Fall." *Chemical and Engineering News*, Volume 80, No. 3, January 21, 2002.

Rumbelow, Donald. *The Complete Jack the Ripper*. London: Penguin Books, 1988.

Shapira, Ian. "A Film by the Son of CIA Spymaster William Colby Has Divided the Colby Clan," *Washington Post*, November 19, 2011.

Shaw, Mark. *The Reporter Who Knew Too Much*. New York: Post Hill Press, 2016.

Silverman, Rosa. "Who Killed Jill Dando? Six Theories Behind the Unsolved Murder of a Much-loved Television Presenter," *Telegraph*, April 25, 2019.

Smith, Alexander. "Fidel Castro: The CIA's 7 Most Bizarre Assassination Attempts." NBC-news.com. https://www.nbcnews.com/storyline/fidel-castros-death/fidel-castro-cia-s-7-most-bizarre-assassination-attempts-n688951 (accessed November 28, 2016).

Snyder, Michael. "From 7 Billion People To 500 Million People—The Sick Population Control Agenda of the Global Elite." EndOfTheAmericanDream.com. http://endoftheamerican-dream.com/archives/from-7-billion-people-to-500-million-people-the-sick-population-control-agenda-of-the-global-elite (accessed October 27, 2011).

Squires, Nick. "Mystery of Missing PM Finally Solved," *Telegraph*, September 3, 2005.

Stebner, Beth. "Bobby Kennedy Assassin Still Claims He Was 'Victim of Mind Control and His Gun Didn't Fire Fatal Shot' in New Appeal after Parole Is Denied." *Daily Mail*, December 15, 2011.

Steiger, Brad. "Ancient Secret Societies, UFOs, and the New World order." Biblioteca Apleyades.net. http://www.bibliotecapleyades.net/sociopolitica/sociopol_brotherhoodss30.htm (accessed January 29, 2008).

———. *Conspiracies and Secret Societies*. Detroit: Visible Ink Press, 2013.

———. "Three Tricksters in Black." *Saga's UFO Report*, winter 1974.

———. "Who Really Killed Abraham Lincoln?" Rense.com. http://www.rense.com/general80/slin.htm (accessed February 11, 2008).

Stuster, J. Dana. "Declassified: The CIA Secret History of Area 51." ForeignPolicy.com. http://blog.foreignpolicy.com/posts/2013/08/15/declassified_the_cias_secret_history_of_area_51 (accessed August 15, 2013).

Thomas, Gordon. "Microbiologists with Link to Race-Based Weapon Turning Up Dead." *American Free Press*. http://www.americanfreepress.net/08_09_03/Microbiologists_With/microbiologists_with.html (accessed August 9, 2003).

———. "The Secret World of Dr. David Kelly." RumorMillNews.com. http://www.rumormillnews.com/cgi-bin/archive.cgi?noframes;read=35765 (accessed August 21, 2003).

Thomas, Kenn. *Maury Island UFO: The Crisman Conspiracy*. Lilburn, GA: IllumiNet Press, 1999.

Thomas, Kenn, and Jim Keith. *The Octopus*. Portland, OR: Feral House, 1996.

Warren Commission. *A Concise Compendium of the Warren Commission Report on the Assassination of John F. Kennedy*. New York: Popular Library, 1964.

Watson, Paul Joseph. "The Population Reduction Agenda for Dummies." PrisonPlanet.com. http://www.prisonplanet.com/the-population-reduction-agenda-for-dummies.html (accessed June 26, 2009).

Watson, Traci. "Conspiracy Theories Find Menace in Contrails," *USA Today*, March 7, 2001.

Webby, Sean, and Lisa Krieger. "Pizza Delivery May Have Been Ambush: Suspect Later Found Dead," *San Jose Mercury News*, February 28, 2002.

White, Jeremy B. "CIA Tried to Kill Fidel Castro on Day of JFK's Assassination," *Independent*, November 10, 2017.

Wilkinson, Sophie. "Harvard Biochemist Don C. Wiley Disappears in Memphis," *Chemical and Engineering News*, Vol. 79, No. 49, December 3, 2001.

Wilmut, Ian. "John Clark: Pioneering Scientist Whose Entrepreneurial Skills Paved the Way for Dolly the Sheep." *Guardian*, August 25, 2004.

Wilson, Julie. "Wave of Holistic Doctor Deaths Continues, as Florida Chiropractor Suddenly Dies Despite Being 'Hearty and Healthy.'" NaturalNews.com. http://www.naturalnews.com /052975_holistic_doctor_deaths_thermography_cancer_detection.html (accessed February 15, 2016).

WND. "1984 Vision of '1984' Becoming a Reality." WND.com. http://www.wnd.com/2014/05/ 1984-predictions-about-police-state-now-reality/ (accessed May 21, 2014).

Wood, Robert M., and Nick Redfern. *Alien Viruses.* Rochester, NY: Richard Dolan Press, 2013.

Zetter, Kim. "April 13, 1953: CIA OKs MK-ULTRA Mind-Control Tests," *Wired,* April 13, 2010.

INDEX

Note: (ill.) indicates photos and illustrations.